W9-BVL-722

ANCHORAGE, DENALI
& THE KENAI PENINSULA

DON PITCHER

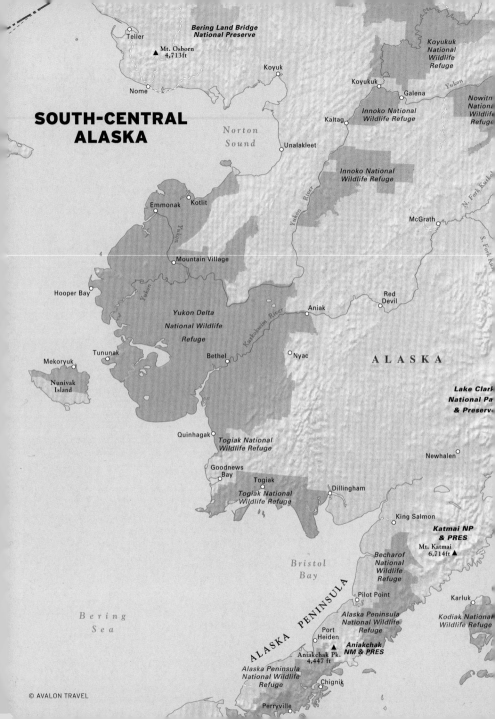

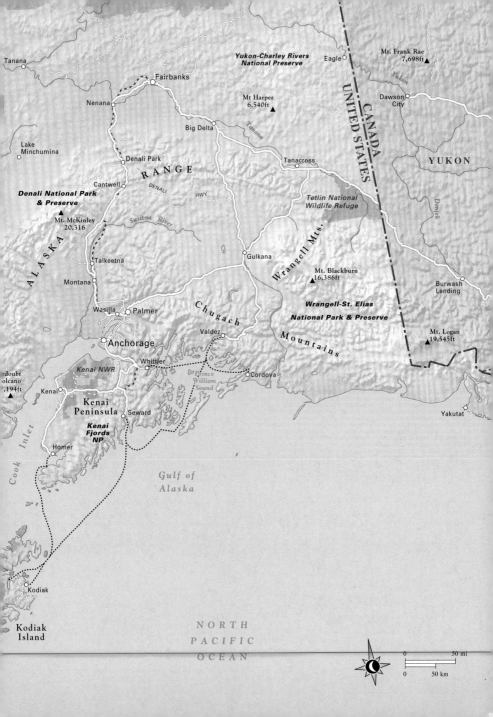

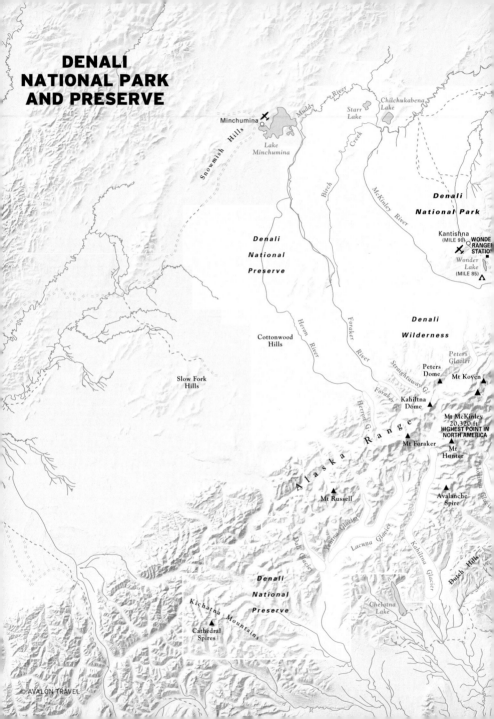

DENALI NATIONAL PARK AND PRESERVE

Minchumina

Lake Minchumina

Snowmish Hills

Muddy River

Birch Creek

Starr Lake

Chilchukabena Lake

McKinley River

Denali National Park

Kantishna (MILE 90)

WONDER RANGER STATION

Wonder Lake (MILE 85)

Denali National Preserve

Cottonwood Hills

Heron River

Foraker River

Denali Wilderness

Peters Glacier

Straightaway Gl.

Peters Dome

Mt Koyen

Kahiltna Dome

Slow Fork Hills

Foraker

Heron Gl.

Mt McKinley 20,320 ft HIGHEST POINT IN NORTH AMERICA

Mt Foraker

Mt Hunter

Alaska Range

Mt Russell

Avalanche Spire

Dall Glacier

Yentna Glacier

Lacuna Glacier

Kahiltna Glacier

Dutch Hills

Denali National Preserve

Kichatna Mountains

Cathedral Spires

Chelatna Lake

© AVALON TRAVEL

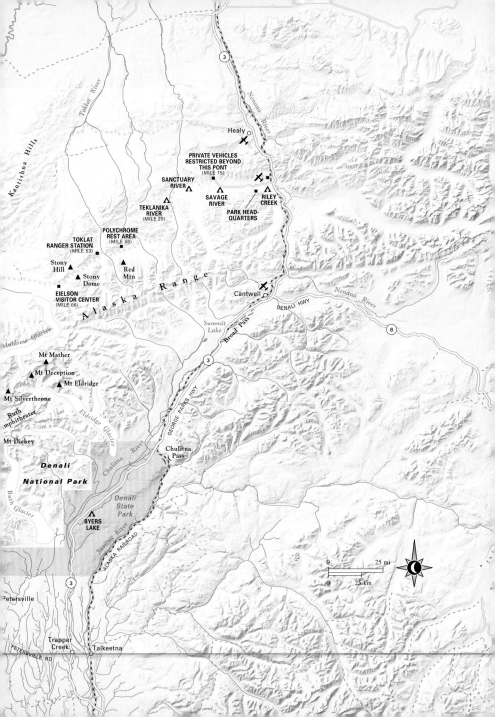

Contents

Discover Anchorage, Denali & the Kenai Peninsula

There is something about Alaska that has always stirred the imagination. From the first migrants who crossed the Bering land bridge during the ice ages to today's travelers escaping the madness of city life, Alaska draws people from the world over to see its wonders: dramatic mountains and immense glaciers, rivers thick with salmon, northern lights dancing across a velvety winter sky.

First-time visitors to Alaska quickly discover how vast the state is, and how difficult it is to see everything in a short period of time. One could easily spend several weeks in Alaska's Inside Passage or remote Bush Alaska without ever coming close to the Anchorage area, but doing so misses one of the most diverse, accessible, and fascinating regions of the state.

This guide is for those Alaska travelers who are looking for a way to kayak next to glaciers, fish for halibut, explore remote backcountry areas, and watch brown bears catching salmon, but who also enjoy a fine Anchorage restaurant, snowboarding at Alyeska Resort, or staying at a luxurious bed-and-breakfast. You could spend an evening in Anchorage dining on king crab and sampling French wines, and the next day take a one-hour floatplane ride to a cabin where the only sounds are singing loons and

droning mosquitoes. The Anchorage, Denali, and Kenai Peninsula region—commonly called South-Central Alaska—is the most accessible part of Alaska, providing an excellent introduction to this magnificent, diverse state.

Anchorage is the natural focal point for travelers visiting South-Central Alaska. The city's international airport has scheduled flights from a dozen U.S. cities, plus direct international flights from Frankfurt, Vancouver, Seoul, Reykjavik, and Vladivostok. Many independent travelers fly into Anchorage and use this city of a quarter-million people as a base to explore surrounding areas, most notably Denali National Park to the north, and the Kenai Peninsula to the south. The Alaska Railroad connects the city with Seward, Talkeetna, Denali, and Fairbanks, and all the major rental car companies have operations at the airport.

I hope this guide opens the doors to this truly unique, amazing, and beautiful part of Alaska. If you haven't visited Alaska before, you're in for a treat. If you have, you will almost certainly want to return.

Planning Your Trip

▶ WHERE TO GO

Anchorage and Vicinity

Anchorage is home to nearly half the state's population, an international airport, and a multitude of cultural attractions. Especially notable are the Anchorage Museum, the largest museum in the state, and the Alaska Native Heritage Center. A paved trail skirts the city's shoreline, and great hiking is a short drive away within massive Chugach State Park. Spend Saturday or Sunday at the downtown Anchorage Market and Festival, where you'll find hundreds of vendors selling everything from Native artwork to birch syrup.

Head south along Turnagain Arm, with its enormous tides and beluga whales, to Portage Glacier and the ski resort town of Girdwood.

North of Anchorage is the Matanuska-Susitna Valley, home to fast-growing Wasilla and Palmer. Beyond lies Hatcher Pass with its pretty alpine country and historic mine buildings.

Denali National Park and Vicinity

Alaska's most loved national park, Denali National Park is 175 air miles north of Anchorage. The park's crowning jewel is 20,320-foot Mount McKinley. A narrow dirt road open only to tour buses courses through the heart of Denali, providing opportunities to see caribou, brown bears, wolves, and other wildlife, plus amazing Alaska Range vistas. Hop on a shuttle bus for an all-day ride into the park: It's an 8-hour round-trip to Eielson Visitor Center, famous for its Mount McKinley views. Or take the 11-hour round-trip to Wonder Lake and the old mining settlement of Kantishna.

The quaint town of Talkeetna, halfway

Anchorage's Performing Arts Center

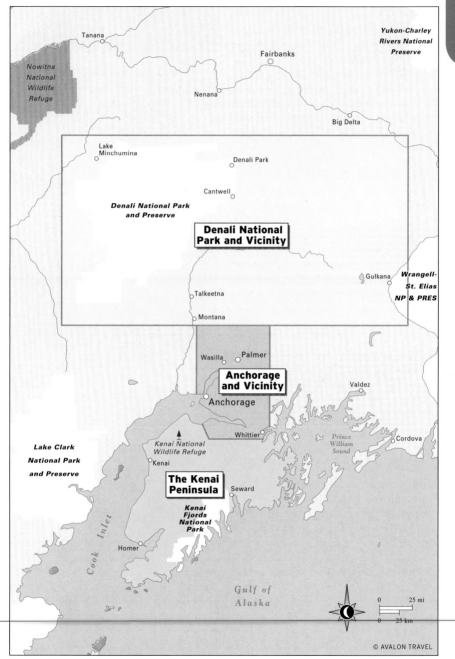

Tanana

Yukon-Charley
Rivers National
Preserve

Fairbanks

Nowitna
National
Wildlife
Refuge

Nenana

Big Delta

Lake
Minchumina

Denali Park

Cantwell

Denali National Park
and Preserve

**Denali National
Park and Vicinity**

Gulkana Wrangell-
St. Elias
NP & PRES

Talkeetna

Montana

Wasilla Palmer

**Anchorage
and Vicinity**

Valdez

Anchorage

Whittier Prince
William
Sound Cordova

Lake Clark
National Park
and Preserve

Kenai National
Wildlife Refuge

Kenai

**The Kenai
Peninsula**

Seward

Kenai
Fjords
National
Park

Cook Inlet

Homer

Gulf of
Alaska

0   25 mi

0   25 km

© AVALON TRAVEL

between Anchorage and Denali, has historic buildings and fun shops, but is best known as a base for flightseeing trips to Denali, including exciting glacier landings.

Beautiful Denali Highway is a mostly gravel 126-mile route that slices east to west along the magnificent Alaska Range. Denali State Park is virtually unknown outside Alaska, but its alpine country affords fine views of Mount McKinley.

The Kenai Peninsula

Extending south and west from Anchorage, the Kenai Peninsula is a recreational paradise, with fishing, hiking, rafting, sightseeing, and camping options galore. The peninsula is dominated by Chugach National Forest, Kenai National Wildlife Refuge, and Kenai Fjords National Park. The last of these is based in Seward, where you can join boat or kayak trips, visit the Alaska SeaLife Center, or hike to Exit Glacier.

Tiny Hope is an almost-ghost town with an abundance of historic log cabins, plus great hiking trails and river rafting. Kenai and Soldotna are bases for fishing, including the famed sockeye salmon combat fishing on the Kenai River. The town of Homer is a premier destination for fishing, sea kayaking,

IF YOU HAVE . . .

- **THREE DAYS:** Visit Anchorage.
- **ONE WEEK:** Add Denali National Park and Talkeetna.
- **TWO WEEKS:** Add Homer, Seward, and other parts of the Kenai Peninsula.

Kenai National Wildlife Refuge

and hiking, with notable lodges, restaurants, and art galleries, some of which can be found along the Homer Spit.

▶ WHEN TO GO

Alaska is primarily a summer destination, and the vast majority of its 1.5 million annual visitors travel mid-May through mid-September, with the peak in July and August. The advantages of summer travel are obvious: long days and warmer weather, not to mention the return of salmon and the emergence of bears and other wildlife. Summer has its drawbacks though, including mosquitoes, high lodging prices, and crowded venues.

Because of Alaska's northern location, spring arrives late, and much of the state does

not green up until mid-May. The road into Denali National Park is closed by snow until late May, and the landscape can be bleak before leaves emerge.

Fall comes early. Autumn colors (primarily yellows on the aspen, birch, and willows, with reds and oranges in alpine areas) typically peak in early September in Denali, and a couple of weeks later in south-central Alaska. Days shorten dramatically by October—en route to the December 21 winter solstice—but longer nights also make Alaska's famous

Dall sheep in Denali State Park

northern lights visible. Winter visitors come to view them, and to watch such events as the Iditarod. Denali can be bitterly cold in winter, but Anchorage and points south are typically milder, especially by mid-February, as the days begin to lengthen.

▶ BEFORE YOU GO

With the right planning, an Alaskan adventure can be the trip of a lifetime. Book well ahead for shuttle bus trips into Denali National Park and for lodging around the park. Many of the larger chain hotels in Anchorage provide substantial discounts if you reserve in mid-winter for the following summer. Leave some time in your schedule to relax, even if you have just a week. Do your research by reading this guide, checking out the websites of places you might want to visit, and requesting a copy of the *Alaska State Vacation Planner* (907/929-2200 or 800/862-5275, www.travelalaska.com).

Iditarod in Anchorage

Be careful of moose when driving.

northern lights near Talkeetna

Explore Anchorage, Denali & the Kenai Peninsula

The following itineraries offer the best that south-central Alaska has to offer. You'll want to spend two to four days in Anchorage; decide whether to explore the city at the beginning or the end (or at both ends) of your trip. Using Anchorage as a travel hub, you can visit Denali National Park or travel along the Kenai Peninsula, visiting towns like Seward and Homer, while mixing travel by train, bus, car, boat, and air. Be sure to take at least one boat excursion, whether it's halibut fishing in Homer, rafting the Kenai River, glacier spotting from Whittier, or wildlife and glacier tours out of Seward.

▶ THE BEST OF ANCHORAGE

Day 1

Fly into Anchorage, get a rental car, then find your hotel and settle in. Copper Whale Inn or Anchorage Grand Hotel are attractive and reasonably priced downtown lodging options. Or book a couple of nights at SpringHill Suites Anchorage University Lake for in-town lodging with an out-of-town lake and mountain view.

If you're planning on doing some outdoor excursions, check out the gear at REI, then grab some lunch at Middle Way Café next door. Get oriented by heading to the downtown Log Cabin Visitors Center and

autumn in Chugach State Park

the nearby Alaska Public Lands Information Center. Enjoy a fine seafood dinner at Simon & Seaforts, where you can sip a nighttime cocktail as the sun arcs across the summer sky over Cook Inlet.

Day 2

Drop by Side Street Espresso downtown for an espresso and croissant. Spend the day exploring the Anchorage Museum and the Alaska Native Heritage Center. There's a free shuttle between the two, and you can save money by purchasing a joint ticket. If the weather cooperates, take an easy walk along the Tony Knowles Coastal Trail. It offers great vistas across Cook Inlet and is readily accessible from downtown. Overnight in Anchorage again.

Day 3

Take a day hike in Chugach State Park. Head to the Glen Alps parking lot for access to Flattop Mountain Trail—a steep climb with a big reward at the end—or the easier saunter up the trail to Powerline Pass. The Flattop

Mountain Shuttle provides transportation from downtown if you want to leave the driving to someone else. A great dinner option is the ever-popular Moose's Tooth Pub & Pizzeria.

Day 4

Start your day with brunch at Snow City Café and browse downtown Anchorage's shops. If you're in town on a weekend, be certain to take in the huge Anchorage Market and Festival at 3rd Avenue and E Street downtown.

H2Oasis Indoor Waterpark is a treat for families with kids. Couples should head to Marx Bros. Café for the ultimate Alaskan fine dining experience. For a night out, visit crazy-busy Chilkoot Charlie's in Midtown or Humpy's Great Alaskan Alehouse downtown.

Onward Travel

From Anchorage, you can travel north to Denali National Park. Going south, Portage Glacier and Girdwood are popular day trips from Anchorage, but they can also make good stops en route to the Kenai Peninsula (see page 18).

► EXPLORING DENALI

Denali National Park is about 240 miles north of Anchorage, a five-hour trip by car. The best way to travel to Denali, though, is by train, where you can relax and enjoy the scenery. The Alaska Railroad runs trains from Anchorage to Denali, with stops at Wasilla and Talkeetna in between. You can take the eight-hour ride straight to Denali, but stopping for a night in Talkeetna is highly recommended.

Day 1

From Anchorage, go to the Alaska Railroad depot and hop on the morning Denali Star train headed north, arriving in Talkeetna three hours later. Upgrading to the luxurious

GoldStar railcars costs more, but they have open-air viewing platforms to take in the grand scenery along the way. If The Mountain (Mount McKinley, of course) is out, book a flightseeing trip to the park from a charter company like Sheldon Air Service or K2 Aviation. Flights with a glacier landing are particularly memorable. Head to dinner at Wildflower Café on Talkeetna's Main Street, and spend the night at Denali Overlook Inn, five miles outside of Talkeetna.

Day 2

Get breakfast and a to-go lunch at Talkeetna Roadhouse. Next, explore the funky historic buildings in town, starting with Nagley's

BEAR-VIEWING

Katmai National Park

Bear-viewing is a booming business in Alaska, and visitors never forget their first sighting. Most folks choose a package trip to areas where the bears have become somewhat habituated to the presence of humans—but there are more adventurous opportunities as well.

The most famous places to see and photograph brown bears are **Denali National Park, Katmai National Park,** and **McNeil River.** Some boats and planes also offer bear-viewing day trips to coastal Lake Clark National Park.

World-famous **Brooks Camp** within Katmai National Park (907/246-3305, www.nps.gov/katm) is one of the few places where large numbers of visitors can see wild bears throughout the summer. Bear activity centers on the Brooks River and particularly Brooks Falls, where those legendary bear-with-jumping-salmon photos are taken. Air taxis in Anchorage, Homer, and Soldotna all provide floatplane flights to Naknek Lake, just a short hike from the river.

One of Alaska's best-known places to see bears is **McNeil River State Game Sanctuary** on the Alaska Peninsula approximately 100 air miles west of Homer and adjacent to Katmai National Park. This state sanctuary—made famous in *National Geographic* specials—allows just 10 visitors per day to the viewing area. The application process is highly competitive, with just 10 percent of applicants actually getting permission to visit McNeil. It's managed by the **Alaska Department of Fish and Game** (907/267-2189, www.wild-life.alaska.gov), with complete details on access and the application process at their website.

Two other popular places to see brown bears are **Silver Salmon Creek** and **Chinitna Bay** within **Lake Clark National Park** (907/781-2218, www.nps.gov/lacl), on the Alaska Peninsula southwest of Anchorage. Access is by air from Anchorage, Soldotna, or Homer, or check out lodges in the park, including **Silver Salmon Creek Lodge** (907/252-5504 or 888/872-5666, www.silversalmoncreek.com) and **Lake Clark Bear Camp** (800/544-2261, www.greatalaska.com).

In addition to the official bear-viewing areas, quite a few air-taxi operators fly out of Anchorage, Homer, and Soldotna on daylong trips in search of brown bears. Most of these head to the outer coast, landing on beaches within Katmai National Park and Preserve. These once-in-a-lifetime day trips typically cost $600-700 per person.

A number of private lodges and camps offer multi-night stays in bear-filled locations. One of the best is **Hallo Bay Bear Lodge** (907/235-2237, www.hallobay.com), a unique camp setting in the heart of Katmai National Park with access by air from Homer. Also recommended is another Homer-based operation, **Katmai Coastal Bear Tours** (907/235-8337 or 800/532-8338, www.katmaibears.com). The company uses two large boats as floating lodges for photographers, cinematographers, and others who use skiffs to go ashore along the Katmai coast.

a warm welcome in Talkeetna

Nagley's Store, Talkeetna

Store, open since the 1920s. Then hop aboard the *Denali Star* once more, where you'll arrive at Denali National Park by late afternoon. From the train depot, find the Denali Salmon Bake shuttle and ride into nearby Healy. Stay at Earth Song Lodge and join the pub fun at 49th State Brewery.

Day 3

This is your day to explore Denali National Park by tour bus. Advance reservations are absolutely necessary for this all-day adventure (many people book several months ahead of time to be sure of a space). Many buses turn around at Eielson Visitors Center (eight hours round-trip), where you'll get a fine view of Mount McKinley if it isn't obscured by clouds. You could also ride to Wonder Lake and back (11 long hours) or take a shorter wildlife-focused tour on one of the park's tan buses. You're likely to see grizzlies, moose, caribou, Dall sheep, and the occasional wolf along the way. Return to your hotel for a second night.

If you'd like to spend more time in Denali, plan ahead by making a reservation at one of the park's six campgrounds, like Riley Creek Campground or Savage River Campground.

Day 4

If you have decided to spend two full days at Denali, use today to try a short but tough hike on Eielson's steep Alpine Trail, or hop on a park bus and head to Wonder Lake, where you can hike the easy McKinley Bar Trail.

If you're planning on returning to Anchorage today, visit the sled dog demonstrations or do a short hike in the morning (try the Horseshoe Lake Trail for a chance at seeing beavers). Take the noon *Denali Star* train south; you'll arrive back in Anchorage that evening.

Backcountry Travel

Denali is backcountry wilderness: vaster and wilder than most people have ever visited. If you're planning on venturing

caribou in Denali National Park

into the backcountry during your visit to Denali, you'll want to visit the Backcountry Information Center at the park. For more information see page 147.

For more information see page 147.

▶ THE BEST OF THE KENAI PENINSULA

The Kenai Peninsula is the Alaska that most people dream about. Distances here are great, but it's worth traversing them to see highlights like Exit Glacier and the towns of Soldotna and Homer. This itinerary generally alternates driving days with more active and adventurous days. You can add additional days in any location if you want to pack in more excursions—or if you prefer a more leisurely pace.

En Route to the Kenai Peninsula
DAY 1: PORTAGE GLACIER
AND GIRDWOOD

Drive south from Anchorage, stopping at Potter Marsh to watch for Arctic terns and other birds. Continue along Turnagain Arm, famous for its bore tides, beluga whales, and cliff-traipsing Dall sheep.

Get a filling lunch at The Bake Shop in Girdwood and drive south to Portage, where you can visit the Alaska Wildlife Conservation Center to see brown and black bears, bison, moose, and other critters up close. Take an hour-long cruise to Portage Glacier and visit the Begich, Boggs Visitor Center to learn more about glaciers and climate change.

Backtrack a few miles to Girdwood and overnight at Hotel Alyeska, part of the Alyeska Resort. Take the resort's tram to dinner at Seven Glaciers Restaurant, high above Turnagain Arm.

From Portage Glacier, you can drive onward to Seward (90 miles, driving time about two hours), or you can take a day cruise to Prince William Sound out of Whittier and spend another night in Girdwood.

UNDERSTANDING THE DENALI MAZE

mountain biking in Denali National Park

Denali National Park requires considerable planning. Here are some tips to make your trip go as smoothly as possible.

- **Book your shuttle bus first.** These all-day tour buses fill early, so make reservations (www.reservedenali.com) as soon as you have travel dates for the park.

- **Book train travel on the Alaska Railroad** if you're traveling by train from Anchorage to Denali.

- **Reserve lodging or campsites early as well,** especially for the peak of the season in July and August.

- **Plan at least three days** in the Denali area. The park is an all-day drive or train ride from Anchorage (or two days if you stop in Talkeetna). The Park Road itself is an all-day ride if you want to reach Eielson Visitor Center or Wonder Lake. You'll want downtime to explore areas around the park entrance or to camp inside the park.

- **Bring a big lunch, water, light jacket, camera, and binoculars** on the shuttle bus ride.

- **Take a natural history tour to learn more.** Although shuttle bus drivers stop for wildlife, you'll learn much more about the park by joining one of the nature tour buses. They're a bit more expensive, but worth it.

- **Reserve a campsite** at one of Denali National Park's seven campgrounds. Riley Creek Campground at the entrance is open to cars and RVs, and some other campgrounds allow limited vehicle access, but three of the campgrounds are only accessible via bus.

- **Backcountry campers need to plan for wilderness conditions.** There are only a handful of trails within Denali; much of the country is relatively open tundra. You'll need a backcountry permit and a reservation for a camper bus to your starting point, and you must attend a safety briefing.

- **Carry bear spray on all hikes.** Although brown bear attacks are extremely rare, it's always wise to carry "bear mace" as a precaution. Talk with rangers for safety tips when hiking in bear country.

- **Rent a mountain bike** if you want to really explore the Park Road. They're available just outside the park entrance, and can be carried onto camper buses. Reservations are necessary, since only two bikes are allowed per bus.

- **Visit in early September,** when fall colors dominate the landscape and fewer travelers crowd the shuttle buses and campgrounds.

- **Try for the Road Lottery.** As fall comes to Denali, the Park Road is opened to private vehicles for four days in mid-September. A total of 400 cars are allowed, with the winners chosen at random. You'll need to apply by June 30; find details at the park website (www.nps.gov/dena).

From Whittier, take a day cruise to see glaciers.

DAY 2: DAY CRUISE FROM WHITTIER

Drive south to Portage and through the tunnel to the little town of Whittier, a popular port for cruise ships and day tours. Two companies, Major Marine Tours and Phillips Tours and Cruises, have all-day boat tours to the spectacular glaciers of western Prince William Sound. You can opt for a leisurely five-hour glacier tour to Blackstone Bay. Seals lounge on the icebergs, and several active glaciers are visible at once.

The Kenai Peninsula

DAY 3: SEWARD AND EXIT GLACIER

Head south over scenic Turnagain Pass to Seward. Get a latte and check out the artwork at Resurrect Art Coffeehouse Gallery, then make the 12-mile drive north to Exit Glacier. In an hour or two you can explore the country around this fast-retreating glacier, or opt for an all-day hike to massive Harding Ice Field.

Reward yourself with a seafood dinner at nearby Exit Glacier Salmon Bake or head back to Seward for a hearty dinner of barbecue ribs at Smoke Shack. Stay at Alaska Paddle Inn just south of Seward on Lowell Point.

DAY 4: DAY CRUISE FROM SEWARD

Take a half-day wildlife boat tour around Resurrection Bay or an all-day trip to Northwestern Fjord or Aialik Bay within Kenai Fjords National Park.

In the late afternoon, visit Seward's Alaska SeaLife Center, where enormous tanks house puffins, seals, and playful sea lions. Enjoy a seafood dinner at Ray's Waterfront or a beer and grilled halibut at Seward Brewing Company, and spend a second night in Seward.

DAY 5: COOPER LANDING

From Seward, drive north to the tiny settlement of Cooper Landing along the Kenai River. Take the day to relax with a float trip on the Kenai River from Alaska River

Denali Mountain Morning Hostel and Lodge is a good option for budget travelers.

Alaska is a notoriously expensive place to visit. It's easy to spend $225 a night for an Anchorage or Denali hotel, and when you add in high fuel and food prices, car rental costs, a flightseeing trip, a day of bear-viewing, and a boat tour, you're starting to talk serious money. Fortunately, there *are* ways to explore Southcentral Alaska without watching your credit card explode in flames.

- **Take buses whenever possible.** Anchorage's People Mover city buses provide inexpensive connections to the airport, and Valley Mover buses continue north to the Mat-Su Valley. Private buses are a good bargain, connecting all major towns and cities in the region.

- **Many Anchorage and Denali hotels provide free airport or train shuttles.** Hotels at the entrance to Denali National Park provide inexpensive shuttles from campgrounds and RV parks to shops and restaurants.

- **Public campgrounds are found throughout the region, and in Anchorage.** It costs just $22 to camp at Denali's Riley Creek Campground, or you can

pay $250 for a hotel room just a mile away.

- **Make car rental reservations well ahead, and check Travelocity or Expedia for the best rates.** Many companies offer discounts if you have a Costco or AAA card.

- **Hostels offer an inexpensive lodging option.** Bent Prop Inn & Hostel Downtown (Anchorage), Denali Mountain Morning Hostel and Lodge (near the park), Nauti Otter (Seward), and Seaside Farm Hostel (Homer) are all great choices.

- **Save money by cooking your own meals.** Most hotels provide in-room microwaves and small refrigerators, and many also include a decent breakfast. Hostels (and a few hotels) have full kitchens for guests.

- **Book your hotel stay well in advance for the best prices.** Although most mom-and-pop outfits don't lower their prices for advance bookings, the bigger hotels in Anchorage and Denali often offer early bird discounts of 10 percent or more.

Adventures or go for an hour-long trail ride with Alaskan Horsemen Trail Adventures.

Kingfisher Roadhouse has delicious meals with a rustic setting and an enclosed deck facing Kenai Lake.Settle in for the night at Alaska Heavenly Lodge.

DAY 6: SOLDOTNA AND KENAI

Grab an early breakfast at Gwin's Lodge. Continue driving along the Sterling Highway, stopping at Mile 55 to ride the self-propelled Russian River Ferry across the river where salmon anglers stand shoulder to shoulder for "combat fishing" during the peak of the sockeye run.

Take the scenic route west from here by turning onto Skilak Lake Loop Road. This pretty 16-mile dirt road crosses the heart of Kenai National Wildlife Refuge, with campgrounds and hiking trails. If you have the time, take one of these hikes: the Bear Mountain Trail is a short one with impressive views.

Back on the Sterling Highway, continue west to Soldotna, where you can browse the handmade goods at Birch Tree Gallery and let the kids run wild at Soldotna Creek Park. Once you're back in the car, continue on the Sterling Highway until the Kenai Spur Highway junction, where you'll turn north to the small city of Kenai. Stay at Daniels Lake Lodge B&B, with its cozy lakeside cabins, and eat dinner with the locals at Louie's Steak & Seafood.

DAY 7: KENAI, NINILCHIK, AND ON TO HOMER

In the morning, head over to the Kenai Visitors and Cultural Center for local information, then visit Veronica's Café for great breakfast blintzes and espresso. Wander a bit farther west to a series of beautiful sand dunes along Cook Inlet at the mouth of the Kenai River.

Drive south from Kenai via Kalifornsky Beach Road, turning south on the Sterling

Skilak Lake, in Kenai National Wildlife Refuge

Transfiguration of Our Lord Russian Orthodox Church, Ninilchik

Highway at Kasilof. As you're driving, look across the Inlet for views of snowy mountains and active volcanoes.

Around 25 miles later, you'll find yourself in Ninilchik, home to the Transfiguration of Our Lord Russian Orthodox Church, located on a dramatic hilltop facing the volcanic summit of Mount Illiamna. Pause at The Buzz Café for a caffeine boost if you need it.

It's another 45 miles south to the small city of Homer, where the Sterling Highway ends. Stop at the big hilltop overlook just before you reach Homer for an all-encompassing vista across Kachemak Bay, and spend the night at Driftwood Inn or Kenai Peninsula Suites. For a great dinner, head to Fat Olives.

DAY 8: HOMER

After breakfast at Two Sisters Bakery, walk down the street to Bishops Beach for a stroll, then head to Islands and Ocean Visitor Center and the Pratt Museum for excellent introductions to the area.

Homer's most-loved destination is the four-mile-long Homer Spit. This natural peninsula of land extends into Kachemak Bay, with a busy boat harbor and a cluster of shops, galleries, restaurants, campgrounds, and lodging at the end. Two good Spit dinner options are Finn's Pizza or Boardwalk Fish and Chips.

DAY 9: DAY TRIPS FROM HOMER

This is a day that could go in three completely different directions. If you have the cash, hop on one of the all-day bear-viewing flights from Homer to Katmai National Park. Sea kayaking is a less expensive option: True North Kayak Adventures has an all-day trip that includes a water taxi to Yukon Island, where you join a guided kayak adventure. The third option is to join an early morning halibut fishing charter boat (find one through Central Charters & Tours). You're almost certain of getting your limit, and fish over 100 pounds are occasionally pulled in. Coal Point Seafood will process, freeze, and ship your catch.

sea kayakers in the Cook Inlet, with Mount Iliamna

For dinner, check out Wasabi's for Asian fusion cuisine or Mermaid Bistro for slow food with focus on fresh, local fare.

DAY 10: RETURN TO ANCHORAGE VIA HOPE

It's a five-hour, 225-mile drive to Anchorage, but if you get going early enough you can still have fun along the way. Take the Hope Highway detour to the historic town of Hope, with its quaint log buildings and great hiking trails. An easy day hike follows the shore of Turnagain Arm to Gull Rock, or for something more challenging, the 38-mile Resurrection Pass Trail begins a few miles from Hope. After your detour to Hope, return to the Seward Highway for the drive to Anchorage.

Seaview Café in Hope

ANCHORAGE AND VICINITY

Anchorage is an eminently enjoyable *and* affordable place to hang out. It certainly has one of the most flower-filled downtowns of any American city; visitors are always impressed with the summertime bounty of blooms. You can easily fill a whole day touring downtown, or just lying around a park for the one day in four that the sun shines. Explore Anchorage's far-flung corners, such as the resort town of Girdwood, south of the city (popular for winter skiing and summer hiking); rapidly growing Matanuska-Susitna Valley (home to the towns of Palmer and Wasilla); and grand mountain country at Hatcher Pass.

Of course, you can simply breeze into town, make your connection, and quickly "get back to Alaska." But if you want a fully rounded experience of the 49th state, get to know Anchorage, *urban* Alaska, and come to your own conclusions.

HISTORY

In June 1778, Captain James Cook sailed up what's now Turnagain Arm in Cook Inlet, reaching another dead end on his amazing search for the Northwest Passage. But he did dispatch William Bligh (of HMS *Bounty* fame) to explore, and he saw some Tanaina Indians in rich otter skins. George Vancouver, who'd also been on Cook's ship, returned in 1794 and noted Russian settlers in the area. A century later, prospectors began landing in the area and heading

© KEN GRAHAM PHOTOGRAPHY / VISIT ANCHORAGE

HIGHLIGHTS

LOOK FOR ◖ TO FIND RECOMMENDED SIGHTS, ACTIVITIES, DINING, AND LODGING.

◖ **Anchorage Museum:** Alaska's largest and finest museum has fascinating exhibits, the kid-friendly Imaginarium, and a fine café (page 34).

◖ **Alaska Native Heritage Center:** Learn about the state's native peoples through exhibits, demonstrations, and cultural presentations at this large facility (page 37).

◖ **Anchorage Market and Festival:** This downtown gathering is packed with Alaskan arts and crafts, great food, and live music every weekend (page 42).

◖ **Chugach State Park:** Who would imagine that you could get into the wilderness so quickly from Anchorage? Lots of wonderful hiking trails are here, especially the climb up Flattop Mountain (page 71).

◖ **Turnagain Arm:** South of Anchorage, this long inlet is a great place to watch for beluga whales and bore tides or see Dall sheep on the cliffs (page 74).

◖ **Crow Creek Mine:** Just a few miles from Alyeska Ski Resort in Girdwood are picture-perfect log cabins from this authentic old mine where you might find gold in the creek (page 77).

◖ **Portage Glacier:** This is one of the state's most-visited glaciers. A boat tour across Portage Lake leaves hourly from the visitors center (page 82).

◖ **Alaska State Fair:** Where else can you find a demolition derby, supersized turkey legs, enormous peonies, and 100-pound cabbages (page 94)?

◖ **Hatcher Pass:** This beautiful area is perfect for hiking in the summer or cross-country skiing when the snow flies. Take time to explore the weathered old buildings of Independence Mine State Historical Park (page 104).

north to Southcentral Alaska's gold country, and in 1902 Alfred Brooks began mapping the Cook Inlet for the U.S. Geological Survey. In 1913, five settlers occupied Ship Creek, the point on the inlet where Anchorage now stands.

A year later, Congress passed the Alaska Railroad Act, and in April 1915 the route for the federally financed railroad from Seward to Fairbanks was made official: It would pass through Ship Creek, where a major staging area for workers and supplies would be located. This news traveled fast, and within a month a

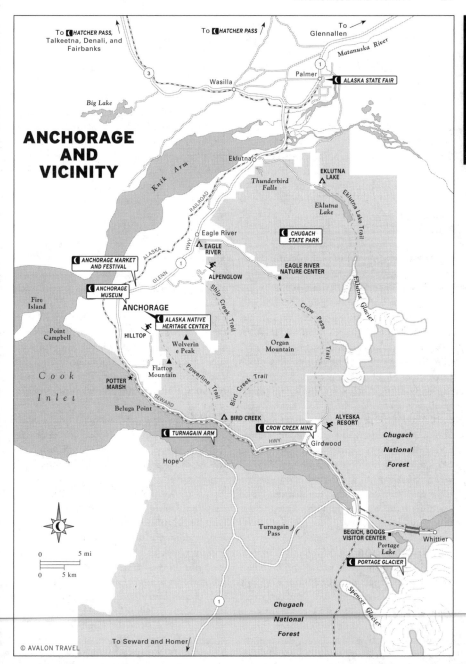

ANCHORAGE AND VICINITY

To **CHATCHER PASS**, Talkeetna, Denali, and Fairbanks

To **CHATCHER PASS**

To Glennallen

Matanuska River

Wasilla

Palmer

ALASKA STATE FAIR

Big Lake

Eklutna

EKLUTNA LAKE

Thunderbird Falls

Eklutna Lake

RAILROAD

Eagle River

CHUGACH STATE PARK

EAGLE RIVER

ALASKA

ANCHORAGE MARKET AND FESTIVAL

HWY

GLENN

1

ALPENGLOW

EAGLE RIVER NATURE CENTER

Eklutna Lake Trail

Eklutna Glacier

ANCHORAGE MUSEUM

Fire Island

ANCHORAGE

ALASKA NATIVE HERITAGE CENTER

Ship Creek Trail

Crow Pass Trail

Point Campbell

HILLTOP

Wolverine Peak

Organ Mountain

Cook Inlet

Flattop Mountain

Powerline Trail

POTTER MARSH

SEWARD

Bird Creek Trail

Beluga Point

BIRD CREEK

TURNAGAIN ARM

CROW CREEK MINE

HWY

ALYESKA RESORT

Girdwood

Chugach National Forest

Hope

Turnagain Pass

BEGICH, BOGGS VISITOR CENTER

Portage Lake

Whittier

0   5 mi

0   5 km

PORTAGE GLACIER

Spencer Glacier

Chugach National Forest

To Seward and Homer

© AVALON TRAVEL

ramshackle tent city of nearly 2,000 railroad job seekers had sprung up. Things developed so quickly that in July the U.S. Land Office auctioned off 650 parcels at the new town site. The settlement, renamed Anchorage, grew quickly, with water, telephone and power lines, sidewalks, and schools in place within a year.

Slumps and Spurts

Railroad laborers, earning 37 cents per hour (low for Alaska), went on strike in 1916, after which the minimum wage was raised to 45 cents per hour. The population continued to boom, topping out at around 7,000 in 1917. With World War I and completion of the southern portion of the railroad, the number of people dropped below 2,000 in 1920, when the town incorporated, electing its first mayor and city council. Through the 1930s, Anchorage held steady at 3,000-4,000 people, but World War II changed that in a hurry. The town's strategic location led to a huge influx of military personnel when the Army's Fort Richardson and the Army Air Corps's Elmendorf Field were constructed outside of town. By 1950, Anchorage was a prosperous small city of over 11,000. In the following decade Anchorage also experienced the postwar boom, with the attendant shortages of housing and modern conveniences, which created the city's own construction mini-boom. In 1957, when Richfield Oil discovered black gold on the Kenai Peninsula, the oil companies started opening office buildings in the city, and the economy stabilized.

Since Statehood

Much of Anchorage collapsed in the incredible Good Friday Earthquake of March 27, 1964, which lasted an interminable five minutes, registering 9.2 on the Richter Scale. The north side of 4th Avenue wound up 8-10 feet lower than the south side of the street. A very rich residential section on the bluff overlooking Knik Arm

was destroyed. Nine people were killed and upward of $300 million in damages were recorded. Anchorage was rebuilt, and because only a few large buildings survived the quake, nearly everything in the city was put up after 1964.

Though the pipeline doesn't come within 300 miles of Anchorage, oil money towers over the city in the form of tall office buildings scattered around town. The military still plays an important role in the local economy, with Elmendorf Air Force Base and Fort Richardson right on the margins of town, and military jets and surveillance planes a common presence in the sky. Tourism also affects Anchorage enormously, especially in the summer months when the city is a waypoint for many travelers. Anchorage fancies itself quite the cosmopolitan city, boasting dozens of arts organizations, a modern performing arts center, a 16-theater cinema with stadium seating, plus many fancy hotels, restaurants, cafés, and bars catering to the thousands of suits who fill the skyscrapers that gleam in the light of the midnight sun. Indeed, if Juneau is bureaucratic Alaska, and Fairbanks is rank-and-file Alaska, then Anchorage is corporate and commercial Alaska.

CLIMATE

Two of the deciding factors in choosing Anchorage as a main construction camp for the Alaska Railroad were mild winters and comparatively low precipitation. The towering Alaska Range shelters Cook Inlet Basin from the frigid winter breath of the Arctic northerlies; the Kenai and Chugach Mountains cast a rain shadow over the basin, allowing only 15-20 percent of the annual precipitation that communities on the windward side of the ranges get. Anchorage receives around 20 inches of annual precipitation (10-12 inches of rain, 60-70 inches of snow), while Whittier, 40 miles away on the Gulf side of the Chugach, gets 175 inches. Anchorage's winter temperatures rarely drop much below 0°F, with only an occasional cold streak, compared with Fairbanks's frequent -40°F; its summer temperatures rarely rise above 65°F, compared with Fairbanks's 80s and 90s.

PLANNING YOUR TIME

Anchorage is an outstanding base for travelers to Alaska's heartland, with Denali National Park, the Kenai Peninsula, and a multitude of other attractions within a day's drive. The state's largest airport provides flights to all regions of the globe, and the Alaska Railroad has daily trains north to Denali and Fairbanks or south to Seward and Whittier. The city has long served as a hub for travelers, but it also offers many attractions not available elsewhere, and one could easily spend two or three days just exploring local museums, hiking trails, shops, and restaurants.

The city's highlights include its outstanding **Anchorage Museum** (the state's largest), the **Alaska Native Heritage Center,** the Alaska Heritage Museum, and an abundance of good restaurants, hip coffeehouses, hopping bars, **H2Oasis Indoor Water Park** for the kids, and two minor-league baseball teams—all that you might expect from the state's largest city. And don't forget the always-packed **Anchorage Market and Festival** every summer weekend, with locally made crafts, tasty finger food, live music, and even a bit of fresh produce from the farmers.

There are also attractions you would only find in an Alaskan city: a wonderful coastal trail that starts right downtown; great hiking in nearby **Chugach State Park**; fascinating **Turnagain Arm** with its enormous tides and beluga whales; and places to outfit yourself for any adventure in the Alaskan outdoors. Anchorage is within striking distance of some of the most exciting and extensive hiking, climbing, fishing, kayaking, river rafting, flightseeing, and wilderness areas.

To the south, the town of Girdwood is home to Alyeska Resort—Alaska's only significant ski area—and funky **Crow Creek Mine,** where you still might find a gold nugget in your pan. A bit farther south is the much-photographed **Portage Glacier,** accessed by a tour boat from the Forest Service visitors center. Accessed through a long tunnel, the town of **Whittier** serves as a launching point for glacier sightseeing tours and sea kayaking adventures.

North of Anchorage the Glenn Highway passes a tiny Tanaina Native Alaskan village where Eklutna Historical Park houses a picturesque graveyard filled with spirit houses before emerging in the Matanuska-Susitna Valley (Mat-Su, for short), where the pastures and farms of the past are giving way to homes and strip malls for folks fleeing Anchorage's housing prices and crowding. The valley's two main towns are booming Wasilla and semirural Palmer, home to a fun musk ox farm and the **Alaska State Fair,** a 12-day blast starting in late August. North of the valley, the Talkeetna Mountains rise abruptly, bisected by a road over Hatcher Pass, where **Independence Mine State Historical Park** provides a base for day hikes or wintertime skis.

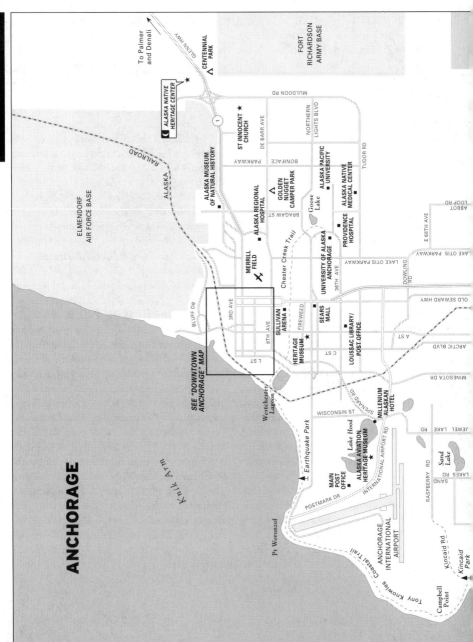

ANCHORAGE

To Palmer and Denali

CENTENNIAL PARK

★ ALASKA NATIVE HERITAGE CENTER

FORT RICHARDSON ARMY BASE

ELMENDORF AIR FORCE BASE

GLENN HWY

RAILROAD

ALASKA

MULDOON RD

DE BARR AVE

NORTHERN LIGHTS BLVD

ST INNOCENT CHURCH ★

BONIFACE PARKWAY

ALASKA MUSEUM OF NATURAL HISTORY

ALASKA REGIONAL HOSPITAL

BRAGAW ST

GOLDEN NUGGET CAMPER PARK ▲

ALASKA PACIFIC UNIVERSITY

ALASKA NATIVE MEDICAL CENTER

TUDOR RD

ABBOT LOOP RD

Goose Lake

Chester Creek Trail

PROVIDENCE HOSPITAL

E 68TH AVE

MERRILL FIELD ✈

UNIVERSITY OF ALASKA ANCHORAGE

36TH AVE

LAKE OTIS PARKWAY

DOWLING RD

BLUFF DR

3RD AVE

SULLIVAN ARENA

FIREWEED

SEARS MALL

OLD SEWARD HWY

8TH AVE

A ST

ARCTIC BLVD

SEE "DOWNTOWN ANCHORAGE" MAP

L ST

HERITAGE MUSEUM ■

LOUSSAC LIBRARY/ POST OFFICE ■

C ST

MINESOTA DR

Westchester Lagoon

JEWEL LAKE RD

Knik Arm

Earthquake Park ▲

WISCONSIN ST

SPENARD RD

MILLENIUM ALASKAN HOTEL ●

SAND LAKE RD

LAKES RD

Sand Lake

RASPBERRY RD

SAND

Lake Hood

ALASKA AVIATION HERITAGE MUSEUM ★

INTERNATIONAL AIRPORT RD

Pt Woronzof

MAIN POST OFFICE ■

POSTMARK DR

INTERNATIONAL AIRPORT RD

ANCHORAGE INTERNATIONAL AIRPORT

Tony Knowles Coastal Trail

Kincaid Rd

Kincaid Park ▲

Campbell Point

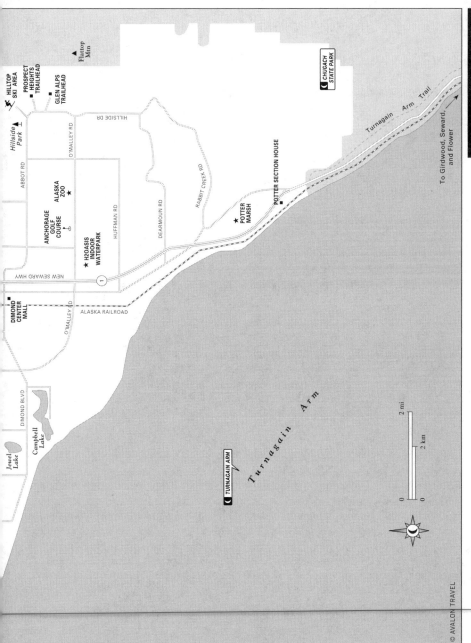

Flattop Mtn

HILLTOP SKI AREA
PROSPECT HEIGHTS TRAILHEAD
GLEN ALPS TRAILHEAD

CHUGACH STATE PARK

Turnagain Arm Trail

To Girdwood, Seward, and Flower

Hillside Park

HILLSIDE DR

O'MALLEY RD

ABBOT RD

ALASKA ZOO

RABBIT CREEK RD

POTTER SECTION HOUSE

ANCHORAGE GOLF COURSE

DEARMOUN RD

HUFFMAN RD

POTTER MARSH

H2OASIS INDOOR WATERPARK

NEW SEWARD HWY

1

DIMOND CENTER MALL

O'MALLEY RD

ALASKA RAILROAD

DIMOND BLVD

Campbell Lake

Jewel Lake

TURNAGAIN ARM

Turnagain Arm

0   2 mi

0   2 km

© AVALON TRAVEL

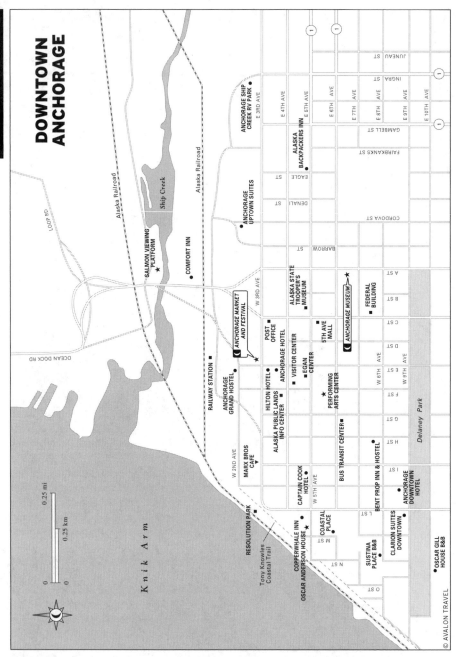

DOWNTOWN ANCHORAGE

0.25 mi
0.25 km

Knik Arm

LOOP RD

Alaska Railroad

Ship Creek

SALMON VIEWING PLATFORM ★

COMFORT INN ●

OCEAN DOCK RD

Alaska Railroad

ANCHORAGE SHIP CREEK RV PARK ●

E 3RD AVE

JUNEAU ST
INGRA ST
E 4TH AVE
E 5TH AVE
E 6TH AVE
E 7TH AVE
E 8TH AVE
E 9TH AVE
E 10TH AVE

ALASKA BACKPACKERS INN ●

GAMBELL ST
FAIRBANKS ST
EAGLE ST

ANCHORAGE UPTOWN SUITES ●

DENALI ST
CORDOVA ST

BARROW ST

W 3RD AVE

ALASKA STATE TROOPER'S MUSEUM ■

ANCHORAGE MARKET AND FESTIVAL ★

POST OFFICE ●

ANCHORAGE HOTEL ●

VISITOR CENTER ■
EGAN CENTER ■

5TH AVE MALL

ANCHORAGE MUSEUM ★

FEDERAL BUILDING ■

A ST
B ST
C ST
D ST

RAILWAY STATION ■

ANCHORAGE GRAND HOSTEL ●

HILTON HOTEL ●

ALASKA PUBLIC LANDS INFO CENTER ■

PERFORMING ARTS CENTER ★

W 8TH AVE
W 9TH AVE

E 8TH AVE
E 9TH AVE

E ST
F ST

Delaney Park

W 2ND AVE

MARX BROS CAFE ●

BUS TRANSIT CENTER ■

G ST
H ST

CAPTAIN COOK HOTEL ●

BENT PROP INN & HOSTEL ●

I ST

ANCHORAGE DOWNTOWN HOTEL ●

W 5TH AVE

RESOLUTION PARK ●

Tony Knowles Coastal Trail

COPPERWHALE INN ●

OSCAR ANDERSON HOUSE ★

COASTAL PLACE ●

SUSTINA PLACE B&B ●

CLARION SUITES DOWNTOWN ●

K ST
L ST
M ST
N ST
O ST

OSCAR GILL HOUSE B&B ●

© AVALON TRAVEL

ANCHORAGE

© AVALON TRAVEL

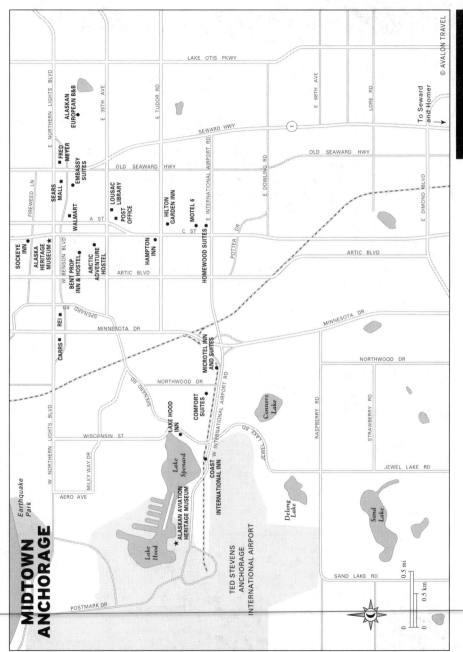

MIDTOWN ANCHORAGE

LAKE OTIS PKWY

E NORTHERN LIGHTS BLVD

E 36TH AVE

ALASKAN EUROPEAN B&B

E TUDOR RD

E 68TH AVE

LORE RD

To Seward and Homer →

SEWARD HWY

1

FRED MEYER

OLD SEAWARD HWY

E INTERNATIONAL AIRPORT RD

E DOWLING RD

FIREWEED LN

EMBASSY SUITES

OLD SEAWARD HWY

SEARS MALL

LOUSAC LIBRARY

A ST

WALMART

POST OFFICE

HILTON GARDEN INN

MOTEL 6

C ST

E DIMOND BLVD

SOCKEYE INN

ALASKA HERITAGE MUSEUM ★

W BENSON BLVD

HAMPTON INN

HOMEWOOD SUITES

POTTER DR

ARTIC BLVD

BENT PROP INN & HOSTEL

ARCTIC ADVENTURE HOSTEL

ARTIC BLVD

SPENARD RD

REI

MINNESOTA DR

MINNESOTA DR

CARRS

NORTHWOOD DR

MICROTEL INN AND SUITES

W NORTHERN LIGHTS BLVD

SPENARD RD

NORTHWOOD DR

W INTERNATIONAL AIRPORT RD

RASPBERRY RD

STRAWBERRY RD

LAKE HOOD INN

COMFORT SUITES

Connors Lake

WISCONSIN ST

LAKE HOOD

JEWEL LAKE RD

JEWEL LAKE RD

Earthquake Park

MILKY WAY DR

Lake Spenard

COAST INTERNATIONAL INN

Delong Lake

Sand Lake

AERO AVE

ALASKAN AVIATION HERITAGE MUSEUM ★

Lake Hood

TED STEVENS ANCHORAGE INTERNATIONAL AIRPORT

SAND LAKE RD

POSTMARK DR

0.5 mi

0.5 km

0

ANCHORAGE

Sights

It doesn't take long to get the hang of downtown Anchorage. The blocks are square, with the lettered streets (A through L) going north-south and the numbered avenues (starting at 2nd Ave., just up the hill from the tracks) running east-west. Once you get east of the lettered streets they start over again using alphabetized names (Barrow, Cordova, Denali, Eagle, Fairbanks).

Beyond downtown, the city of Anchorage sprawls across the Anchorage Bowl, with hillside homes peering down on the masses below. A number of neighborhoods are scattered around Anchorage, but most travelers are likely to spend their time in downtown and **Midtown,** a collection of malls, shopping centers, supermarkets, fast-food joints, bars, movie theaters, discount stores, gas stations, and other businesses just a 20-minute walk or a 10-minute bus ride south of downtown. Midtown encompasses the area within Northern Lights and Benson Boulevards between Minnesota Drive and Old Seward Highway. It isn't exactly a tourist attraction, but this, along with shopping malls on the south and east end of town, is where locals—and others looking to save money—spend their cash. Another large shopping district is along Dimond Boulevard in South Anchorage, where all the stalwarts are: Best Buy, WalMart, Costco, Sam's Club, Sports Authority, and more.

DOWNTOWN
Town Square (5th Ave. and G St.) on the spacious front lawn of the Performing Arts Center is a fine flower-filled field of fecundity. It's a wonderful place to meet up with friends or just relax on a sunny summer day.

◖ Anchorage Museum
A massive $106 million expansion in 2009 transformed the Anchorage Museum (625 C St., 907/929-9200, www.anchoragemuseum. org, daily 9am-6pm May-Sept.; Sun. noon-6pm, Tues.-Sat. 10am-6pm the rest of the year, $12 adults, $9 seniors, students, and military, $7 ages 3-12, younger children free) into the state's largest—170,000 square feet—and finest museum. One very popular feature is the kid-friendly **Imaginarium Discovery Center,** with 80 hands-on science exhibits, including an amazing high-tech magic-planet globe that displays today's weather patterns (and much more), live marine touch tanks (with sea stars, crabs, and anemones), an air cannon, and pulley chairs. Exhibits focus on Alaskan science, especially earthquakes and volcanoes.

WILDERNESS IN THE CITY

In Anchorage, it's surprisingly easy to get away from busy city streets to the wilderness at the city's borders. Here are a few city getaways:

- Walk or bike the **Tony Knowles Coastal Trail.**
- Climb **Flattop Mountain** within massive Chugach State Park.
- Drive along **Turnagain Arm** to watch for beluga whales and bore tides.
- Go mountain biking in **Kincaid Park.**
- Check out the **Alaska Zoo.**
- Ride the **aerial tramway** to the top of Mount Alyeska for great hikes and fine dining.
- Visit the **Alaska Botanical Garden.**
- Catch a king, silver, or pink salmon in **Ship Creek,** right in the heart of Anchorage.
- Visit the **Alaska Wildlife Conservation Center** near Portage to see brown bear, moose, and other wildlife up close.

© KEN GRAHAM PHOTOGRAPHY.COM/ANCHORAGE MUSEUM

Anchorage Museum

Also on the first level is the **Thomas Planetarium** ($6 adults, $4 kids). This isn't one of those boring point-out-the-stars shows, but a fun 3-D trip beyond the solar system. Especially fun is Pink Floyd's Dark Side of the Moon music and light show. Other highlights include a gallery of Alaskan art that features Sydney Laurence's 6-by-10-foot oil painting of Mount McKinley. The upper levels contain galleries with contemporary Native Alaskan art, Alaskan history, and rotating shows that change every few months. Don't miss the second-floor collection of some 600 archaeological pieces on long-term loan from the Smithsonian Museum—they're the highlight of the museum. The upper levels are devoted to changing exhibitions, with fine mountain and city vistas from the fourth level.

In addition to exhibits, the Anchorage Museum has a gift shop and historical photos in the resource center. Enjoy an upscale lunch at trendy **Muse** (907/929-9210, www. marxcafe.com, Tues.-Sun.). In the summer, free hour-long tours are offered four times a day, and local artists sell their crafts in the atrium during June and July. Outside is a two-acre commons, perfect for summer afternoon picnics or letting the kids run around. The Anchorage Museum and Alaska Native Heritage Center have teamed up to offer the **Alaska Cultural Pass** ($29), providing entrance to both of these facilities plus a free shuttle; get tickets at either facility.

Museums and Historic Buildings

Anchorage is pretty short on historical buildings since much of the city was destroyed in the 1964 quake and most of the city's development and growth has taken place since the 1970s. The neighborhood around 2nd Avenue at F Street includes several of the original town-site homes constructed in the early 1900s, and historical panels describe the city's early days.

A few other structures survive from quieter

times, including the **Oscar Anderson House Museum** (420 M St., 907/274-2336, www.anchoragehistoricproperties.org, tours: Mon.-Fri. noon-5pm June-mid-Sept., $3 adults, $1 kids), open for 45-minute tours. This refurbished little bungalow—built in 1915 by Anchorage's first butcher—is the oldest frame residence in this young city. Outside of the summer months, it reopens during the first two weekends of December, when it is festooned with traditional Swedish Christmas decorations. The Tony Knowles Coastal Trail passes right in front of the Oscar Anderson House, and adjacent is tiny **Elderberry Park,** a pleasant place to relax on a sunny afternoon, with picnic and playground facilities.

Across the street from the old Federal Building is the **4th Avenue Theater** (630 W. 4th Ave.), built in 1947 and one of the few structures to survive the 1964 earthquake. It's closed to the public. Up the street and right next to the log cabin visitors center is **Old City Hall** (4th Ave. near E St., 907/276-4118, Mon.-Fri. 8am-5pm, free), housing the offices of the ACVB. Step inside the lobby to view a few exhibits and historic photos from early Anchorage.

The **Alaska State Trooper Museum** (245 W. 5th Ave., 907/279-5050, www.alaskatroopermuseum.com, Mon.-Fri. 10am-4pm, Sat. noon-4pm, free) is worth visiting to check out the gleaming black 1952 Hudson Hornet patrol car.

Immediately north of downtown is the **Alaska Railroad Depot** (411 W. 1st Ave.), where you can book train travel or check out the 1907 train engine out front.

Delaney Park

Known as the "park strip," early in Anchorage's history, enjoyable Delaney Park (between 9th and 10th Aves. from L St. to Barrow St.) marked the boundary where the town stopped and the wilderness started. In 1923 the strip

where the park is today was cleared as a fire-break. Since then it has served as a golf course, an airstrip, and now hosts half a dozen softball games every night of summer, tennis and basketball courts, and large grassy sections for Frisbee, Hacky Sack, tai chi, sunbathing, or people-watching. Right next to the park is a cage housing **Star, the pet reindeer** (corner of 10th Ave. and I St.). The owners have had a succession of reindeer here since 1962; this is number six.

Resolution Park

A very popular stop for tour buses, visitors on foot, and the occasional (probably drunk) local is Resolution Park (west end of 3rd Ave. at L St.). This tiny city park consists of a viewing platform centered around a statue of Captain James Cook, who encountered what is now called Cook Inlet in 1778. The park is named for his ship, the *Resolution.* On clear days you'll delight in the mountain-scape vistas. Mount McKinley (many locals call it Denali) rises 125 miles to the north, and the low mountain just northwest across Cook Inlet is aptly named Sleeping Lady (the maps call it Mount Susitna). Behind it, and just a bit south, stands a chain of active volcanoes that dump ash on Anchorage every few years, including Mount Spurr and Mount Redoubt. If you have eagle eyes and crystalline weather, you might pick out a third volcano, Mount Iliamna, far to the southwest. Out of sight is yet a fourth volcano, Mount Augustine, which last spewed ash in 1986.

Tony Knowles Coastal Trail

This is one of Anchorage's highlights, a wonderful 11-mile asphalt track that wends its way along the shore from downtown past the airport to Kincaid Park at Point Campbell, where the Knik and Turnagain Arms meet. From downtown, the trail is accessible from the west ends of 2nd, 5th, and 9th Avenues, with additional access at Westchester Lagoon, Earthquake

Park, Point Woronzof, and Kincaid. Stroll the trail a ways, at least through the tunnel, beyond which you leave downtown behind and emerge into a new world: the grand sweep of the Arm, tidal flats, railroad tracks, and a residential neighborhood. On warm summer evenings this trail is more like a freeway, with people on every kind of wheels imaginable: bike riders, inline skaters, skateboarders, and babies in carriages. In winter they trade the wheels for skis. The Coastal Trail gets especially crowded around duck-filled **Westchester Lagoon,** a mile south of downtown, which is also the city's favorite wintertime ice skating rink.

A second paved path intersects the Coastal Trail at Westchester Lagoon, the **Chester Creek Trail,** which creates another greenbelt across Anchorage. This one heads east along the creek, continuing for five miles to the University of Alaska at Anchorage campus.

BEYOND DOWNTOWN

Earthquake Park, out on West Northern Lights Boulevard near the airport, has interpretive signs about the Big One on Good Friday 1964, and a view of the skyline and the Chugach Mountains. But the views are even more dramatic from **Point Woronzof,** another mile or so out. Tony Knowles Coastal Trail parallels the coast along Earthquake Park and Point Woronzof; it continues from downtown all the way south to **Kincaid Park.** And speaking of Kincaid, the trails here are a destination for hikers and mountain bikers all summer, and cross-country skiers when the snow flies.

Covering 11 acres of land, the **Alaska Botanical Garden** (Campbell Airstrip Rd. off Tudor Rd., 907/770-3692, www.alaskabg.org, daily during daylight hours year-round, $7 adults, $5 age 3-18, younger children free) is home to more than 1,100 varieties of plants. An information kiosk is at the entrance, and a pleasant one-mile nature trail leads through the perennial, rock, wildflower, and herb gardens.

Join a guided tour of the garden daily at 1pm (plus Wed. at 6pm) June-August.

◖ Alaska Native Heritage Center

Located on a 26-acre site facing the Chugach Mountains, the Alaska Native Heritage Center (8800 Heritage Center Dr., Glenn Hwy. and Muldoon Rd., 907/330-8000 or 800/315-6608, www.alaskanative.net, daily 9am-5pm mid-May-mid-Sept., closed in winter, $25 adults, $21 seniors and military, $17 ages 7-16, younger children free) provides an excellent introduction to Native Alaskan culture in the state. A joint Alaska Cultural Pass ($29) provides access to both the Anchorage Museum and the Heritage Center. The central "Welcome House" has a variety of exhibits and is used for concerts and demonstrations. Outside, five traditional village settings have been recreated around a small lake, and Native Alaskan guides explain Alaska's various cultures. The Heritage Center is east of downtown near the intersection of the Glenn Highway and Muldoon Road. A free shuttle runs from the downtown Log Cabin Visitors Center and the Anchorage Museum five times daily in the summer.

Alaska Heritage Museum

Housed in the lobby of the Wells Fargo bank in Midtown, and officially called the Alaska Heritage Museum at Wells Fargo (Northern Lights Blvd. and C St., 907/265-2834, www.wellsfargohistory.com, Mon.-Fri. noon-5pm June-Sept., Mon.-Fri. noon-4pm in winter, free), this is one of the state's largest privately owned collections of Alaskan artifacts and books. It will keep you spellbound for hours, if you have the time. Be sure to check out the 3.2-pound (!) gold nugget found in 1963 near Ruby, Alaska. Other highlights include many Native Alaskan baskets, parkas made from bird skins and walrus intestines, Sydney Laurence's paintings, Nome and Fairbanks newspapers from the early 1900s, and bookcases filled with rare books and maps. This little gem of a museum is not to be missed.

Alaska Museum of Natural History

Located off Mountain View Drive on the northeast end of town, the Alaska Museum of Natural History (201 N. Bragaw St., 907/274-2400, www.alaskamuseum.org, Mon.-Sat. 10am-5pm, $5 adults, $4 seniors and military, $3 ages 3-12, younger children free) houses kid-friendly exhibits on polar dinosaurs, the Ice Age, birds, and geology.

Alaska Aviation Heritage Museum

The Alaska Aviation Heritage Museum (4721 Aircraft Dr., 907/248-5325, www.alaskaairmuseum.org, daily 9am-5pm mid-May-mid-Sept.; Wed.-Sat. 9am-5pm, Sun. noon-5pm in winter, $10 adults, $8 seniors, $6 ages 5-12, younger children free) is off the Lake Hood exit from International Airport Road. This unusual museum displays 30 vintage aircraft in three connected hangars—from a 1928 Stearman up to an old Alaska Airlines 737—as well as Japanese artifacts from the World War II Aleutian Island battles and historical photos. The theaters show videos on early Alaskan aviation, and the museum fronts on **Lake Hood,** the world's largest seaplane base, where floatplanes take off and land almost constantly in the summer.

Alaska Zoo

Located two miles east of New Seward Highway, the zoo (4731 O'Malley Rd., 907/346-2133, www.alaskazoo.org, daily 9am-9pm June-Aug., daily 9am-6pm May and Sept., daily 10am-5pm March, April, and Oct., daily 10am-4pm Nov.-Feb., $12 adults, $9 seniors and military, $6 ages 3-17, younger children free) is connected by a free shuttle bus from the Transit Center. The zoo has nice grounds, enjoyable shady paths, and all the Alaskan animals, plus a number of more exotic critters. If you have kids, they'll enjoy it, especially the star attractions: Ahpun and Louie, the polar bears. You can watch the bears' underwater antics through the glass of their swimming pool, or check out the polar bear cam on the zoo's website.

Entertainment and Events

NIGHTLIFE

The best sources for Anchortown action are the Friday *Anchorage Daily News* (www.adn.com/play) and the *Anchorage Press* (www.anchoragepress.com), a free weekly newspaper available in racks all over town. Anchorage has joined many other American cities by banning smoking in bars and virtually all other indoor places.

Bars in Anchorage are typically open until 2am.

Bars and Clubs

Anchorage is a *Cheers*-type town, with lots of corner bars and local pubs tucked away. Downtown, a popular place is **F Street Station** (4th Ave. and F St., 907/272-5196), which also serves good-value lunches and dinners. **Darwin's Theory** (426 G St., 907/277-5322) attracts a fun after-work crowd. There is free hot pepper schnapps—if you can stomach it—when the bartender rings the bell (quite often some evenings).

Popular Anchorage sports bars include **Peanut Farm** (5227 Old Seward Hwy., 907/563-3283, www.wemustbenuts.com, Sun.-Thurs. 6am-2:30am, Fri.-Sat. 6am-3am), **Crossroads Lounge** (1402 Gambell St., 907/276-9014, Sun.-Thurs. 10am-2:30am,

Fri.-Sat. 10am-3am), and **Eddie's Sports Bar** (6300 Old Seward Hwy., 907/563-3970).

Anchorage's favorite downtown bar is **Humpy's Great Alaskan Alehouse** (610 W. 6th Ave., 907/276-2337, www.humpys.com/anc, Mon.-Thurs., 11am-2am, Fri. 11am-2:30am, Sat. 10am-2:30am, Sun. 10am-2am). Drop by on any night of the week to rub shoulders (and arms, legs, and other body parts—it gets mighty crowded) with a hip, raucous, and youthful crowd. The bar has dozens of microbrews on tap, the kitchen cranks out pub fare, bands play nightly, and there's never a cover charge. Humpy's is a must-see place if you're staying downtown, especially if you're single (or pretending to be).

Chilkoot Charlie's (2435 Spenard Rd. at Fireweed Ln., 907/272-1010, www.koots.com, daily 11:30am-close) is a ramshackle building where you can do some serious jumping up and down to real rock and roll and generally have a night of good, raunchy fun. There are three separate dance floors and 10 (!) bars inside. It's big enough to get lost in. The main stage has loud and very live rock, while the other dance floors are filled with folks dancing to DJ Top 40 or whatever else is hot. 'Koots is a love-it-or-hate-it sort of place; if you aren't into the cruising and pickup scene, try elsewhere. But you should at least go here to say you didn't miss the most famous place in town. 'Koots gets extremely crowded on weekend nights (cover charge), so you may have to wait quite a while to get in if you come after 10pm. You can't miss Chilkoot Charlie's: just look for the tall lighted windmill.

Blues Central Chef's Inn (825 W. Northern Lights Blvd., 907/272-1341, www.bluescentral.org, Sun.-Thurs., 11am-2:30am, Fri.-Sat. 11am-3am) is truly Anchorage's blues central, with live bluesy bands nightly. The bar attracts leather-clad bikers and others. There is good food (especially the French dip) and great blues tunes.

McGinley's Irish Pub (645 G St., 907/279-1782, www.mcginleyspub.com, daily 11am-close) has Guinness on tap, weekend bands, and no cover.

Several Anchorage bars offer a quiet and romantic atmosphere. If you luck into a clear evening, have packed something a little dressy, and don't mind blowing two days' budget on a beer, head up to the **Crow's Nest** (4th Ave. and K St., 907/276-6000, http://captaincook.com, Mon.-Sat. 5pm-midnight) atop the Captain Cook Hotel—the view is worth the effort. The **Fancy Moose Lounge** (4800 Spenard Rd., 907/266-2249, www.millenniumhotels.com/milleniumanchorage, daily 11am-1am) at the Millenium Alaskan Hotel has an upscale bar with outdoor seating overlooking Lake Hood.

Gay and Lesbian Nightlife
Mad Myrna's (530 E. 5th Ave., 907/276-9762, www.madmyrnas.com, Sun.-Thurs. 4pm-2:30am, Fri.-Sat. 4pm-3am) has drag shows on Fridays, karaoke Thursdays, and DJ tunes on Fridays and Saturdays. **The Raven** (708 E. 4th Ave., 907/276-9672) is a pool-shootin' joint.

PERFORMING ARTS
Anchorage's active cultural scene centers on the downtown **Alaska Center for the Performing Arts** (5th Ave. and G St., 907/263-2900, www.myalaskacenter.com, tours Wed. 1pm, free), better known as "the PAC," short for Performing Arts Center, an unusual brick-and-glass building with colorful Olympic-like rings of light around the top. Inside are three auditoriums with wonderful acoustics. Two IMAX films are screened throughout the summer: one on wolves, the other on the Great Land. The latter is narrated by Charlton Heston, so check your National Rifle Association guns at the door. In addition, the center has an interesting slide show on the northern lights.

PAC has events throughout the year, including modern dance, ballet, Broadway

ANCHORAGE

© DON PITCHER

Alaska Center for the Performing Arts

musicals, comedy troupes, opera, and concerts by nationally known artists, along with winter performances by the **Anchorage Concert Association** (907/272-1471, www.anchorageconcerts.org), **Anchorage Symphony Orchestra** (907/274-8668, www.anchoragesymphony.org), the **Anchorage Concert Chorus** (907/274-7464, www.anchorageconcertchorus.org), and the **Anchorage Opera** (907/279-2557, www.anchorageopera.org).

Call 907/566-2787 for a recording of upcoming events at the PAC and elsewhere. Tickets are available at the PAC box office, in Carrs stores, and at 800/478-7328 or www.centertix.net. Check Friday's *Anchorage Daily News* (www.adn.com/play) for upcoming events.

Anchorage is a city that showers appreciation on traveling musicians who come out of their way to visit the city, particularly those with a folk-rock bent. Many of Anchorage's best performances arrive courtesy of **Whistling Swan Productions** (907/263-2787, www.

whistlingswan.net); visit their website for upcoming shows.

For plays, check out productions by **Cyrano's Off-Center Playhouse** (413 D St., 907/274-2599, www.cyranos.org), **Out North Contemporary Art House** (3800 DeBarr Rd., 907/279-3800, www.outnorth.org), and **Anchorage Community Theatre** (1133 E. 70th Ave., 907/344-4713, www.actalaska.org).

MOVIES

The downtown **Alaska Center for the Performing Arts** (5th Ave. and G St., 907/263-2900, www.myalaskacenter.com, daily on the hour 9am-9pm summer, $9 adults, $8 seniors and military, $7 kids) offers photo shows on the northern lights.

Bear Tooth Theatrepub (1230 W. 27th Ave., 907/276-4200, www.beartooththeatre. net, Mon.-Thurs. 10:30am-10pm, Fri.-Sat. 10:30am-11pm, Sun. noon-10pm, $4 movies) has a winning combination: inexpensive second-run and art-house movies, tasty light meals (including tacos, nachos, salads, burritos, and pizzas), plus brewery-fresh draft beer. It's a great place with a family atmosphere, and it's run by the same geniuses that created Moose's Tooth Pub & Pizzeria. You can eat downstairs and drink while watching the movie; upstairs is reserved for underage kids.

It also has a restaurant area (very noisy) in the lobby, for those who just want a meal in a family setting, and the adjacent **Bear Tooth Grill** (Mon.-Fri. 11am-11:30pm, Sat.-Sun. 10am-11:30pm, $12-18), with a big brunch and dinner menu of fish tacos, burgers, Mexican platters, pasta, and salads. Since reservations are not available you may face a lengthy wait on weekends. Parking for these Bear Tooth venues can be a problem on weekend nights, but they have a parking lot a block down the street. Whatever you do, don't park across the street from the theater, where a tow truck driver takes pleasure in hauling cars away.

See what's showing at local theaters by visiting www.anchoragemovies.com. Anchorage's main theater action is the **Century 16** (36th Ave. and A St., 907/929-3456), where all 16 theaters have stadium seating and reclining chairs. Other Anchorage multiplexes include **Totem 8** (3131 Muldoon Rd., 907/566-3329), **Fireweed 7** (Fireweed Ln. and New Seward Hwy., 907/566-3328), and **Dimond Center 9** (Dimond Mall, Dimond Blvd. and Old Seward Hwy., 907/566-3327).

FESTIVALS AND EVENTS

Winter is the time for Anchorage's best-known events, the Iditarod and Fur Rendezvous, but the city is certainly full of life in the summer. Check the Anchorage Convention and Visitors Bureau website (www.anchorage.net) for a complete listing of events.

Summer

Every Wednesday and Friday at noon, head downtown for free **Music in the Park** (4th Ave. and E St., 907/279-5650, www.anchoragedowntown.org, Wed. and Fri. at noon), next to the visitors center. Other events take place here most other weekday afternoons in the summer.

Several times each summer, the big parking lot at **Moose's Tooth Pub & Pizzeria** (3300 Old Seward Hwy., 907/258-2537, www.moosestooth.net) becomes a stage for acclaimed bands such as Wilco, G. Love, Cake, Silversun Pickups, and Michael Franti. The biggest event is usually the Moose's Tooth Anniversary Party in late July. Check their Facebook page for upcoming events, and be sure to get tickets in advance.

The **Arctic Thunder Air Show** (907/552-7469, www.jber.af.mil/arcticthunder, June) at Joint Base Elmendorf-Richardson features a stunning performance by the Air Force's Thunderbirds.

Three Barons Renaissance Faire (3400 E. Tudor Rd., 907/868-8012, www.3barons.org,

early June) takes place at Hilltop Ski Area, and the crowd gets into the act by pelting rotten acting with rotten tomatoes.

Alaska's biggest marathon is the **Mayor's Midnight Sun Marathon** (www.mayorsmarathon.com, late June), which attracts a serious cadre of runners on the summer solstice.

On Independence Day, there's a **Fourth of July parade** (9th Ave. and K St., www.anchoragejuly4thcelebration.com) downtown in the morning, but when the fireworks show starts at midnight the sky still isn't very dark!

Also in early July, the **Bear Paw Festival** (downtown Eagle River, 907/694-4702, www.bearpawfestival.org, early July) comes to nearby Eagle River, with a classic car show, races, a chili cook-off, carnival rides, and the state's biggest parade.

Winter

In recent years, tourism to Alaska has increased in the winter months as visitors discover what Alaskans already know: that winter opens up a panoply of outdoor options. Several companies specialize in winter tours and activities; see the visitors center for brochures.

The **Anchorage Folk Festival** (campus of the University of Alaska Anchorage, www.anchoragefolkfestival.org, late Jan.) is a major winter diversion, with free concerts that fill two consecutive weekends.

The **Fur Rendezvous** (907/274-1177, www.furrondy.net, last weekend in Feb. and the first weekend in Mar.) is one the city's biggest annual events, with all sorts of fun activities during this 10-day-long festival. A carnival packs a downtown lot, and there are fireworks, snow sculpture and ice carving contests, dress balls, concerts, dog-pulling contests, the world championship sled dog race, and a very popular run-with-the-reindeer event (slightly) modeled after the running of the bulls in Pamplona.

The one Alaskan event that always attracts national attention is the **Iditarod Trail Sled**

ANCHORAGE

Dog Race (starts in downtown Anchorage, 907/376-5155, www.iditarod.com, early Mar.) from Anchorage to Nome.

Another very popular event is the **Great Alaska Shootout** (Sullivan Arena, 1600 Gambell St., 907/786-1250, www.goseawolves.com, Nov.) basketball tournament that features seven top college teams and the lowly University of Alaska Seawolves. This one gets national media attention because it's so early in the year.

The **Nordic Skiing Association of Anchorage** (907/276-7609, www. anchoragenordicski.com) keeps dozens of miles of local trails groomed, and puts on such events as the **Tour of Anchorage** (www.tourofanchorage.com, early Mar.). The **Ski for Women** (www.alaskaskiforwomen.org, early Feb.) on Super Bowl Sunday is the largest North American ski event for women, attracting more than 1,500 participants.

Spring Carnival and Slush Cup (Girdwood, 907/754-1111, www.alyeskaresort.com, mid-April) is a wet and wild event for skiers and boarders as they try to cross a slushy pond at Alyeska Resort.

Shopping

Although big-city folks sometimes complain that Anchorage doesn't have the fancy boutiques they're accustomed to finding, it *does* have just about every other sort of place—from Sam's Club to Nordstrom. The city is a car haven, so many of these stores are scattered in the various shopping malls that help give Anchorage its urban sprawl.

◖ ANCHORAGE MARKET AND FESTIVAL

Anchorage's finest and freshest produce can be found at the Anchorage Market and Festival (3rd Ave. and E St., 907/272-5634, www.anchoragemarkets.com, Sat.-Sun. 10am-6pm mid-May-mid-Sept.), held at the downtown parking on weekends. More than 300 vendors offer local arts and crafts, a diverse mix of finger food—everything from salmon quesadillas to sweet funnel cakes—and, of course, produce. Live music and entertainment add to the allure. Be sure to stop by the **Kahiltna Birchworks** (907/733-1309, www.alaskabirchsyrup.com) booth, where you'll find distinctive and flavorful birch syrups and caramels created from Michael and Dulce East's home in the Alaskan bush.

There is also a smaller **Wednesday Market** (Northway Mall, 3101 Penland Blvd., 907/272-5634, Wed. 9am-4pm July-early Oct.).

MALLS

Downtown Anchorage's **5th Avenue Mall** (320 W. 5th Ave., 907/258-5535) includes two big stores—J. C. Penney and Nordstrom—along with Alaska's only official Apple store and several dozen storefronts on four levels.

The city's largest mall is **Dimond Center** (Dimond Blvd. and Old Seward Hwy., www. dimondcenter.com) on the south side. In Midtown, **The Mall at Sears** (Northern Lights Blvd. and Seward Hwy., www.mallatsears. com) has good variety. Anchorage has all the megastores, including WalMart, Fred Meyer, Costco, Sam's Club, Lowes, Home Depot, Toys 'R' Us, Barnes & Noble.

GIFTS AND NATIVE ART

Much of downtown is given over to shops selling tourist doodads, particularly along 3rd and 4th Avenues, where you'll find everything from $5 made-in-China trinkets to $20,000 sculptures.

One People (425 D St., 907/274-4063,

The Anchorage Market and Festival takes place every summer weekend.

www.onepeoplegifts.com) has a fine selection of Native Alaskan art in a convenient downtown location. Also check out the nonprofit **Alaska Native Arts Foundation** (500 W. 6th Ave., 907/258-2623, www.alaskanativearts.org), which represents hundreds of artists. One of the finest places to buy Native Alaskan crafts is the out-of-the-way **Alaska Native Medical Center Gift Shop** (4315 Diplomacy Dr. off East Tudor Rd., 907/729-1122, www.anmc.org). Excellent grass baskets, dolls, masks, yo-yos, and more are sold on consignment. Another recommended place is the gift shop at the **Alaska Native Heritage Center** (8800 Heritage Center Dr., Glenn Hwy. and Muldoon Rd., 907/330-8000 or 800/315-6608, www.alaskanative.net, Mon.-Fri. 10am-2pm).

An unusual (and very expensive) purchase to consider is *qiviut:* caps, scarves, shawls, sweaters, or baby booties, hand-knitted by Native Alaskans from the wool of domestic musk oxen (the musk ox farm is outside of Palmer). Many times warmer and lighter than wool, these fine knits can be seen and salivated over at **Oomingmak Co-op** (604 H St., 907/272-9225 or 888/360-9665, www.qiviut.com).

SWEETS

Alaska Wild Berry Products (5225 Juneau St., 907/562-8858 or 800/280-2927, www.alaskawildberryproducts.com, Mon.-Sat. 10am-8pm, Sun. noon-7pm Jan.-Apr.; Mon.-Thurs. 10am-9pm, Fri.-Sat. 10am-10pm, Sun. 11am-8pm May; Sun.-Thurs. 10am-9pm, Fri.-Sat. 10am-10pm June-Labor Day; Mon.-Thurs. 10am-8pm, Fri.-Sat. 10am-9pm, Sun. 11am-8pm Labor Day-Oct.; Mon.-Sat. 11am-9pm, Sun. 11am-8pm Nov.-Dec.) has a large chocolate factory and gift shop on Juneau Street near the corner of Old Seward Highway and International Airport Road. This is a fun place for chocoholics; there's even a 20-foot melted-chocolate waterfall, free taste samples, and a free shuttle from downtown. Fifteen-minute tours are given throughout the day, and this is a very popular stop on the Anchorage tour-bus circuit. The big gift shop offers all the standard tourist stuff (and then some), while the theater shows an award-winning 30-minute film ($8) about Alaska.

GALLERIES

On the **First Friday** of each month Anchorage's art scene comes alive with openings, hors d'oeuvres, and the chance to meet regional artists at a dozen or so galleries. Check the Friday *Anchorage Daily News* or the weekly *Anchorage Press* for details.

Anchorage's premier gallery is the **International Gallery of Contemporary Art** (427 D St., 907/279-1116, www.igcaalaska.org, Tues.-Sun. noon-4pm), with something new each month from top regional artists.

Three good places to buy original artwork in Anchorage are **Artique** (314 G St., 907/277-1663 or 800/848-1312, www.artiqueltd.com), **Arctic Rose Gallery** (420 L St., 907/279-3911, www.arcticrosegallery.com), and the jam-packed **Aurora Fine Arts Gallery** (314 G St., 907/277-1663 or 800/848-1312, www.aurorafineart-alaska.com).

It isn't exactly art work, but **Stewart's Photo Shop** (531 W. 4th Ave., 907/272-8581, www.stewartsphoto.com) has the most complete selection of photographic equipment in the state. It's right downtown across from the visitors center.

OUTDOOR OUTFITTERS

Anchorage is an excellent place to stock up on outdoor gear before heading into Alaska's bush. The biggest place to shop—and one of the best—is **REI** (1200 W. Northern Lights Blvd., 907/272-4565, www.rei.com) on the corner of Northern Lights Boulevard and Spenard Road. REI stands for Recreation Equipment Inc. This Seattle-based cooperative has a knowledgeable staff that offer free clinics and

talks throughout the year. You can also rent canoes, kayaks, stand up paddleboards, tents, backpacks, sleeping bags, stoves, bear-proof containers, skis, snowshoes, and other outdoor equipment from REI.

Another excellent outdoor store with a technically adept staff is **Alaska Mountaineering & Hiking** (2633 Spenard Rd., 907/272-1811, www.alaskamountaineering.com)—better known as AMH—just a block from REI. Though much smaller, AMH often has equipment that is unavailable elsewhere. This is where the hard-core climbers and backcountry skiers go.

Check the bulletin boards at AMH and REI for used gear and travel partners. Or cross the street to **Play it Again Sports** (2636 Spenard Rd., 907/278-7529, www.playitagainsports.com), where used equipment of all sorts is available, from backpacks and tents to baseball gloves and fishing poles. They also buy used gear if you need a little cash on your way out of town.

Downtown shoppers head to the **Army/Navy Store** (320 W. 4th Ave., 907/279-2401, www.classicalaska.com) for more traditional Alaskan outdoor clothing and boots. **B&J Commercial** (2749 C St., 907/274-6113, www.bnjsg.com) has a downstairs packed with sport and commercial fishing supplies. This is where you'll find really heavy-duty clothing and equipment at fair prices.

BOOKS AND MUSIC

Alaska's largest independent bookstore is **Title Wave Books** (1360 W. Northern Lights Blvd., 907/278-9283 or 888/598-9283, www.wavebooks.com), next to REI. Offering a fine choice of new and used titles, this is a great hangout spot, with a literate crowd and an adjacent Kaladi Brothers shop to sip coffee and surf the Internet. Also in Midtown is **Metro Music and Books** (530 E. Benson Blvd., 907/279-8622), with a big selection of used and new CDs, any of which you can listen to before deciding to buy.

In Midtown, **Barnes & Noble** (200 E. Northern Lights Blvd., 907/279-7323 or 888/279-7323, www.barnesandnoble.com) has a wide array of books, magazines, Kindles, and CDs, plus a Starbucks.

SEAFOOD

The best places to find fresh fish, clams, crab, and other Alaskan specialties are **10th & M Seafoods** (1020 M St., 907/272-3474 or 800/770-2722, www.10thandmseafoods.com) and **New Sagaya's** (900 W. 13th Ave., 907/274-6173, www.newsagaya.com). If you've caught your own fish, 10th and M will store your catch in their freezers for a fee. For smoked salmon, drop by **Alaska Sausage & Seafood** (2914 Arctic Blvd., 907/562-3636 or 800/798-3636, www.alaskasausage.com).

Recreation

SUMMER
Hiking and Horseback Rides

One of the most popular hiking trails in Alaska is the 1.5-mile path to the summit of **Flattop Mountain** in Chugach State Park. The trailhead is on the southeastern edge of Anchorage, so you'll need a car to get there.

The **Mountaineering Club of Alaska** (MCA, meetings at BP Energy Center, 900 E. Benson Blvd., www.mtnclubak.org, membership $15) holds meetings at 7:30pm on the third Wednesday of each month. Visitors are welcome to enjoy the presentations. Members can go along on any of their frequent outings.

Horse Trekkin Alaska (907/868-3728, www.horsetrekkinalaska.com) offers horseback rides in Anchorage parks.

Biking

Anchorage has 200 miles of urban cycling and jogging trails; pick up bike trail maps at the downtown visitors center. A delightfully easy ride—it's all paved—goes 11 miles from the west end of 2nd Avenue along the **Tony Knowles Coastal Trail,** past Westchester Lagoon, Earthquake Park, and Point Woronzof, and then all the way to Kincaid Park at Point Campbell, out on the western tip of the city. The **Chester Creek Trail** meets the Coastal Trail at Westchester Lagoon and takes you almost five miles to Goose Lake, where you can take a dip if you're hot. Or just bomb around to wherever the wind blows you. Note, however, that the major Anchorage arteries are not especially bike-friendly, so you may want to stick to the side streets to avoid contending with exhaust fumes and speeding pickup trucks. Dirt biking and hiking trails abound within **Kincaid Park, Hillside Park,** and **Far North Bicentennial Park,** or you can head up **Powerline Pass Trail** inside Chugach State Park or to **Eklutna Lake** (bike rentals available on-site).

The city of Anchorage produces a helpful free **bike map,** available at the Log Cabin Visitors Center or online at www.muni.org. City buses all have front bike racks. One of the newest innovations is the advent of fat tire bikes, with out-sized balloon tires for riding on snow and other soft surfaces. They're sold in local bike shops and are becoming increasingly common on winter trails throughout Alaska. Based in Anchorage, the **Arctic Bicycle Club** (907/566-0177, www.arcticbike.org) organizes races and tours and has a very helpful website.

For mountain bike rentals, head to **Downtown Bicycle Rental** (333 W. 4th Ave., 907/279-3334, www.alaska-bike-rentals.com, May-Sept.), or two shops within a block of each other on L Street: **Bike Anchorage** (440 L St., 907/746-4644 or 800/952-8624, www.lifetimeadventures.net, May-Sept.) and **Pablo's**

Bicycle Rentals (501 L St., 907/250-2871, www.pablobicyclerentals.com, May-Sept.). All three are close to the Coastal Trail and also rent a variety of other bikes.

Glacier Tours

Several companies have downtown Anchorage offices promoting boat day-tours to glaciers in Prince William Sound (via Whittier) or Resurrection Bay (via Seward). These include Prince William Sound tours from **Phillips Tours and Cruises** (519 W. 4th Ave., 907/276-8023, www.phillipscruises. com) and **Major Marine Tours** (1800 Premier Ct., 907/274-7300 or 800/764-7300, www. majormarine.com), plus Resurrection Bay trips from **Prince William Sound Cruises and Tours** (877/777-4051, www.princewilliam-sound.com) and Major Marine Tours (1800 Premier Ct., 907/274-7300 or 800/764-7300, www.majormarine.com). The companies can arrange bus transport to the starting points in Seward or Whittier, or you can ride the Alaska Railroad. Also popular are the day trips from Anchorage to Portage Glacier operated by **Gray Line of Alaska** (888/425-1737, www.graylinealaska.com).

Flightseeing

The best way to get a bird's-eye view of the Anchorage area is from a bird's-eye vantage point: in an airplane. Anchorage has a large number of companies offering flightseeing. Visit the flightseeing links on www.anchorage.net for a complete listing or peruse their brochures at the visitors center. Three respected Lake Hood operations have been around for many years: **Rust's Flying Service** (907/243-1595 or 800/544-2299, www.flyrusts.com), **Regal Air** (907/243-8535, www.regal-air. com), and **Ellison Air** (907/243-1959, www.el-lisonair.com). Also check out **Spernak Airways** (907/272-9475, www.spernakair.com), located at Merrill Field.

Typical flights include a 90-minute flight over the Chugach Mountains and Knik Glacier ($245 pp or $295 pp with lake landing); a three-hour flight over Prince William Sound and Columbia Glacier ($345 pp, includes a remote water landing); and a three-hour flight over Mount McKinley ($385). Rust's has a bear viewing flight to Lake Clark National Park ($595 pp for a 6-hour trip), plus a trip to watch the bears at Brooks Camp within Katmai National Park ($795 pp for a 10-12-hour trip).

The air taxis also feature fly-in fishing trips, primarily to the Susitna River area, where Rust's has rental cabins available. Charter service may be the way to go if you have a group of four or more people and a specific destination, such as a public cabin in Chugach National Forest.

Talkeetna Aero Services (907/683-2899 or 888/733-2899, www.talkeetnaaero.com, $595 pp) has a unique Denali day trip from Anchorage that includes a scenic flight to Healy (just outside the park entrance), an all-day bus trip into the park, lunch, and a return flight to Anchorage. It's a great way to see the park if you don't have time for a longer trip to Denali.

Rock Climbing

Alaska Rock Gym (4840 Fairbanks St., 907/562-7265, www.alaskarockgym.com) has climbing walls, classes, a pro shop, locker rooms, and a weight room. For the real thing, most folks head south to Turnagain Arm, which is also popular with ice climbers in the winter. Talk to folks at **Alaska Mountaineering & Hiking** (AMH, 2633 Spenard Rd., 907/272-1811, www.alaskamountaineering.com) or **REI** (1200 W. Northern Lights Blvd., 907/272-4565, www.rei.com) for details on other climbing options.

Fishing

Although Anchorage sits along Cook Inlet, wild tides and strong winds create notoriously treacherous conditions. As a result, there are no charter-boat fishing operations out of Anchorage. A popular salmon-fishing stream, **Ship Creek,** flows right through downtown and has good runs of king salmon (late May-July) and silver salmon (Aug.-mid-Sept.). It's probably the only place where you can catch kings within sight of office high-rises. But watch out for the quicksand-like mud at the mouth of the creek; it can trap unwary anglers. You can also rub shoulders with fellow anglers in mid-summer at **Bird Creek,** 25 miles south of town on the Seward Highway.

To figure out where the fish are running, or what the local regulations are, call **Alaska Fish and Game** (recorded message 907/267-2510) or visit the **Public Lands Information Center** (605 W. 4th Ave., 907/644-3661 or 866/869-6887, www.alaskacenters.gov, daily 9am-5pm late May-early Sept., Mon.-Fri. 10am-5pm in winter) downtown for a copy of the fishing regulations. Both the *Anchorage Daily News* (www.adn.com/outdoors) and the *Anchorage Press* publish weekly fishing reports for the Anchorage area.

Increasingly popular are fly-in fishing trips. All the local air-taxi services offer guided or unguided trips to nearby rivers and lakes for world-class salmon fishing.

Rafting

Two companies lead white-water trips down the wild Six Mile Creek near Hope: **Chugach Outdoor Center** (907/277-7238 or 866/277-7238, www.chugachoutdoorcenter.com) and **Nova Riverrunners** (907/745-5753 or 800/746-5753, www.novalaska.com).

Swimming

If you're lucky enough to be in Anchorage during a hot spell and want to cool off under the bright blue sky, head out to **Lake Spenard/ Lake Hood** (take Spenard Rd. toward the airport, then right on Lakeshore Dr.), the two are actually one connected lake. In the southwest

corner of the city, **Jewel Lake** (Dimond Blvd. between Jewel Lake and Sand Lake Rds.) also has swimming. The most developed outdoor swimming is at **Goose Lake** (on Northern Lights Blvd. between Lake Otis Pkwy. and Bragaw St.), near the University of Alaska Anchorage, accessible on the bike trail and with basketball courts, a changing room and toilets, and a snack bar.

Anchorage is a good place to experience Alaska's love affair with Olympic-size indoor pools. There are seven to choose from, including five at the various high schools; call 907/343-4474 for locations and times. Other pools are at **Alaska Pacific University** (APU) and the **University of Alaska Anchorage** (UAA, Wells Fargo Sports Complex, 907/786-1231, www.uaa.alaska.edu/recreation/sportscomplex, $5). With its high ceiling, taut diving boards, and hard-bodied swimmers, the UAA pool is easily the finest in Alaska, and your entrance fee also provides access to the other facilities here, including a fine ice rink, a weight room, saunas, racquetball courts, and a gym.

If you have children, don't miss **H2Oasis Indoor Waterpark** (1520 O'Malley Rd., 907/522-4420 or 888/426-2747, www.h2oasiswaterpark.com, daily 10am-9pm late May-early Sept., Mon., Wed., and Fri. 3pm-8pm, Sat.-Sun. 10am-8pm in winter, closed Thanksgiving and Christmas, $25 ages 13 and up, $20 ages 3-12, free for younger children with a paying adult), a cavernous indoor water park near the intersection of O'Malley Road and New Seward Highway on the south end of Anchorage. On busy weekends half the kids in town seem to be here, splashing in the wave pool, shooting jets of water at each other from the pirate ship, gliding down the lazy river, zipping through the body slide, and riding several fast water rides, including the roller coaster-like Master Blaster. Hot tubs are reserved for the over-16 set. Towel and swimsuit rentals are available, and the food court sells snacks.

ANCHORAGE

Golf

There are four Anchorage-area public golf courses: **Anchorage Golf Course** (3651 O'Malley Rd., 907/522-3363, www.anchoragegolfcourse.com, 18 holes) on lower hillside in South Anchorage; **Russian Jack Springs Course** (5200 DeBarr Rd., 907/343-6992, 9 holes); **Tanglewood Lakes Golf Club** (11701 Brayton Dr., 907/345-4600, 9 holes); and **Moose Run** (27000 Arctic Valley Rd., 907/428-0056, www.mooserungolfcourse.com, 36 holes).

Spectator Sports

Anchorage has not one but two semipro baseball teams: the **Anchorage Bucs** (E. 16th Ave. and Cordova St., 907/561-2827, www.anchoragebucs.com) and the **Anchorage Glacier Pilots** (E. 16th Ave. and Cordova St., 907/274-3627, www.glacierpilots.com). That means there's usually a game worth watching from June to early August. Past players have included such pro stars as Reggie Jackson, Dave Winfield, Mark McGuire, and Randy Johnson. Games take place at Mulcahy Stadium.

WINTER

Contrary to popular belief, Alaska—and Anchorage in particular—does not go into hibernation for the long months of winter. Instead, many locals look forward to the cold and snow because of the wonderful outdoor activities they bring. Anchorage is a national center for cross-country skiing, dogsledding, skijoring (skiing behind a dog), hockey, and all sorts of other winter fun.

Visitors soon discover what the residents already know—the city is blessed with excellent facilities for all of these. There are dogsled racetracks; dozens of miles of free groomed ski trails; several excellent ice rinks; and three downhill ski areas, including the state's best resort, Alyeska. Add in such events as the Iditarod, Fur Rendezvous, and the college

and semipro hockey games, and it's easy to see why more and more visitors are coming to Anchorage in the winter.

Downhill Skiing and Sledding

Alpine skiers and snowboarders head 37 miles south of Anchorage to **Alyeska Resort** (Girdwood, 907/754-1111 or 800/880-3880, www.alyeskaresort.com) for the finest skiing to be found, and some of the deepest snow at any American resort.

Hilltop Ski Area (Abbott Rd. near Hillside Dr., 907/346-1407, ski hotline 907/346-2167, www.hilltopskiarea.org, $30 ($32 with night skiing) adults, $28 ages 8-18, $16 for kids under 8) is right on the edge of town and consists of a small chairlift and a rope tow. It has lights for night skiing, plus a small lodge with rentals and a snack bar, and it's a favorite place to learn skiing and boarding or to play around without the 45-minute drive to Alyeska.

A bit farther afield is **Arctic Valley** (907/428-1208, www.skiarctic.net, weekends and holidays early Nov.-mid-Apr., $32 adults, $26 ages 8-18, free for seniors and kids under 8). There are two chairlifts and a T-bar, providing a wide range of slopes and conditions.

Downhill skis and snowboards can be rented from several places in Anchorage, including REI and the ski areas.

Sledders of all ages play on the steep powerline slope that cuts along the road up to **Arctic Valley,** with parents taking kids back uphill in their cars. Another great sledding hill, with a 600-foot run, is in **Centennial Park.** Popular short sledding hills are at **Kincaid Park** and **Service High School.**

Cross-Country Skiing

Any Anchorageite over the age of four seems to be involved in cross-country skiing in one form or another. The city is laced with trails that serve as summertime cycling and jogging paths and wintertime ski routes. Most of these are groomed, with set tracks for traditional cross-country skiers and a wider surface for the skate-skiing crowd. Skijorers are also often seen on the Coastal Trail in this dog-happy town (dogs aren't allowed on most ski trails).

The **Nordic Skiing Association of Anchorage** (907/276-7609, www.anchoragenordicski.com) is Alaska's largest cross-country association, and its website has all sorts of information on the sport. Pick up *The Alaska Nordic Skier* (published Oct.-Apr.) at local ski shops and newsstands.

The best-known cross-country area is **Kincaid Park** (9401 Raspberry Rd.), where a convoluted maze of paths cover the rolling terrain, offering fun for all levels of ability. One of the top three competitive ski venues in the United States, Kincaid often hosts national meets. You can warm up inside the Kincaid chalet and enjoy the vistas of Sleeping Lady and Mount McKinley.

Russian Jack Springs Park (near Debarr Rd. and Boniface Pkwy.) has many more groomed ski trails, as well as a small rope tow and a warming house. Several more miles of groomed trails await at **Hillside Park** (off Abbott Rd.) next to Hilltop Ski Area; watch out for the moose here. All these trails are groomed for both traditional cross-country and the faster skate skis, which are becoming increasingly popular. Rent cross-country skis from **REI** (1200 W. Northern Lights Blvd., 907/272-4565, www.rei.com) or **AMH** (2633 Spenard Rd., 907/272-1811, www.alaskamountaineering.com).

Backcountry Skiing

If you're more ambitious—and have the wheels to get there—you'll find incredible backcountry skiing all around Anchorage. The Chugach Mountains offer an endless choice of skiing options that last from mid-October all the way into late June in some places. Note, however, that these areas are *not* for novices, so don't

head out without knowing about and being prepared for such dangers as avalanches and hypothermia. Quite a number of skiers (and more snowmobilers) have died in mountain avalanches near Anchorage. Even such favorites as the nearby summit of Flattop Mountain have taken a high human toll over the years.

The best-known backcountry areas are in Chugach State Park and at Turnagain Pass and Hatcher Pass. Pick up a winter routes map for **Chugach State Park** (park headquarters Mile 115 Seward Hwy., 907/345-5014, www.alaskastateparks.org) from the state park office. **Turnagain Pass** is 60 miles southwest of Anchorage on the way to Seward. The west side of the road is open to snowmobilers, but tele-skiers avoid them by heading to the east side. There's a big parking lot, and from here you can continue into the open meadows or high into the mountains for deep untracked powder.

Located 70 miles northeast of Anchorage, **Hatcher Pass** (907/745-2827) is a favorite backcountry area and serves as a training area for the U.S. National Cross-Country Ski Team. The road can sometimes be a bit treacherous if you don't have studded tires, so be sure to call the park for road conditions. Just downhill from Hatcher Pass, **Government Peak Recreation Area** (www.matsugov.us/projects/hatcherpass) has outstanding trails groomed for skate and classic skiers.

Ice Skating and Hockey

Anchorage is wild about ice-skating and hockey. The **UAA Seawolves** (907/786-1293, www.uaa.alaska.edu) and the semi-pro **Alaska Aces** (907/258-2237, www.alaskaaces.com) attract crowds all season.

The area has four indoor rinks. All are open year-round and offer skate rentals as well as instruction: **Ben Boeke Ice Arena** (334 E. 16th Ave., 907/274-5715, www.benboeke.com) in the Sullivan Arena, which features an Olympic-sized hockey rink; **Dempsey**

ANCHORAGE

Anderson Ice Arena (1741 W. Northern Lights Blvd., 907/277-7571, www.sullivanarena.com); UAA Sports Center (2801 Providence Dr., 907/786-1233); and Dimond Ice Chalet (800 E. Dimond Blvd., 907/344-1212, www.dimondicechalet.com) in the Dimond Mall.

Ice Climbing

When winter arrives, local waterfalls freeze over, creating perfect conditions for ice climbing. Anchorage has an active community of climbers, with the primary focus along Turnagain Arm between Anchorage and Girdwood. Dozens of icefalls here attract locals; visit Alaska Ice Climbing (www.alaskaiceclimbing.com) for details, or stop by REI (1200 W. Northern Lights Blvd., 907/272-4565, www.rei.com) or AMH (2633 Spenard Rd., 907/272-1811, www.alaskamountaineering.com). If you've never climbed before, take an ice climbing class from The Ascending Path (907/783-0505, www.theascendingpath.com, $250 pp for a seven-hour excursion). All gear is provided.

Accommodations

As might be expected in a city of nearly 300,000 people, Anchorage has a wide range of lodging options. Unfortunately, most of these also have Alaskan-sized prices. A good one-stop place to begin your search for local lodging is the Anchorage Convention and Visitors Bureau website (www.anchorage.net).

Anchorage is a spread-out city, and much of the lodging recommended in this guide is in Midtown rather than downtown, making a rental car a wise investment. Parking may or may not be available at downtown locations, so ask ahead to be sure. Add a 12 percent lodging tax to the rates listed in this guide.

Be sure to make Anchorage lodging reservations far ahead for July-August. If summertime prices in Anchorage seem too high, try using online resources such as Priceline. Check websites such as www.biddingfortravel.yuku.com to get an idea of the deals other folks are getting on Priceline.

UNDER $100

⬛ Bent Prop Inn & Hostel Downtown (700 H St., 907/276-3635, www.bentpropinn.com/downtown, dorm rooms: $35 pp first night, $30 subsequent nights; $65 d; parking $4/day) is *the* downtown place for budget travelers. The owners are very friendly and keep a clean, well-run operation. It has the perfect location: just a few steps from the Transit Center, and downtown's many restaurants, bars, and attractions are within walking distance. The hostel has 22 dorm rooms containing 4-8 bunks in each. Several private rooms with double beds are also available. The hostel contains a huge central kitchen, showers, laundry facilities, a TV room, sitting room, free computers and Wi-Fi, and luggage storage. Lockers are provided in each room, so bring a padlock. There is no curfew, but quiet time is enforced after 10pm. Call at least two weeks ahead for summer reservations to be sure of a space. Note: this is a hostel, so don't expect a lot of privacy since the walls are thin. Upgrading to a private room here makes for a better night's sleep.

⬛ Bent Prop Inn & Hostel Midtown (3104 Eide St., 907/222-5220, www.bentpropinn.com/midtown, dorm rooms: $30 pp first night, $25 subsequent nights; semi-private rooms: $35 pp first night, $30 subsequent nights), in an apartment building two blocks from WalMart and many other businesses in Midtown Anchorage, has the same owners as Bent Prop Inn & Hostel Downtown. This hostel has four dorm-style rooms. Dorm guests have access to a common kitchen, TV room, and laundry, with free computers, lockers, and Wi-Fi. Quiet is enforced after 10pm, but there is no curfew. Also available are eight semi-private units. These are full apartments with three single beds in each bedroom, plus private baths and entrances, a full kitchen, lockers, free parking, a living room with TV, and Wi-Fi. Call at least two weeks ahead for summer reservations to be sure of a space. Airport pickup may be available.

Located in Midtown just off C Street, **Arctic Adventure Hostel** (337 W. 33rd Ave., 907/562-5700, www.arcticadventurehostel.com, dorm rooms: $22 pp; $45 d) is a clean, quiet, and friendly place with a full kitchen, Wi-Fi, guest computers, laundry, free parking and storage, and no curfew. The hostel has six dorm rooms that house two or three people per room. The 18 private rooms with a double or queen bed are a better deal.

Another reasonable option is **Spenard Hostel International** (2845 W. 42nd Pl., 907/248-5036, www.alaskahostel.org, $27 pp; tents: $21 s or $37 d), with 43 bunks spread over eight rooms. There is no curfew, but alcohol is not allowed either. The hostel has three kitchens, four baths, laundry facilities, and Wi-Fi. They rent mountain bikes ($20/day) and have space for tents. Sheets and blankets are provided. Call for reservations 2-4 weeks ahead of your visit if arriving on a midsummer weekend.

Popular with international travelers **Alaska Backpackers Inn** (327 Eagle St., 907/277-2770, www.alaskabackpackers.com, dorm rooms: $25-30 pp; $60-65 s, $70-75 d) has a variety of rooms in two buildings close to downtown. The main building contains very clean dorm-style rooms with four beds or two beds, as well as private rooms. The rooms share a dozen bathrooms and a big downstairs kitchen with food lockers. Other amenities include Wi-Fi, laundry facilities, and a game room. The annex building has rooms with

private baths, fridges, and micr[...] is no kitchen here, but you can [...] the main building a half-block a[...]

A European style hotel in [...] neart of Midtown, **Sockeye Inn** (303 W. Fireweed Ln., 907/771-7300, www.sockeyeinn.com, $79 s or $89 d) contains attractive rooms with queen or king beds, full fridges, small flat screen TVs, and Wi-Fi. Each floor has 20 rooms with six baths, and guests have access to a communal kitchen and laundry. The two upper levels are for extended stays, with weekly rates ($300 for one person or $325 for two). There are also two apartment-style units ($500/week), each with a king bed, private bath, and full kitchen. Call several weeks ahead for midsummer reservations since the hotel fills quickly.

$100-200

Creekwood Inn (2150 Gambell St., 907/258-6006 or 800/478-6008, www.creekwoodinn-alaska.com, $99 d, $125-140 kitchen suites) is a no-frills Midtown place with a mix of older budget rooms (standard units with microwaves and fridges) and kitchen suites. Wi-Fi is available. A major renovation in 2012 and 2013 will bring larger rooms, queen beds, and updated furnishings, but prices will also increase.

Motel 6 (5000 A St., 907/677-8640 or 800/466-8656, www.motel6.com, $150 d) has predictable Midtown accommodations, Wi-Fi, and an airport shuttle, but no microwaves or fridges in the rooms.

Close to the airport, **Microtel Inn & Suites** (5205 Northwood Dr., 907/245-5002 or 888/680-4500, www.microtelinn.com, $160 d) is one of the better reasonably-priced options. Continental breakfast, an airport shuttle, two hot tubs, and Wi-Fi are included with the large guest rooms.

It's hard to beat the location for **Copper Whale Inn** (440 L St., 907/258-7999 or 866/258-7999, www.copperwhale.com, $185 d with shared bath, $220 d with private bath;

arking $15/day), right on the edge of downtown with a flower-packed back patio overlooking Cook Inlet. Next door is Simon and Seafort's, one of the city's finest restaurants, and a seasonal kiosk rents bikes out front. This attractively appointed inn has two guest rooms that share a bath, while the other 13 small guest rooms have private baths. A filling buffet breakfast is included, along with Wi-Fi. Pay for hotel parking or take your chance with the parking meters.

A good, moderately priced hotel, **Coast International Inn** (3450 Aviation Ave., 907/243-2233 or 800/663-1144, www.coasthotels.com, $189-197 for up to four) is close to Lake Hood and the airport. Amenities include spacious rooms, queen or king beds, a patio where you can watch floatplanes take off, a 24-hour airport shuttle, a walk-in freezer for fish and game storage, and Wi-Fi.

If you're looking for plenty of space, the 19-unit **Anchorage Uptown Suites** (234 E. 2nd Ave., 907/762-5922, www.anchorageuptownsuites.com, $159-199 d) has one-bedroom apartments, which are nicely appointed with full kitchens, big bathrooms, and Wi-Fi. German is spoken, and some units have fireplaces or whirlpool tubs.

A friendly, family-run hotel, **Anchorage Downtown Hotel** (826 K St., 907/258-7669 or 866/928-7669, www.anchoragedowntownhotel.com, $189-237 d, off-season from $80) has 15 rooms with fridges, microwaves, Wi-Fi, and continental breakfast. There is no elevator, the rooms are small, and lower level units lack views, so request a third-floor room if climbing steps is not an issue. Off-season rates are very reasonable.

Inlet Tower Suites (1200 L St., 907/276-0110 or 800/544-0786, www.inlettower.com, $169 d, suites: $209 d) is a 14-story tower atop a hill halfway between downtown and Midtown. The hotel began life as an apartment building in 1953 and was one of the few large buildings

to come through the 1964 earthquake in good shape. Guest rooms are large and nicely furnished, with great views of the mountains or Cook Inlet from higher levels. There are rooms with queen beds, microwaves, and fridges as well as king suites with a separate living room. Free airport, downtown, or railroad transportation is included, along with an exercise facility and Wi-Fi. Pub House Restaurant is on the premises, and it's just a block to the New Sagaya's gourmet market.

OVER $200

One of my favorite Anchorage hotels, **Dimond Center Hotel** (700 E. Dimond Blvd., 907/770-5000 or 866/770-5002, www.dimondcenterhotel.com, $219 d), has a less-than-appealing location next to WalMart and the Dimond Mall on the south side of town. But, inside you'll find a gorgeous lobby, custom-designed furnishings, and luxurious rooms with plush beds and 42-inch flat-screen TVs. Even the baths are special, with soaking tubs and windows opening into the main room. A full hot breakfast is included, and the hotel has guest computers and Wi-Fi, guest passes to a nearby athletic club, plus free airport and train station shuttles.

Right in the heart of town close to the railway depot, the 31-room **Anchorage Grand Hotel** (505 W. 2nd Ave., 907/929-8888 or 888/800-0640, www.anchoragegrand.com, $199 d) is a cozy all-suites place with friendly service, full kitchens, free parking, Wi-Fi, and a business center. A continental breakfast and newspaper are left at your door each morning.

Anchorage Hotel (330 E St., 907/272-4553 or 800/544-0988, www.historicanchoragehotel.com, $209-219 d, suites: $259 d) is a classy, small 26-room hotel built in 1916 and now on the National Register of Historic Places. There are standard guest rooms (small in size) and two-room suites. The hotel has Wi-Fi, continental breakfast, an exercise facility, large-screen TVs, and a staff that speaks Spanish and Japanese.

Hotel Captain Cook (939 W. 5th Ave., 907/276-6000 or 800/843-1950, www.captaincook.com, from $280 d, suites: $295-650 d), occupies an entire block, with three towers and three restaurants. The hotel is owned by the family of late governor Wally Hickel, who also served as President Nixon's Secretary of the Interior in the 1970s. The hotel's 550 rooms follow a nautical theme (befitting the name), and the building has an old-money feeling with dark woods and lots of suits and power ties. Amenities include concierge service, Wi-Fi, and a full athletic club with a hot tub, sauna, and indoor pool. Rooms range from standard guest rooms to junior suites and all the way up to an executive suite on tower 3.

A tiny three-room boutique hotel, **Coastal Place** (540 Coastal Pl., 907/891-0188, www.coastalplace.com, $220 d) has a convenient downtown location and ultra-luxurious accommodations. The red building was built in 1941, but has been totally renovated with spacious rooms, hardwood floors, gas fireplaces, private baths, fridges, blackout shades, and Wi-Fi. It benefits from friendly owners, too.

ALL-SUITES HOTELS

Anchorage's all-suites hotels are geared to business travelers and families looking for more space who don't mind the big-box hotel atmosphere. These places typically have one room with two queen beds and a separate sitting room with a pullout sofa, plus a microwave and a fridge. All also include indoor pools, hot tubs, exercise facilities, a breakfast buffet, Wi-Fi, and shuttles to the airport and train station.

One of the nicest Anchorage lodging choices, **Embassy Suites** (600 E. Benson Blvd., 907/332-7000, www.embassysuites.com, $309-429 d) gets kudos for spacious upscale suites with a separate bedroom and kitchenette, friendly staff, and such amenities as a fitness center, indoor pool and hot tub, hot breakfasts, Wi-Fi, free transport, valet service, and more. It's in Midtown with a phalanx of malls in all directions.

Close to the UAA campus, **K SpringHill Suites Anchorage University Lake** (4050 University Lake Dr., 907/751-6300 or 888/287-9400, www.springhillsuites.com, $209-279 d) is an excellent option if you have a car. The hotel fronts on University Lake, with a big patio providing a fine view of the Chugach Mountains. It's the most natural setting for any Anchorage hotel. Rooms are modern, large, and stylish, with separate sleeping and working areas, plus fridges, microwaves, and Wi-Fi. Hotel amenities include a hot breakfast, business center, indoor pool and whirlpool, and fitness center. Rates are fairly reasonable—especially considering the setting and amenities—for studios with one king or two queen beds and for larger studio units.

Centrally located in Midtown and nicely maintained, **Homewood Suites** (101 W. 48th Ave., 907/762-7000 or 800/225-5466, www.anchorage.homewoodsuites.com, $299-309 d) features suites with full kitchens, a hot breakfast buffet, indoor pool, exercise facility, free shuttle to airport and around town, a complimentary light dinner Monday-Thursday evenings (with wine), laundry, and Wi-Fi.

Quite a few recently built Midtown and downtown places have similar facilities and prices, including spacious modern rooms, hot breakfast buffets, indoor swimming pools, hot tubs, fridges, microwaves, exercise facilities, business centers, laundries, Wi-Fi, and a complimentary airport shuttle. All of the following offer variations on these themes: **Comfort Suites International Airport** (2919 W. International Airport Rd., 907/243-8080, www.choicehotels.com, $219-249 d), **Clarion Suites Downtown** (1110 W. 8th Ave., 907/222-5005 or 888/469-6575, www.clarionhotel.com, $229-249), **Hilton Garden Inn** (4555 Union

Square Dr., 907/562-7000 or 800/445-8667, www.hiltongardeninn.com, $279-299 d), and **Hampton Inn** (4301 Credit Union Dr., 907/550-7000 or 800/426-7866, www.hamptoninn.com, $279-299 d).

BED-AND-BREAKFASTS AND GUESTHOUSES

Anchorage has dozens of B&Bs, including luxurious hillside homes with spectacular vistas, snug downtown places, and rent-out-the-spare-room suburban houses. An excellent starting point when looking for a local B&B is the **Anchorage Alaska B&B Association** (907/272-5909 or 888/584-5147, www.anchorage-bnb.com). Its website has links to 30 or so B&Bs, with location and price details. See the *Official Guide to Anchorage* (available from the Visitors Information Center downtown or online at www.anchorage.net) for a fairly complete listing of local B&Bs, or take a look at the blizzard of B&B brochures filling visitors center racks.

Downtown Bed-and-Breakfasts

Built in 1913, **Oscar Gill House B&B** (1355 W. 10th Ave., 907/279-1344, www.oscargill.com, $115-135 d) is a historic home facing the downtown Park Strip. Two attractive guest rooms share a bath, while the largest has its own. Guests appreciate the central location, full breakfasts, friendly owners, and grandma's-house atmosphere. Call well ahead since Gill House fills fast.

Close to downtown in one of the nicer sections of Anchorage, **◖ Wildflower Inn** (1239 I St., 907/274-1239 or 877/693-1239, www.alaska-wildflower-inn.com, $129-139 d, add $15 pp for extra guests) is a charming two-story home built in the 1940s. Rooms are elegantly appointed, flowers decorate the exterior, a delicious breakfast is included, and the B&B has Wi-Fi. The Wild Iris room has a queen bed and private bath with jetted tub,

and two suites contain queen or king beds, private baths, and sitting rooms with double futons. A gourmet grocer—New Sagaya's—is just across the street.

A lovely home furnished in the Arts and Crafts style, **Parkside Guest House** (1302 W. 10th Ave., 907/683-2290, www.parksideanchorage.com, June-mid-Sept., $185 d with shared bath, $225 d with private bath) has an excellent location just off the Park Strip. The four rooms are small but beautifully appointed, with a continental breakfast, Wi-Fi, and laundry. The family who owns Parkside also owns famed Camp Denali and North Face Lodge within Denali National Park.

The primary attraction for **Susitna Place B&B** (727 N St., 907/274-3344, www.susitnaplace.com, $115-145 d, suites: $175-200 d) is its location on the west edge of downtown with a sweeping view of Sleeping Lady, Cook Inlet, and Mount McKinley. Seven reasonably priced guest rooms have shared or private baths. And there are two suites, which include private baths with jetted tubs, fireplaces, and private decks. A buffet breakfast is provided, and the B&B has a big communal area and Wi-Fi.

Beyond Downtown Bed-and-Breakfasts

Close to the airport, **Lake Hood Inn** (4702 Lake Spenard Dr., 907/258-9321 or 866/663-9322, www.lakehoodinn.com, $169-189 d) is a recently built custom B&B with four guest rooms, private baths, a continental breakfast, fridges, and Wi-Fi. Some rooms include private balconies, and there's a big waterside deck for sunny afternoons. This is the perfect spot to watch floatplanes taking off or landing on busy Lake Hood, and headphones are provided so you can listen to the control tower. Owner Bill Floyd's Cessna 180 is docked just a few feet away.

At **Alaskan European B&B** (3107 Cottonwood St., 907/258-2746, www.

alaskaeuropeanbb.com, $129-159 d) the owners hold true to their name with fluency in Dutch, German, Italian, and French. The B&B is a favorite of international Mount McKinley climbers (who can spread out their gear in the backyard). It's within walking distance from Midtown shops and restaurants, and has a comfortable living room, full European-style breakfasts, and Wi-Fi. Two downstairs rooms share a bath, and the third upstairs room has a king bed and private bath.

Elderberry B&B (8340 Elderberry, 907/243-6968, www.elderberrybb.com, $125-150 d) provides reasonable accommodations near the airport. The three guest rooms all have private baths, and a full breakfast is included, along with a big-screen TV in the sunroom and Wi-Fi.

Located on a lush three-acre Hillside spread, **Alaskan Frontier Gardens B&B** (Hillside Dr. at Alatna, 907/345-6556, www.alaskafrontiergardens.com, $125 d, suites: $175-225 d) is known for its beautiful gardens, Alaskan artifacts, accommodating host, big breakfasts, and friendly dogs. Amenities include private baths, TVs, fridges, and Wi-Fi. Two guest rooms are available, along with two suites with gas fireplaces. The Ivory suite is larger than some apartments, and also has a whirlpool tub and sauna.

A modern tri-level Hillside home, **Alaska House of Jade B&B** (3800 Delwood Pl., 907/337-3400, www.alaskahouseofjade.com, May-Sept., $140-160 d, add $20 pp for extra guests) contains five large rooms and suites, gourmet Alaskan breakfasts, private baths, and Wi-Fi. Owners Yves and Dee Mamoune are world travelers, fluent in French and Hebrew, plus some Spanish and Japanese.

Guesthouses

Find more than 50 Anchorage vacation rentals online at **VRBO** (www.vrbo.com).

Downtown Guest House (1238 G St., 907/279-2359, www.downtownguesthouse. com, $150 for up to 4) is an immaculate and peaceful two-bedroom apartment with a full kitchen, Internet access, and laundry. It's just a block or so from New Sagaya's (gourmet food, coffees, and deli) and a short walk from downtown. It's highly recommended, but with just one unit you'll need to book well ahead for the busy summer season. Tell Clark and Mitzi I sent you.

CAMPING

The city-run **Centennial Park Campground** (8300 Glenn Hwy., 907/343-6986, www.muni.org, late May-mid-Sept., $25 plus $5 for showers) has 100 spaces for tents and RVs (no hookups). Take Muldoon Road south from the Glenn Highway, take the first left onto Boundary Avenue, then the next left onto the highway frontage road for 0.5 miles to the campground. It's a 15-minute drive from downtown Anchorage in a less-safe part of town. Other than this, the closest public campgrounds are Eagle River Campground, 13 miles northeast of Anchorage, or Bird Creek Campground, 25 miles south.

Anchorage Ship Creek RV Park (150 N. Ingra St., 907/277-0877 or 800/323-5757, www.alaskarv.com, May-Sept., tents $29, RVs $49-57) is close to downtown, with laundry, showers, Wi-Fi, and a gift shop. Sites are jammed together and the railroad tracks are nearby, so expect noise.

Golden Nugget RV Park (4100 DeBarr Rd., 907/333-2012 or 800/449-2012, www.goldennuggetcamperpark.com, year-round, RVs $48, no tents) has an East Anchorage location with 215 sites, Wi-Fi, showers, laundry, and clean restrooms. It's across from Costco.

Creekwood Inn (2150 Gambell St., 907/258-6006 or 800/478-6008, www.creekwoodinn-alaska.com, year-round, RVs $43, no tents) has a Midtown location fairly close to stores and restaurants. It's somewhat run down, with quite a few old RVs parked for extended periods. However, it offers showers, laundry, Wi-Fi, cable TV, and a freezer for your fish.

Many travelers also park RVs for free in the Fred Meyer and Sam's Club parking lots, but check with store managers for any restrictions.

Food

Anchorage's size and diverse population are mirrored in a wide range of places to eat, from grab-a-bite fast-food joints to high-class (and high-priced) gourmet restaurants. To reach many of the best places, you'll need a vehicle or knowledge of bus schedules, but there are several fine restaurants right downtown. Pick up the free *Restaurant & Entertainment Guide* from racks around town. Note: Smoking has been banned in Anchorage restaurants.

BREAKFAST

Looking for a great downtown breakfast? Join the throngs at the spacious **C** **Snow City Café** (1034 W. 4th Ave., 907/272-2489, www.snowcitycafe.com, daily 7am-4pm late May-early Sept.; Mon.-Fri. 7am-3pm, Sat.-Sun. 7am-4pm in winter, $9-14), where meals are ample, reasonably priced, and dependably good. Breakfast and lunch items are available all day. Try the Kodiak benedict, the crabby omelet, or one of the day's breakfast specials. Get here early on weekends to avoid a lengthy wait; make reservations through Opentable. com. Lunchtime sandwiches—including a tasty chicken salad BLT—bring in the legal staff from nearby offices along "lawyer row." The café also has free Wi-Fi.

If you're in Midtown, head to **Middle Way Café** (1200 W. Northern Lights Blvd., 907/272-6433, Mon.-Fri. 7am-6pm, Sat.-Sun. 8am-6pm, $8-12) for yummy French toast, huevos rancheros, breakfast burritos, omelets, vegan specials, and more in a noisy and colorful setting. Big art decorates the wall at this trendy café sandwiched between REI and Title Wave Books. The café is also extremely

popular for lunch, lattes, and smoothies. There is free Wi-Fi onsite.

An old-time favorite, **Gwennie's Old Alaska Restaurant** (4333 Spenard Rd., 907/243-2090, www.gwenniesrestaurant.com, $8-14) specializes in breakfast (available all day), especially sourdough pancakes and reindeer sausage. Meals are Alaska-size, so those with small appetites may want to split an order. Memorabilia crowds the walls on this sprawling two-story place, and big tables fill with families filling up.

BAKERIES

Some of the best Anchorage breads and pastries come from **Europa Café** (601 W. 36th Ave., 907/563-5704, Mon.-Fri. 6am-6pm, Sat. 7am-6pm, Sun. 9am-5pm, $8), where the 15 daily thick-crusted artisan breads compare favorably to anything you might find in France. The cases are filled with pastries and cakes, and the café is popular for lunchtime sandwiches and soups.

COFFEE AND TEA

Anchorageites love strong coffee, and the town is packed with espresso stands and cafés—including the commonplace Starbucks versions. Tucked away in a Midtown shopping mall, **Café del Mundo** (341 E. Benson Blvd., 907/274-0026, www.cafedelmundo.com, Mon.-Fri. 6am-8pm, Sat. 7am-8pm, Sun. 8am-6pm, $4-7) is a favorite of the business crowd, and is a relaxing place to while away a morning reading a book or surfing the web (free Wi-Fi). Alaska's first coffee roaster—it was established in 1975—Café del Mundo is now owned by the big boy in town, Kaladi Brothers.

Upscale **Terra Bella** (601 E. Dimond Ave., 907/562-2259, www.terrabellacoffee.com, daily 7:30am-6pm, $4-8) has a good selection of sandwiches, paninis, and salads. They're in a Southside strip mall across from Dimond Mall. Free Wi-Fi is available.

A personal favorite is the local chain of nine **Kaladi Brothers** (downtown New Sagaya's location: 900 W. 13th Ave., 907/274-6173, www.kaladi.com, Mon.-Sat. 6am-8pm, Sun. 8am-7pm) espresso shops, which includes branches inside the New Sagaya's grocery stores and adjacent to Title Wave Books. All have free Wi-Fi. Many other Alaskan coffee shops buy their espresso beans from Kaladi Brothers, and they've even opened a shop in Seattle—the heart of enemy (Starbucks) territory.

There are literally hundreds of coffee shops in Anchorage, but tiny **Side Street Espresso** (412 G St., 907/258-9055, Mon.-Sat. 7am-3pm, $3-6) has its own unique atmosphere. Friendly and frumpy, with a mish-mash of tables and chairs, the café is decorated with the often-political daily drawings of co-owner George Gee. You'll find occasional music and monthly art shows, but there is no Wi-Fi here and credit cards are not accepted.

LUNCH AND QUICK MEALS

Anchorage's proliferation of fast food eateries are scattered across town, particularly in the Midtown area. Downtown's **5th Avenue Mall** (320 W. 5th Ave., 907/258-5535, Mon.-Fri. 10am-9pm, Sat. 10am-8pm, Sun. 11am-6pm) is home to dozens of shops of all types. Take the elevator to the 4th floor for the food court, where fast-food eateries of all persuasions—from Thai to frozen yogurt—await. The Nordstroms store on the second level has a popular café ($8-10) with lunchtime soups, salads, and paninis.

Urban Greens (304 G St., 907/276-0333, www.urbangreensak.com, 9am-3pm Mon.-Fri., $9-10) is arguably Anchorage's best sandwich shop, where the subs are made with hoagies from French Oven Bakery. Try the bootlegger club with turkey, pastrami, mortadella, and Swiss cheese.

Housed within the Anchorage Museum, **Muse** (625 C St., 907/929-9210, www.marxcafe.com, Mon.-Wed. 11am-3pm, Thurs.-Sat. 11am-9pm, Sun. noon-4pm, $12-16) is a colorful café with tall windows and outside tables on the patio. Muse is managed by Marx Bros. Café, with a creative and fresh menu of homemade soups, salads, and sandwiches. Brunch includes delicious Alaskan eggs Benedict with king crab, and be certain to try the venison brochettes. For lunch, you can get an affordable bowl of soup with bread. Muse hosts live music during First Friday art openings.

Don't miss perpetually crowded **L'Aroma Bakery and Deli** (Midtown: 3700 Old Seward Hwy.; near downtown: 900 W. 13th Ave., www.laromabakery.com, $5-12), at both New Sagaya's stores, for panini sandwiches, small pizzas baked in wood-fired ovens, sushi, spring rolls, a salad bar, Chinese specials, and American "comfort food" (mac and cheese, meatloaf, lasagna, and so on), along with freshly baked breads and sweets. You're guaranteed to find something that appeals. Eat here or get it to go.

Middle Way Café (1200 W. Northern Lights Blvd., 907/272-6433, Mon.-Fri. 7am-6pm, Sat.-Sun. 8am-6pm, $6-11) hides out next to the REI store but always manages to fill up when lunch arrives. Look for today's specials on the board, order at the counter, and wait for your name to be called. The menu includes vegetarian sandwiches and wraps, burgers, salads, fruit smoothies, and daily specials. The barista will make a mocha while you wait or serve a big slice of carrot cake. There is free Wi-Fi here.

Spenard Roadhouse (1049 W. Northern Lights Blvd., 907/770-7623, www.spenardroadhouse.com, Mon.-Fri. 11am-11pm, Sat.-Sun. 9am-11pm, $9-18) is a busy, noisy lunch place in Midtown near REI. The bacon jam burger (with Cambozola cheese and grilled apple) is popular with carnivores, or order the spicy Thai chicken curry, rockfish and chips, or a cubano sandwich. There's a happy hour menu on weekdays ($7 appetizers), and the Roadhouse stays open late for an after-the-movie bite. Breakfast (only available on weekends) includes berry apple crepes, veggie Benedict, and hangover helper—with beef, fried egg, chedder, bacon, tomato, onion, and fries. The bar features the largest bourbon selection in Alaska. There are no reservations, so you may end up waiting awhile for a table. Spenard Roadhouse is owned by the same folks who bring you Sacks Café and Snow City Café, two of Anchorage's most-loved restaurants.

In the summer, several vendors have **downtown carts** (in front of the old Federal Building on 4th Avenue). The best of these—look for the queue—is the vendor of reindeer sausage and grilled onions. On weekends in the summer your best downtown bet is the weekend **Anchorage Market and Festival** (3rd Ave. and E St., 907/272-5634, www.anchoragemarkets.com, Sat.-Sun. 10am-6pm mid-May-mid-Sept.).

Anchorage's two top burger-and-fries joints are **Arctic Roadrunner** (2477 Arctic Blvd., 907/279-7311, Mon.-Fri. 10:30am-8pm, Sat. 11am-7pm, $5-8) and **Tommy's Burger Stop** (W. Benson Rd. at Spenard Ave., 907/561-5696, Mon.-Fri. 10:30am-8pm, Sat. 11am-8pm, Sun. noon-4pm, $7-12).

AMERICAN

Off the beaten path in a strip mall on the east side of town, **Paris Bakery Café** (500 Muldoon Rd., 907/337-2575, www.parisbakeryandcafe. com, Tues.-Thurs. 9am-9pm, Fri.-Sun. 8am-9pm, $25-35) looks like an All-American diner, but serves American and French fare. Breakfast choices include omelets, eggs Benedict, stuffed French toast, and freshly baked croissants,

along with lunchtime quiches, sandwiches, and salads. Dinner entrées include filet mignon, pork au jus, and halibut King Louis, but the real surprise comes during twice-monthly six-course tasting dinners ($40 pp). The bakery cases are filled with French pastries and breads, all made from scratch.

PIZZA AND ITALIAN

Anchorage has all the national pizza chains, and the "Pizza" listing in the Yellow Pages includes some 60 different places. Among these, **Pizza Olympia** (2809 Spenard Rd., across from REI, 907/561-5264, www.pizzaolympia.us, Mon.-Fri. 11am-11pm, Sat. 3pm-11pm, $15-25) is a personal favorite. Four generations of the Maroudas family run this place with authentic affection, rolling out such unique offerings as garlic and feta cheese pizzas and all the standard Greek specialties.

Two excellent pizza options are **Moose's Tooth Pub & Pizzeria** (3300 Old Seward Hwy., 907/258-2537, www.moosestooth.net, daily 10:30am-1am May-early Sept.; Mon.-Fri. 11am-11pm, Sat.-Sun. 11am-midnight in winter, $13 and up) and **L'Aroma Bakery & Deli** (Midtown: 3700 Old Seward Hwy.; downtown: 900 W. 13th Ave., www.laromabakery. com) in New Segaya stores. Other good pizza places include **Sorrento's** (610 E. Fireweed Ln., 907/278-3439, Mon.-Thurs. 3:30pm-10pm, Fri. 3:30pm-11pm, Sat. 2pm-11pm, Sun. 2pm-10pm, $15-25), with the best southern Italian food in Anchorage, and **Fletcher's** (in Hotel Captain Cook, 5th Ave. and K St., 907/276-6000, www.captaincook.com, daily 11:30am-1am, $12-14), where Anchorage waiters and cooks go after work.

For delicious northern Italian dinners with an Alaskan twist, visit the small **CampoBello Bistro** (601 W. 36th Ave., 907/563-2040, www.campobellobistro.com, Mon. 11am-2:30pm, Tues.-Fri. 11am-2:30pm and 5pm-9pm, Sat. 5pm-9pm, $16-35). This is a relaxing and romantic spot for lunch or dinner; try the duck a'la orange or shrimp and scallops Florentine.

For creative Tuscany-meets-Alaska fare in the heart of town, head to **Ristorante Orso** (737 W. 5th Ave., 907/222-3232, www.orso-alaska.com, Mon.-Thurs. 11:30am-2:30pm and 5pm-10:30pm, Fri. 11:30am-2:30pm and 5pm-11pm, Sat. 11am-2:30pm and 5pm-11pm, Sun. 11am-2:30pm and 5pm-10:30pm, $21-40). This popular restaurant exudes energy, and the menu encompasses wild mushroom ravioli (made fresh), lamb osso bucco, halibut cheek piccata, and a spicy calamari appetizer, along with a dessert selection that stars a wonderful molten chocolate cake and distinctive oatmeal stout carrot cake. Lunches include a grilled Alaskan salmon BLT, and tasty cod fish and chips. Return for a weekend brunch of eggs Benedict atop risotto crab cakes or baked French toast stuffed with cream cheese, ricotta, and blueberries. The bar serves ales from nearby Glacier BrewHouse (same owners), plus a fine choice of wines by the glass or bottle. Dinner reservations are recommended.

CHINESE

Many of Anchorage's Chinese restaurants are actually run by Korean Americans, who make up a large ethnic community in the city.

Charlie's Bakery (2729 C St. at Northern Lights Blvd., 907/677-7777, Mon.-Sat. 11am-8:30pm, $10-15) does have breads, éclairs, and other baked goods, but that's not the main attraction at this plain-Jane shop tucked into a Midtown strip mall. The menu covers plenty of Chinese options and daily specials—from pork spare ribs with black bean sauce to barbeque eel with rice—but it's the dim sum that attracts aficionados looking for a fix of crystal dumplings or barbeque pork steamed buns. Service can be slow, and there's often a wait on Saturdays.

In the heart of Midtown across from the Sears store, **Panda Restaurant** (605 E. Northern Lights Blvd., 907/272-3308, www.akpandarestaurant.com, Mon.-Fri. 11am-11:30pm, Sat.-Sun. noon-9:30pm, $12-15) has a big Chinese menu and equally impressive fish tank. Service is fast and portions are ample, making this a great place for takeout. Be sure to check the board for the specials of the day; they're usually your best bargain.

Twin Dragon Mongolian Bar-B-Que (612 E. 15th Ave., 907/276-7535, daily 11am-10pm, $15) is a fun place where you fill a plate with veggies and meat and watch the chefs do their show. It's reasonable too.

Surrounded by a world of WalMart and other megastores, **China Lights** (9220 Old Seward Hwy., 907/522-5700, www.chinalight-sak.com, daily 11am-10pm, $15) has a large and very popular buffet for lunch or dinner; it is the best Chinese/Korean/Japanese buffets in Anchorage. Crab legs and sushi rolls are the real buffet attractions.

THAI AND VIETNAMESE

Anchorage has quite a few Thai restaurants—seven at last count. None of these measures up to what you'd find in Thailand (or Berkeley, for that matter), but several are well worth a visit. Hip locals rave about **Thai Kitchen** (3405 E. Tudor Rd., 907/561-0082, www.thaikitchenak.com, Mon.-Fri. 11am-3pm and 5pm-9pm, Sat. 5pm-9pm, Sun. 5pm-8:30pm, $9-12), tucked away in a strip mall on Tudor Road near Bragaw Street. With 120 choices on the menu, you're sure to find something to your taste, but favorites include Popeye chicken or any of the spicy soups. Get there early since it closes at 9pm, even on weekends.

Housed within an old Pizza Hut building in Midtown, **Chiang Mai Ultimate Thai** (3637 Old Seward Hwy., 907/563-8900, www.chiangmaiak.com, Mon.-Fri. 11am-9pm, Sat. 4pm-9pm, $12-15) is a family-friendly spot decorated with Thai linen and portraits of the royal family. Meals are consistently great, service is super-friendly, and the prices are fair. Favorites include fresh rolls, volcano chicken, and pad see-iew. Everything is made fresh while you wait.

Also recommended is **Thai Orchid Restaurant** (219 E. Dimond Ave., 907/868-5226, www.thaiorchidalaska.com, Mon.-Sat. 11am-3pm and 4:30pm-9pm, $11-15), with the best pad Thai in town and a diverse and inexpensive menu that includes many vegetarian choices. It's across the road from Costco.

Anchorage's best known Vietnamese restaurant is **Ray's Place** (2412 Spenard Rd., 907/279-2932, www.raysplaceak.com, Mon.-Fri. 10am-3pm and 5pm-9pm, $9-11). Pho chicken soup, pork cold noodle salad, seafood sauté noodles, and sautéed lamb curry with vegetables are a few favorites from Ray's extensive menu. Don't come here on a weekend; Ray's is closed all day Saturday and Sunday.

INDIAN AND MIDDLE EASTERN

Bombay Deluxe (555 W. Northern Lights Blvd., 907/277-1200, www.bombaydeluxe.com, Mon.-Sat. 11am-2pm and 5pm-9:30pm, Sun. 5pm-9:30pm, $13-18) has an ample weekday lunch buffet and free delivery. It's the state's only restaurant with a traditional clay tandoor oven.

Aladdin's (4240 Old Seward Hwy. at Tudor Rd., 907/561-2373, www.aladdinsalaska.com, Wed.-Sat. 5pm-10pm, $15-21) serves traditional Mediterranean dishes from North Africa and the Middle East, including moussaka, lamb couscous, seafood kebab, and various vegetarian specialties. The restaurant has a strong local following.

Alaska's only Tibetan restaurant, **Yak & Yeti Himalayan Restaurant** (3301 Spenard Rd., 907/743-8078, www.yakandyetialaska.com, Mon.-Wed. 11am-2:30pm, Thurs.-Fri. 11am-2:30pm and 5pm-8:30pm, Sat. 5pm-8:30pm,

$11-16) is a relaxing Midtown spot with a mix of vegetarian and meaty dishes. Kids appreciate the lhasa momos (Tibetan beef dumplings), and grownups rave over the spicy goat curry and pork vindaloo.

JAPANESE

Get the finest fresh sushi, tempura, and teriyaki from **Yamato Ya** (3501 Old Seward Hwy., 907/561-2128, www.yamatoyasushi.com, Mon.-Fri. 11am-3pm and 4pm-10pm, Sat. 4pm-10pm, Sun. 4pm-9pm), across from Moose's Tooth. Sushi rolls range from a kappa maki ($4) to a dragon roll ($16).

Kumagoro (533 W. 4th Ave., 907/272-9905, daily 11am-11pm mid-May-early Sept., daily 11am-10pm early Sept.-mid-May, $15-30) is a plant-bedecked downtown restaurant with house-made udon noodle soups and an evening-only sushi bar. The restaurant fills up for lunch with the business crowd.

Just two doors away from the old-time charm of Café Paris is its exact opposite, the trendy pan-Asian **Ginger** (425 W. 5th Ave., 907/929-3680, www.gingeralaska.com, Mon.-Fri. 11:30am-2pm and 5pm-10pm, Sat.-Sun. 11am-2:30pm and 5pm-10pm, $16-31), with hardwood floors, stylish black tables, and big art on the walls. Ginger's menu encompasses everything from Panang beef curry to duck breast chinois; be sure to sample the spicy tuna tower appetizer. The lunchtime express menu has a couple of specials ($9), and the bar has eight brews on tap.

MEXICAN

The oldest Mexican restaurant in Alaska, in existence for over 60 years, **La Cabaña** (312 E. 4th Ave., 907/272-0135, www.alaskalacabana.com, daily 11am-11pm, $13-20) is a good lunch place, with tasty halibut fajitas.

La Mex (2552 Spenard Rd., 907/274-7511, www.lamexalaska.com, Mon.-Thurs. 11am-10pm, Fri. 11am-11pm, Sat. noon-11pm,

$13-17) is popular for evening nachos and margaritas, or for full meals. The service is fast, and the steaks aren't bad either. Check out the bar with its 17,000 tiles, and head here for a big choice of lunch specials.

In business since 1972, **Mexico in Alaska** (7305 Old Seward Hwy., 907/349-1528, www.mexicoinalaska.com, Mon.-Fri. 11am-10pm, Sat. noon-10pm, $15-18) is one of the more authentic south-of-the-border spots, but it's a long way out if you don't have a car. There are quite a few vegetarian offerings for non-carnivores.

If you're looking for the quick version, **Taco King** (112 W. Northern Lights Blvd., 907/276-7387, www.tacokingak.com, Mon.-Sat. 10am-11pm, Sun. noon-10pm, $6-9) is an authentic Mexican taqueria serving fat burritos and tacos. Order at the counter and then slather it up with your choice of salsas and sour cream. You'll never want to go Taco Bell after this! They deliver too.

On the east side of Anchorage, **El Rodeo** (385 Muldoon Rd., 907/338-5393, www.elrodeoak.com, Mon.-Fri. 11am-10pm, Sat. noon-10pm, Sun. noon-9pm, $12-15) isn't much to look at on the outside, but inside, the Mexican food is tasty and service is friendly. Choose from such standards as chicken burritos, beef enchiladas, or mini chimis dinner (deep fried tortillas filled with shredded beef, guacamole, and sour cream), or head to the big Tuesday-Friday lunchtime buffet.

ORGANIC AND VEGETARIAN

In the heart of Spenard, **Organic Oasis** (2610 Spenard Rd., 907/277-7882, www.organicoasis.com, Mon.-Sat. 11am-9pm, Sun. 1pm-6pm, $10-16) serves organic wraps and sandwiches (even a few with meat), fresh-squeezed juices, smoothies, and other lunch and dinner fare. Freshly baked breads, housemade chai teas, and vegan specialties are here, but you'll also find elk burgers, portabella stuffed chicken breast, and pizzas. The enjoyable, airy setting is right

next to Inner Dance Yoga studio and across from the Oriental Healing Arts Center. There's a baby grand piano and live music four nights a week.

The grocery store **Natural Pantry** (3801 Old Seward Hwy., 907/770-1444, www.naturalpantry.com, Mon.-Sat. 9am-9pm, $5-10) has a café serving organic smoothies, fresh juices, and light lunches.

SEAFOOD

One of the city's most popular seafood-focused restaurants, **Kinley's** (3230 Old Seward Hwy., 907/544-8953, www.kinleysrestaurant.com, Mon. 5pm-10pm, Tues.-Fri. 11:30am-10pm, Sat. 5pm-10pm, $18-28) provides an upscale dining experience. Start with the bacon-wrapped dates or calamari steak appetizers (half price 4pm-6pm) before moving on to a main course of almond crusted halibut, seared Kodiak scallops, braised lamb shank, or filet mignon. For lunch, sandwiches (including a popular halibut BLT), ahi tuna tacos, and Parisian salads are featured. Choose from more than 100 beers and a wide choice of wines by the glass, but don't miss the excellent desserts, including an espresso-soaked moca bourbon pecan torte. Reservations are recommended, especially on Friday and Saturday nights. Kinley's is next door to the incredibly popular Moose's Tooth Pub & Pizzeria, providing a good dining alternative if the queue at the Tooth is too long.

STEAK

As you might guess, Anchorage has several of the meat-lover chain restaurants, including Black Angus, Cattle Company, Lone Star Steakhouse, and Outback Steakhouse. Anchorage's old-time steakhouse, **C Club Paris** (417 W. 5th Ave., 907/277-6332, www.clubparisrestaurant.com, Mon.-Sat. 11:30am-2:30pm and 5pm-10pm, Sun. 5pm-10pm, $19-32) has been an unstylish fixture on the downtown scene since 1957. The atmosphere is dark—the building once housed a mortuary—and one wall is lined with photos of the famous and infamous visitors who've eaten here over the decades. Super-tender filet mignon is the house specialty ($38 for the 14-ounce version, and worth it), but other items are somewhat cheaper, including Alaskan seafood, freshly ground burgers, sandwiches, and salads. The resident butcher who slices 500 or more steaks every week cuts all meat on the premises. This is one of the few union-shop restaurants in Anchorage and many of the staff have been here for 15 or more years. Reservations are recommended.

BREWPUBS AND WINE BARS

Anchorage's food-and-booze scene is thriving, with a surprising variety of options from which to choose. Right downtown, **◖Glacier BrewHouse** (737 W. 5th Ave., 907/274-2739, www.glacierbrewhouse.com, Mon.-Fri. 11am-11pm, Sat.-Sun. 10am-11pm mid-May-mid-Sept., reduced winter hours, $23-35) is a lively and noisy place that overflows most evenings; reservations are recommended if you want to avoid the two-hour weekend wait. The central fireplace and open ceilings provide a relaxing setting, and you can watch hard-working chefs in the open kitchen. House dinner favorites include herb crusted halibut, a BrewHouse blue salad, and wood-oven fired pizzas, notably the Thai chicken pizza with grilled chicken, three cheeses, toasted peanuts, fresh cilantro, and sweet Thai chili sauce. The bar pours a dozen or so specialty ales made in the behind-the-glass brewery. Lunch specialties include sandwiches, salads, and pizzas. The weekend brunch features crab cake Benedict, oatmeal stout waffles, Alaskan seafood scramble, and even breakfast pizzas. There's free Wi-Fi, too.

A few blocks away is **Snow Goose Restaurant** (717 W. 3rd Ave., 907/277-7727, www.alaskabeers.com, daily 11:30am-11pm in summer, reduced winter hours, $16-30), with

halibut, pork, steak, and more downstairs, plus an upstairs pub where the outdoor patio overlooks Cook Inlet; that white triangle in the distance is Mount McKinley. Snow Goose always has several homebrews from its Sleeping Lady Brewery (on the premises), along with a substantial wine selection.

◖Moose's Tooth Pub & Pizzeria (3300 Old Seward Hwy., 907/258-2537, www.moosestooth.net, daily 10:30am-1am May-early Sept.; Mon.-Fri. 11am-11pm, Sat.-Sun. 11am-midnight in winter, pizza $13 and up) is *the* Anchorage place for pizza and beer, hands down. The huge parking lot fills with cars most evenings, and you're likely to endure a wait for a table—up to two hours in the summer—since they don't take reservations. (Get a slice to go if you're in a hurry, but these are only available weekdays 10:30am-2pm) Distinctive pizzas are all made from scratch and baked in a stone oven. Crowd favorites include blackened rockfish, chicken ranch, and Santa's little helper. Caesar salads and homemade mushroom soup are also popular. The 15 or so prize-winning beers from their own Broken Tooth Brewery make the perfect accompaniment to pizza. Moose's Tooth hosts nationally known bands in the parking lot a couple of times each summer.

The same people own the equally popular **Bear Tooth Theatrepub** (1230 W. 27th Ave., 907/276-4200, www.beartooththeatre.net, Mon.-Thurs. 10:30am-10pm, Fri.-Sat. 10:30am-11pm, Sun. noon-10pm, $8-12). It's a great family option for nachos, burritos, and pizzas. You can take in a movie ($4) while you eat.

You won't go wrong with a meal at tiny **◖F Street Station** (325 F St., 907/272-5196, daily 11am-1am, $17), with reasonably priced, ultrafresh daily seafood specials, fast service, Guinness on draught, and a convivial white-collar atmosphere. Try the perfectly cooked beer-batter halibut or the New York steak and fries. Be sure to ask the bartender the story behind the huge hunk of Tillamook sharp cheddar that's always on the counter. And despite the sign, you can cut the cheese (so to speak). This is a bar, so it's not for kids after 8pm. If I had to choose one Anchorage restaurant, this would be the place! F Street's only problem is its popularity, so you'll probably end up waiting a bit—sometimes quite awhile—and sharing your table.

They don't brew their own beers, but **Humpy's Great Alaskan Alehouse** (610 W. 6th Ave., 907/276-2337, www.humpys.com, Mon.-Thurs. 11am-2am, kitchen closes at midnight; Fri. 11am-2:30am, kitchen closes at 1am; Sat. bar 10am-2:30am, kitchen 9am-1am; Sun. bar 10am-2am, kitchen 9am-midnight, $12-20) attracts a 20-something crowd with more than 50 brews on tap and a pub menu of halibut burgers, salads, pastas, nachos, and other crunchy fare. Live bands play nightly in this perpetually packed, no-cover-charge hangout.

The industrial chic setting for **Midnight Sun Brewing Co.** (8111 Dimond Hook Dr., 907/344-1179, www.midnightsunbrewing. com, daily 11am-8pm, under $12) is reflected in 20 or so unusual craft beers, including the award-winning Arctic Devil Barleywine Ale. The brewery's upstairs loft serves an eclectic mix of sandwiches and salads, along with daily hot dishes such as taco Tuesdays and *posole* Thursdays (a hearty Mexican stew). Midnight Sun is out of the way on the south end of Anchorage near New Seward Highway and E. Dimond Boulevard. There are free brewhouse tours Thursdays at 6pm.

Anchorage's trendiest wine bar, **Crush Wine Bistro and Cellar** (9343 W. 6th Ave., 907/865-9198, www.crushak.com, Mon.-Thurs. 11:30am-10pm, Fri.-Sat. 11:30am-midnight, $9-15) is a love-it or hate-it place. Popular with 20-somethings, it's crowded, urbane, noisy, and stylish, with a limited menu that includes a beef and hominy empanada, a Niçoise salad, and

a surprisingly good mac and cheese. Sample a flight of three wines ($12) or head upstairs for wines to go.

FINE DINING

Several of Anchorage's fine-dining establishments are described elsewhere, including Ristorante Orso (737 W. 5th Ave., 907/222-3232, www.orsoalaska.com) and Club Paris (417 W. 5th Ave., 907/277-6332, www.clubparisrestaurant.com). Reservations are strongly advised or required for all of the following restaurants.

Simon & Seaforts (420 L St., 907/274-3502, www.simonandseaforts.com, Mon.-Thurs. 11am-10pm, Sat. 4:30pm-11pm, Sun. 4:30pm-10pm, $27-40) has an eclectic menu, efficient service, and splendid views. Simon's serves daily fresh fish specials and aged prime rib; wonderful cracked wheat sourdough bread comes with each meal. Lunch (try the Cajun chicken fettuccine) is considerably less expensive than dinner. If you don't have dinner reservations, head to the more relaxed bar, where the menu is more limited but still diverse enough to satisfy. Once in the bar, check out the collection of single-malt Scotch whiskies, said to be one of the largest in the nation.

A much smaller and quieter place than Simon's, the elegant 🍷**Marx Bros. Café** (627 W. 3rd Ave., 907/278-2133, www.marxcafe. com, Tues.-Sat. 5:30pm-10pm May-Sept.; Tues.-Thurs. 6pm-9:30pm, Fri.-Sat. 5:30pm-10pm in winter, $34-52) has been in business since 1979. The Caesar salad—made at your table—is especially memorable. The menu changes daily, but it's always innovative, and the big wine list and good dessert selection complement the meal. Reservations are essential at this dinner-only café; book well ahead of your visit to be assured of a table.

🍷 **Sacks Café** (328 G St., 907/274-4022, www.sackscafe.com, Mon.-Thurs. 11am-2:30pm and 5pm-10pm, Fri.-Sat.

11am-2:30pm and 5pm-10:30pm, Sun. 10am-2:30pm and 5pm-10pm, $24-34) crafts some of Anchorage's finest lunches and dinners, and is especially popular with the business crowd and for weekend brunches. You'll find an arty decor, creative cooking, and heady talk. The menu changes frequently, but typically includes Alaskan scallops, halibut, or salmon, baked penne pasta, pan seared duck breast, pork tenderloin medallions, and lunchtime Thai chicken sandwiches or jambalaya. Desserts are great too. Brunch features huevos rancheros, freshly squeezed orange juice, and poached eggs on crab and scallop cakes. Reservations are essential for dinner, though they aren't taken for the wine bar.

Crow's Nest (939 W. 5th Ave., 907/343-2217, www.captaincook.com, Mon.-Sat. 5pm-9:30pm, $38-52) sits atop the Hotel Captain Cook, 20 floors above the masses, with fine dining and prices (and a view) to match. Order off the sky-high menu, and ask the sommelier for assistance in choosing a matched wine from the restaurant's 10,000-bottle wine cellar. This is one of the only places in Alaska where you can't eat in Carhartt work clothes; not only would you stand out from the rest of the crowd, there's also a dress code. Reservations are strongly recommended. A bit old fashioned for my taste, but perfect for an anniversary or milestone birthday celebration.

Don't let the strip-mall setting for ◖ **Jens'** (701 W. 36th Ave., 907/561-5367, www.jensrestaurant.com, Mon. 11:30am-2pm, Tues.-Fri. 11:30am-2pm and 6pm-10pm, Sat. 6pm-10pm, $24-45) throw you off—this is a great European-style bistro with an Alaskan twist. The atmosphere is art-filled, and the food is equally beautiful, from the grilled rockfish to the filet mignon a la Wellington. Attentive service, a nice wine list, and delectable desserts complete the picture. Reservations are

recommended. It's easy to spend well over $150 for two people, but you'll go away satiated and happy. You can also hang out at the wine bar, which serves appetizers until midnight (and can get noisy).

It's pretty far off the main tourist trails, but **Kincaid Grill** (6700 Jewel Lake Rd., 907/243-0507, www.kincaidgrill.com, Tues.-Sat. 5pm-10pm, $28-36) is well worth the detour. Telegenic owner-chef Al Levinsohn—whom you might recognize from his Food Network appearances—has created a playful setting with a wine bar and an ever-changing menu. Alaskan seafood is always on the menu, along with rack of lamb, gumbo, and chocolate bourbon soufflé. The location, in a corner strip mall next to a tanning place, leaves something to be desired, but the food is sumptuous.

GROCERIES

Carrs/Safeway has 10 stores scattered around Anchorage, including one at the Sears Mall in Midtown (600 E. Northern Lights Blvd., 907/297-0600, www.safeway.com, 24 hours daily). Grocery prices are generally a bit lower at the four big **Fred Meyer** stores, including one at Northern Lights Boulevard and New Seward Highway (1000 E. Northern Lights Blvd., 907/264-9600, www.fredmeyer.com, daily 7am-11pm). Most Carrs/Safeway and Fred Meyer stores have delis, fresh sushi, salad bars, ATMs, and in-store Starbucks outlets.

A distinctive gourmet grocer is **New Sagaya's** (3700 Old Seward Hwy., 907/561-5173 or 800/764-1001, and 900 W. 13th Ave., 907/274-6173, www.newsagaya.com, daily 6am-10pm mid-May-early Sept., 6am-9pm early Sept.-mid-May), where the featured attractions include exotic produce and Asian foods, outstanding delis, L'Aroma Bakeries, Kaladi Coffee, live crab and oysters, and fresh-from-the-sea seafood.

Information and Services

VISITOR INFORMATION

Start your tour of downtown at the **Anchorage Convention and Visitors Bureau** (ACVB, corner of 4th Ave. and F St., 907/274-3531, www. anchorage.net, daily 7:30am-7pm June-Aug., daily 8am-6pm May and Sept., daily 9am-4pm Oct.-Apr.), a sod-roofed log cabin that's commonly referred to as the **Log Cabin Visitors Center.** The cabin isn't actually the main place for information; go out the back door to a more spacious visitors center where you'll find a plethora of brochures from around the state and helpful staff. Be sure to pick up a copy of the fat *Anchorage Big Wild Life,* which includes a downtown walking tour and an Anchorage-area driving tour, plus details on sights, attractions, activities, lodging, restaurants, and more.

For a quick one-hour introduction to the city, hop on one of the red **Anchorage City Trolley Tours** (corner of 4th Ave. and F St., 907/276-5603 or 888/917-8687, www.alaska-trolley.com, daily departures on the hour 9am-5pm May-Sept., $15 adults, $8 ages 6-12, free for younger kids). Tours begin in front of the Log Cabin Visitors Center.

The ACVB also maintains two **Airport Visitors Centers:** one near the baggage area in the **domestic terminal** (907/266-2437, daily 9am-4pm mid-May-mid-Sept.) and the other in the **international terminal** (907/266-2657, daily 9am-4pm mid-May-mid-Sept.).

ALASKA PUBLIC LANDS INFORMATION CENTER

Kitty-corner from the ACVB is the old Federal Building, which now houses the Alaska Public Lands Information Center (APLIC, 605 W. 4th Ave., 907/644-3661 or 866/869-6887, www.alaskacenters.gov, daily 9am-5pm late May-early Sept., Mon.-Fri. 10am-5pm in winter, free). This is a great starting point to learn about federal lands in Alaska. a Park Service ranger on staff, and the center also hosts eight other agencies, including national forests, wildlife refuges, and Bureau of Land Management areas. Displays introduce you to Alaska's wildlife and wild places, the touchscreen kiosk features interactive maps, daily historical walks are offered throughout the summer, the bookstore has a great selection of Alaskan titles, and there's even free Wi-Fi. You can also book Kenai Fjords National Park cabins here, and the auditorium opens for daily 2pm nature talks and high-definition nature videos all summer. Take a look around this old building to find classic Depression-era paintings of Alaska. The only problem with APLIC is access: Because it's also a courthouse, all visitors will need to go through screening at the entrance. It's a minor hassle, but generally not a long delay.

A few blocks away is the **Department of Natural Resources Public Information Center** (550 W. 7th Ave., 12th floor, 907/269-8400, www.alaskastateparks.org, Mon.-Fri. 10am-5pm). The information center has helpful staff and details on state parks, public-use cabins, where to pan for gold, state land sales, and much more.

CONVENTION CENTERS

Near the Performing Arts Center are **Egan Civic and Convention Center** (555 W. 5th Ave., 907/263-2800, www.anchorageconventioncenters.com) and the beautiful **Dena'ina Civic and Convention Center** (600 W. 7th Ave., 907/263-2850, www.anchorageconventioncenters.com).

LIBRARIES

The **Z. J. Loussac Library** (36th Ave. and Denali St., 907/261-2975, http://lexicon.

anchorage.ak.us, Mon.-Thurs. 10am-8pm, Fri.-Sat. 10am-6pm) is a spacious facility out in Midtown. You could easily lose an afternoon just wandering among the stacks, enjoying the cozy sitting room on Level 3, studying the huge relief map of the state, browsing among the paintings hanging on the walls, or picking a book at random from the large Alaskana collection. Getting to the Alaskana section is an adventure in its own right—the architects did everything they could to make it difficult to reach: up two flights of stairs, across a long connecting walkway, and then back down two levels. And it's back out the same way, since there is no exit here! The library has computers for free Internet access, but you may have to wait awhile.

INTERNET ACCESS

Local libraries all have computers and free Wi-Fi access. The Anchorage airport and many local businesses—especially hotels, B&Bs, and restaurants—have free Wi-Fi. These include: **Café del Mundo** (341 E. Benson Blvd., 907/274-0026, www.cafedelmundo.com, Mon.-Fri. 6am-8pm, Sat. 7am-8pm, Sun. 8am-6pm); **Middle Way Café** (1200 W. Northern Lights Blvd., 907/272-6433, Mon.-Fri. 7am-6pm, Sat.-Sun. 8am-6pm); **Organic Oasis** (2610 Spenard Rd., 907/277-7882, www.organicoasis.com, Mon.-Sat. 11am-9pm, Sun. 1pm-6pm); **Glacier BrewHouse** (737 W. 5th Ave., 907/274-2739, www.glacierbrewhouse.com, Mon.-Fri. 11am-11pm, Sat.-Sun. 10am-11pm mid-May-mid-Sept., reduced winter hours); **Peanut Farm** (5227 Old Seward Hwy.,

907/563-3283, www.wemustbenuts.com); and Kaladi Brothers Coffee.

BANKING

As might be expected, ATMs can be found practically anywhere, including most grocery stores. **Wells Fargo** (320 W. 5th Ave., 907/265-2016) has a booth inside the 5th Avenue Mall to exchange traveler's checks or foreign currency for greenbacks.

MEDICAL SERVICES

Alaska's three largest hospitals are in Anchorage. Of the first two, **Alaska Regional Hospital** (2801 DeBarr Rd., 907/276-1131, www.alaskaregional.com) and **Providence Alaska Medical Center** (3200 Providence Dr., 907/562-2211, www.providence.org), Providence has a better reputation and is a nonprofit. The modern **Alaska Native Medical Center** (4315 Diplomacy Dr., 907/257-1150, www.anmc.org) is perhaps the finest facility in Alaska, but is only for Native Alaskans.

To find a doctor, call the **physician referral services** offered by Providence (907/261-4900) and Alaska Regional (907/264-1722 or 800/265-8624).

Several "Doc-in-a-box" offices are scattered around Anchorage, but you're likely to see a physician's assistant rather than a doctor. Try **Alaska Health Care Clinic** (3600 Minnesota Dr., 907/279-3500), **Urgent Care** (5437 E. Northern Lights Blvd., 907/333-8561), or **Primary Care Associates** (4100 Lake Otis Pkwy., 907/562-1234, www.primarycareak.com).

Getting There and Around

GETTING THERE
Air

Almost everybody who flies into Alaska from the Lower 48 lands at **Anchorage International Airport** (907/266-2525, www.anchorageairport.com), even if just to connect to other carriers to travel around the state. The airport is six miles southwest of downtown, and officially it is Ted Stevens Anchorage International Airport in honor of the U.S. senator who for decades brought home federal funds for Alaskan projects, including the airport. All this money shows, with big windows facing the mountains and a classy design. There is free Wi-Fi here, too.

If you have time to kill while waiting for a flight, head upstairs to the **observation deck** for a quiet space decorated with Native art; look for the stairs next to Starbucks. It's a great place to catch a few Zs, watch the planes come and go, or surf the web.

An **information booth** (907/248-0373, daily 9am-5pm summer) is near the baggage area; if it's closed, check the racks for free brochures. You can store luggage and even frozen fish nearby.

The **People Mover** bus 7 (907/343-6543, www.peoplemover.org, daily, $1.75 adults, $1 ages 5-18) runs from the lower level into downtown Anchorage almost hourly, seven days a week. There's always a line of cabs ($20-25 to downtown) waiting out front as you exit the baggage claim area.

The Alaska Railroad has a terminal at the airport that is used by cruise ship companies, with passengers flying into Anchorage and riding the train to Whittier or Seward, where they disembark for their cruise to Southeast Alaska (or vice versa). In addition to passengers, the airport serves as a vital link for air cargo companies. Both Federal Express and UPS have major international terminals, and hundreds of cargo flights land and refuel each week.

DOMESTIC

Many of the big domestic carriers fly into and out of Anchorage from the Lower 48, including **Alaska Airlines** (800/426-0333, www.alaskaair.com), **American** (800/433-7300, www.aa.com), **Delta** (800/221-1212, www.delta.com), **Frontier** (800/432-1359, www.flyfrontier.com), **JetBlue** (800/538-2583, www.jetblue.com), and **United** (800/241-6522, www.united.com).

Most of these flights arrive via Seattle, but Alaska Air also has year-round nonstop flights to Chicago, Denver, Honolulu, Kansas City, Las Vegas, Los Angeles, and Portland, Oregon, with connecting service via Seattle to most Western cities and all the way to Atlanta, Dallas, Houston, Philadelphia, Boston, Washington, D.C., Miami, Newark, Orlando, and a number of Mexican cities. Delta flies nonstop year-round to Salt Lake City, and United flies to San Francisco and Denver.

Summer-only nonstop Anchorage flights arrive from Chicago (American), Dallas (American), Denver (Frontier), Long Beach (JetBlue), San Francisco (Virgin America), and Philadelphia (U.S. Airways). In addition, **Sun Country Airlines** (800/359-6786, www.suncountry.com) has seasonal charters between Anchorage and Minneapolis.

INTERNATIONAL

The following companies offer nonstop international service into Anchorage: **Air Canada** (888/247-2262, www.aircanada.com) from Vancouver, **Korean Air** (800/438-5000, www.koreanair.com) from Seoul, **Condor Airlines** (800/524-6975, www.condor.com) from Frankfurt, **Iceland Air** (800/223-5500,

© DON PITCHER

Anchorage International Airport

www.icelandair.us) from Reykjavik, and **Vladivostok Air** (www.vladivostokavia.ru/en) to Vladivostok in Russia. **Alaska Air** flies to destinations across Mexico (with a stop in Los Angeles or San Diego).

REGIONAL AIRLINES

Alaska's largest regional airline is **Era Alaska** (907/266-8394 or 800/866-8394, www.flyera. com) with direct flights connecting Anchorage with Bethel, Cordova, Homer, Kenai, Kodiak, Valdez, Nome, Fairbanks, Aniak, Dillingham, Unalakleet, and Galena. From these hubs flights continue to dozens of smaller villages across the state.

PenAir (907/771-2640 or 800/448-4226, www.penair.com) flies from Anchorage to Aniak, Cold Bay, Dillingham, Dutch Harbor, Iliamna, King Salmon, McGrath, Pribilof Islands, Sand Point, and Unalakleet.

Grant Aviation (907/243-3592 or 888/359-4726, www.flygrant.com) provides daily flights connecting Anchorage with Kenai and Valdez.

Alaska Railroad

Anchorage is a major stop for the Alaska Railroad, with service north all the way to Fairbanks and south to Seward and Whittier. The Alaska Railroad train depot (411 W. 1st Ave., 907/265-2494 or 800/544-0552, www. alaskarailroad.com) is just down the hill from the center of Anchorage. Its daily express to Fairbanks has prices comparable to those of the tour buses but is a much more comfortable, historical, enjoyable, and leisurely ride. The **Denali Star train** (departs Anchorage daily 8:15am mid-May-mid-Sept., $117 one-way to Denali, $167 one-way to Fairbanks) runs from Anchorage to Denali (arriving 4pm) and Fairbanks (arriving 8pm). The train also stops in Wasilla and Talkeetna, where you can hop off, but you're not allowed to check any luggage—only what you can carry on.

Take the **Coastal Classic train** (daily mid-May–mid-Sept., $79 one-way, $125 round-trip; kids half-price) south to Seward for a fantastic over-the-top voyage across the Kenai Peninsula. The route diverges from the highway near Portage and then winds steeply into the Kenai Mountains past several glaciers. The Anchorage to Whittier **Glacier Discovery train** (departs Anchorage 9:45am mid-May–mid-Sept., $89 round-trip) is a three-hour ride. Both of these trains also stop in Girdwood, but only hand-carried baggage is allowed from there.

The Alaska Railroad also offers **GoldStar** double-decker coaches with open-air viewing platforms for an old-fashioned luxury rail experience to Seward ($134 one-way), Denali ($202 one-way), and Fairbanks ($277 one-way). Both **Princess Tours** (206/336-6000 or 800/426-0500, www.princesslodges.com) and **Gray Line of Alaska** (907/277-5581 or 888/425-1737, www.graylinealaska.com) hook their super-dome cars to the back of the express for a similar experience. These are mostly for the cruise ship crowd, but they also sell seats to independent travelers.

Buses

A number of bus companies head out from Anchorage to other parts of the state, and most will carry bikes for an extra charge. Try a city bus for a cheaper option if you're just heading to Palmer or Wasilla from Anchorage.

Alaska/Yukon Trails (907/479-2277 or 800/770-7275, www.alaskashuttle.com, daily late Apr.–Sept., $75 one-way to Denali) has a daily Anchorage-Talkeetna-Denali-Fairbanks run.

Interior Alaska Bus Line (907/883-0207 or 800/770-6652, www.interioralaskabusline.com) provides year-round service three times a week from Anchorage to Tok, continuing north to Fairbanks.

Anchorage Denali Express (907/376-1992 or 877/376-1992, www.anchoragedenaliexpress.com, daily early June–mid-Sept., $86

one-way to Denali) has daily runs between downtown Anchorage and Denali.

Park Connection (907/245-0200 or 800/266-8625, www.alaskacoach.com) provides summertime bus service connecting Anchorage with Seward, Whittier, Talkeetna, and Denali.

The Stage Line (van stop 412 W. 53rd Ave., Anchorage, 907/868-3914, www.stagelineinhomer.com, Mon.-Fri. in summer, once a week in winter) runs vans between Anchorage and Cooper Landing ($54), Soldotna ($70), and Homer ($90). Drivers can stop almost anywhere along the route to pick up or drop off passengers. The anchorage van stop is a bit far from downtown, but drivers often have packages to deliver and can drop you closer to your Anchorage destination.

Seward Bus Lines (bus stop 539 3rd Ave., 907/563-0800 or 888/420-7788, www.sewardbuslines.net, daily year-round, $40 one-way to Seward; daily summer-only, $30 one-way to Whittier) provides year-round bus service to Seward and summer-only service to Whittier. In Anchorage, buses stop on 3rd Avenue but can take you directly to your hotel for an extra $5.

The **Alaska Bus Guy** (907/720-6541, www.alaskabusguy.com, daily summer, twice-weekly winter, $85 one-way to Denali, $67 one-way to Talkeetna) operates an environmentally friendly hydrogen-hybrid van with service from Anchorage to Denali or Talkeetna.

GETTING AROUND
City Buses

People Mover (907/343-6543, www.peoplemover.org, Mon.-Fri. 6am-10pm, Sat. 8am-8pm, Sun. 9:30am-6:30pm, $1.75 adults, $1 ages 5-18, free downtown, $5 day pass), Anchorage's public bus system, covers the entire Anchorage Basin. Weekday service is extensive, with all routes operating. On Saturday, most lines run, but Sunday service is only offered on certain routes. Visit the **Transit Center** (6th Ave. and G St., Mon.-Fri. 7am-6pm), where you can pick up a *Ride Guide* timetable of all routes. Exact fare is required, and transfers are valid only on a different bus traveling in the same direction within two hours of the time of receipt. People Mover buses are free all day in the downtown area; just get on board and ride. A day pass—good for unlimited rides—is sold on all buses. All buses have front bike racks.

All People Mover buses can transport wheelchairs, or call the **Anchor Rides** program (907/343-7433) for special transportation needs. You'll need to call at least a day in advance.

Valley Mover (907/892-8800, www.valleymover.com, $7) has commuter runs connecting Anchorage with Wasilla.

Taxis

Taxis are expensive: Most charge $2 per flag drop plus $2.50 per mile thereafter. **Yellow Cab** (907/222-2222, www.akyellowcab.com) and **Anchorage Checker Cab** (907/276-1234) are the two main companies. There's always a line of waiting cabs outside the airport if you are just arriving and need a way into Anchorage; the fare is $20-25 to downtown.

Car Rentals

Anchorage is car-happy, so rental cars can be very hard to come by. Make car reservations as much as two months ahead to be sure of a car in the peak season. Most of the major companies (Alamo, Avis, Budget, Dollar, Enterprise, Hertz, National, and Thrifty) operate from the Anchorage airport, with free shuttles from the south terminal. If you rent a car here you'll add an extra 29 percent tax to the rate (versus 18 percent in town). Especially for long rentals, it's usually best *not* to get a rental car from the airport.

The best rates are frequently through **Payless** (907/243-3616 or 800/729-5377,

www.paylesscar.com), **Budget** (907/243-6492 or 800/248-0150, www.budget.com), **Alaska Car & Van Rental** (907/243-4444, www.alaskacarandvan.com), **Denali Car Rental** (907/276-1230 or 800/757-1230, www.akdenalicarrental.com), **Dollar** (907/248-5338 or 800/800-4000, www.dollar.com), **Thrifty** (907/276-2855 or www.thrifty.com), or **High Country Car & Truck Rental** (a.k.a. E-Z Rent-A-Car, 907/562-8078 or 888/685-1155, www.highcountryanchorage.com).

Most car rental companies prohibit driving on the McCarthy Road, Denali Highway, and other rough roads, but many drivers also ignore these rules. If you're traveling in the winter, ask for a car with studded tires, which are—surprisingly—not on many Anchorage rental cars.

When making a reservation, be sure to mention if you have a AAA or Costco card; you can often save substantially on the rates. Don't even think of renting a car in Anchorage and leaving it elsewhere in Alaska; the charges are sky-high for this luxury.

RV Rentals

Quite a few places let you rent honkin' Alaska-size RV land yachts—the ones you sit behind for miles as they waddle down the road at 30 mph and get 4 miles to the gallon. Recreational vehicles may be of some value for groups of six or more, but are completely unnecessary for smaller groups.

The following Anchorage companies rent RVs: **Great Alaskan Holidays** (907/248-7777 or 888/225-2752, www.greatalaskanholidays.com), **Clippership Motorhome Rentals** (907/562-7051 or 800/421-3456, www.clippershiprv.com), **ABC Motorhome Rentals** (907/279-2000 or 800/421-7456, www.abcmotorhome.com), and **Alaska Motorhome Rentals/Alaska Travel Adventures** (907/789-0052 or 800/323-5757, www.bestofalaskatravel.com).

Tour Buses

At least a half-dozen tour companies are happy to sell you bus tours of Anchorage and the surrounding area; get their brochures from the visitors center. The largest companies—**Gray Line of Alaska** (907/277-5581 or 888/452-1737, www.graylinealaska.com) and **Princess Tours** (206/336-6000 or 800/426-0500, www.princess. com)—also offer a wide range of other package trips on land, sea, or air throughout Alaska.

Boats

Although there are no boat tours out of Anchorage, it *is* a good place to check out boat trips across Prince William Sound and out of Seward. Several tour companies offer trips that include a bus from Anchorage to Whittier, boat across the Sound, and flight or bus ride back to Anchorage. Or get to Whittier on your own and hop on one of these tour boats.

The **Alaska Marine Highway** (907/465-3941 or 800/642-0066, www.dot.state.ak.us/amhs) ferry does not reach Anchorage, but you can connect up with the system in Whittier via the Alaska Railroad or in Homer by bus.

Vicinity of Anchorage

◖ CHUGACH STATE PARK

Alaska's second-largest chunk of state-owned land, Chugach State Park (park headquarters Mile 115 Seward Hwy., 907/345-5014, www. alaskastateparks.org) encompasses nearly half a million acres—half the size of Delaware. The park covers the entire Chugach Range from Eagle River, 25 miles north of Anchorage, to Girdwood, 35 miles south. It could take a committed hiker years to explore all of its trails, ridges, peaks, and passes. From the short but steep 1.5-mile trail up Flattop Mountain in Anchorage to the 25-mile trek from the Eagle River Nature Center over Crow Pass down to Girdwood, there are a wide range of trails to choose from, each varying in length, elevation, difficulty, access, and congestion.

Pick up hiking brochures at the Alaska Public Lands Information Center in Anchorage, decide on a trail, then dress for rain. The clouds often sit down on these city-surrounding mountaintops, and when it's sunny and hot in Anchorage, it could be hailing only a few minutes away on the trails. But don't let that stop you. This whole park is within a few miles of where half of Alaska's population huddles, but up in these mountains it's easy to pretend you're a hundred years behind the crowds, and all the hustle and bustle on the Inlet flats is far in the future.

Hillside Trails

Two trailheads on the city's southeastern outskirts give access to a network of crisscrossing and connecting trails in the section of the range that hems in Anchorage Bowl. They're all off Hillside Drive, which skirts a suburb of sparkling glass houses and gorgeous views of the skyline, inlet, and Mount Susitna to the west. City buses do not reach the park in this area, so you'll really need a vehicle ($5 day-use parking) to get to the Hillside trailheads.

For the **Glen Alps Trailhead,** drive south on New Seward Highway and turn east toward the mountains on O'Malley Road. Follow it to Hillside Drive, where you turn right, then left on Upper Huffman Road. In 0.5 miles, go right again onto aptly named Toilsome Hill Drive. Toil steeply uphill for 2.5 miles to reach the Glen Alps parking lot ($5 day-use). On warm summer weekends every space in the lot fills with cars, so get here early or take the **Flattop Mountain Shuttle** (907/279-3334, www.hike-anchorage-alaska.com, May-Oct.,

© DON PITCHER

cottonwood trees in Chugach State Park

$22 round-trip) from downtown. Take a look from the nearby overlook, and then head up the **Flattop Mountain Trail** for even better views. This extremely popular 1.5-mile trail gains 1,500 feet and is very steep near the top as you scramble through the boulders.

Also from the Glen Alps Trailhead are several moderate and very scenic hikes: **Little O'Malley Peak,** 7.5 miles round-trip; the **Ramp and Wedge,** 11 miles round-trip; and **Williwaw Lakes,** 13 miles round-trip. A great mountain bike route is the 11-mile (one-way) **Powerline Pass Trail** that also takes off from the Glen Alps Trailhead and goes over 3,550-foot Powerline Pass all the way to the Indian Creek Trailhead on Turnagain Arm.

Continue north on Hillside Drive past Upper Huffman Road and take a right on Upper O'Malley Road. The second left leads to **Prospect Heights Trailhead,** where the **Wolverine Peak Trail** leads to the top of this 4,455-foot mountain (11 miles round-trip).

You'll discover great views of the Alaska Range and Anchorage, but go in late summer when the snow has melted.

Naturalist guides from **The Ascending Path** (907/783-0505, www.theascendingpath.com, half-day hike $89 pp, two-person minimum, full day $120 pp) lead an array of day hikes in the Anchorage area, including ones from the Glenn Alps Trailhead.

Eagle River Area

Take the Eagle River exit 13 miles north of Anchorage on the Glenn Highway, then your first right onto Eagle River Road, a dazzling, paved 11-mile ride right into the heart of Chugach State Park. Rafters and kayakers on the Class II Eagle River can put in at two access points (Miles 7.5 and 9) along this road. The road ends at the **Eagle River Nature Center** (907/694-2108, www.ernc.org, Wed.-Sun. 10am-5pm May-Sept., Fri.-Sun. 10am-5pm in winter, parking $5), which features a "close-up corner" with furs and a track book, as well as an aurora display and a gift shop. Park rangers lead 1.5-hour hikes (daily 1pm June-Aug.). The **Rodak Nature Trail** (0.5 miles round-trip) is a wide gravel route with informative signs on snow, glaciers, the forest, and the sun. It's 15 minutes well spent. For a longer walk, take the seven-mile **River Trail** along the Eagle River.

Eklutna Lake

Twenty-six miles north of Anchorage on the Glenn Highway is the exit for Eklutna Lake, a favorite weekend destination. Narrow and winding Eklutna Road follows the Eklutna River 10 miles to the lake, where you'll find a pleasant small **campground** ($10) with outhouses and a large picnic area. The 14-mile **Lakeside Trail-Eklutna Glacier Trail** starts nearby, skirting the west side of Eklutna Lake and then climbing to this very scenic glacier. Three side trails lead off the main route to Twin Peaks, Bold Ridge, and East Fork of Eklutna

River. This is an outstanding mountain biking area in summer, and a popular wintertime skiing and snowmobiling trail. Most of the route is also open to ATVs (Sun.-Wed.), so you may not have peace and quiet. Experienced skiers may want to continue beyond Eklutna Glacier via a multiglacier traverse that takes them 31 miles to Crow Pass. The **Mountaineering Club of Alaska** (www.mtnclubak.org) has three huts along the way.

Kayak and bike rentals are available near the Eklutna Campground from **Lifetime Adventures** (907/746-4644 or 800/952-8624, www.lifetimeadventures.net), along with a popular paddle-and-peddle option: you kayak across the lake and return along the trail by mountain bike ($80 pp).

Also from the Eklutna exit, you can follow the access road a mile south to scenic **Thunderbird Falls** (if you're heading north from Anchorage, there's a marked Thunderbird Falls exit before you reach the Eklutna exit). The trail takes you on an easy one-mile hike up Thunderbird Creek. Follow your ears to the falls.

Crow Pass

For one of the longest and most scenic hikes in the park, head out on the 25-mile **Crow Pass Trail.** This trail (also known as the Historic Iditarod Trail) provided a turn-of-the-20th-century overland route from Seward through the Chugach to the Interior gold mining town of Iditarod. The gradual climb to Crow Pass fords several streams, including Eagle River midway along the trail. It might be wise to camp overnight and cross the river in the morning, when the glacial runoff is lower. Raven Glacier and Crystal Lake are scenic highlights near Crow Pass, where you leave Chugach State Park and continue in immense Chugach National Forest. The Forest Service's popular **Crow Pass Cabin** (518/885-3639 or 877/444-6777, www.recreation.gov, $35/night)

is an A-frame structure on the summit. From the cabin it's four miles down to the trailhead on rough Crow Creek Road, then another five miles to the Alyeska Ski Resort access road. Experienced skiers sometimes use the Iditarod and Crow Pass Trails for a winter traverse of the mountains, but be aware that avalanche danger can be very high.

Camping and Cabins

Developed state park campgrounds are found at **Eklutna Lake** ($10) and **Eagle River** (907/746-4644 or 800/952-8624, www.lifetimeadventures.net, $20) north of Anchorage, and at **Bird Creek** ($15) to the south. All three have four-day limits, outhouses, and water, and are generally open May-September. Located just off the Hiland Road exit, 12 miles north of Anchorage, is the often-full Eagle River Campground; make reservations in advance.

A wonderful **cabin** (www.dnr.alaska.gov/parks, $50) is available on the shore of Eklutna Lake, and three **yurts** and an **eight-person cabin** (907/694-2108, www.ernc.org, $65) are near the Eagle River Nature Center.

NORTH OF ANCHORAGE

Chugach State Park includes several popular destinations north of Anchorage around Eklutna Lake and Eagle River.

Arctic Valley

Six miles north of Anchorage along the Glenn Highway is the exit to Arctic Valley Road, which climbs seven steep miles to the parking lot at the Alpenglow ski area. A trailhead about a mile before road's end leads to long **Ship Creek Trail,** which, with a little cross-country hiking, hooks up with Bird Creek and Indian Creek Trails via the passes of the same names. It's 22 miles from Arctic Valley to Indian Creek Trailhead. Plan on 2-3 days to do this traverse. From the Alpenglow parking lot a two-mile trail goes up to **Rendezvous Peak,** an easy hike with great views of the city, the inlet, and even Mount McKinley if you're lucky.

Eklutna Historical Park

This park (Eklutna Rd. exit off Glenn Hwy., 907/688-6026, www.eklutnahistoricalpark. org, Mon.-Sat. 10am-5pm mid-May-Sept., $5 adults, $3 kids) is one of those surprising discoveries just off the Glenn Highway. Take the Eklutna Road exit (26 miles northeast of Anchorage) and cross back over the highway to Eklutna Village. Russian Orthodoxy is strongly overlaid on Native Alaskan culture from this point, at the site of the first Tanaina (a branch of the Athabascans) settlement on the Inlet, down through the western Kenai Peninsula, Kodiak, and the Aleutians. The ancestors of most of these Indians were converted by Russian missionaries, and **St. Nicholas Russian Orthodox Church**—a miniature log chapel that dates from the 1830s and

was reconstructed in the 1970s—is the oldest building in the Anchorage area. Nearby is a newer and larger church. Both are set against a backdrop of 80 or so colorful **spirit houses** that sit atop Native Alaskan graves. Informative half-hour tours are offered, and you can stroll the grounds at other times. A small gift shop sells Native Alaskan crafts and souvenirs.

◖ TURNAGAIN ARM

Cook Inlet bends east from Anchorage, becoming Turnagain Arm. The inlet was named by Captain James Cook's master, William Bligh, who later captained the ill-fated HMS *Bounty*. The Seward Highway curves around Turnagain Arm, past the town of Girdwood and the turnoff to Portage Glacier and Whittier, and finally south over the Kenai Mountains to Seward, 127 miles away. The Turnagain Arm stretch is exceptionally scenic, but traffic is often heavy, so drive carefully and keep your headlights

© DON PITCHER

spirit houses at Eklutna Historical Park

© DON PITCHER

Kenai Mountains, near the head of Turnagain Arm

on at all times. Many people have lost their lives in traffic accidents on this narrow highway jammed against the cliffs, so always use extreme caution. Travelers will find places to watch birds, beluga whales, Dall sheep, and rock climbers, and you can stop for hikes or to fish along the way.

Potter Marsh Area

On the south end of Anchorage, wedged between the Seward Highway and hillside homes, Potter Marsh is a great spot to look for migrating and nesting birds, moose, and spawning salmon. A boardwalk extends into the marsh, providing views of Canada geese, trumpeter swans, and even the flyin'-fool Arctic terns. Bring binoculars and a light jacket for the often-breezy conditions. This marsh was created when the railroad builders installed an embankment to protect the track from Turnagain Arm's giant tides, which dammed the freshwater drainage from the mountains.

A mile south on the other side of the highway is the **Potter Section House** (115 Seward Hwy., 907/345-5014, Mon.-Fri. 8am-4:30pm year-round, free), a small railroad museum of interpretive displays and signs outside and inside the restored original "section" house. This is also headquarters for Chugach State Park; get brochures on local trails here. Check out the nine-foot rotary snowplow once used to clear avalanches. A small gift shop sells railroad memorabilia and books.

Turnagain Arm Trail

Across the highway from Potter Section House is the parking lot for **Potter Creek Trailhead,** the first access to the Turnagain Arm Trail, which parallels the highway for over nine miles, with good opportunities to see Dall sheep, moose, and spruce grouse. The trail began as a turn-of-the-20th-century wagon road built to transport railroad workers and supplies. This is a very popular early summer path since its south-facing slopes lose the snow early. In three miles is **McHugh Creek,** an always-crowded day-use area and trailhead for the seven-mile hike up to **Rabbit Lake.** You can continue south along the Turnagain Arm Trail past three more trailheads all the way to **Windy Corner Trailhead,** nine miles from your starting point and not far from Beluga Point.

Beluga Point

Twenty miles south of Anchorage is Beluga Point, a good place to see the small white beluga whales cavorting in Turnagain Arm in late May and late August; they follow salmon into these shallow waters. Unfortunately, overhunting by Native Alaskans caused the population of belugas to plummet in the 1990s, and they still have not recovered.

Look behind you for the Dall sheep that often wander close to the highway in this area. Or just have a picnic and wait for the Cook Inlet's famous bore tides. The tides here, at 30 feet, are among the world's highest, and the lead breaker can be up to 6 feet high, a half-mile across, and can move at over 10 miles per hour. This is the only bore tide in the United States, created when a large body of water (Cook Inlet) is forced by strong tidal action into a narrow shallow one (Turnagain Arm). Look for a series of small swells (2-3 feet high, larger depending on the wind) that crash against the rocks and send up a mighty spray. Bore tides peak when tides are largest, during the new or full moon phases. The bore tide passes Beluga Point roughly two hours after low tide in Anchorage—check the tide tables online or pick up a tide chart from local outdoor stores. One warning: Never go out on the Turnagain Arm mudflats at any time. The mixture of glacial silt and mud creates quicksand; people have drowned after getting their feet stuck in the mud and being inundated by the incoming tide. Don't take a chance!

Indian and Bird Creeks

Twenty-five miles south of Anchorage, and right before Turnagain House Restaurant in Indian, take a left on the gravel road and head 1.5 miles to the **Indian Valley Trailhead.** This trail, which follows Indian Creek over Indian Pass (especially rewarding during Indian summer), is five miles of easy walking on a well-maintained path. You can then continue for several miles of undeveloped hiking until you hook up with the Ship Creek Trail, which runs 22 miles to Arctic Valley north of Anchorage. The Powerline Pass Trail goes 11 miles from the Glenn Alps trailhead to Indian Creek Trail; look for the signed turnoff 100 yards up the Indian Valley Trail. Historic **Indian Valley Mine** (27301 Seward Hwy. Mile 104, 907/653-1120, www.indianvalleymine.com, daily 9am-9pm mid-May-mid-Sept., $1 pp) has summertime gold panning, historic buildings, a little museum, and a gift shop.

Two miles down the highway from Indian is the Bird Creek area, where dozens of cars line the roadside on July-August afternoons. They're all here trying to hook a silver salmon in this very productive creek. A half-mile north of the creek is a parking area for **Bird Ridge Trail,** which climbs straight up this 3,500-foot promontory in less than two miles.

Also nearby is the **Bird Creek Campground** (Seward Hwy. Mile 101, 907/269-8400, $15), a surprisingly pretty place just off the busy Seward Highway. Campsites are just a few feet from Cook Inlet. This thickly forested campground is often full of anglers working Bird Creek. The **Bird to Gird Bike Trail** runs right through the middle of the campground, continuing north for three miles to Indian and south three miles to Girdwood along the old highway.

GIRDWOOD

The town of Girdwood is officially part of the hectic Anchorage municipality, but feels a world away. Located 37 miles south via the

© DON PITCHER

historic Crow Creek Mine in Girdwood

unique and inexpensive souvenirs or gift items; they also burn until the cows come home.

◀ CROW CREEK MINE

The gravel Crow Creek Road leads from Girdwood three miles to Crow Creek Mine (Crow Creek Rd., 907/229-3105, www.crow-creekgoldmine.com, daily 9am-6pm mid-May-Sept., $10 adults, free for kids under 7; add $10 to adults and kids fee to pan for gold), one of the earliest gold strikes in Alaska (1896) and Southcentral Alaska's richest mine. The area was actively mined until World War II, producing over 45,000 ounces of gold. There's still a lot of gold to be found, and the creek attracts both casual panners looking for a flake of gold and those who come with metal detectors and large suction dredges. (When I last visited, a German tourist had just discovered a pea-sized nugget of gold.) Eight of the original mine buildings have been restored by the Toohey family and are filled with all sorts of flotsam and jetsam from the past. If you pay the additional fee to pan for gold, a pan and instructions are provided. There's a little gift shop, panning equipment rental, and overnight campsites ($10, no hookups). It's a pretty place with a rich history, and a must stop in the Girdwood area.

Continue another four miles out on Crow Creek Road beyond Crow Creek Mine to the **Crow Pass Trailhead.** It's an invigorating and beautiful 3.5 miles to the pass, with a 2,000-foot elevation gain. The trail is in the alpine area for much of the route and passes old mining ruins and a **Forest Service cabin** (www.recreation.gov, $45). A half-mile beyond the pass is Raven Glacier, where you enter Chugach State Park.

Seward Highway, the original town was leveled by the 1964 earthquake. A cluster of businesses stands along the highway, providing a rest stop for travelers, but new Girdwood and the Alyeska Resort sit at the end of a three-mile access road (Alyeska Highway). This winter resort is a favorite destination for locals, package tourists, unsuspecting travelers, and the occasional backpacker who likes a quick ride to the alpine tundra in the summer.

Sights

Adjacent to The Bake Shop, **Girdwood Center for Visual Arts** (Olympic Mountain Loop, 907/783-3209, www.gcvaonline.org, daily 11am-5pm summer, Wed.-Sun. 11am-5pm winter) is a co-op gallery with pottery, paintings, photography, glasswork, jewelry, and other locally crafted pieces.

Stop off at the **Alaska Candle Factory** (on the access road, 0.5 mile from Seward Hwy., 907/783-2354). Their candles are not only

Entertainment and Events

NIGHTLIFE

Après-ski partiers head to the **Sitzmark Bar & Grill** (Alyeska Hwy., 907/754-2256, www.

alyeskaresort.com, Sun.-Thurs. 11am-midnight, Fri.-Sat. 11am-2am in winter) at Alyeska Resort for a pitcher of beer and the chance to dance the night away to live bands on winter weekends; Sitzmark is closed in the summer.

FESTIVALS AND EVENTS

The big summertime event is **Girdwood Forest Fair** (www.girdwoodforestfair.com, early July), an annual event for more than 35 years. Hundreds of folks show up to buy arts and crafts, graze through the food booths, and listen to bands cranking out the tunes from two separate stages. It's a three-day party that seems to attract every free-spirited hippie left in Alaska. No dogs, politicians, or religious orders are allowed.

Skiing and snowboarding events fill the winter calendar at Alyeska Resort; the most fun for spectators is the **Spring Carnival and Slush Cup** (Alyeska Hwy., 907/754-1111, www.alyeskaresort.com, late Apr.), when costumed skiers and boarders blast downhill and attempt to make it across a slushy pond. There are lots of cold, wet folks at this one.

Recreation
SUMMER

First, check out **Alyeska Resort** (Alyeska Hwy., 907/754-1111, www.alyeskaresort.com) and the impressive lobby of the enormous Hotel Alyeska. Next, catch a ride 2,300 feet up Mount Alyeska on the **aerial tramway** (907/754-2275 or 800/880-3880, www.alyeskaresort.com, $20). On top are two restaurants. The two 60-passenger tram cars are entirely wheelchair accessible. Follow the well-marked trail to the alpine overlook onto cute Alyeska Glacier. If you have reservations to dine at Seven Glaciers restaurant, the tram ride is free. There is also a tram-and-lunch special to Glacier Express Café ($30); the tram office has details.

The resort's **Downhill Bike Park** utilizes chairlifts and the tram to access a maze of fast and fun bike trails. A day pass for the chairlifts ($20) and bike rentals are available at the day lodge or from **Girdwood Ski & Cyclery** (1553 Alyeska Hwy., 907/783-2453, www.girdwoodskicyclery.com). A paved path parallels the road to the Hotel Alyeska, and Crow Creek Road provides an easy dirt road for mountain bikers. The paved 13-mile **Bird to Gird Bike Trail** follows the shore of Turnagain Arm north from Girdwood.

Naturalist guides from **The Ascending Path** (907/783-0505, www.theascendingpath.com, $69 pp for 2-3-hour hike) lead an array of day hikes from their yurt office next to the base of the tram. **Nature hikes** are an easy introduction to the forests around Girdwood. More adventurous trips include a tram ride and alpine hike ($139 pp for 3 hours), a hike to Crow Pass ($120 pp for 5 hours), and **ice climbing classes** on Byron Glacier ($250 pp for 10 hours). One of their most popular hikes includes a ride on the Alaska Railroad to Spencer Glacier ($359 pp for nine hours, including rail, lunch, and guide), where a van takes you up a gravel road to an overlook where you begin a hike to the glacier. At the glacier's edge you learn about travel on the ice, strap on crampons and a helmet, and head out for two hours of exploration of the cravasses, ice caves, and other glacial features. Ascending Path also offers a number of other less expensive but still interesting hikes in the Spencer Glacier area.

Alaska Paragliding (907/301-1215, $195) takes novices on exciting tandem paragliding rides from the top of the tram.

Alpine Air (907/783-2360, www.alpineairalaska.com) has helicopter flightseeing, tours of Prince William Sound, and a very popular two-hour dog mushing adventure ($459 adults, $429 kids) that includes a glacier landing and the chance to drive a team of sled dogs.

WINTER

Alaska's primary center for downhill skiing and boarding, **Alyeska Resort** (Alyeska

Hwy., 907/754-1111 or 800/880-3880, www. alyeskaresort.com, Sun.-Wed. 10:30am-5:30pm winter, Thurs.-Sat. 10:30am-9:30pm winter, reduced hours early and late in the season) encompasses the ski and snowboard area, a large hotel, and several restaurants. The resort covers 500 skiable acres and has 60 trails, a 60-passenger tram, eight chairlifts, two pony lifts, and a tubing park. Most of the ski runs are at the intermediate or advanced level. In addition to abundant natural snowfall (depths generally exceed 10 feet), there is snowmaking capability on the lower slopes.

Alyeska Resort generally opens for skiing and snowboarding around Thanksgiving and closes at the end of April. Full-day lift tickets cost $65 adults, $50 ages 13-18 and seniors, and $30 ages 6-12. The half-day rate is $55 for adults, but kids pay the full-day rate. On Thursday-Saturday there's night skiing for $20 extra. A half-day ticket plus night skiing will run you $65. There are discounts for children, students, families, and multiday passes. Downhill skis, snowboards, cross-country skis, snowshoes, and ice skates (for use on the skating pond) can be rented in the day lodge, where you can also get expensive cafeteria food. More cafeteria fare, along with an elaborate restaurant and lounge, is on top of the mountain. Ski and snowboarding classes at all levels are available. Traffic between Anchorage and Girdwood can back up on winter weekends, so head out early if you're driving. Call 907/754-7669 or visit www.alyeskaresort.com for the latest snow conditions. Hot tip: Costco stores in Anchorage often have discounted Alyeska ski passes; they're a great deal for families.

Based in Girdwood, **Chugach Powder Guides** (907/783-4354, www.chugachpowder-guides.com) leads heli-skiing adventures into some of the wildest mountain country anywhere. The company also provides snowcat skiing at Alyeska Resort, accessing areas away from the groomed runs.

Cross-country skiers will find five kilometers of groomed trails in the flats around Hotel Alyeska. Get details from the **Girdwood Nordic Ski Club** (www.skigirdwood.org).

Accommodations

Because of its resort status, Girdwood has a large number of lodging options, from basic hostel rooms to high-end suites. Add a 12 percent lodging tax to all rates quoted.

The luxurious 307-room **Hotel Alyeska** (Alyeska Hwy., 907/754-1111 or 800/880-3880, www.alyeskaresort.com, $279-319 d, $329-1,300 suites) is an eight-story 304-room hotel where nicely appointed rooms include heated towel racks, fridges, ski-boot storage boxes, Wi-Fi, and safes. Other in-hotel amenities include three restaurants, a fitness center, a large indoor swimming pool, a sauna, and a hot tub. The tram to the top of Mount Alyeska is right out the back door. Lodging rates vary, with the lowest prices for small rooms on level three. Suites vary dramatically in price. Be sure to ask if they have any discounted rates and packages; your savings can be substantial.

Heading toward the resort on the access road, go right on Timberline, pass gorgeous ski chalets, then turn right again on Alpina. Around a couple of curves is the **Alyeska Hostel** (227 Alta Dr., 907/783-2222, www.alyeskahostel.com, $21 pp dorm rooms, $50 d private rooms, $75-100 cabin for four). This is a great place with a coed dorm, two private rooms, and a summer-only cabin, plus a full kitchen and two baths, and Wi-Fi. The hostel gets noisy, and even the private rooms aren't all that private; one is a tiny loft with a curtain for a door. It's not great for families, but fine for single travelers and young couples. Reservations are recommended in the summer and mid-winter, especially for the private room and cabin. There is no lockout and no curfew, but no alcohol either.

One of the finest B&B's in Alaska, ◖**Hidden Creek B&B** (739 Vail Dr., 907/783-5557, www.

hiddencreekbb.com, $185-225 d) is a beautiful modern craftsman home with three nicely appointed rooms containing Stickley furniture. There's a hot tub out back, a gas fireplace in the common area, a wet bar, and Wi-Fi. Enjoy a gourmet Alaskan breakfast in the morning. Friendly innkeepers Ron and Michelle Tenny are knowledgeable about Alaska, but have also traveled extensively around the globe. Kids under age five are not allowed.

Just two blocks from the ski lifts, **Bud and Carol's B&B** (211 Brighton Rd., 907/783-3182, www.budandcarolsbandb.com, $130 d) has two guest rooms, each with a queen bed, private bath, full kitchen, private entrance, a hearty continental breakfast, and Wi-Fi.

Alyeska Accommodations (907/783-2000 or 888/783-2001, www.alyeskaaccommodations.com) is the best source for condo, chalet, and home rentals, representing several dozen places around Girdwood. Two organizations provide descriptions and helpful links to websites for most local B&Bs and guesthouses: **Girdwood Bed-and-Breakfast Association** (907/222-4858, www.gbba.org) and the **Alyeska/Girdwood Accommodations Association** (907/222-3226, www.agaa.biz).

Food

At the intersection of the Girdwood Spur Road and Seward Highway is a little strip mall with a variety of services, including a gas station-convenience store, a coin laundry, a video store, and a restaurant. Travelers heading south to Seward or north to Anchorage stop here before pushing back out on the highway. **Alpine Café & Bakery** (1 Alyeska Hwy., 907/783-2550, daily 6am-10pm mid-May-Sept., daily 8am-8pm in winter) serves breakfast, lunch, and dinner, but it is best known for the display cases filled with pastries. There's always a queue on winter mornings as the pre-ski gang comes in to inject sugar and caffeine into their veins.

In business since 1962, famous **Double Musky Inn** (Crow Creek Rd., 907/783-2822, www.doublemuskyinn.com, Tues.-Thurs. 5pm-10pm, Fri.-Sun. 4:30pm-10pm early Dec.-late Oct., $28-37) is 0.25 miles up Crow Creek Road on the left. It's crowded and loud, with long waits, a tacky New Orleans-meets-Alaska decor, and brief visits from your server. They don't take reservations either. Despite these drawbacks, the food is dependably good, if not stellar. Featured attractions are shrimp etouffee, rack of lamb, and the house specialty, French pepper steak. Save space for the ultra-rich Double Musky pie.

At the Alyeska resort is **The Bake Shop** (Alyeska Hwy., 907/783-2831, www.thebakeshop.com, Sun.-Fri. 7am-7pm, Sat. 7am-8pm, $6-17), a fine spot for lunch or an after-ski warm-up. Homemade sourdough bread, hearty soups, sandwiches, omelets, hefty sweet rolls, ice cream, coffee, and pizza fill out the menu. The front yard is packed with flowers, including some enormous peonies.

Get espresso or surf the Internet on the computers at **Java Haus** (907/783-2827, www.girdwoodjava.com, Mon.-Thurs. 7am-2pm, Fri.-Sun. 7am-5pm), a couple of doors away. Smoothies, wraps, and panini sandwiches are also here.

Down the hill on Arlberg Street is **◖ Jack Sprat Restaurant** (165 Olympic Mountain Loop, 907/783-5225, www.jacksprat.net, Mon.-Fri. 5pm-10pm, Sat.-Sun. 10am-10pm, $21-36), which has tall windows and a relaxed, lively setting just a short walk from the ski slopes. Dinners include everything from lamb osso bucco to vegetable tagine and baked ricotta cavatelli, with a decadent orange creamsicle panna cotta for dessert. Brunches are available on weekends, featuring crepes, red flannel hash, sausage omelet, and eggs Benedict.

Across from the post office on Hightower Road, **Chair 5 Restaurant** (5 Lindblad Ave., 907/783-2500, www.chairfive.com, daily 11am-11pm, $15-30) is a townie spot for very good pizzas, halibut and chips, rib-eye steaks, and daily specials. The bar (open till 2am) has a great choice of single malt scotches and microbrews. There are no reservations and the place gets busy on weekends, so grab a beer and enjoy a game of pool or sports on the TVs.

Just around the corner from Chair 5, **Casa del Sol** (158 Holmgren Pl., 907/783-0088, www.girdwood-casadelsol.com, daily 8am-midnight, $16-28) serves reasonably priced Southwest border fare all day. The sauces are all made here, and there's a small deck out front that's a popular spot for relaxing with a beer. In addition to burritos, tacos, enchiladas, and carne asada, the menu includes breakfast items such as cor fritters and juevos rancheros, plus seafood and steak for dinner. The local laundromat is in the same building, hence the restaurant's other title, Laundromex.

Silvertip Grill (165 Hightower Rd., 907/783-2584, www.silvertipgrill.com, daily 9am-midnight, $11-14) has the best burgers in town, with live music on weekends. Breakfast is served all day and features chicken fried steak with housemade reindeer sausage gravy.

On top of the mountain, **Seven Glaciers Restaurant** (Alyeska Hwy., 907/754-2237, www.alyeskaresort.com, daily 5pm-10pm in summer, variable winter hours, $49-75) offers excellent food with one of the best views you're ever likely to get while dining. Sitting on a crag at 2,303 feet above sea level, you can see the valley below, across to the Crow Pass area, and up Turnagain Arm. Main courses include ginger-citrus encrusted halibut, Alaskan king crab, and Wagyu beef New York steak. You can opt for the chef's tasting menu with five courses ($79 pp), plus wine pairings ($45). It's *très élégant,* but not at all stuffy or pretentious. The seven-minute tram ride gives you the chance to survey the area, and if you have dinner reservations (required), the tram ride is free.

The local grocery store, **Crow Creek Mercantile** (1 Hightower St., 907/783-3900, Mon.-Fri. 7am-midnight, Sat.-Sun.

8am-midnight) has all the basics, plus deli sandwiches, video rentals, liquor, firewood, and propane.

Information and Services
Girdwood doesn't have a visitors center, but you'll find information online at www.girdwoodalaska.com. In addition to the resort, the town has several restaurants, a grocery store, a post office, a library, and a laundry with showers. Both the library and the coin laundry have Internet access.

The Forest Service's **Glacier Ranger District office** (907/783-3242, www.fs.usda.gov/chugach, Mon.-Fri.) is on the left as you drive into town from the Seward Highway. It can provide details and maps for hikers, anglers, sea kayakers, and other recreation enthusiasts heading into Chugach National Forest.

Getting There and Around
The **Alaska Railroad** (907/265-2494 or 800/544-0552, www.alaskarailroad.com) connects Girdwood with Anchorage daily in the summer, but the trains stop at a small shelter out near the Seward Highway. You'll need to make advance reservations for a pickup in Girdwood, and only carry-on luggage is allowed.

Glacier Valley Transit (907/754-2547, www.glaciervalleytransit.com, year-round, $1) provides morning and evening bus transportation throughout Girdwood, from the Seward Highway to Alyeska, and most other points around the valley. Buses have wintertime ski and snowboard racks.

The Stage Line (907/868-3914, www.stagelineinhomer.com) will stop in Girdwood on the way to Anchorage, Homer, or Seward, but call ahead.

Alaska Wildlife Conservation Center
One of the most popular visitor attractions in Alaska, the 140-acre Alaska Wildlife

ANCHORAGE

© DON PITCHER

brown bears at the Alaska Wildlife Conservation Center

Conservation Center (907/783-2025, www.alaskawildlife.org, daily 8am-8pm mid-May-mid-Sept., daily 10am-5pm mid-Sept.-Feb., daily 10am-6pm Mar.-mid-May, $13 adults, $9 children, military, and seniors, maximum $35 per vehicle) sits along Turnagain Arm just across the Seward Highway from the turnoff to Portage Glacier. This nonprofit game farm for orphaned and injured Alaskan animals houses brown and black bears, wood bison, moose, elk, musk oxen, Sitka black-tailed deer, lynx, caribou, coyote, bald eagles, and even Snickers the famous (on YouTube at least) porcupine. It's a hit with all ages, providing an up-close look at animals you normally see from a distance—if at all. Visit in early summer for the chance to watch those ever-cute moose and musk ox babies.

🄲 PORTAGE GLACIER

Fifty miles south of Anchorage on the Seward Highway is the turnoff to Portage Glacier and Whittier. A six-mile access road takes you through Portage Valley to Portage Glacier. A town that stood on this corner was destroyed when the 1964 earthquake dropped the land 6-10 feet. Saltwater from Turnagain Arm inundated the area, killing the still-standing trees; the remaining buildings are gradually disintegrating. Portage Glacier is one of the more popular tourist attractions in Southcentral Alaska, so be ready to share the ride with busloads of cruise ship travelers.

An info booth along the Seward Highway has details on Whittier, and it sells tickets for various tour options, including the Alaska Railroad's scenic trips to Grandview.

Visitors Center

The Forest Service's **Begich, Boggs Visitor Center** (907/783-2326, www.fs.usda.gov/chugach, daily 9am-6pm late May-mid-Sept., closed in winter) is named after Nicholas Begich (U.S. representative from Alaska and father of current U.S. Senator Mark

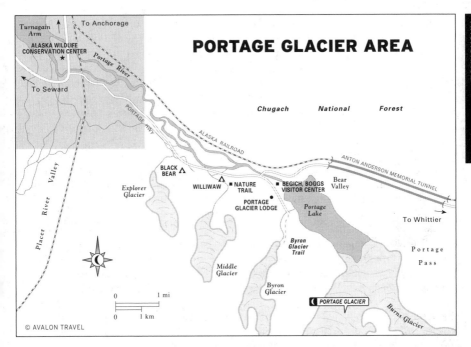

PORTAGE GLACIER AREA

Turnagain Arm

To Anchorage

ALASKA WILDLIFE CONSERVATION CENTER ★

Portage River

To Seward

Chugach   National   Forest

PORTAGE HWY

ALASKA RAILROAD

BLACK BEAR ∧

WILLIWAW ∧

■ **NATURE TRAIL**

PORTAGE GLACIER LODGE

■ **BEGICH, BOGGS VISITOR CENTER**

Bear Valley

ANTON ANDERSON MEMORIAL TUNNEL

To Whittier

Portage Lake

Explorer Glacier

Placer   River   Valley

Byron Glacier Trail

Portage Pass

Middle Glacier

Byron Glacier

(**PORTAGE GLACIER**

Burns Glacier

0   1 mi

0   1 km

© AVALON TRAVEL

Begich) and Hale Boggs (majority leader of the U.S. Senate and father of journalist Cokie Roberts), whose plane disappeared in the area in 1972. They were never found. A large picture window overlooks the narrow outlet of Portage Lake. When the visitor center first opened, the glacier was readily visible, but it is now out of sight around a corner, and in recent years the number of icebergs entering the lake has decreased greatly as it continues to shrink.

The visitor center boasts an amazing array of displays, including an ice cave, a small iceberg hauled in from the lake, an engrossing relief map of local ice fields, and everything you ever wanted to know about glaciers, including displays on glacial motion and crevasses. Don't miss the vial of tiny iceworms, which inhabit the surfaces of glaciers, feeding on pollen grains and red algae and surviving within a delicate, near-freezing temperature range. There's also good footage of iceworms in a pair of interesting glacier films (shown every hour, $5 adults, kids free).

During the summer, Forest Service naturalists lead half-mile "iceworm safari" nature walks (assuming funding is available). The **fish platform** near Williwaw Campground is a good place to see spawning red and chum salmon in late summer.

Seeing the Glacier

To see Portage Glacier, you'll need to hop onboard the 200-passenger ***Ptarmigan* tour boat** (907/277-5581 or 888/452-1737, www.graylinealaska.com, $34 adults, $17 kids); catch it at the dock near the visitor center. Operated by Gray Line of Alaska and staffed by Chugach National Forest naturalists, these one-hour cruises across Portage Lake start at 10:30am, with the last tour at 4:30pm. Gray Line offers the option to combine the boat tour with round-trip bus transportation from Anchorage ($79 adults, $39 kids), including a stop at Alyeska.

Hiking

Two hikes are within walking distance of the visitor center. The **Moraine Loop Trail,** accessible from the path to the lodge, is a five-minute stroll through typical moraine vegetation; Portage Glacier occupied this ground only 100 years ago. Follow the access road past the visitor center (south) just under a mile. At the back of the parking lot starts the **Byron Glacier Trail,** an easy 0.75-mile walk along the runoff stream to below this hanging glacier.

At Williwaw Campground, the 1.25-mile **Williwaw Nature Trail** provides an easy introduction to the area, and **Trail of the Blue Ice** continues to the Begich, Boggs Visitor Center.

Camping

Two seasonal Forest Service campgrounds near Portage contain woodsy sites. **Black Bear Campground** ($14) has 13 sites for tent camping and is not recommended for RVs. The larger **Williwaw Campground** (518/885-3639 or 877/444-6777, www.recreation.gov, $18) has 60 tent and RV sites (no hookups), plus a wheelchair-accessible observation platform where spawning salmon are visible in the summer. Williwaw's sites can be reserved ($9 fee).

WHITTIER

Named for poet John Greenleaf Whittier, this town of 300 friendly people has a picturesque mountains-and-bay setting. Unfortunately, the town itself is anything but poetic. Thousands of tourists pass through this settlement every week, but very few choose to spend much time in this strange place where the entire population lives in concrete high-rises and the wind never seems to stop. Whittier *does* have a gorgeous setting and lots of great outdoorsy things to do on nearby Prince William Sound. So

come here for the surrounding land, but don't expect to fall in love with the town, no matter how poetic the name.

All the businesses in Whittier are clustered around the harbor within a short walk from each other, so addresses are relatively meaningless (and thus have not been provided).

History

While less well known than the Alaska Highway, the construction of the railway to Whittier was one of the great engineering feats of World War II. Two tunnels, 1 mile and 2.5 miles long, were carved through the Chugach Mountains to link the military bases in Anchorage and Fairbanks to a secret saltwater port. Seward, the main ice-free port in Southcentral Alaska at that time, was considered too vulnerable to Japanese attack, so in 1941-1943 the Army blasted through the mountains and laid the tracks that would ensure the flow of supplies for the defense of Alaska. After the defeat of Japan, the military pulled out of Whittier, but a year later they were back as the Cold War began with the Soviet Union. Whittier became a permanent base, and large concrete buildings were built at that time. The 14-story Begich Tower (completed in 1954), an unlikely skyscraper in this small village, is near another anomaly, the "City under One Roof," which once housed 1,000 personnel and was the largest building in Alaska. Why did they build high-rises? To lessen the need for snow removal in a place where the snow sometimes tops 14 feet.

The base was deactivated in 1960, and the buildings were heavily damaged in the 1964 earthquake. One of them is still vacant, but Begich Tower has been restored and converted into condos. A third high-rise, Whittier Manor, was privately built in the 1950s and later turned into more condos. The military presence today is limited to an oil pipeline that supplies

© DON PITCHER

boat harbor in Whittier

military installations in Anchorage. Ships from Princess Cruises and Carnival Cruise Line stop in Whittier, but most of their passengers quickly depart the town.

For nearly half a century the town of Whittier was connected to the road system only via the Alaska Railroad. This changed in 2000, when an $80 million project made it possible for cars to drive in directly from the Seward Highway through two tunnels, one of which is shared with the railroad.

Sights

Most travelers never get farther than the tourist action on the waterfront, where boats of all sizes bob in the picturesque harbor.

Follow the signs for Whittier down past the dry dock, then go left across the tracks onto Whittier Street. Take a right on Glacier Avenue to the **Begich Tower.** In its 198 condos live most of the town's population; the rest reside in the 70 condos at **Whittier Manor.** Many are owned by Anchorageites who use them for weekend and summer getaways, boosting Whittier's summer population to nearly 1,000.

Continue a quarter-mile out on Eastern Avenue to quiet and scenic **Smitty's Cove,** where one of Whittier's few freestanding residences sits. You'll get a great view across Passage Canal of waterfalls, a kittiwake rookery, and Billing's Glacier.

The little **Prince William Sound Museum** (100 Whittier St., 907/472-2354, www.pws-museum.org, daily 10am-6pm late May-early Sept., $3 adults, $2 kids) is in the Anchor Inn building. It houses historic photos and items from Whittier's past.

Festivals and Events

The main Whittier event is the **Fourth of July celebration** featuring a parade, a picnic, games for kids, and fireworks.

On Father's Day, the **Tunnel Walk to Whittier** (mid-June) is a March of Dimes

ANCHORAGE

© DON PITCHER

Glacier cruises depart from Whittier.

fundraiser where participants walk the 2.5-mile tunnel from Bear Valley to Whittier.

Shopping

With an exterior in all sorts of Alaskan memorabilia, **Log Cabin Gifts** (Harbor Triangle, 907/472-2501, May-Sept.) features arts and crafts items, ivory, and watercolors by the owner, Wilma Buethe Wilcox. You can pet, photograph, and even feed the two pet **reindeer** next door. Also check out **Sound Ideas** (907/472-2535, www.whittierfudge.com, daily mid-May-mid-Sept.) for gifts and homemade fudge.

Recreation
BOAT TOURS

Whittier is a popular departure point for day trips to the glaciers of Prince William Sound mid-May-late September. **Phillips Tours and Cruises** (907/276-8023 or 800/544-0529, www.26glaciers.com, $159 adults, $99 kids)

operates the 4.5-hour 26-Glacier Cruise. The trip aboard its 340-passenger *Klondike Express*—a high-speed three-deck catamaran—covers a lot of ground but still allows plenty of time to linger at the faces of several glaciers. A hot lunch is included, there's a bar on board, and the lounges provide plenty of room inside should the weather be less than perfect. The schedule is timed so that you can ride the train from Anchorage and back (an additional $89 adults, $45 kids) or take a bus (an additional $50 adults, $25 kids).

Major Marine Tours (907/274-7300 or 800/764-7300, www.majormarine.com, daily, $119 adults, $60 ages 2-11, younger children free; with buffet dinner: $138 adults, $69 kids) takes visitors on a leisurely 4.5-hour voyage into stunning Blackstone Bay. If you want to include the filling salmon and prime rib buffet, the cruise price goes up. The company also offers a five-hour cruise to Surprise Glacier in Harriman Fjord onboard a high-speed

© DON PITCHER

Log Cabin Gifts in Whittier

catamaran ($149 adults, $75 kids; with buffet dinner: $168 adults, $85 kids). A Chugach National Forest ranger is onboard all Major Marine cruises.

In addition to these large operators, a number of locals offer small-boat trips into Prince William Sound. The prices may be a bit higher, but you get a more personal journey. Recommended for sightseeing, fishing, water taxis, and kayak drop-offs are **Lazy Otter Charters** (907/345-1175 or 800/587-6887, www.lazyotter.com), **Prince William Sound Taxi** (907/440-7978, www.princewilliam-soundtaxi.com), and **Aquetec** (907/362-1291, www.whittierwatertaxi.com).

HIKING

The most popular Whittier trail is up to **Portage Pass.** In the early days when gold was discovered around Hope on the Kenai Peninsula, Hope-bound hopefuls would boat to this harbor, portage their supplies over the glacier pass, and float down Turnagain Arm to their destination. This highly recommended day hike from Whittier affords splendid views of Passage Canal, Portage Glacier, and the Chugach Mountains. On a clear day, the views of the glacier from the Portage Pass area are far superior to those from the Portage Visitors Center.

This trail starts near the oil tanks and tunnel entrance at the foot of Maynard Mountain. Cross the tracks on the dirt road to the left. Take the road to the right and climb southwest along the flank of the mountain up a wide easy track. If you walk briskly, you can be at Portage Pass (700 feet) in less than an hour. There are places to camp or picnic beside Divide Lake, but beware of strong winds at the pass. From the lake follow the stream down toward the glacier, then find a way via a tributary on the right up onto one of the bluffs for a view of Portage Lake. Deep crevasses in the blue glacial ice are clearly visible from here. Portage Glacier has receded far enough that the gold-rush route is no longer traversable because of the lake; you must go back the way you came. This hike is highly recommended; allow a minimum of three hours round-trip. There is no clear trail beyond Divide Lake, so you must find your own way. Do not attempt to walk on the glacier itself, as the crevasses can be deadly.

SEA KAYAKING

A seasonal Forest Service information station is usually housed in the yurt next to the boat harbor; stop by for details on sea kayaking and other outdoor options. If it isn't here, get kayaking information from the Ranger Station in Girdwood (907/783-3242). Although it is possible to paddle from Whittier to the heart of Prince William Sound, most people prefer to get a boat ride out so that they can spend more time near the glaciers and wild country that make this such a special place. A number of local water taxis provide these services, transporting sea kayaks, paddlers, and their gear, then picking them up several days later.

Two companies offer kayak rentals and guided day trips: **Alaska Sea Kayakers** (907/472-2534 or 877/472-2534, www.alaskaseakayakers.com) and **Prince William Sound Kayak Center** (907/472-2452 or 877/472-2452, www.pwskayakcenter.com). Take an easy three-hour paddle to the kittiwake rookery ($80 pp) or take an all-day Blackstone Glacier trip ($340 pp, four-person minimum). Multiple-night trips are available, and Prince William Sound Kayak Center also has stand up paddleboard rentals and lessons.

Accommodations

June's Whittier Condo Suites (100 Kenai St., 907/841-5002 or 888/472-6001, www.whittiersuitesonline.com, from $155 one-bedroom unit, $275 three-bedroom unit), consists of a dozen condo suites on the 14th and 15th floors of Begich Tower, ranging from one-bedroom apartments to three-bedroom units that sleep six.

It's hard to miss the **Inn at Whittier** (Harbor Rd., 907/472-3200, www.innatwhittier.com, $169-249 d, suites: $299 for 4 guests), an elaborate New England-style building right on the harbor. Owned by Hooper Bay Native Corporation, the hotel has 23 standard rooms and a pair of two-story townhouse suites. Wi-Fi is available, but service can be spotty when those giant cruise ships pull in nearby.

Camping

Whittier's **Creekside Campground** (100 Kenai St., 907/472-2670, www.whittierparking.com, late May-early Oct., $20) next to Begich Tower is plentiful, with secluded spots for tents and RVs, and a shelter for cooking and socializing in the rain. There are no hookups or running water, but you can use bathrooms on the first floor of Begich Tower, and showers are available at the harbormaster's office. A walking trail leads uphill from the campground to a high point over Whittier.

Food

In addition to grilled halibut, glacier burgers, sandwiches, salads, and espresso, **Café Orca** (907/472-2549, www.alaskacafeorca.com, daily 11am-9pm May-Sept., $8-14) has a pleasant waterside deck with picnic tables for sunny mornings.

With windows facing the harbor, **Lazy Otter Café** (907/345-1175 or 800/587-6887, www.lazyotter.com, daily 6:30am-6pm mid-May-mid-Sept.) serves espresso, breakfast sandwiches, seafood chowder, sandwiches, and sweets. If you're heading out on the water, ask for a box lunch ($15).

Inn at Whittier (Harbor Rd., 907/472-3200, www.innatwhittier.com, daily breakfast, lunch, and dinner in summer, daily lunch and dinner in winter, $19-28) has a fantastic location, with tall windows fronting on the boat harbor.

Gourmet entrées include blackened prawns, beef short rib, lemon papperdelle, and more, or choose lighter fare from the tavern menu.

Swiftwater Seafood Cafe (907/472-2550, www.swiftwaterseafoodcafe.com, Sun.-Thurs. 11:30am-9pm, Fri.-Sat. 11:30am-10pm early May-early Sept., $12-18) is popular for fish-and-chips, halibut burgers, and seafood chowder.

The owners of Swiftwater Seafood Cafe also own **Varley's Ice Cream and Pizza Parlor** (907/472-2547, www.swiftwaterseafoodcafe.com, daily 11am-9pm early May-early Sept.), serving ice cream cones, shakes, malts, sundaes, hot dogs, and homemade pizza by the slice or pie. It gets crowded on those rare sunny days.

China Sea Restaurant (Harbor Triangle #6, 907/472-3663, daily 11am-11pm mid-May-Sept., buffet $11) has an all-you-can-eat lunch buffet with soup and salad bar. They have good harbor views, too.

Practicalities

Get local information from the chamber website (www.whittieralaskachamber.org).

Anchor Inn (100 Whittier St., 907/474-2354 or 877/870-8787, www.anchorinnwhittier.com) has a small grocery store, but don't miss the **Harbor Store** (Harbor View Rd., 907/244-1996), a combination grocery, dry goods, clothing, sporting goods, laundromat, hardware, bait-and-tackle, supermarket, and department store—all in an ATCO trailer. The **post office** (100 Kenai St.) is on the first floor of Begich Tower; the library is in the fire hall. Get showered at the Harbor Office, next to Hobo Bay.

Getting There

Whittier is accessible by boat, ferry, train, or car. Drivers get here by turning from Seward Highway at Mile 79 (50 miles south of Anchorage) onto Portage Glacier Highway. The road to Whittier splits off near the Begich, Boggs Visitor Center and heads through a 400-foot tunnel before emerging into Bear Valley. Here you'll find a staging area for access to the 2.5-mile **Anton Anderson Memorial Tunnel** (907/472-2584 or 877/611-2586, www.tunnel.alaska.gov, eastbound toll $12 autos, $20 RVs, heading west is free) that is shared by both trains and cars. It's the longest auto tunnel in North America, and one of the only tunnels in the world where the same roadbed is used by both rail and auto traffic. The tunnel is open to one-way travel throughout the day, but only for 15 minutes out of each hour in each direction (and not at all when trains are transiting the tunnel). Ferry travelers and anyone else on a tight schedule should check the tunnel times in advance to make sure they don't miss their connections.

The tunnel is not recommended for anyone with claustrophobia, and you will be driving on an odd roadbed over the railroad tracks. There are pullouts for emergency use, and enormous fans to clean the air after trains pass through. Once you reach Whittier, there is **parking** (www.whittierparking.com, $10/day, $5 if you're on one of the glacier cruises; free first two hours of parking).

Avis (907/440-2847, www.avisalaska.com, mid-May-mid-Sept.) has one-way car rentals available if you want to put your car on the ferry to Valdez and end back in Anchorage.

TRAIN AND BUS

The **Alaska Railroad** (907/265-2494 or 800/544-0552, www.akrr.com, daily in summer, $89 round-trip) connects Whittier with Anchorage, departing Anchorage at 9:45am and arriving in Whittier at 12:45pm. The northbound train leaves Whittier at 6:45pm and arrives in Anchorage at 9:15pm. This makes an excellent day trip from the city. A trivia note: The route to Whittier was used in scenes from the 1986 film *Runaway Train*.

Seward Bus Lines (907/563-0800 or

ANCHORAGE

888/420-7788, www.sewardbuslines.net, daily, $30 one-way) provides bus service between Anchorage and Whittier.

FERRY

The **Alaska Marine Highway** (907/465-3941 or 800/642-0066, www.dot.state.ak.us/amhs) has daily ferry service connecting Whittier with Valdez and Cordova on both the high-speed **Chenega** and the older (and much slower) **Aurora,** where a Forest Service naturalist is on board. In addition, the **Kennicott** has a once-a-month summer sailing across the Gulf of Alaska from Whittier to Yakutat, continuing south to Juneau and then all the way to Prince Rupert, British Columbia.

Matanuska-Susitna Valley

The Parks Highway heads north from Anchorage to Denali and Fairbanks, but before you're even close to either of these, the road takes you through the heart of the Matanuska-Susitna Valley, named for the two rivers that drain this part of Alaska. Originally established as an agricultural center, the Mat-Su is now primarily a bedroom community for Anchorage, with reasonably priced homes and fast-spreading semi-urban sprawl. Two towns dominate the valley: The old farming settlement of Palmer is along the Glenn Highway 42 miles from Anchorage, while Wasilla rears its ugly face 40 miles north of Anchorage along the Parks Highway.

PALMER

For its first 20 years, Palmer (pop. 8,000) was little more than a railway depot for Alaska Railroad's Matanuska branch. Then in May 1935, during the height of both the Depression and a severe drought in the Midwest, the Federal Emergency Relief Administration of President Franklin D. Roosevelt's New Deal selected 200 farming families from the relief rolls of northern Michigan, Minnesota, and Wisconsin and shipped them here to colonize the Matanuska Valley. Starting out in tent cabins, the colonists cleared the dense virgin forest, built houses and barns, and planted crops pioneered at the University of Alaska's

Agricultural Experimental Station. These hardy transplanted farmers endured the inevitable first-year hardships, including disease, homesickness, mismanagement, floods, and just plain bad luck. But by the fall of 1936 the misfits had been weeded out, 120 babies had been born in the colony, fertile fields and long summer days were filling barns with crops, and the colonists celebrated with a three-day harvest festival, the forerunner of the big state fair. In a few more years, Palmer had become not only a flourishing town but also the center of a bucolic and beautiful agricultural valley that was and still remains unique in Alaska.

Driving into Palmer from Wasilla along the Palmer-Wasilla Highway is a lot like driving into Wasilla from the bush on the Parks Highway time warp. The contrast between Palmer, an old farming community, and Wasilla, with its helter-skelter development, is startling. Suffice it to say that Palmer is more conducive to sightseeing.

Today, downtown Palmer is a blend of the old and new, with Klondike Mike's Saloon just up the street from a fine Tuscany-inspired bistro. Palmer is also home to the **National Outdoor Leadership School's** Alaska campus (907/745-4047, www.nols.edu). From this base, NOLS offers a range of courses that involve backpacking, sea kayaking, and mountaineering in remote parts of Alaska.

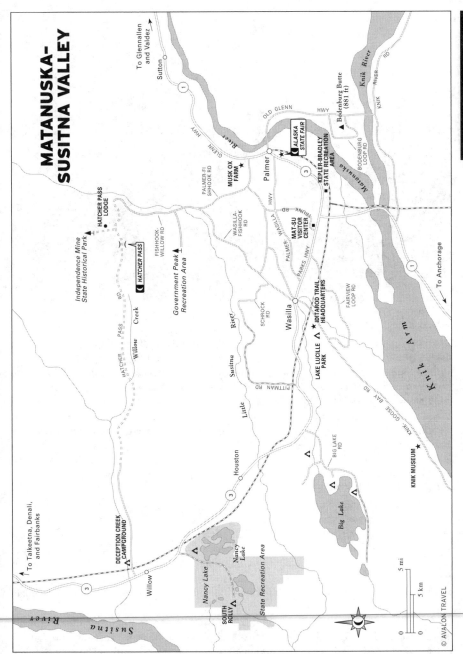

MATANUSKA-SUSITNA VALLEY

To Glennallen and Valdez

Sutton

To Anchorage

To Talkeetna, Denali, and Fairbanks

Independence Mine State Historical Park

HATCHER PASS LODGE

HATCHER PASS

Government Peak Recreation Area

Willow Creek

HATCHER PASS RD

FISHHOOK-WILLOW RD

WASILLA-FISHHOOK RD

PALMER FISHHOOK RD

MUSK OX FARM

Palmer

ALASKA STATE FAIR

OLD GLENN HWY

Bodenburg Butte (881 ft)

BODENBURG LOOP RD

Knik River

KNIK RIVER RD

KEPLER-BRADLEY STATE RECREATION AREA

Matanuska

GLENN HWY

River

PALMER-WASILLA HWY

WASILLA RD

TRUNK RD

MAT-SU VISITOR CENTER

PARKS HWY

IDITAROD TRAIL HEADQUARTERS

FAIRVIEW LOOP RD

Wasilla

SCHROCK RD

LAKE LUCILLE PARK

Susitna River

Little

PITTMAN RD

Houston

BIG LAKE RD

Big Lake

KNIK-GOOSE BAY RD

KNIK MUSEUM

Knik Arm

DECEPTION CREEK CAMPGROUND

Willow

Nancy Lake

Nancy Lake State Recreation Area

SOUTH ROLLY

Susitna River

5 mi

5 km

© AVALON TRAVEL

ANCHORAGE

© DON PITCHER

a Matanuska-Susitna Valley farm near Palmer

Sights

Colony House (316 E. Elmwood Ave., 907/745-1935, www.palmerhistoricalsociety.org, Tues.-Sat. 10am-4pm summer only, $2 adults, $1 children) is just up the block from the Palmer Visitors Information Center. Built by the Beylund family, who moved here in 1935 from Wisconsin, it has been restored and filled with period furnishings to provide a window into the life of the Matanuska colonists.

Continue another block east on East Elmwood to visit the appropriately named **Church of a Thousand Logs** (713 S. Denali St., 907/745-3822), built by the colonists in 1936-1937 and still in use.

FAIRGROUNDS AND FARMS

Heading north through downtown, take a right on Arctic Avenue, which turns into the Old Glenn Highway. About a mile south of town on the Glenn Highway is the **Alaska State Fairgrounds.** At the fairgrounds is **Colony**

Village (2075 Glenn Hwy., 907/745-4827, Mon.-Sat. 10am-4pm, free), which preserves some of Palmer's early buildings, including houses (one built in 1917 in Anchorage), several barns, a church, and a post office.

Five miles south of Palmer on the Old Glenn Highway, **Bodenberg Loop Road** is a five-mile drive through some of the most gorgeous valley farmland, with 6,400-foot **Pioneer Peak** towering behind. To see some of the original colony farms, head three miles north out along the Glenn Highway to **Farm Loop Road.** The valley's best-known crop isn't mentioned in any of the tourism brochures: marijuana. The local version (Matanuska Thunder) has a reputation as big as Alaska and is some of the most potent in the nation. It was formerly grown outside, but today nearly all grow-operations are indoors under lights.

Knik River Road splits off the Old Glenn Highway at Mile 9. Turn here and drive four miles to the trailhead for the **Pioneer**

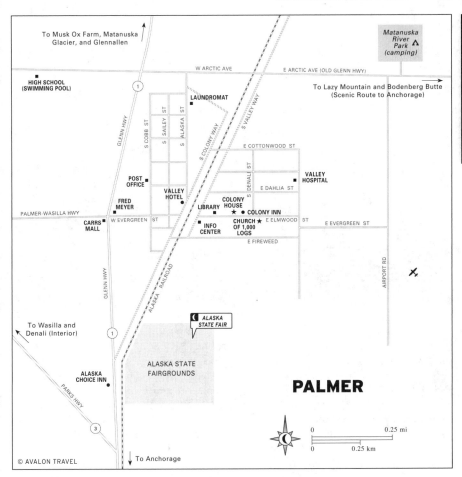

To Musk Ox Farm, Matanuska
Glacier, and Glennallen

*Matanuska
River
Park
(camping)*

W ARCTIC AVE

E ARCTIC AVE (OLD GLENN HWY)

HIGH SCHOOL
(SWIMMING POOL)

To Lazy Mountain and Bodenberg Butte
(Scenic Route to Anchorage)

LAUNDROMAT

S COBB ST

S SAILEY ST

S ALASKA ST

S COLONY WAY

S VALLEY WAY

E COTTONWOOD ST

GLENN HWY

POST
OFFICE

VALLEY
HOTEL

FRED
MEYER

S DENALI ST

E DAHLIA ST

VALLEY
HOSPITAL

PALMER-WASILLA HWY

CARRS
MALL

W EVERGREEN ST

LIBRARY

COLONY
HOUSE

★ COLONY INN

CHURCH ★
OF 1,000
LOGS

E ELMWOOD ST

E EVERGREEN ST

INFO
CENTER

E FIREWEED ST

AIRPORT RD

ALASKA RAILROAD

GLENN HWY

To Wasilla and
Denali (Interior)

ALASKA
STATE FAIR

ALASKA
CHOICE INN

PARKS HWY

ALASKA STATE
FAIRGROUNDS

PALMER

0   0.25 mi

0   0.25 km

© AVALON TRAVEL

To Anchorage

Ridge-Knik River Trail, which climbs a staggering 5,100 feet in less than six miles. Beyond this alpine ridge, only experienced rock climbers should consider heading to the twin summits of Pioneer Peak.

Seven miles south of Palmer on the Old Glenn Highway is the **Reindeer Farm** (5561 S. Bodenburg Loop Rd., 907/745-4000, www.reindeerfarm.com, daily 10am-6pm May-late Sept., $7 adults, $5 children), where tours are offered daily. The farm has 150 or so reindeer, along with elk, horses,

a bull moose, and bison. Children especially love the chance to pet a baby reindeer. Horseback rides ($65 for a one-hour ride) are also possible.

Entertainment and Events
NIGHTLIFE
Klondike Mike's Dance Hall & Saloon (820 S. Colony Way, 907/745-2676) has live rock and roll in a rustic—and smoke-filled—Alaskan setting. Also check the lineup at **Vagabond Blues** (642 S. Alaska St., 907/745-2233),

ANCHORAGE

© DON PITCHER

water tower in Palmer

which comes alive on weekends when singer-songwriter musicians pack the house.

PALMER FRIDAY FLING
The Palmer Friday Fling (across from the downtown visitors center, 907/745-2880, www.palmerchamber.org/events, Fri. 10am-5pm mid-May-mid-Aug.) features local produce, food, crafts, and musical entertainment.

COLONY DAYS
Colony Days (downtown Palmer, 907/745-2880, second weekend in June) includes a downtown parade, arts and crafts booths, bed races, foot races, and games. The main wintertime event is the **Colony Christmas Celebration** (downtown Palmer, 907/745-2880, Dec.), with a lighted parade held on the second Friday and Saturday of December, along with reindeer sled rides, caroling, arts and crafts, visits with Santa, and fireworks.

◖ ALASKA STATE FAIR
Don't miss Alaska's biggest summertime event, a 12-day party to bring down the curtain on summer that draws 300,000 visitors annually. The state fair (2075 Glenn Hwy., 907/745-4827 or 800/850-3247, www.alaskastatefair.org, $13 adults, $8 seniors and youths, free for kids under age six, parking $5) cranks up the next to the last Thursday in August and continues through Labor Day. On a weekend it may seem as though half of Anchorage has driven up to the fair. Long lines of cars wait to turn into the open field parking lots around the grounds, and crowds throng the 4-H displays, livestock auctions, horse shows, and carnival rides. There's live music daily, a rodeo, a demolition derby, three nights of fireworks, and lots of food and craft booths. Favorites always include the roasted corn on the cob, sickly sweet elephant ears, supersized turkey legs, and finger-lickin' halibut tacos. One big

MEET THE MUSK OX

© DON PITCHER

The musk ox farm in Palmer is a great place to view these unusual animals up close.

While in Palmer, take the opportunity to visit the world's only domestic **musk ox farm** (Mile 50 Glenn Hwy., 907/745-4151, www.muskoxfarm.org, daily 10am-6pm May-mid-Sept., $11 adults, $9 seniors, $5 ages 6-17, free for younger children) and see 50 or so of these fascinating prehistoric Arctic creatures up close. During the half-hour tour you learn, among other things, that these exotic animals were hunted nearly to extinction in the early 1900s but have been reestablished in northwestern and arctic Alaska.

The musk ox wool is collected here, shipped back east to be spun, then distributed to Native Alaskan villages to be woven into *qiviut* wool products. *Qiviut* is eight times warmer than sheep's wool and much softer and finer even than cashmere. Scarves, stoles, caps, and tunics are sold in the showroom; don't miss the display of little squares of *qiviut*, cashmere, alpaca, and wool from sheep, camels, and llamas to compare the softness.

The farm opens on Mother's Day in May (a great time to see the calves) and remains open all summer. Get there by taking the Glenn Highway north of town to Mile 50 and following the signs. Admission includes a half-hour tour of this nonprofit facility.

attraction is the gargantuan vegetables, including 125-pound pumpkins, 10-pound onions, and 2-pound radishes. The cabbage weigh-off makes front-page news in Alaska each year; a world record was set in 2012 when a Palmer man grew a 138-pound cabbage.

The **Alaska Railroad** (907/265-2494 or 800/544-0552, www.alaskarailroad.com) has direct train service from Anchorage to the fairgrounds during the state fair; it's a great way to avoid the traffic jams and parking hassles. The round-trip prices ($54 adults, $47 seniors,

$27 ages 6-12, $22 ages 2-5, free for younger children) include entrance to the fairgrounds.

Recreation

Two excellent hikes are accessible off the Old Glenn Highway east of Palmer. Heading north from downtown, go right on Arctic Avenue, which becomes the Old Glenn Highway. Just beyond the bridge across the Matanuska River, go left onto Clark-Wolverine Road, then continue about a mile until the next junction. Take a right on Huntley Road, go about a mile, bear right at the fork, and then drive 0.25 miles to the trailhead for **Lazy Mountain.** It's a two-mile hike to the summit of this 3,270-foot mountain with views of the Matanuska Valley.

A better view and a shorter hike are to the top of **Bodenberg Butte** (881 ft.). Keep going south on the Old Glenn Highway, pass the first right onto the Loop Road, and take the second right. A parking lot ($3) is 0.25 miles up the road, and a 40-minute trek rewards you with a 360-degree view of the farm-filled valley, Chugach, the Talkeetnas, Knik Glacier, and some of the uncleared forest, which graphically illustrates what the colonists confronted in "clearing the land."

Swimming is available at Palmer High School's **indoor pool** (1170 W. Arctic Ave., 907/745-5091, www.matsugov.us). The **Palmer Golf Course** (Lepak Ave., 907/745-4653, www.cityofpalmer.org) is an 18-hole course along the Matanuska River.

The **Mat-Su Miners** (2075 Glenn Hwy., 907/745-6401, www.matsuminers.org) play semiprofessional baseball on the Alaska State Fairgrounds throughout the summer. They're part of the Alaska Baseball League.

Meekins Air Service (907/745-1626, www.meekinsairservcie.com, $85 pp for half-hour flight, with a three-person minimum) provides flightseeing trips toward the Talkeetna Mountains.

Accommodations

Lodging is reasonable in Palmer—at least by Alaska standards. Visit the **Mat-Su Bed & Breakfast Association's** website (www.alaskabnbhosts.com) for links to local places, including a daily vacancy listing in the summer.

Located downtown, **Valley Hotel** (606 S. Alaska St., 907/745-3330 or 800/478-7666, $85 d, larger rooms $110) has been here since 1948. There a 43 small guest rooms, now with Wi-Fi, and a few larger ones with two queen beds. There is no elevator, the furnishings are aging, and the baths are tiny. Downstairs you'll find a popular 24-hour café plus a lounge and a liquor store.

The **Colony Inn** (325 E. Elmwood Ave., 907/745-3330 or 800/478-7666, $100 d) is one of the older buildings in the valley, built in 1935 as a teachers' dormitory for the Matanuska Valley Colony. Today this historic structure has been transformed into a 12-room hotel with a central sitting room with a fireplace and wingback chairs. The spacious rooms contain antiques, quilts, microwaves, flat screen TVs, a queen or two twin beds, and jetted tubs, along with Wi-Fi. It's managed by the Valley Hotel, which is where you register.

Located a mile west of Palmer, **River Crest Manor B&B** (2655 N. Old Glenn Hwy., 907/746-6214, www.rivercrestmanor.com, $110-120 d) is a quiet colonial-style bed-and-breakfast with an extraordinary view of Pioneer Peak and the Chugach Mountains; private baths, Wi-Fi, and full breakfast are included.

Set on 15 acres with a spectacular Pioneer Peak backdrop, ◖ **Alaska's Harvest B&B** (2252 N. Love Dr., 907/745-4263, www.alaskasharvest.com, $110-125 d, suite $145 d) is an exquisite place to relax. Four guest rooms have private or shared baths and kitchenettes, and the 900-square-foot suite includes a king bed, a day bed, a kitchenette, and a private bath. All guest rooms are stocked for breakfast, and a guest computer and Wi-Fi are available.

More dramatic mountain and glacier vistas are at the modern and immaculately maintained **Alaska Garden Gate B&B** (950 S. Trunk Rd., 907/746-2333, www.gardengatebnb.com, studio apartments $139-169 d, cottages $159-179 d). Three studio apartments and four one-bedroom cottages all contain private entrances, full kitchens, queen or king beds, flat screen TVs, and Wi-Fi. A continental breakfast is provided.

Camping

Palmer has one of the most luxurious city campgrounds in Alaska. **Matanuska River Park** (on East Arctic Ave. about 0.5 miles east of town, 907/745-9631, www.matsugov.us, late May-early Oct., tents $10, RVs $15 with hookups) occupies a lush site full of big old cottonwoods and wild roses. There's lots of space among the 86 campsites, which are usually not crowded except at state fair time. Surrounding the campground is a day-use area, complete with picnic tables, softball and volleyball, horseshoe pits, and a nature trail around the ponds. The park also has potable water, flush toilets, coin-operated showers, firewood, trails, river access, and an observation deck.

A popular area for fishing, hiking, canoeing, and biking, **Matanuska Lakes State Recreation Area** (Glenn Hwy. Mile 36, Lifetime Adventures: 907/746-4644 or 800/952-8624, www.lifetimeadventures.net, $10) consists of three large lakes and eight smaller ones. It's just west of Palmer. Make camping reservations through Lifetime Adventures; reservations must be made at least seven days in advance of your stay. Canoe rentals are available.

Kepler Park Campground (1.5 miles east of the Parks and Glenn Hwys. interchange, 907/745-3053, www.keplerpark.com, $18) is adjacent to Kepler and Bradley Lakes. The lakes are stocked with trout, and the family-friendly campground has paddle boats, canoes, and rowboats for rent. There are no RV hookups.

Three miles south of Palmer off the Old Glenn Highway, **Mountain View RV Park** (1405 N. Smith Rd., 907/745-5747 or 800/264-4582, www.mtviewrvpark.com, $35 RVs, $22 tents) has a quiet year-round location with showers, laundry, and Wi-Fi.

Fox Run RV Campground (4466 S. Glenn Hwy., 907/745-6120 or 877/745-6120, www.foxrunlodgealaska.com, $29 RVs, $19 tents) is just east of the Parks and Glenn Highway intersection, so expect some traffic noise. The RV park sits on the shore of pretty Matanuska Lake, with rowboat and canoe rentals, showers, laundry, Wi-Fi, and even massage therapists. It's open all year, with cabins, rooms, and lakefront efficiencies available.

Food

Vagabond Blues (642 S. Alaska St., 907/745-2233, Sun. 7am-6pm, Tues.-Sat. 6am-8pm, $5-10) is a longtime favorite, serving pastries, espresso, and tasty lunches—including vegan and gluten-free variations. You won't go wrong ordering a big hunk of freshly baked bread and an enormous bowl of today's soup served in hand-painted pottery. Occasionally, there is live music, too.

Turkey Red (550 S. Alaska St., 907/746-5544, www.turkeyredak.com, Mon.-Sat. 7am-9pm, $14-31) is Palmer's standout restaurant, with an open, modern feel and an emphasis on fresh, local, and organic ingredients. Owner-chef Alex Papasavas hails from Tuscany, crafting a Mediterranean-Alaskan menu that includes portobello mushroom pasta, moussaka, New York strip steak, and chicken bruschetta.

If you just want a good down-home halibut sandwich or dinner of chicken, pork, steak, scallops, pizzas, or pasta, head to **Open Café** (606 S. Alaska St., 907/745-3330, daily 24 hours, $18-25) at the Valley

Hotel. Especially popular are grilled halibut dinners, deep fried prawns, and Philly steak sandwiches. Try corned beef hash, eggs, and hash browns for breakfast.

Palmer has a 24-hour **Carrs** grocery store (corner of the Glenn Hwy. and the Palmer-Wasilla Hwy., 907/745-7505, daily 24 hours), and the **Fred Meyer** (650 N. Cobb St., 907/761-4200, daily 7am-11pm) is just up the street.

Information and Services

Start your visit at the **Palmer Visitors Information Center** (723 S. Valley Way, 907/745-8878, www.palmermuseum.org, daily 9am-6pm May-Sept.; Wed.-Fri. 10am-5pm, Sat. 10am-2pm in winter). Inside, load up with brochures, check out the gift shop, and wander downstairs to the little museum depicting the colonists' lives.

The **Matanuska-Susitna Convention and Visitors Bureau** (7744 Visitors View Ct., 907/746-5000, www.alaskavisit.com, daily 8:30am-6:30pm mid-May-mid-Sept.) has a large visitors center just north of the junction of the Parks and Glenn Highways, and six miles south of Wasilla. Take the Trunk Road Exit and follow the CVB signs. Inside you'll find a plethora of brochures and stuffed critter heads lining the walls, plus free Wi-Fi.

The **Palmer Public Library** (655 S. Valley Way, 907/745-4690, www.cityofpalmer.org, Mon. and Wed. 10am-8pm, Tues. and Thurs. 10am-6pm, Fri.-Sat. 10am-2pm) has public-use computers.

Take showers in downtown Palmer at **Wash Day Too** (127 S. Alaska St., 907/746-4141).

Mat-Su Regional Medical Center (2500 S. Woodworth Loop, 907/746-8600, www.matsuregional.com) occupies the hilltop just off the Parks Highway at Trunk Road.

Getting There and Around

Mat-Su Community Transit, better known as **MASCOT** (907/376-5000, www.matsutransit.

com, $2.50), has weekday service throughout the valley, with connections to **Valley Mover** (907/892-8800, www.valleymover.com, $7) for commuter runs to Anchorage.

Knik Glacier

Visible approximately seven miles up the Knik River Road, this unusual and impressive riverside glacier is primarily accessible by airboat. **Knik Glacier Tours** (907/745-1577, www.knik-glacier.com, $100 adults, $50 kids), runs four-hour airboat trips that include two hours at a camp next to the glacier, with kayaks for those who want to explore on their own. Overnight stays ($225 pp including meals) are possible in the fully outfitted camp.

In 2012, a National Guard helicopter was flying over Knik Glacier when the crew noticed something strange on the ice below. Investigators later discovered the remains of a 1952 plane crash, when a C-124A Globemaster cargo plane crashed, killing all 52 people on board. The wreckage had been buried by heavy snow shortly after the crash, and it wasn't until its rediscovery 60 years later that some of the remains could be removed.

Knik River Lodge (907/745-5002 or 877/745-4575, www.knikriverlodge.com, May-mid-Sept. and Mar.-Apr., $135-159 d) has 15 modern cabins 11 miles out on Knik River Road. All include private baths, decks, microwaves, fridges, Wi-Fi, and continental breakfasts. Also here is a surprisingly good restaurant (lunch and dinner daily, $23-46)—in a yurt!—with a changing menu that emphasizes locally grown produce, meats, and seafood. It features specials such as beef Wellington and rack of lamb; reservations are required. The lodge offers summertime dog mushing ($485 pp) on Troublesome Glacier. Unlike larger glacier dog sledding operations elsewhere in Alaska, these are personalized trips. In addition, the lodge runs four-hour heli-hiking trips (in summer, $385 pp), along with heli-skiing in March and April.

WASILLA

In 2008 the town of Wasilla vaulted into the big time as the home of Alaska's then-governor (and U.S. vice presidential candidate), Sarah Palin. Her meteoric rise to fame brought international attention to Wasilla. Wasilla is also home to the gorgeous mountains at nearby Hatcher Pass. You may not be able to see Russia from here, but you can see Alaska from Wasilla.

In 1977, Wasilla consisted of a landing strip and a grocery store that advertised the convenience of flying in from the bush, buying Matanuska Valley produce, and flying out again—without the hassles of Anchorage. Then, when the capital looked like it might be moved to Willow, 25 miles up the highway, Anchorageites began to discover Wasilla's quiet, beauty, and affordable land, and contractors took advantage of the town's lax restrictions on development. And develop it did, with a vengeance. During 1980-1982, the town's population of 1,200 doubled, then doubled again in 1982-1984. Stores, malls, and fast-food chains popped up faster than you could say "We do chicken right." Teeland's General Store was jacked up, moved from the corner it had sat on for over 60 years, and unceremoniously dumped in a parking lot around the block to make way for a 7-Eleven. The original airstrip, which had kept Wasilla on the map for so long, was moved out from the middle of all the hustle and bustle of town.

The unbridled growth continues today, as relatively low real estate prices and good roads make the area a favorite of Anchorage commuters wanting a piece of the suburban lifestyle. In the 1990s, Wasilla's WalMart proved so popular that after just a few years WalMart built a new and much larger version across the highway. It's been followed by Target and Walgreens stores, plus dozens of strip-type buildings crowding the highway. Driving south into and through Wasilla on the Parks

© DON PITCHER

Wasilla's town-site park gives visitors a glimpse into the city's history.

ANCHORAGE

Highway is like passing through any southern California suburb.

Sights

Make sure to visit **Dorothy Page Museum and Historical Park** (323 N. Main St., 907/373-9071, www.cityofwasilla.com/museum, Tues.-Fri. 8am-5pm year-round, $3 adults, children under 13 free) on Main Street just off the Parks Highway. The museum houses historical photos and artifacts from early settlers and the Iditarod, plus interesting downstairs exhibits of the mining era, including a diorama of Independence Mine. The adjacent old **town-site park** contains a schoolhouse, a bunkhouse, a smokehouse, a steam bath, a blacksmith shop, and a cache. Just up the street is **Teeland's Store** (405 E. Herning Ave.), built in 1917, one of the oldest buildings in Alaska. Today the beautifully restored structure houses a sandwich shop.

About four miles north of town at Mile 47, take a left at the sign and head 0.75 miles down to the **Museum of Alaska Transportation and Industry** (3800 W. Museum Dr., 907/376-1211, www.museumofalaska.org, daily 10am-5pm mid-May-early Sept., $8 adults, $5 ages 3-17, free children under age 3, $18 families). This museum houses an extensive collection of antiques relating to Alaskan aviation, railroading, fishing, mining, and road transportation. Take a gander at the "Chitina auto railer," an old car built to run on rail tracks. Outside are wooden boats, farm machinery (much of it still running), ancient snowmobiles, and several rail cars.

Knik Museum (Knik Rd., 907/376-7755, Thurs.-Sat. 1pm-6pm, Sun. 1pm-5pm June-Aug., $5 adults, $2 kids, $10 family) is 14 miles from Wasilla. Housed in a century-old building, it exhibits items from the Knik gold rush of 1897-1917 and the Iditarod Trail.

Wasilla is the headquarters for the 1,049-mile Iditarod Trail Sled Dog Race from Anchorage to Nome. The **Iditarod headquarters** (907/376-5155 or 800/545-6874, www.iditarod.com, daily 8am-7pm mid-May-mid-Sept.; Mon.-Fri. 8am-5pm winter, free) includes a log museum containing race memorabilia, Native Alaskan artifacts, videos, and dog-mushing equipment. Also here is Togo, the stuffed sled dog who led Leonhard Seppala's team during the 1925 serum delivery to Nome. Find Togo and friends two miles out on Knik Road. A fee is charged to go for a ride on a wheeled dogsled.

Shopping

The **Wasilla Farmers Market** (old Wasilla town site, 907/376-5679, Wed. 11am-6pm June-mid-Sept.) takes place weekly in summer.

Recreation

Lakeshore Park at Wasilla Lake right off the highway has swimming (not too cold), picnic tables, and a view of the craggy Chugach Mountains—a great place to set up your tripod. A less crowded day-use lake area is at **Matanuska Lakes State Recreation Site** (Glenn Hwy.) just beyond the junction of the Parks and Glenn Highways, heading toward Palmer.

Wasilla's big **Brett Memorial Ice Arena** (9746 E. Bogard Rd., 907/376-9260, www.matsugov.us) has year-round skating and hockey. For the unfrozen version, swim at the **Wasilla High School pool** (701 W. Bogard Rd., 907/376-4222).

Accommodations
MOTELS

Several motels are strung along the Parks Highway. On the north end of Wasilla is **Trout's Place Hotel** (2201 E. Parks Hwy., 907/376-4209, www.windbreakalaska.com, $79 d) with 10 budget guest rooms.

Alaskan View Motel (2650 E. Parks Hwy., 907/376-6787, www.alaskanviewmotel.com,

THE LAST GREAT RACE

The most Alaskan of all Alaskan events is the Iditarod Trail Sled Dog Race from Anchorage to Nome. The "Last Great Race" is run each March, attracting 60 or more of the world's best mushers, each with a team of up to 20 dogs. With a top prize of $70,000 and a $500,000 purse for the top 20 teams, the race has become an event with an international following.

Today's Iditarod Trail Sled Dog Race is run on the historic Iditarod Trail, a path that had its origins in the 1908 discovery of gold along a river the Ingalik Native Alaskans called *hidedhod*, meaning "distant place." Thousands of miners flooded into the region following the find, and trails were cut from Seward to the new boomtown of Iditarod so that mail and supplies could be brought in and gold shipped out. Once the gold ran out after a few years, the miners gradually gave up and left, and the old town began a long slow return to quietude. But other events would eventually bring Iditarod back to life in a new form.

During the winter of 1925, a diphtheria epidemic broke out in Nome, and the territorial governor hurriedly dispatched a 20-pound package of life-saving antitoxin serum to halt the disease's spread. Regular boat mail would take 25 days, and the only two airplanes in Alaska were open-cockpit biplanes. With temperatures far below zero and only a few hours of light each day (it was mid-January), that option was impossible. Instead, the package was sent by train from Seward to Nenana, where mushers and their dogs waited to carry the antitoxin on to Nome. What happened next is hard to believe: A Herculean relay effort by 20 different mushers and their dogs brought the vaccine to Nome in just six days. They somehow managed to cover the 674 miles in conditions that included whiteout blizzards, 80 mph winds, and temperatures down to -64°F. The incident gained national attention, and President Coolidge thanked the mushers, presenting each with a medal and $0.50 for each mile traveled.

Long after this heroic effort, two more people entered the picture: Dorothy Page ("Mother of the Iditarod") and Joe Redington Sr. ("Father of the Iditarod"). In 1967 the two organized a commemorative Iditarod race over a small portion of the trail. Six years later they set up a full-blown dogsled race from Anchorage to Nome, a distance that is officially called 1,049 miles. It took winner Dick Wilmarth 20 days, 49 minutes, and 41 seconds to make it under the Nome archway. At the finish line, Wilmarth lost his lead dog, Hot Foot. Fourteen days later the dog wandered into his master's home in Red Devil—500 miles from Nome.

Over the years the race has become much more professional and far faster. The record run of 9 days, 58 minutes, and 6 seconds was set by Doug Swingley in 2000. And this was even with two mandatory layovers of 10 hours along the way. The Iditarod is certainly one of the most strenuous events in the world. With below-zero temperatures, fierce winds, and all the hazards that go with crossing the most remote parts of Alaska in winter, the race is certainly not for everyone. Despite this, the Iditarod has gained a measure of fame as one in which both women and men are winners. Between 1985 and 1993, five of the nine winners were women, and the late Susan Butcher won four of these races. (After Butcher won the race three consecutive years, T-shirts began appearing in local stores saying "Alaska: where men are men, and women win the Iditarod.")

The Iditarod has not one but two actual starts. The official start is from 4th Avenue in downtown Anchorage, where several thousand onlookers cheer each team that leaves the starting line. The mushers and dogs race as far as Eagle River (25 miles), where they're loaded into trucks and driven to the "restart" in Willow. (This is to avoid having to sled over the thin snow conditions around Palmer and open water on the Knik River.) At the restart, the fastest teams into Eagle River leave first, creating chaotic conditions when several 20-dog teams are pulling to the start at once. From here on, it's 1,000 miles of wilderness.

The **Iditarod Trail Committee** (Knik Rd., 907/376-5155 or 800/545-6874, www.iditarod. com) has its headquarters in Wasilla, where they have a museum of race memorabilia and offer wheeled dogsled rides in the summer.

$115-125 d) is a little two-story log building across from Kendall Ford. It's convenient for shopping and dining, and windows frame the Chugach Range. Amenities include in-room fridges, microwaves, and Wi-Fi.

Alaska's Select Inn (3451 Palmdale Dr., 907/357-4768 or 888/357-4768, www.alaskaselectinn.com, $129-139 d, suites $149 d) is a recently built place with spacious guest rooms and suites, all with full kitchens, flat-screen TVs, and Wi-Fi.

Best Western Lake Lucille Inn (1300 W. Lake Lucille Dr., 907/373-1776 or 800/780-7234, www.bestwestern.com/lakelucilleinn, $170 d, suites $280-300 d) has 54 roomy guest rooms and suites, many with private balconies overlooking the lake. Guests will also appreciate the fitness center, sauna, business center, Wi-Fi, and continental breakfasts.

In a quiet residential area, **Agate Inn** (4725 Begich Cir., 907/373-2290 or 800/770-2290, www.agateinn.com, $139 d, suites $195-275; guesthouses $225 for a two-bedroom that sleeps four, $375 for a three-bedroom home) is three miles from Wasilla on the Palmer-Wasilla Highway. A variety of lodging options are scattered across four buildings: motel-type rooms with king beds, apartment suites with full kitchens, and two guesthouses. A continental breakfast is provided, along with Wi-Fi. The six pet reindeer on the grounds are a favorite of guests, and two handicap-accessible units are available.

VACATION HOMES AND CABINS

Tollers' Timbers (3251 E. Toller Ct., 907/746-1438 or 800/795-1438, www.alaskavacationcabins.com, $139-169, add $15 pp for extra guests) consists of four attractive vacation homes on a peaceful 14-acre spread halfway between Palmer and Wasilla. Each home is equipped with a full kitchen, private bath, laundry, continental breakfast, and Wi-Fi. The

smallest cottage sleeps two, while the largest home has space for seven comfortably.

In a beautifully landscaped wooded area, **Alaska Kozey Cabins** (351 E. Spruce Ave., 907/376-3190, www.kozeycabins.com, $129 d, add $20 pp for extra guests—maximum six) has modern two-bedroom log cabins, each with a full kitchen, bath, and Wi-Fi.

BED-AND-BREAKFASTS

Visit the website for **Mat-Su Bed & Breakfast Association** (www.alaskabnbhosts.com) for links to local B&Bs, including a daily vacancy listing in the summer.

Lake Lucille B&B (235 W. Lakeview Ave., 907/357-0352, www.alaskaslakelucillebnb.com, $119 d) is a gracious home right on the shore of Lake Lucille, just a short distance from Wasilla. There are four guest rooms (with private or shared baths); you can combine two rooms into a four-person family suite ($179 d). A light breakfast starts each day.

For something more uniquely Alaskan, stay at **Pioneer Ridge B&B** (1830 E. Parks Hwy., 907/376-7472 or 800/478-7472, www.pioneerridge.com, $139-179 d, cabin $99 d). This distinctive former dairy barn sits on a hill in the country south of Wasilla. Six guest rooms with shared or private baths are available, along with a rustic cabin (bath in the main house). A buffet breakfast is served in the common room, where you can also play a game of pool, watch a video, listen to the player piano, surf the web, or simply relax. There's a big deck, and atop the house is a unique (and rather bizarre) glass-enclosed Aurora Room with a fireplace and 360-degree views.

CAMPING

The city-run **Lake Lucille Park** (1401 S. Endeavor St., 907/373-9010, www.cityofwasilla.com, mid-May-Sept., $10) is an 80-acre natural area with trails and campsites two miles south of Wasilla off Knik-Goose Bay Road. There are no RV hookups.

There's another public campground at **Finger Lake State Recreation Site** (Bogard Rd., $15), six miles east of Wasilla. Make reservations through Lifetime Adventures (907/746-4644 or 800/952-8624, www.lifetimeadventures.net); canoe rentals are available.

Open year-round, **Big Bear RV Park** (2010 S. Church St., 907/745-7445, www.bigbearrv.net, $25-32 RVs, $18 tents, $50 cabins) has RV and tent sites, plus a laundry, basic cabin rentals, and Wi-Fi. Showers are $5 if you aren't camping here.

Many RVers park for free in local shopping mall lots.

Food

Perhaps because of all the early-morning commuters to Anchorage, Wasilla seems to have an espresso stand on almost every corner—along with an equal number of gun shops. So put your gun in its holster and cruise over to **Espresso Café** (1265 Seward Meridian, 907/376-5282, Mon.-Fri. 5am-7pm, Sat. 6am-7pm, Sun. 6am-6pm) for coffee, comfy chairs, and free Wi-Fi. It's across from WalMart, of course.

Windbreak Café (2201 E. Parks Hwy., 907/376-4484, www.windbreakalaska.com, Mon.-Sat. 6am-10pm, Sun. 7am-10pm) is a good choice for home-cooked meals, prime rib, and seafood. Breakfast is served all day, with plenty of bang for the buck.

Chepo's Fiesta (731 W. Parks Hwy., 907/373-5656, www.cheposfiesta.com, Sun.-Thurs. 11am-10pm, Fri.-Sat. 11am-11pm, $13-15) serves Mexican food in a fun setting. It's on the north end of Wasilla in yet another strip mall.

Mekong Thai Cuisine (473 W. Parks Hwy., 907/373-7690, www.mekongthaiwasilla.com, Mon.-Thurs. 11am-3pm and 5pm-8:30pm, Fri.-Sat. 11am-3pm and 5pm-9pm, closed Sun.) serves excellent Thai meals. **Sakura Sushi** (991 S. Hermon Rd., 907/373-2212, daily 11am-10pm) has very good sushi; try the dragon roll. Service can be a bit slow, especially on weekends.

Occupying a little yellow house across from the museum in "old town" Wasilla, **The Grape Tap** (322 N. Boundary St., 907/376-8466, www.thegrapetap.com, Tues.-Sat. 5pm-10pm, $18-40) is the town's fine-dining establishment. A romantic downstairs lounge has 25 different boutique wines by the glass ($7-18), along with champagne cocktails. The menu (available downstairs as well) includes filet mignon, tenderloin au Poivre, and seafood Peppernada, but be sure to also order an appetizer of Not so Cheap Dates stuffed with chevre cheese and wrapped in bacon. Everything is handmade from scratch; no canned sauces here. When summer comes, The Grape Tap opens a big back patio and lawn to relaxing outdoor dining with occasional live music.

Adjacent to Settlers Bay Golf Course eight miles out Knik-Goose Bay Road, **Settlers Bay Lodge** (5801 S. Knik-Goose Bay Rd., 907/357-5678, www.settlersbaylodge.com, daily 4pm-10pm, $23-42) is a destination spot for locals who appreciate the towering windows, deck-with-a-vista dining, and menu of steaks, seafood, and pasta along with daily specials.

Information and Services

The **Wasilla Chamber of Commerce** (415 E. Railroad Ave., 907/376-1299, www.visitwasilla.org, Mon.-Fri. 11am-5pm) is housed in the historic train depot. Built in 1911, the quaint building has railroad memorabilia and brochures from local businesses. Drop in to have your photo taken with a cardboard cutout of Sarah Palin, but this is probably as close as you'll get. She spends most of her time in Arizona now, like a true Alaskan.

Adjacent to the museum, the **Wasilla Public Library** (391 N. Main St., 907/376-5913, www.cityofwasilla.com/library, Mon. 2pm-6pm, Tues. and Thurs. 10am-8pm, Wed. and Fri. 10am-6pm, Sat. 1pm-5pm) is a good place to stop and check your email or use the Internet.

Getting There and Around

Mat-Su Community Transit, better known as **MASCOT** (907/376-5000, www.matsutransit.com, $2.50), has weekday service throughout the valley, while **Valley Mover** (907/892-8800, www.valleymover.com, $7) has commuter runs to Anchorage.

◖ HATCHER PASS

This is one of the most beautiful parts of the Mat-Su Valley region and a wonderful side trip from either the Parks Highway north of Wasilla or the Glenn Highway at Palmer. It's a 49-mile drive, starting in Palmer and ending at Mile 71 on the Parks Highway (30 miles north of Wasilla).

Most folks get to Hatcher Pass from the Palmer end. Hatcher Pass Road (also called Fishhook-Willow Rd.) begins in rolling forest-and-farm country and then climbs along the beautiful Little Susitna River, which is popular with experienced kayakers who enjoy Class V white water. After passing Motherlode Lodge, the road climbs steeply uphill to Independence Mine State Historical Park at Mile 17, where the pavement ends, before topping out at 3,886-foot Hatcher Pass and Summit Lake in an area of vast vistas, high tundra, excellent hiking, and backcountry camping. Then it's downhill through pretty forests along Willow Creek all the way to the Parks Highway; this route was originally a wagon road built to serve the gold mines. The road is paved from Palmer all the way to Independence Mine, and for 10 miles from the Willow side; the rest is gravel. A bike path follows the road along the Little Susitna River section, and campsites can be found at Deception Creek, two miles from the Parks Highway.

Independence Mine State Historical Park

It's hard to imagine a park that better combines the elements of the Alaska experience: scenery, history and lore, and that noble yellow metal, gold. This mine is very different from the panning, sluicing, deep-placer, and dredging operations seen in Interior Alaska. This was "hard-rock" mining, with an intricate 21-mile network of tunnels under Granite Mountain. The miners drilled into the rock, inserted explosives (which they set off at the end of shifts to give the fumes time to dissipate before the next crew went in), then "mucked" the debris out by hand, to be sorted, crushed, amalgamated, and assayed.

Hard-rock or "lode" mining is often preceded by panning and placer mining. Prospectors who first took gold from Grubstake Gulch, a tributary of Willow Creek, in 1897 noticed the gold's rough unweathered nature, which indicated a possible lode of unexposed gold nearby. In 1906, Robert Lee Hatcher staked the first lode claim, and his Alaska Free Gold Mine operated until 1924. In 1908 the Independence Mine opened on the mountain's east slope, and over the next 25 years it produced several million dollars' worth of gold. In 1937 the two mines merged into the Alaska Pacific Consolidated Mining Company, which operated Independence Mine at peak production through 1942, when World War II shut it down. A series of private sales and public deals with the Alaska Division of Parks culminated in 1980, leaving the state with 271 acres, including the whole mining camp, and deeding 1,000 acres to the Coronado Mining Corporation, which has active operations in the area.

cross-country skiers at Independence Mine

A couple of dozen camp buildings are in various stages of ruin and refurbishing. Start at the **Independence Mine Visitor Center** (7278 E. Bogard Rd., 907/745-2827 or 907/745-3975, www.alaskastateparks.org, daily 11am-6pm late May-early Sept., parking $5) in the rehabilitated house of the camp manager. Take some time to enjoy the excellent displays: historic charts, an overview of gold mining, a "touch tunnel" complete with sound effects, and wage summaries for workers and management. Park personnel lead guided tours (daily at 1 and 3pm, $6). At other times, just wander the site on your own; interpretive signs describe the various buildings. Independence Mine State Historical Park is a must-see on any Alaskan itinerary.

Winter Recreation

Just downhill from Hatcher Pass, **Government Peak Recreation Area** (www.matsugov.us/projects/hatcherpass) is a new Nordic skiing area with outstanding trails groomed for skate and classic skiers. Access is off the Palmer-Fishhook Road and Edgerton Parks Road. Additional Nordic ski trails are maintained next to Independence Mine.

Hatcher Pass Road isn't plowed beyond Independence Mine State Historical Park in winter, but you can park here to play; it's a special favorite of snowmobilers, snowboarders, and skiers. Snowboarders and skiers often catch a ride up the hill to a point below the mine site and then head downhill on ungroomed trails. On a winter weekend you'll see dozens of kids boarding down, with parents and friends waiting at the bottom to drive them back up for another run. The road typically reopens to cars in early June.

Accommodations and Food

A number of lodging options are scattered along the southern section of Hatcher Pass Road north of Palmer. **Hatcher Pass B&B** (9000 N. Palmer Fishhook Rd., 907/745-6788 of 877/745-6788, www.hatcherpassbb.com, cabins $114 d, chalets $159, add $15 per person for additional guests—maximum 6) has delightful log cabins with kitchenettes and private baths. There are small "sourdough" cabins and large two-bedroom chalets. Cabins are fully stocked for make-it-yourself breakfasts.

Just downhill from Independence Mine is **Hatcher Pass Lodge** (907/745-5897, www.hatcherpasslodge.com, daily 8am-8pm late May-early Sept., Sat. 8am-8pm, Fri. and Sun. noon-6pm in winter, $17-35; cabins $100-165, guest rooms $95 d). This A-frame lodge is a good spot for breakfasts, sandwiches, pizzas, steaks, soups, and halibut, with a sunset view to die for. Be sure to try the house specialty, fondue made with Swiss Gruyère and Emmentaler cheeses, Kirschwasser, and French bread ($27). There are nine cozy cabins for up to four people each and three tiny upstairs guest rooms; breakfast is available for guests. Also on the grounds

© DON PITCHER

© DON PITCHER

Hatcher Pass Lodge

is a creek-side sauna for guests ($25/hour). The lodge is open daily all year. Speaking from personal experience, this is the perfect place for a summer wedding. The lodge also maintains six miles of groomed ski trails in the winter for both classical and skate skis; more adventurous backcountry skiers and snowboarders head up the steep (and avalanche-prone) slopes that rise on three sides.

NORTH TO DENALI

It's a long 195-mile drive from Wasilla (237 miles from Anchorage) to Denali National Park on the Parks Highway. After the first few miles, the developments peter out and roadside attractions shift from fast food, gun shops, and video stores to the real Alaska of forests and mountains. The land is a seemingly endless birch and spruce forest, with a smattering of half-finished plywood homesteads covered in blue tarps, their yards piled high with firewood. The road follows a gradual climb toward the magnificent Alaska Range that seems to grow in magnitude the farther north you get. Mile after mile of pink fireweed flowers brighten the roadside in midsummer.

Big Lake

The Big Lake area (907/892-6109, www.biglakechamber.org) is a popular recreation destination, especially on summer weekends when many Anchorageites head to summer homes here. Access is via 9-mile-long Big Lake Road, which splits off the Parks Highway at Mile 52 (10 miles north of Wasilla). Don't expect quiet along this large and scenic lake. In summer, Big Lake is Jet Ski central 24 hours a day, and when winter arrives the snowmobile crowd comes out for more motorized mayhem. Big Lake was near the center of the 1996 Miller's Reach Fire that blackened 37,500 acres and destroyed over 400 buildings.

Three state park campgrounds (907/317-9094, www.dnr.alaska.gov, $10) are in the area:

Rocky Lake State Recreation Site, Big Lake North State Recreation Site, and **Big Lake South State Recreation Site.**

Operated by four-time Iditarod champion Martin Buser, **Happy Trails Kennels** (Mile 4.5 West Lakes Blvd., 907/892-7899, www.buserdog.com, $38 adults, $18 kids) has 1.5-hour kennel tours and demonstrations all summer.

A luxurious lakeside resort, **Alaska Sunset View Resort** (5268 S. Big Lake Rd., 907/892-8885, www.alaskasunsetviewresort.com, $240-385 d) is popular for weddings and retreats. Ten immaculate guest rooms are available, with such perks as a continental breakfast, whirlpool tubs, pool table, gourmet kitchen, laundry, exercise facility, and Wi-Fi. The owners also have **Creekside Lodge** ($1,350/night), a large and very private six-bedroom log home on 10 acres of land; it is a favorite of honeymooners. On the grounds of Alaska Sunset View Resort, **Boathouse Restaurant** (5268 S. Big Lake Rd., 907/892-8595, www.akboathouse.com, Mon.-Sat. 5pm-10pm, Sun. 11am-7pm, $25-37), serves a surf-and-turf menu with such favorites as Louisiana style crab cakes, Alaskan scallops, or tomahawk rib-eye, along with big Sunday brunches.

If you're camping in the area, **Doc Rockers Laundromat** (3462 S. Big Lake Rd., 907/892-1800) has showers.

Houston

This gathering of 1,800 or so souls 58 miles from Anchorage includes the usual lineup of suspects: gas, groceries, cafés, lodging, an RV park, a coin laundry, and air-taxi operators, but it is best known for its **fireworks stands.** Five of these behemoths—it's especially hard to miss Gorilla Fireworks—sit on the edges of town, pulling families from Anchorage looking for fun on the 4th of July. Amazingly, they're all owned by the same family! It's illegal to shoot off fireworks almost anywhere in Alaska. Of course, this is one of those legal niceties that is widely ignored.

Little Susitna River Campground (Mile 57 Parks Hwy., 907/892-6812, $10) is an Alaska Department of Fish and Game facility on the south side of Houston.

Nancy Lake State Recreation Area

Access to Nancy Lake is from Mile 67 of the Parks Highway, just south of Willow and 25 miles north of Wasilla. This flat, heavily forested terrain is dotted with over 100 lakes, some interconnected by creeks. As you might imagine, the popular activities here are fishing, boating, and canoeing, plus a comfortable campground and a couple of hiking trails. As you might also suspect, the skeeters here are thick in early summer.

Follow Nancy Lake Road a little more than a mile to **Nancy Lake State Recreation Site Campground** ($10). A half-mile past the kiosk is the trailhead to several **public-use cabins** (907/745-3975, www.alaskastateparks.org, $45). Reserve months ahead to be sure of getting one of these exceptionally popular cabins. Just under a mile beyond this trailhead is the **Tulik Nature Trail,** an easy walk that takes about an hour. Keep an eye out for loons, beavers, and terns, and watch for that prickly devil's club. **South Rolly Lake Campground** (Mile 6.5 Nancy Lake Rd., no phone, $10), at South Rolly Lake, has 98 campsites and 12 picnic sites, as well as a small boat launch.

The **Tanaina Lake Canoe Route** begins at Mile 4.5 on Nancy Lakes Road. This leisurely 12-mile, two-day trip hits 14 lakes, between most of which are well-marked portages, some upgraded with boardwalks over the muskeg. Hunker down for the night at any one of 10 primitive campsites (campfires allowed in fireplaces only). Another possibility, though it requires a long portage, is to put in to the Little Susitna River at Mile 57 on the Parks Highway and portage to Skeetna Lake, where you connect to the southern leg of the loop trail.

Tippecanoe (South Rolly Campground along Nancy Lake, 907/495-6688, late May-early Oct., $32/day) rents canoes for local lakes. The canoes are stashed on 14 nearby lakes, so you don't even need to transport them. Tippecanoe provides paddles and life jackets.

Willow

At Mile 69 is Willow (pop. 2,000), a roadside town that you'll miss if you sneeze. It has gas, groceries, hardware, a café, and air service. Back in 1980, Alaskans voted to move the state capital here. A multibillion-dollar city was planned and real estate speculation went wild. When a second vote was held in 1982 to decide whether to actually spend the billions, however, the plan was soundly defeated.

Willow's big event comes in early March, as the **Iditarod Trail Sled Dog Race** slides through town. The race officially begins in Anchorage, but after a 25-mile run to Eagle River, the dogs are trucked north for the "restart" at Willow Lake. Just west of here the teams move completely away from the road system and are in wilderness all the way to Nome.

Both **Willow Air Service** (907/495-6370 or 800/478-6370, www.willowair.com) and **Denali Flying Service** (907/495-5899) offer scenic flights over Knik Glacier, Hatcher Pass, and Mount McKinley from Willow.

Operated by Iditarod veteran Vern Halter, **Dream a Dream Dog Farm** (Mile 65 Parks Hwy., 907/495-1197 or 866/425-6874, www.vernhalter.com, $89 pp for two people) has summertime kennel tours and demonstrations in Willow. Kennel and dog lot tours include a cart ride pulled by the dogs.

Right along the creek, **Willow Creek Resort** (Mile 71.5 Parks Hwy., 907/495-6343, www.willowcreekresortalaska.com, May-Sept., RVs $36,

tents $23; cabins $115 d, add $20 pp for extra guests) has spaces for RVs and tents, plus a laundry, showers, Wi-Fi, and raft rentals. The basic cabin comes with a kitchenette but no bath. **Northern Lights Adventures** (Mile 62 Parks Hwy., 907/495-6562, www.northernlightsadventures.com, $80 d including breakfast) has comfortable modern cabins.

North to Talkeetna

Off the Parks Highway is the turnoff to **Willow Creek State Recreational Area** (Mile 71 Parks Hwy., no phone, camping $10), four miles down the Susitna River access road. There are 140 campsites, but don't expect a quiet night's repose in the wilderness here if the salmon are running, which they do for most of the summer. The boat launch attracts fishing parties at all hours of the day and night, as well as lots of RVs with their inevitable generator noise. Still, it's a pretty and handy place to spend the night if it's getting late and you plan to travel over the exceptionally scenic Hatcher Pass to Independence Mine State Historical Park. Find additional camping along nearby Deception Creek, two miles up Hatcher Pass Road.

Mat-Su RV Park (Mile 91 Parks Hwy., 907/495-6300, www.matsurvpark.com, May-Sept., RVs $35, tents $17) has a convenience store, laundry, showers, restrooms, and Wi-Fi.

Big Susitna B&B (Mile 92 Parks Hwy., 907/495-6324, www.bigsusitnabnb.com, $97 d) has two rooms with shared baths and full breakfasts in a comfortable log home. The owners are Iditarod veterans.

The privately run **Montana Creek Campgrounds** (Mile 97 Parks Hwy., 907/733-5267 or 877/475-2267, www.montanacreekcampground.com, RVs $40-45, tents $28-33) provides wooded sites on both sides of this popular salmon-fishing creek.

DENALI NATIONAL PARK AND VICINITY

Spectacular Denali National Park is near the center of Alaska, 235 miles north of Anchorage and 125 miles south of Fairbanks. The park covers nearly six million acres of land on both sides of the Alaska Range, and is part of the vast Interior Alaska terrain of boreal forests, tundra, and towering mountains.

The Parks Highway connecting Anchorage with Denali and Fairbanks is the only paved route through this country. Other roads are more limited: a dirt road extends 90 miles through Denali National Park, and the gravel Denali Highway turns east from Cantwell paralleling the Alaska Range to Paxson, but the rest of the land has few roads.

One of the wonderful aspects of Alaska's

Interior is its vastness. Although Talkeetna and the entrance to Denali National Park are both packed with travelers all summer long, it's amazingly easy to escape the crowds and find yourself in a land that seems unchanged from time immemorial. Take the time to pull off the highway and fish a bit on one of the creeks or climb a hill for the view. You won't regret it!

PLANNING YOUR TIME

It's a very scenic five-hour drive (eight relaxing hours by train) from Anchorage to the entrance to **Denali National Park.** The big draws are 20,320-foot Mount McKinley (often obscured by clouds), a grand landscape of open tundra and boreal forests, and

HIGHLIGHTS

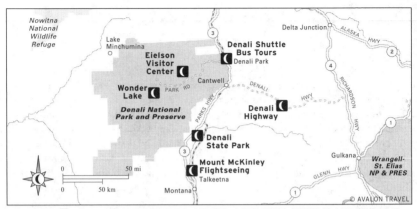

LOOK FOR 【 TO FIND RECOMMENDED SIGHTS, ACTIVITIES, DINING, AND LODGING.

【 **Mount McKinley Flightseeing:** Talkeetna is the base for several air charter operators with flights over McKinley that include a bush plane landing on Ruth Glacier (page 115).

【 **Denali State Park:** This 325,000-acre park affords breathtaking views of Mount McKinley from backcountry trails and roadside pullouts (page 127).

【 **Denali Highway:** This 136-mile mostly gravel road provides dramatic views of the Alaska Range and access to vast stretches of wild country (page 129).

【 **Denali Shuttle Bus Tours:** This is the only way to reach the heart of Alaska's most famous park. Grizzlies, moose, wolves, and Dall sheep are commonly seen and you may even see Mount McKinley in all its glory (page 140).

【 **Eielson Visitor Center:** A four-hour one-way ride by shuttle bus, this modern eco-friendly visitor center provides spectacular views of Denali when the mountain is out (page 144).

【 **Wonder Lake:** Near the end of the Park Road, Wonder Lake is famous for picture-perfect views of the mountain (page 144).

the chance to watch grizzly bears, moose, wolves, Dall sheep, and caribou. Private cars are not allowed on the 92-mile Park Road, but **shuttle and tour buses** provide a wonderful way to see the park or to access remote areas for hiking and camping. Be sure to book your bus well in advance of your trip since the seats often fill up.

It's 8 hours round-trip to **Eielson Visitor Center,** where most buses turn around, or a challenging 11 hours round-trip to **Wonder Lake,** deep inside the park. Plan to take at least two days—more if at all possible—to explore

the park; one day for a ride into the park, and the second for a half-day ranger-led Discovery Hike or other trek. Add another day for a float down the Nenana River just outside the park entrance and to take in the sled dog demonstrations and other activities.

Talkeetna is a delightful destination, with outstanding vistas across to Mount McKinley and a quaint historic downtown filled with mountaineers and outdoor enthusiasts. Several air-taxi operators offer Mount McKinley flightseeing trips that often include a glacier landing. Farther north is the **Denali Highway,**

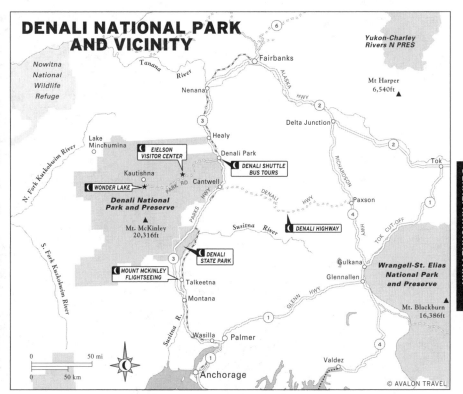

DENALI NATIONAL PARK

---

a partly paved, mostly gravel 126-mile route that cuts east to west along the magnificent Alaska Range. One could easily spend several days hiking backcountry routes, camping beneath the midnight sun, and fishing the lakes and streams along the Denali Highway.

Talkeetna

The outdoorsy and youthful town of Talkeetna (pop. 900) lies at the end of a 14-mile side road that splits away from the Parks Highway 98 miles north of Anchorage. Two closely related phenomena dominate this small bush community: The Mountain, and flying to and climbing on The Mountain. On a clear day, from the overlook a mile out on the Spur Road, Mount McKinley and the accompanying Alaska Range scrape the sky like a jagged white wall.

All summer, local flightseeing and air-taxi companies take off in a continuous parade to circle Mount McKinley, buzz up long glaciers or even land on them, then return to Talkeetna's busy airport to drop off passengers whose wide eyes, broad smiles, and shaky knees attest to the excitement of this once-in-a-lifetime thrill. In late April-early July, these same special "wheel-and-ski" planes might be delivering an American, European, Japanese,

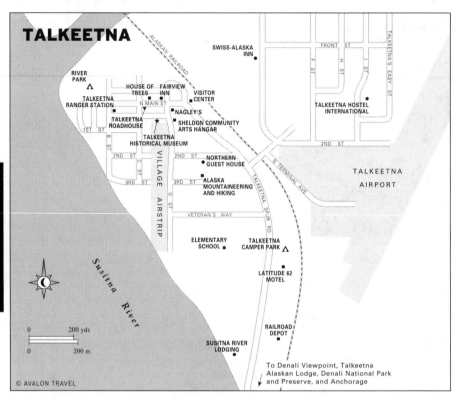

or Korean climbing expedition to the Kahiltna Glacier (elev. 7,000 ft.), from which—if they're lucky—they inch their way up the popular West Buttress route 13,000 feet to the peak. On a clear day, if you're anywhere within striking distance, make a beeline for Talkeetna and be whisked away to some of the most stunning and alien scenery you'll ever see.

If you visit Talkeetna early in the summer you'll find a peculiar mixing of people: the earthy locals with their beards and rusty pickups, the mountaineers—mostly male—decked in color-coordinated Gore-Tex, and the busloads of cruise ship passengers who unload on the south side of town and wander through town.

Talkeetna ("where the rivers meet"), nesting at the confluence of the Talkeetna, Chulitna,

and Susitna Rivers, was originally settled by trappers and prospectors who paddled up the Susitna River to gain access to rich silver, coal, and fur country around the Talkeetna Mountains. The settlement got a boost when the railroad was pushed through in the early 1920s, and it still remains a popular stop on the route. In 1965 the Spur Road from the Parks Highway to Talkeetna was completed, providing further access to the town.

This is one of the few Alaskan villages that still looks the way people imagine Alaskan towns should look, with rustic log buildings lining Main Street and a local population that embraces both grizzled miners and back-to-the-earth tree huggers. Talkeetna men easily win the prize for the highest number of beards

© DON PITCHER

Talkeetna welcome sign

per capita anywhere in Alaska! Local bumper stickers proclaim "Talkeetna, where the road ends and life begins." If you ever saw *Northern Exposure* on TV, this is the place it's rumored to have been modeled on.

SIGHTS

At mile 13 of the Talkeetna Spur Road (one mile south of town), a turnout provides a good view of **Mount McKinley and the Alaska Range.** Across the road is the driveway for Talkeetna Alaskan Lodge, where the spacious back deck provides even more striking vistas of The Mountain.

Talkeetna is a walk-around town, with most of the action within a couple of blocks of Nagley's Store and the Fairview Inn. Start your tour of town at **Nagley's Store** (13650 E. Main St., 907/733-3663, www.nagleysstore. com), a red log building that first opened in the 1920s and moved to the present site in 1945. The crowded interior has limited groceries,

espresso, and a genuine old-time atmosphere. Head up the stairs for outdoor supplies and to check out the noisy parakeets and zebra finches. The walls are lined with old photos, furs, traps, and snowshoes, and you can use the computer to check email. Look around for **Stubbs,** Talkeetna's unofficial mayor asleep in his cat box. Stubbs periodically wanders through town, frequenting West Rib Deli and Pub, directly behind Nagley's. You might be sitting at the bar in the evening when suddenly a cat jumps up to drink from his specially labeled wine glass filled with catnip-laced water. Only in Talkeetna!

The town's other icon—**Fairview Inn** (101 Main St., 907/733-2423, www.denali-fairview. com)—sits kitty-corner across the road. Locals sit on the benches out front most afternoons, and music spills out when evening comes. Built in 1923, it's a great place to soak up the old-time atmosphere, and it's entirely smoke-free. But it *is* a bar, so kids don't belong. President Warren Harding ate lunch at the Fairview during his Alaska visit in 1923; it was one of the last meals he had before falling ill and dying.

For a graphic and detailed look at the history of the town and its connection to The Mountain, check out the excellent **Talkeetna Historical Museum** (907/733-2487, www.tal-keetnahistoricalsociety.org, daily 10am-6pm mid-May-Sept., by appointment the rest of the year, $3 adults, children under 12 free). Take a left after Nagley's Store; the museum is a half-block down the side street on the right in a red schoolhouse built in 1936. Inside are all sorts of local artifacts—including a horse-hide coat from the 1890s—but more interesting is the old railroad section house out back, which now houses an enormous relief map of Denali surrounded by photos and the stories of climbers, including several famous adventurers who lost their lives on this treacherous peak. Other exhibits show the gear climbers use, such as the required "clean mountain cans" for

DENALI NATIONAL PARK

DENALI NATIONAL PARK

Nagley's Store

transporting human waste. Return at 1pm for a Park Service ranger talk on climbing Mount McKinley.

ENTERTAINMENT AND EVENTS

Fairview Inn (101 Main St., 907/733-2423, www.denali-fairview.com) has live bands five nights a week in the summer, and on winter Saturdays.

The **Sheldon Community Arts Hangar** (downtown behind Nagley's, 907/733-2321 or 800/478-2321, June-Aug., showtimes daily 3 and 7pm) hosts plays and other events in the summer, including showings of a video on the life of legendary bush pilot Don Sheldon, who used this building as his airplane hangar.

Talkeetna loves to party, especially on the **Fourth of July** with a parade and other events. All summer long you can find music in the downtown park during **Live at 5** (Fri.) performances.

Winter arrives with a vengeance this far

north, and **Talkeetna Winterfest** (Dec.) brightens spirits, especially those of the many local bachelors. The main events are a Wilderness Woman Contest that includes all sorts of wacky activities, followed later that evening by a Bachelor Society Ball during which local bachelors are bid on by single women, many of whom drive up from Anchorage for the chance. It has all the sexual energy of a male-stripper night, except that some of the men are considerably less fit and keep their clothes on (at least during the bidding). This is one of Alaska's most authentic winter events, representing the skewed ratio of men to women and the oddball nature of small-town Alaska.

SHOPPING

Talkeetna's **Artisans Open Air Market** (no phone, Sat.-Mon. 10am-6pm summer) has booths selling jewelry, clothing, and local crafts. It's in front of the Sheldon Community Arts Hangar behind Nagley's.

The Dancing Leaf Gallery (Main St. near Nagley's, 907/733-5323, www.thedancingleafgallery.com) has a fine selection of local and Alaskan art in a lovely timber frame building.

Several local shops are worth a visit, including the downtown **Denali Images Art Gallery** (22336 S. Talkeetna Spur, 907/733-2026), which displays wildlife and nature images from a half-dozen local photographers.

Find paintings by David Totten at **Wildlife North Art Gallery** (Mile 10 Talkeetna Spur Rd., 907/733-5811, www.davidtotten.com).

Kahiltna Birchworks (Mile 1 Talkeetna Spur Rd., 907/733-1409 or 800/380-7457, www.alaskawildharvest.com, daily mid-May-mid-Sept.) is a unique local business where owners Michael and Dulce East produce distinctively tart-sweet birch syrup and other products. They tap more than 10,000 birch trees each spring, using a sophisticated maze of tubing to produce 140,000 gallons of sap and 1,300 gallons of golden syrup. This is the

© DON PITCHER

Talkeetna Historical Museum

world's largest producer of birch syrup; okay, there isn't a lot of competition out there. Taste a sample or buy a bottle of syrup at their facility, check out the Alaskan-made gifts, or get scoops of birch flavored Matanuska Creamery ice cream topped with berry toppings. Have a picnic on the porch. Visit in early May to watch them in full production mode.

RECREATION
◖ Mount McKinley Flightseeing

Talkeetna is famous as a launching point for flights over Mount McKinley, and on a clear summer day a constant parade of planes takes off from the airport on the edge of town. The flight services in town offer a bewildering array of possibilities, including short scenic flights, glacier landings, drop-off hiking or fishing, wildlife-viewing, overnight trips, and flights to, around, or over the top of The Mountain. Rates vary according to the type of airplane, length of the flight, and how many

people there are in your group. Most outfits will try to match you up with other folks to maximize your flightseeing dollar. Be flexible in your plans, since weather is infinitely variable and is always the most important consideration when it comes to flying you safely. There are one-hour flights ($200 pp, $275 pp with a glacier landing), but the most popular tours are 1.25 hours long ($250-265 pp, $325-340 pp with a glacier landing). A 1.5-hour flight ($385 pp with a glacier landing) to the summit of Mount McKinley offers a good chance to see the climbers. Given the choice, I'd always pay a bit more for the glacier landing on any of these. It turns a spectacular flight into a once-in-a-lifetime adventure.

Reservations are recommended, but not always necessary, so stop by the airport for details and current weather conditions around The Mountain. Note that the climbing season on Mount McKinley runs from early spring until mid- or late June, and the flight services

DENALI NATIONAL PARK

Talkeetna is the primary starting point for Denali flightseeing trips.

© DON PITCHER

are busiest then. As always with bush flying, risks are involved, and fatalities have taken the lives of some of the best local pilots and climbers over the years. Your odds (not to mention the vistas) are probably better if you wait until a clear day to fly.

A number of charter companies provide service to Mount McKinley from the Talkeetna Airport. **K2 Aviation** (907/733-2291 or 800/764-2291, www.flyk2.com) and **Talkeetna Air Taxi** (907/733-2218 or 800/533-2219, www.talkeetnaair.com) are the largest operators. Talkeetna Air is a favorite of climbers, and provides translations for Korean and Japanese travelers. K2 provides printed material translated in multiple languages to help identify features during the flight. K2 offers a unique fly-in trip that includes a floatplane trip to remote Moraine Lake where you hike into the backcountry. These four-hour trips ($495 pp) are only offered after ice melts from the lake in mid-June.

Owned by Holly Sheldon—daughter of famed pilot Don Sheldon—**Sheldon Air Service** (907/733-2321 or 800/478-2321, www.

sheldonairservice.com) is an excellent small family operation offering a personal touch.

Based at Fish Lake, **Alaska Bush Floatplane Service** (Mile 9 Talkeetna Spur Rd., 907/733-1693 or 877/710-8807, www.alaskafloatplane.com) offers flightseeing into Denali, but is better known for fly-in hiking, bear-viewing, and fishing at remote lakes.

Talkeetna Aero Services (907/683-2899 or 888/733-2899, www.talkeetnaaero.com) has flightseeing from Talkeetna (no glacier landings from here), with a larger operation out of Healy that goes by the name of Denali Air.

River Trips

Denali View Raft Adventures (907/733-2778 or 877/533-2778, www.denaliviewraft.com) has 3-hour Susitna River trips ($105 adults, $65 children), 2-hour Talkeetna River floats ($75 adults, $49 children), and a unique 4.5-hour trip that starts with a train ride upriver followed by a float and lunch on the Susitna River ($169 adults, $110 children).

Talkeetna River Guides (907/733-2677 or

800/353-2677, www.talkeetnariverguides.com) offers two-hour Talkeetna River natural history floats ($79 adults, $59 children) and four-hour Chulitna River trips ($129 adults, $109 children). They primarily book customers from the large hotels.

Mahay's Riverboat Service (907/733-2223 or 800/736-2210, www.mahaysriverboat.com) has a popular two-hour jet-boat tour up the Susitna River ($65 adults, $49 children). Longer trips are also offered, including a five-hour run into Devil's Canyon ($155 adults, $116 children).

The fishing in Talkeetna is excellent all summer long; rainbow trout, grayling, Dolly Varden, and all five species of Pacific salmon are there for the catching. Local riverboat services can supply you with a fishing guide or drop you off along the river for the day or overnight. The visitor center has rack cards from most local guides, including **Phantom Salmon Charters** (907/733-2322, www.phantomsalmoncharters.com).

Ziplining

Talkeetna's newest adventure is **Denali Zipline Tours** (13572 E. Main St., 907/733-3988 or 855/733-3988, www.denaliziplinetours.com, $149 adults, $119 ages 10-14, no children under 10 allowed), located in a birch, spruce, and cottonwood forest three miles from town. The course consists of nine ziplines and three sky-bridges, with panoramic views of Denali and the Alaska Range along the way. The highest platform is 60 feet up a tree, and the final zipline—700 feet long—takes you over a small lake. Tours take place several times a day all summer, with a maximum of eight guests for two guides. This is a good rainy day alternative when flights to McKinley are cancelled.

Biking, Hiking, and Canoeing

A paved bike path parallels the Spur Road all the way to Talkeetna. Turn off onto gravel roads at Miles 3 and 12 for out-\ lakes and camping spots. At Mile 13 turnout with an interpretive sign on th ...ska Range and heart-stopping views if the clouds are cooperating. Talkeetna Alaskan Lodge is on the opposite side of the road; stop in for the Mount McKinley view from its back deck even if you aren't overnighting here.

It's hard to miss the florescent green bikes from **Talkeetna Bike Rentals** (22911 S. Talkeetna Spur Rd., 907/354-1222, www.talkeetnabikerentals.com, $20 for three hours), located at the big parking lot just before you enter town. These are primarily for the cruise ship crowd, with three-speeds, cruisers, and trikes, along with tag alongs and baby bugs. They're a bit spendy for a three-hour rental of a cruiser bike.

Two miles south of town, **Talkeetna Lakes Park** (off Comsat Rd., www.matsugov.us) covers more than a thousand acres of forested land around X, Y, and Z Lakes. There is no camping, but the parks have a maze of excellent hiking and biking trails that become cross-country ski trails in winter. Several canoes are stashed at the park; rent one from **Talkeetna Camp and Canoe** (907/733-3355 or 800/318-2534, www.talkeetnacampandcanoe.com, canoes $35/day).

Alaska Nature Guides (907/733-1237, www.alaskanatureguides.com, mid-May-mid-Sept., $59 adults, $39 children) provides excellent three-hour nature walks within Talkeetna Lakes Park. The guides are former national park rangers with years of local experience, and also offer custom birding, photography, and winter snowshoeing trips.

If your kids are bored, take them to the big **Talkeetna Playground** on the south end of town.

Horseback Riding and Dog Mushing

Join a ride through the birch forests through **Talkeetna Horses** (3.1 miles up Montana Creek Rd., off Parks Hwy. Mile 96.1,

907/733-0154, www.talkeetnahorses.com, daily May-mid-Sept., $50 one-hour ride, $65 half-day ride, $100 dinner ride). Dinner rides consist of one hour on horseback plus a steak dinner around a campfire.

Tour the kennels of Iditarod musher Jerry Sousa and take a cart ride behind a team of sled dogs at **Sundog Racing Kennel** (Main St., 907/733-3355 or 800/318-2534, www.sundog-kennel.com, $75 pp two-hour tour, $150 10-mile trip). There are two-hour kennel tours and rides, or for the real deal, join a 10-mile wintertime dog mushing trip.

Another Iditarod competitor, Randy Cummins of **Huskytown Kennel** (30018 Talkeetna Spur Rd., 907/733-4759, www.huskytown.com, $35 pp), has similar tours.

ACCOMMODATIONS

There is a 5 percent lodging tax in Talkeetna; add the tax to the base price of your lodging choice.

Hostels

Right in the center of Main Street, **House of 7 Trees** (Main St., 907/733-7733, late Apr.-early Sept., hostel bunks $25 pp, guest rooms $75-90) is a lovely and clean little place that attracts travelers of all ages and nationalities. Built in 1936, this charming frame home has lots of history, and the friendly owner Pat McGee—a 35-year Talkeetna resident—really knows the area. Her welcoming dog adds to the allure. The back cabin houses six coed hostel bunks, and four private rooms are upstairs in the main house. Three of the private rooms have one queen or two twin beds, and the fourth private room contains a queen and twin bed—all topped with handmade quilts. Guests can access the common room with its baby grand piano, plus the impressive commercial kitchen, two baths (one wheelchair accessible), and the shady yard. Wi-Fi is available. Make reservations a few weeks ahead, especially for summer weekends, but don't call after 9:30pm. There is no alcohol here.

A few blocks east of downtown near the airport, **Talkeetna Hostel International** (22159 S. I St., 907/733-4678, www.talkeetnahostel.com, mid-Apr.-Sept., dorm rooms $22 pp; guest rooms $50-65 d; cabin $50, add $10 pp for extra guests; VW bus $25 s, $35 d; tents $10) is a place with haphazard management that may or may not be to your taste. The location is quiet and shady. Each of the two coed dorm rooms has four beds. There are also private rooms and a very basic cabin with two twin beds and a miniscule loft. Another option (though not recommended) is the ancient VW bus. You can also pitch a tent in the backyard. There are three baths, a kitchen and laundry, guest computer, Wi-Fi, TV, and no curfew.

Hotels

For a taste of the past, stay at **Talkeetna Roadhouse** (corner of Main St. and C St., 907/733-1351, www.talkeetnaroadhouse.com, hostel $20 pp; guest rooms $55-75 s, $65-85 d shared bath; cabin $105 for two, add $10 pp for extra guests, maximum of five), a delightful old Alaskan lodge, constructed in 1917 and in business since 1944. It's best known for home-cooked meals downstairs, but it also has lodging options. Budget travelers and mountaineers appreciate the Roadhouse's four-bed coed hostel with a bath down the hall. Five simple but clean guest rooms have period antiques and shared baths. Out back is a cozy little cabin that sleeps two. It has a fridge, microwave, TV, and gas fireplace, with bathrooms in the main building. Three blocks away is Trapper John's cabin ($130 d), with two double beds, fridge, microwave, running water, and a private bath. Also available is an apartment ($150 d private bath), located over the historic red schoolhouse at the museum.

Latitude 62 Motel (next to the airport and railroad depot, 907/733-2262, www.latitude62.com, $85 d, suite $120 d, offsite cabin $130 d) is a two-story log building on the south end of town with 11 small budget rooms and a suite. The furnishings are older, and there are no phones or TVs, but Latitude does have Wi-Fi, plus a full service restaurant and bar. An offsite log cabin includes a private bath with jetted tub and full kitchen.

Downtown above Wildflower Café, **Main St. Suites** (Main St., 907/733-2694, www.talkeetnasuites.com, summer only, studio $150 d, suite $175 d) consists of a one-bedroom studio and a two-bedroom suite, both with private baths and kitchenettes.

Head across the railroad tracks to **Swiss-Alaska Inn** (22056 S. F St., 907/733-2424, www.swissalaska.com, $108 s, $135-150 d, cabin $165), with 20 motel rooms, homemade quilts, and private baths. There is also a separate cabin with three beds, a kitchenette, and private bath. There is no TV reception, but videos are available along with Wi-Fi. German is spoken, and the adjacent restaurant (open seasonally) serves good breakfasts.

Talkeetna Alaskan Lodge (23601 Talkeetna Spur Rd., 907/733-9500 or 888/959-9590, www.talkeetnalodge.com, mid-May-mid-Sept., $279-315 d, $409 d for rooms that face Mount McKinley; suites $479-569 d) sits atop a hill a mile south of Talkeetna, with spacious, modern rooms. There are also luxury suites, most with gas fireplaces and jetted tubs. The grand lobby includes a stone fireplace and towering windows framing The Mountain, and a fine-dining restaurant is on the premises. There's a free shuttle to town and the train depot. This 200-room Native Alaskan-owned lodge serves up million-dollar views for an upscale clientele, pretty much the opposite of most Talkeetna lodging places. The hotel is packed with cruise ship passengers all summer.

Cabins

Paradise Lodge & Cabins (S. Birch Creek Blvd., 907/733-1471 or 888/205-3553, www.paradiselodge.net, mid-May-early Sept., $115

© DON PITCHER

Talkeetna Alaskan Lodge

d, add $10 pp for extra guests) is aptly named, with a peaceful and secluded location along Fish Lake five miles south of Talkeetna. Four rustic log cabins (with double beds and kitchenettes but no running water) share a bathhouse, or you can stay in the main lodge where two rooms share a bath. Also available is a spacious three-bedroom, four-bath home ($500 for up to eight guests). Wi-Fi is available, but TVs are only in the main lodge. This off-the-grid place (power comes from a generator) is open only in the summer months.

Right in town behind Mountain High Pizza, **Talkeetna Cabins** (22137 C St., 907/733-2227 or 888/733-9933, www.talkeetnacabins.org, cabins $175 d, add $20 pp for extra guests; house $350 for 4 people, add $20 pp for max of 12) consists of four duplex log cabins and a large three-bedroom house, all with new beds, full kitchens, dishes, private baths, laundry, grill, and Wi-Fi.

Susitna River Lodging (23094 S. Talkeetna Rd., 907/733-1505 or 866/733-1505, www. susitna-river-lodging.com, cabins $249 d, lodge rooms $169-189 d, add $15 pp for extra guests) has four lovely cedar cabins and lodge rooms a half-mile south of Talkeetna. All guest rooms and cabins include private baths, kitchenettes, electric fireplaces, BBQ grills, continental breakfast, and Wi-Fi, but no TVs. They're right along the river, and the main lodge has a big porch facing the water.

Looking for a unique wilderness experience? ◖**Caribou Lodge** (907/733-2163, www. cariboulodgealaska.com, Mar.-Nov., $325 pp/day) has a striking location on an unnamed alpine lake near the southeast edge of Denali National Park. It's a 15-minute flight from Talkeetna ($185 pp round-trip), but a world away. Residents for more than 20 years, owners Mike and Pam Nichols provide three simple, but nicely set up cabins for guests. Lodging, meals, canoeing, and guided day hikes—abundant wildlife—are included in the rate. There's a

two-night minimum stay, and multi-night packages are available. Winter guests come for snowshoeing, cross-country skiing, and dramatic northern lights above the summit of Mount McKinley. This is a wonderful introduction to a place where TVs, phones, and the hi-tech world don't intrude. There is no indoor plumbing here!

In a quiet location, **Question Lake Cabin** (Mile 7 Talkeetna Spur Rd., 907/243-7661, www.talkeetnaquestionlakecabin.com, $95 d) sits on the north shore of this lake where you'll hear loons calling many evenings. The rustic cabin is large enough for families, with two beds and a queen futon, plus a kitchenette. The bedside commode and outhouse remind you that this isn't the city.

Talkeetna Lakeside Cabins (35320 S. St. John Dr., 907/733-2349, www.talkeetnalakesidecabins.com, $110-150 d, add $20 pp for extra guests) consists of three immaculate cabins along a private lake a mile off Talkeetna Spur Road. Each has a kitchenette, private bath, and Wi-Fi. There are no TVs, but you can make your own entertainment by rowing around the artificially-constructed lake.

Guesthouses

On a hill facing the Alaska Range away from the noises of town, **Out of the Wild** (22198 S. Freedom Dr., 907/733-2701, www.talkeetnapro.com, $140 d, add $15 pp for extra guests) has a cluster of three architecturally unique guesthouses. Co-owner Brian McCullough (an internationally known mountaineer and guide) built them all by hand, filling each with distinctive furnishings. All three places contain private baths and full kitchens stocked with breakfast supplies, Wi-Fi, and satellite TVs. Spacious Mountain House has three upstairs bedrooms and two baths, Kahiltna Chalet is an elegant cottage perfect for romantic getaways, and Stone Hut features artistic stonework, two bedrooms, and a spiral staircase. Rates are the same for all rooms at Out of the Wild. Kids and dogs are welcome, and rooms are available year-round. The hilltop location is perfect for winter northern lights viewing.

Just two blocks from Main Street, **Northern Guest House** (13712 2nd St., 907/715-4868, www.northernguesthouse.com, $60 s, $80 d, add $20 pp for extra guests) has hard to beat rates. The three guest rooms each contain a private bath and two beds, and guests can use the full kitchen, dining room, and living room, plus the rec room with a ping pong table and piano. A two-bedroom apartment ($95-115 d) contains a kitchen, living room, bath, private deck, and private entrance. Borrow a bike to explore town, or kick back around the enclosed backyard fire pit. There is no Wi-Fi here, however.

Bed-and-Breakfasts

When it comes to Talkeetna B&Bs the old "location, location, location" saying applies, with several places providing Denali vistas to die for.

Five miles from Talkeetna, **◖ Denali Overlook Inn** (29198 S. Talkeetna Spur Rd., 907/733-3555 or 855/733-3555, www.denalioverlookinn.com, open all year, $179-279 d) is a memorable home where the view exceeds your expectations; on a clear day it's impossible to miss Mount McKinley and the rest of the Alaska Range. Five bedrooms—the largest features wall-to-wall windows facing The Mountain—have private baths, and a full menu breakfast is included, along with a guest computer and Wi-Fi. Honeymooners will appreciate privacy at the adjacent two-level cabin ($259 d) with a kitchenette and private bath.

Five miles east of town, **Traleika Mountaintop Cabins** (22216 S. Freedom Dr., 907/733-2711, www.traleika.com, guesthouse $205 d, cabins $175-185 d, add $20 pp for extra guests) has a dramatic location facing Denali. There is a two-bedroom guesthouse and two smaller cabins. All three places include full baths, living rooms, decks, kitchens, and Wi-Fi; the largest sleeps up to eight.

Not far away—with an equally fine vista—is the reasonably priced **Freedom Hills B&B** (Freedom Dr., 907/733-2455 or 888/703-2455, www.gbfreedomhillsbb.com, May-Sept., $130 d shared bath, $150 d private bath), where five guest rooms are in two adjacent homes. There's an enormous deck on the main house for Denali views, and free Wi-Fi. Co-owner and chef Bill Germain creates a delicious breakfast each morning.

Built in 1946 and beautifully maintained, **Fireweed Station Inn** (15113 E. Sunshine Rd., 907/733-1457 or 888/647-1457, www.fireweed-station.com, guest rooms $150 d, suite $205 d, cabin $100 d) is a gorgeous log home off Mile 2 of the Talkeetna Spur Road. A spacious suite occupies the entire upstairs, and downstairs are two guest rooms with private baths. A historic cabin makes a good add-on for larger groups with friends or family in the main lodge. (Cabin guests use a bath in the main building.) All rates include a full breakfast, Wi-Fi, and access to the big deck. Dinners are available upon request. Winter guests can ride the flag-stop train from Anchorage directly to Fireweed Station.

Another wonderful hilltop place with stunning Alaska Range views is **Talkeetna Chalet B&B** (Mile 10.7 Talkeetna Spur Rd., 907/733-4734, www.talkeetnachalet.net, guest rooms $139-189 d, cabins $179 d, add $20 pp for extra guests), three miles from town. Three guest rooms have private baths, and two newly built cabins contain kitchenettes and private baths. Guests can use the first two floors of the home, and amenities include big hot breakfasts, a great room with a large screen TV, Wi-Fi, guest computer, and a large seasonal hot tub on the wraparound deck.

Camping

Find camping at shady **River Park** (end of Main St., no phone, free), but it lacks running water. Also on the river, but a bit farther from town, is

Talkeetna Alaska RV (22763 S. Talkeetna Spur Rd., 907/733-2604, May-Sept., tents and RVs $20, showers $6) with in-the-trees tent and RV sites. There are no hookups, but some sites are right along the Talkeetna River.

Talkeetna Camper Park (22763 S. Talkeetna Spur, 907/733-2693, www.talkeetnacamper.com, Apr.-Oct., RVs $32-38) has 35 wooded RV sites, plus showers and laundry; it's on the right just before you enter town.

FOOD

Talkeetna has turned into quite the spot for great inexpensive food, making it a rarity on the Alaska road system. Most places are downtown, so you can just walk a block or so to see what appeals to you.

Cafés and Diners

At ◖ **Talkeetna Roadhouse** (corner of Main St. and C St., 907/733-1351, www.talkeetnaroadhouse.com, daily 6am-9pm mid-May-mid-Sept., daily 8am-8pm winter, $5-14) long tables make for fun family-style dining with crowds of locals. The chalkboard menu lists two options: "Breakfast" and "Not Breakfast." Breakfast variations—available till 2pm—include Paul Bunyan-size cinnamon rolls, chocolate potato cake, and gargantuan sourdough hotcakes, from a starter that's been in use since 1902! The Not Breakfast options feature reindeer chili, squarebun BBQ pulled pork sandwiches, quiche, lasagna, homemade pasties, mac and cheese, sandwiches, salads, and daily soups. Fresh loaves of bread adorn the bakery cases in the afternoon.

◖ **Flying Squirrel** (Mile 11 Talkeetna Spur Rd., 907/733-6887, www.flyingsquirrelcafe.com, Tues.-Wed. 7:30am-7pm, Thurs.-Sat. 7:30am-9pm, Sun. 8am-6pm late May-late Oct.; closed Mon. year-round plus Tues. in winter, most items under $8, pizzas $10-17) hides in a birch forest four miles from town. Owner Anita Colton's bakery café is definitely worth

the drive! Get a big mug of organic espresso while perusing the cases to see what looks interesting. Daily specials include quiche, soups, hot sandwiches, wraps, desserts, and breads. Pizzas emerge from the brick oven Thursday-Saturday nights in summer (Fri.-Sat. in winter), and the café has free Wi-Fi and gluten-free options.

For an in-town buzz, visit picture-perfect **Coffee a la Mer** (behind the Fairview Inn, 907/315-2891). Built in 1933, the snug cabin has a flower-filled yard and a selection of homemade scones, cookies, bagels, and more.

Quick Bites

A little trailer behind the Fairview Inn, **Payo's Thai Kitchen** (22160 S. Railroad Ave., 907/733-5503, daily 11am-9pm May-Sept., $8-14) serves curries, stir fries, soups, and other Thai favorites, including gang phanang curry, tom yum gai, and shrimp with ginger. A few tables are available outside and beneath the deck.

Looking for a late-night snack? **My Little Dumpling** (next to Wildflower Café, 907/733-3867, daily till 2am in summer, dumplings $10-14) has bowls of pelmeni dumplings, plus smoothies, spring rolls, and a big choice of black, green, and herbal teas. It's a tiny walkup place with a couple of covered picnic tables.

Brewpubs

Twister Creek Restaurant (13605 E. Main St., 907/733-2537, www.denalibrewingcompany.com, daily 11am-10pm mid-May-mid-Sept.; Mon.-Wed. 1pm-9pm, Thurs.-Sun. noon-9pm winter, $13-32) has a big front deck in the heart of town, plus a combined lunch/dinner menu ranging from fish and chips and handmade veggie burgers to prime rib and Thai coconut shrimp curry. There's a good selection of appetizers (try smoked provolone wedges), and the adjacent brewery serves 5-10 of their beers, including Single Engine Red, an Irish red ale. There is free Wi-Fi here, too.

West Rib Deli and Pub (directly behind

Nagley's Store, 907/733-3663, www.westribpub.
info, daily 11:30am-11pm, $7-15) attracts climbers and locals with a tasty pub-grub menu that specializes in burgers, sandwiches, salads, seafood, and nightly specials. Everyone raves about the caribou chiliburger (an Angus burger topped with caribou chili and cheese), or try the veggie mushroom burger. Looking for a real artery clogger? The McKinley Burger drops two half-pound beef patties with Swiss and American cheese, sautéed onion, lettuce, and tomato. The bar serves Alaskan brews and Guinness. There's not much space here, but there is a side deck for summer evenings, and a back room with pool and foosball tables. Looking for the best deal? Meet the locals at the Friday-night burger-and-beer (for just $7). Hang around long enough and you're likely to encounter Stubbs, the stubby-tailed Manx cat who roams through town, garnering attention and food along the way. He's unofficially known as Mayor Stubbs (check him out on Facebook), and has drinks from his own wine glass—filled with catnip-infused water—at West Rib.

Housed in a modern log building, **Wildflower Café** (Main St., 907/733-1275, www.talkeetnasuites.com, daily 11am-9pm mid-May-mid-Sept., Fri.-Sun. 9:30am-9pm Dec.-mid-May, $30-36) serves a pub menu with halibut sandwiches, burgers, soups, salads, pizzas, and fish and chips all day, plus dinner specials such as grilled sesame salmon, pork tenderloin, and grilled chicken breast alfredo. More unusual is the outdoor bar next to Wildflower where you can work your way through 43 different beers on tap! Trivia tip of the day: Wildflower's owner/chef, Jerome Longo, previously served as chef for President George W. Bush.

Pizza

Mountain High Pizza Pie (22165 S. C St., 907/733-1234, www.pizzapietalkeetna.com, daily 11am-10pm May-Sept., Tues.-Sat. noon-8pm Oct.-Apr., pizza by the slice $4, pizzas

Mountain High Pizza Pie

$14-33), in the purple log cabin, is a busy spot for pizza by the slice, calzones, flatbreads, salads, and subs. They have all the standard 15-inch pizzas. The Mountain High version is piled with "everything but the mosquitoes." In summer, the side deck is a great spot to enjoy your pizza with a beer (there are a dozen Alaskan brews on tap); it erupts with live music six nights a week all summer.

Sweets
Adjacent to the Fairview Inn is a seasonal ice cream stand called **Wake and Shake** (Main St., $3-5) with a steam-powered ice cream machine and four daily flavors. Get a cone or shake to go.

Markets
Nagley's Store (907/733-3663, www.nagleysstore.com) opened in the 1920s and is still the main place for (limited) groceries in town, but it has also added such staples of 21st-century life as an ATM, ice cream, and lattes.

Cubby's Marketplace IGA (14 miles south of town at the junction with Parks Hwy., 907/733-5050, Mon.-Sat. 8am-8pm, Sun. 8am-10pm) is the primary grocery store for the region, with a deli, liquor store, and ATM.

INFORMATION
The **Talkeetna Visitor Information Center** (across from the Village Park, 907/733-2688 or 800/660-2688, www.talkeetnadenali.com, daily 9am-7pm mid-May-mid-Sept.) is housed in the historic Three German Bachelors' Cabin, built in 1934. It's on the right side as you come into town. Out front is the funky and much-photographed "Welcome to Beautiful Downtown Talkeetna" sign next to a wheelbarrow overflowing with flowers.

At **Talkeetna/Denali Visitor Center** (intersection of Parks Hwy. and Talkeetna Spur Rd., 907/733-2688 or 800/660-2688, www.talkeetnadenali.com, daily 9am-7pm mid-May-mid-Sept.) look for the giant bear out front.

Both visitor centers are owned by Talkeetna Aero Services, but the always-helpful staff will book flights with any local air taxi, provide current weather conditions on Denali, set up fishing expeditions or guided hikes, book rooms at hotels and B&Bs, or just supply brochures and information on the area. The **Talkeetna Chamber of Commerce** (www.talkeetnachamber.org) has a useful website, and can send out brochures.

The Park Service's log **Talkeetna Ranger Station** (B St., 907/733-2231, www.nps.gov/dena, daily 8am-6pm mid-Apr.-early Sept., Mon.-Fri. 8am-5:30pm mid-Sept.-mid-Apr.) is a pleasant place to watch a climbing video or look over the mountaineering books.

SERVICES
Keep in touch with the outside world via the Internet at the **Talkeetna Public Library** (907/733-2359, www.matsulibraries.org/talkeetna, Mon.-Sat. 11am-6pm) on the south side of town. There's also a single computer upstairs in Nagley's; ask for the password at the counter.

Go to **Sunshine Community Health Center** (Mile 4 Talkeetna Spur Rd., 907/733-2273, Mon.-Sat. 9am-5pm) if the need arises.

Take showers and wash your clothes at **Washi-Washi** (on the south end of town). Showers are also available at **Talkeetna Alaska RV** (907/733-2604, May-Sept., $6).

GETTING THERE AND AROUND
The turnoff to Talkeetna is 100 miles north of Anchorage on the George Parks Highway, and the town is another 14 miles out on Talkeetna Spur Road.

Buses
Several companies provide van transportation connecting Talkeetna with Anchorage ($65 one way), Denali ($65 one way), and Fairbanks ($95 one way). **Alaska/Yukon Trails**

© DON PITCHER

From Talkeetna, continue on to Denali via the Alaska Railroad.

(907/479-2277 or 800/770-7275, www.alaskashuttle.com, late Apr.-Sept.) has a daily run from Anchorage to Talkeetna, Denali, and Fairbanks. **Park Connection** (907/245-0200 or 800/266-8625, www.alaskacoach.com, mid-May-mid-Sept.) provides summertime service connecting Talkeetna with Seward, Whittier, Anchorage, and Denali.

The **Alaska Bus Guy** (907/720-6541, www.alaskabusguy.com) operates an environmentally friendly hydrogen-hybrid van with service from Talkeetna to Anchorage or Denali ($67 one way). It has daily service in the summer and twice-weekly winter runs.

Sunshine Transit (907/733-2273, Mon.-Fri. 7:30am-5:30pm, $3 one way) is a local not-for-profit van service that operates along the Talkeetna Spur Road, stopping at points along the way, including Flying Squirrel Café and the Talkeetna Clinic.

Trains

The **Alaska Railroad** (907/265-2494 or 800/544-0552, www.alaskarailroad.com, $70 one way) *Denali Star* runs from Anchorage to Talkeetna. The train leaves Anchorage every morning at 8:15am and arrives in Talkeetna at 11:05am before continuing north to Denali National Park and Fairbanks. A southbound train leaves Fairbanks at 12:15pm, stopping in Denali, before reaching Talkeetna at 4:40pm. This train continues south to Anchorage, arriving at 8pm.

A local flag-stop train (stops on an as-needed basis), the ***Hurricane Turn*** (Thurs.-Sun. in summer, $96 round-trip), runs the 50 miles from Talkeetna north to Hurricane and back. It's a great way to see the countryside with locals. Winter travelers can get on or off the flag-stop train at points south of Talkeetna as well.

North from Talkeetna

TRAPPER CREEK AND PETERSVILLE ROAD

The minuscule settlement of Trapper Creek (pop. 350) is at Mile 115 of the Parks Highway, and 16 miles north of the junction with Talkeetna Spur Road. Petersville Road splits off at Trapper Creek, providing access to the western end of Denali State Park and offering some of the finest views of Mount McKinley. **Trapper Creek Museum** (a half-mile out on Petersville Rd., 907/733-2555, www.trapper-creekmuseum.com, daily 10am-4pm late May-early Sept., closed winter, donations accepted) has a collection of local historical items and local crafts in a log cabin built in 1959. The museum is on Spruce Lane Farms, which raises miniature horses.

A number of rural subdivisions and homesteads are found along Petersville Road, and this is a popular winter destination for dog mushers and hordes of snowmobilers. The road continues all the way to old mining developments in the Petersville mining camp, 30 miles in, although the last section may not be passable without a high-clearance vehicle. Petersville Road is paved for 10 miles, then gravel the next 9 miles to the site of historic Forks Roadhouse, destroyed in a 2012 fire. The owners hope to rebuild. Beyond mile 19, the road deteriorates, though it's still passable until around mile 35. The State of Alaska is gradually making improvements, but expect several miles of rocks and slow going beyond this. A high clearance vehicle and good tires are recommended, but more than a few rental cars have made the 2.5-hour trek up Petersville Road.

Accommodations

Trapper Creek Inn & General Store (Mile 115 Parks Hwy., 907/733-2302, www.trapper-crkinn.com, $99-139 d, tents $10, RVs $30) has guest rooms, camping sites, groceries, free Wi-Fi, a deli, and a coin laundry with showers.

Set along two ponds, **Gate Creek Cabins** (Mile 10.5 Petersville Rd., 907/733-1393, www.gatecreekcabins.com, $150 d, add $55 for two additional people) has eight modern log cabins—the largest has four bedrooms—with kitchens, private baths, TVs, BBQ grills, and Wi-Fi. They're really more like furnished vacation homes, with all the creature comforts in a peaceful and picturesque setting. Guests can borrow a canoe or paddleboat to cruise the ponds or try a bit of trout fishing. Be sure to ask about the mid-July bear-viewing opportunities. The cabins provide an extremely popular winter base for snowmobilers.

McKinley View B&B (near Mile 114 Parks Hwy., 907/733-1758 or 352/425-2573, www.mckinleyviewlodging.com, $115 s, $135 d) is all about the view. Take a seat on the back deck for dramatic vistas of the Alaska Range and Mount McKinley (when the weather cooperates). Four guest rooms are available, with full breakfasts, private baths and entrances, gracious owners, a guest computer, and Wi-Fi.

Alaska's Northland Inn (0.8 miles out Petersville Rd., 907/733-7377, www.alaskas-northlandinn.com, $120 d, add $30 for additional adults) has a pair of two-level apartments with private baths, full kitchens, two queen beds, continental breakfast (summer only), and Wi-Fi. Relax in the great room with a pool table and satellite TV. In winter, the owners rent snowmobiles and provide groomed cross-country ski trails.

If you want remote, check out **Cache Creek Cabins** (Petersville Rd., 907/733-5200 summer or 907/252-1940 winter, www.cachecreekcabins.com, mid-June-Sept., $55-60 d shared bath, $150 private bath), 39 rugged miles out on the Petersville Road. Six rustic little cabins share a

NORTH FROM TALKEETNA   **127**

common bathhouse, and a nicer two-story cabin sleeps eight and has a private bath. The friendly owners can provide home-cooked meals ($15 breakfast, $15-20 dinner) and gold panning in the creek ($25/day). It's a pretty setting with wonderful views of Denali on the drive in. It is, however, a long and rough ride, so call for current road conditions before heading out.

Food

Also known as Angela's Heaven, **Trapper Creek Pizza Pub** (Mile 116 Parks Hwy., 907/733-3344, Fri.-Wed. 3pm-9pm late May-early Sept., Fri.-Mon. 1pm-8pm winter, $15-29) is well worth a stop. Pizza is the primary draw, but owner Angela Sunjakom comes from German heritage and also makes Hungarian goulash, Greek salads, Russian borsht, sloppy joes, and knockwurst. There's a good selection of German beers too.

◖ DENALI STATE PARK

This 325,240-acre state park (907/745-3975, www.alaskastateparks.org, $5/day trailhead parking) lies just southeast of Denali National Park and Preserve and is bisected by the Parks Highway from Mile 132 to Mile 169. Situated between the Talkeetna Mountains to the east and the Alaska Range to the west, the landscape of Denali State Park varies from wide glaciated valleys to alpine tundra. The Chulitna and Tokositna Rivers flow through western sections of the park, while the eastern half is dominated by Curry Ridge and Kesugi Ridge, a 35-mile-long section of alpine country.

Denali State Park provides an excellent alternative wilderness experience to the crowds and hassles of its federal next-door neighbor. The Mountain is visible from all over the park, bears are abundant, and you won't need to stand in line for a permit to hike or camp while you wait for Mount McKinley's mighty south face to show itself. Several trails offer a variety of hiking experiences and spectacular views.

Sights

Denali State Park is best known for its breathtaking **views of Mount McKinley** and the Alaska Range from pullouts along the Parks Highway. If The Mountain or even "just" some of the lower peaks of the Alaska Range are out, you won't need to read the next sentence to know what or where the sights are. The best viewpoint along the highway in the park, and the most popular, is at Mile 135, where on a clear day you will find an interpretive signboard and crowds of fellow travelers. Set up your tripod and shoot, shoot, shoot. Other unforgettable viewpoints are at Miles 147, 158, and 162.

The **Alaska Veterans Memorial** (Mile 147, within walking distance of Byers Lake Campground) consists of five monumental concrete blocks with stars carved out of them. Turn your back to the monument, and if you're lucky, there's blue-white McKinley, perfectly framed by tall spruce trees.

The western section of Denali State Park lies within the remote **Peters Hills,** an area known for its pristine Mount McKinley vistas and open country. This section is accessed via the Petersville Road.

Recreation

Little Coal Creek trailhead (Mile 164) is five miles south of the park's northern boundary. This is the park's gentlest climb to the alpine tundra—five miles east up the trail by Little Coal Creek, then you cut southwest along Kesugi Ridge, with amazing views of the Range and glaciers; flags and cairns delineate the trail. Watch for bears! The trail goes 27 miles until it hooks up with Troublesome Creek Trail just up from Byers Lake Campground. About halfway there, **Ermine Lake Trail** cuts back down to the highway, an escape route in case of really foul weather.

Troublesome Creek Trail is so named because of frequent bear encounters; in fact,

© DON PITCHER

view of Mount McKinley and the Alaska Range from an overlook in Denali State Park

Troublesome Creek Trail is frequently closed in late summer and early fall because of the abundance of bears. It has two trailheads, one at the northeast tip of Byers Lake (Mile 147), the other at Mile 138. The park brochure describes this 15-mile hike along Troublesome Creek as moderate. It connects with Kesugi Ridge Trail just up from Byers Lake or descends to the easy five-mile **Byers Lake Loop Trail,** which brings you around to both campgrounds. Just down and across the road from the Byers Lake turnoff is a family day-hike along Lower Troublesome Creek—a gentle mile.

Based at Byers Lake, **Alaska Nature Guides** (907/733-1237, www.alaskanatureguides. com, mid-May-mid-Sept., 2.5-hour walks: $54 adults, $39 children; 5.5-hour hikes: $94 adults, $69 children) guides easy 2.5-hour nature walks and more interesting 5.5-hour hikes up Kesugi Ridge (includes lunch and gear). The guides are former national park rangers with years of local experience; the company also provides custom trips for birders and photographers.

Denali Southside River Guides (Byers Lake campground day-use parking lot, 907/733-7238, www.denaliriverguides.com) rents canoes and sit-on-top kayaks at Byers Lake. The company also leads full-day excursions ($249 adults, $179 kids) that combine kayaking, lunch, and rafting.

D&S Alaskan Trail Rides (Mile 133 Parks Hwy., 907/733-2207, www.alaskantrailrides. com, mid-May-late Sept.) has guided horseback rides from their location near Denali State Park. There are two-hour horseback rides ($119). Another option is a two-hour wagon ride with gold panning ($79). (The latter is primarily for cruise passengers staying at the nearby Mt. McKinley Princess Lodge.)

Accommodations
Turn off the highway at Mile 133 for a one-mile side road into **Mt. McKinley Princess**

Lodge (Mile 133 Parks Hwy., 907/733-2900 or 800/426-0500, www.princesslodges.com, mid-May-mid-Sept., $189-200 d). This stylish 460-room retreat is famous for its riverside location and picture-perfect vistas of the Alaska Range and Mount McKinley. Most rooms are filled with Princess cruise passengers, but anyone can stay or eat here. The lodge itself centers around a "great room" with a stone fireplace and enormous windows fronting the mountain. Lodging is in smaller buildings scattered around the grounds; ask for one of the new rooms with a king bed. There's also a small fitness center, two outdoor hot tubs, a restaurant, and a café. Wi-Fi is available only in the main lodge.

Located at the southern edge of Denali State Park, **Mary's McKinley View Lodge** (near Mile 134 Parks Hwy., 907/733-1555, www.mckinleyviewlodge.com, May-late Sept., $79-89 d) has a full service restaurant, great views of The Mountain out the big picture windows, and eight clean but older guest rooms with private baths. You can buy autographed copies of the many books authored by owner Jean Carey Richardson and her late mother, Mary Carey. There is no Wi-Fi here.

Camping and Cabins

Byers Lake Campground ($10) has large and uncrowded sites, water, outhouses, interpretive signs, and beautiful Byers Lake a stone's throw down the road. Also at Byers Lake are two popular **public-use cabins** (907/745-3975, www.alaskastateparks.org, $60). Just under two miles along the Loop Trail from the campground or across the lake by boat is **Lakeshore Campground,** with six primitive sites, outhouses, no running water, but unimpeded views of The Mountain and Range from your tent flap. Across the road and a quarter-mile south, **Lower Troublesome Creek Campground** ($10) has 20 sites and all the amenities of Byers Lake.

◖ DENALI HIGHWAY

The Denali Highway, which stretches 136 miles east-west across the waist of mainland Alaska from Cantwell, from 30 miles south of Denali Park to Paxson at Mile 122 on the Richardson

DENALI NATIONAL PARK

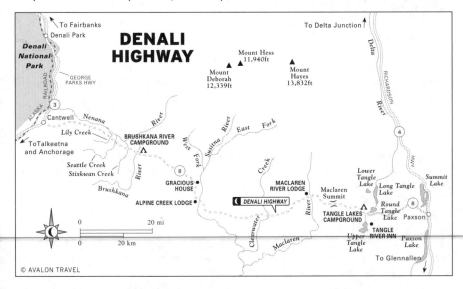

© AVALON TRAVEL

Highway, may be the best-kept secret in Alaska. Originally the Denali Highway was the only road into Denali National Park, and this beautiful side trip has been largely ignored by visitors since the opening of the George Parks Highway in 1971. Denali Highway is paved for 21 miles on the east end of the road (from Paxson to Tangle Lakes) and for three miles on the western end, but the rest is well-maintained gravel, which has received an undeserved bad rap—usually from folks hoping to set world land-speed records on their Alaska vacation.

The Denali Highway offers a varied selection of outstanding scenery and wildlife-viewing opportunities. Much of the route punches through the foothills of the magnificent Alaska Range. This area is part of the home range of the huge 30,000-strong Nelchina caribou herd. In the fall they begin to group in the greatest numbers—sightings of several hundred caribou are not unusual.

The Denali Highway is closed October-mid-May. In the winter it becomes a popular trail for snowmobilers, dog mushers, and cross-country skiers. Die-hard Alaskans also use this trail in the winter for access to unparalleled ice fishing and caribou and ptarmigan hunting.

As always, travelers on the Denali Highway should be prepared for emergencies. Always carry a spare tire and tire-changing tools, water, some snacks, and warm clothing. Towing is available from Paxson, Gracious House, and Cantwell, but it ain't cheap, so take your time and be safe.

History

The Denali Highway began as a "cat" track in the early 1950s when a man named Earl Butcher first established a hunting camp at Tangle Lakes. Known for years as Butcher's Camp, it's now the site of Tangle Lakes Lodge. About the same time, Chalmer Johnson established a camp at Round Tangle Lake. Now known as the Tangle River Inn, this lodge is still operated by the Johnson family.

Cantwell

A minuscule settlement (pop. 160) at the junction of the Parks Highway and Denali Highway, Cantwell began as a railroad settlement, and a cluster of decrepit buildings are strewn along the tracks two miles west of the highway. Cantwell is less than 30 miles south of Denali National Park, and a couple of businesses provide the staples: fuel, food, lodging, and booze. Most folks stop to fill up on the expensive gas, get a soda, and tool on up the highway. There aren't a lot of reasons to stay in Cantwell itself, though the surrounding country is grand.

Denali Sightseeing Safaris (Mile 188 Parks Hwy., 907/240-0357, www.denalisights.com, June-mid-Sept., seven-hour treks $160 adults, $80 children under 13) operates from the igloo on steroids 22 miles south of Cantwell. These unique tours are in customized big-tire trucks that allow them to cross glacial rivers and take you up old mining roads into the spectacular alpine area.

Cantwell Lodge (two miles off Parks Hwy., 907/388-8743, www.cantwelllodgeak.com) houses a café, saloon, liquor store, laundry, showers, and Wi-Fi.

Also two miles from Parks Highway, **Blue Home B&B** (Caribou Ave., 907/768-2020, www.cantwell-bluehome.de, $130 d) has two spotless guest rooms that share a bath, full breakfasts, and Wi-Fi. The owners also speak German.

Bluesberry Inn (Mile 210 Parks Hwy., 907/768-2415, www.bluesberryinn.com, May-Nov., $75 d shared bath, $95-120 d private bath) provides reasonably priced—but very rustic—accommodations. There are dry cabins (they have electricity and heat, but no water) with a shared bathhouse and guest rooms with a double bed and private bath. Most units (except the dry cabins) have TV and Wi-Fi, and hostel-style bunks ($40 pp) may be available.

Backwoods Lodge (0.25 miles up Denali Hwy., 907/768-2231 or 800/292-2232, www.

© DON PITCHER

Denali Sightseeing Safaris operate from this igloo building south of Cantwell.

DENALI NATIONAL PARK

backwoodslodge.com, motel rooms $140-150 d, cabins $110-120 d) has clean, modern motel rooms with fridges, microwaves, TV, and Wi-Fi, and a pair of cabins. Motel rooms contain private baths, but the cabin guests use showers in the lodge.

Park RVs at **Cantwell RV Park** (an open lot near the junction with the Parks Hwy., 907/768-2210 or 800/940-2210, www.alaskaone.com/cantwellrv, mid-May-mid-Sept., tents $19, RVs $28-33). Services include Wi-Fi, showers, laundry, and a dump station.

EAST ON THE DENALI HIGHWAY

About three miles east of the Denali Highway-Parks Highway junction is a turnout with a view of Cantwell and Mount McKinley, if it's out. There's another potential view of the mountain at Mile 13, then in another five miles the highway runs parallel to the Nenana River. The headwaters of the Nenana emanate from a western digit of the ice fields atop the Alaska Range trio of peaks: **Mount Deborah** on the left at 12,339 feet, **Mount Hess** in the middle at 11,940 feet, and **Mount Hayes** on the right at 13,832 feet.

Over the next 10 miles the road crosses Lily Creek, Seattle Creek, and Stixkwan Creek; throw in a line and pull up some grayling or Dolly Varden. At Mile 31 you come to the **Brushkana River,** where the Bureau of Land Management (BLM) has a good free campground right on the river, and over the next 10 miles you get some great views of the three prominent peaks, along with the West Fork Glacier. The southern glaciers off Deborah, Hess, and Hayes feed the Susitna River, which flows west to the Parks Highway, and then south to empty into Cook Inlet across from Anchorage.

Gracious House Lodge and Beyond

Fifty-four miles east of the junction of the

Parks and Denali Highways is **Gracious House Lodge** (Mile 82 Denali Hwy., 907/333-3148, www.alaskaone.com/gracious, June-mid-Sept., guest rooms $135 d private bath; basic rooms $80 s, $105 d with access to showers; RVs $25, tents $15), a friendly mom-and-pop place where welcoming owners Butch and Carol Gratias have run things for more than 55 years. Guest rooms in the lodge are homey and clean and come with a private bath and light breakfast. Simple sleeping rooms come with access to the shower house. Park RVs or pitch a tent; both include showers. The owners can set up air-taxi and guide services, and provide minor tire and mechanical repairs or towing. Phone service into the lodge is via satellite phone, so it's generally best to make reservations through the email listed on their website. The lodge does, however, provide free Wi-Fi.

Five miles farther, you cross the single-lane 1,000-foot-long Susitna River bridge. Farther south, the Susitna is a popular river to float, but passage between here and there is considered impossible because of the impassable Devil's Canyon just downriver from the bridge.

Alpine Creek Lodge (Mile 68 Denali Hwy., 907/743-0565, www.alpinecreeklodge.com, lodge rooms $75 pp shared bath, suites $199 d private bath) has a beautiful setting for wilderness accommodations. Owners Claude and Jennifer Bondy operate this year-round place with reasonably priced lodging. There are 10 lodge rooms with bunk beds and a shared bath, as well as suites with private baths. Nearby are three small cabins ($30 pp for the two smaller cabins; $99 d for larger cabin, add $25 for extra guests) with woodstoves; guests use the bath in the lodge. The largest cabin sleeps up to six. A full breakfast is included in all rates, and hearty lunches and dinners are available. Summertime ATV tours are offered, along with fishing, hiking, and berry picking. In winter—when the lodge is only accessible by snowmobile—northern lights are the big attraction.

At Mile 79, the highway crosses Clearwater Creek; there are pit toilets at a rest stop and camping area here. In six miles is a turnout with a view of numerous lakes and ponds that provide a staging area for waterfowl; look for ducks, cranes, geese, trumpeter swans, and migrating shorebirds.

Maclaren

At Mile 93 out of Cantwell, the road crosses the Maclaren River, a tributary of the Susitna, flowing from the southern ice fields of mighty Mount Hayes. From here to the other end of the Denali Highway, you get occasional views of the three Alaska Range peaks. A mile west of the bridge is Maclaren River Road, which leads 12 miles north to Maclaren Glacier.

Just before the bridge crossing is **Maclaren River Lodge** (Mile 42 Denali Hwy., 907/822-5444, www.maclarenlodge.com, Feb.-Oct.), catering to hikers, hunters, anglers, and sightseers in the summer, and wintertime snowmobilers and dog teams. You can stay overnight in a duplex lodge ($150 for up to five people) with private baths, or in a separate lakeside cabin ($100 d) with a bathhouse. Other options include a pair of basic cabins with bunks ($25 pp), plus old Atco units ($60 d). The lodge has a relaxation area with satellite TV and Wi-Fi. A full-service restaurant (daily 7am-9pm, $10-30) serves burgers, steaks, seafood, and vegetarian specials, and the small bar has beer and wine. All sorts of day trips into the backcountry are offered. Especially popular are the jetboat trip to Maclaren Glacier ($65 pp), where you can camp near the glacier and then canoe back to the lodge.

In another seven miles is Maclaren Summit, at 4,080 feet the second-highest road pass in Alaska. It provides breathtaking views of Mount Hayes and the Maclaren Glacier. Peer through binoculars at the plains below to spot wildlife. Up at the summit you might see rock ptarmigan.

East End

The BLM's **Tangle Lakes Campground** (Mile 113, 907/822-3217, www.blm.gov/ak, free) has water pumps, pit toilets, blueberries in season, and a boat launch for extended canoe trips into the "tangle" (or maze) of lakes and ponds and creeks in the neighborhood.

One mile east of Tangle Lakes Campground is **Tangle River Inn** (Mile 114 Denali Hwy., 907/822-3970 summer or 907/892-4022 winter, www.tangleriverinn.com, mid-May-Sept.). Jack and Naidine Johnson have owned this classic Alaskan lodge since 1970; there's even a mountain named for Naidine nearby! The Johnsons sell gas, liquor, and gifts, and they offer good home cooking three meals a day (daily 7:30am-9pm), a lively bar with pool and foosball tables, simple lodging ($75 d shared bath, $100-150 d private bath), canoe rentals, and fishing gear.

The **Tangle Lakes Archaeological District** begins at Mile 119 and extends back to Crazy Notch at Mile 90. A short hike from the highway to any given promontory along this 30-mile stretch could have you standing at an ancient Athabascan hunting camp where no human footprints have been made for hundreds of years.

At Mile 122, there's a viewpoint from the summit that looks south over a great tundra plain. The three most prominent peaks of the Wrangell Mountains are visible from here: Mount Sanford on the left, Mount Drum on the right, and Mount Wrangell in the middle.

At Mile 125 is a paved turnout with a view of **Ten Mile Lake.** A short trail leads down to the lake, where you can catch trout. A turnout at Mile 129 tacular view of the Alaska Rang The Gulkana and Gakona Glacie from this point. The Denali High..ay joins the Richardson Highway at Paxson.

Paxson

This tiny settlement at Mile 186 of the Richardson Highway and Mile 136 (from Cantwell) of the Denali Highway has two lodging options. **Paxson Lodge** (Mile 185.5 Richardson Hwy., 907/822-3330, www.paxson-lodge.com, $80 s, $100 d) offers gas, meals (daily 7am-9pm), and lodging, in rustic but clean rooms. There's a big deck for summertime dining three meals a day, a liquor store and bar, plus limited Wi-Fi.

Located just north of the highway junction, **Paxson Alpine Tours** (Mile 185.6 Richardson Hwy., 907/822-5972, www.denalihwy.com), guides birding hikes and rents bikes and kayaks. Owners Dr. Audie Bakewell and Jenny Rodina also operate **Denali Highway Cabins** ($160-200 d), with peaceful riverside cabins containing private baths, including a communal kitchen. Interested in glamping? Stay in one of the deluxe wall tents on riverside platforms ($160 d). A large guesthouse ($185 d, add $25 pp for extra guests; three-night minimum) with a full kitchen is also available. Guests have a continental breakfast basket delivered each morning, and guests have access to mountain bikes and the great room with a grand piano, games, and Wi-Fi.

Denali National Park and Preserve

Alaska's most famous tourist attraction, Denali National Park (907/683-2294, www.nps.gov/dena) draws over 400,000 visitors during its brief summer season. Most travelers come to see Mount McKinley, highest peak in North America (20,320 ft.), which towers above the surrounding lowlands and 14,000-17,000-foot peaks. Although it's visible only one day in three, and often shrouded for a week or more at a time, those who get lucky and see mountain experience a thrill equivalent to its majesty and grandeur. Those who don't are usually consoled by lower snowcapped mountains and attending glaciers, high passes and adrenaline-pumping drops off the road, tundra vistas and "drunken forests," and an incredible abundance of wildlife, including caribou, moose, sheep, and bears. But even if the mountain is socked in, the grizzlies are hiding, and the shuttle-bus windows are fogged up, you're still smack in the middle of some of the most spectacular and accessible wilderness in the world. It was the call of the wild that brought you out here in the first place; all you have to do is step outside and answer.

THE LAND

The Alaska Range is a U-shaped chain that extends roughly 600 miles from the top of the Alaska Peninsula (at the head of the Aleutians) up through the park and down below Tok. It's only a small part, however, of the coastal mountains that include California's Sierra Nevada, the Northwest's Cascades, the Coast Mountains of British Columbia, Yukon's St. Elias Range, and eastern Alaska's Wrangell Range. The Park Road starts out a bit north of the Alaska Range and follows the U 90 miles southwest toward its heart—Mount McKinley. One thing that makes the mountain so spectacular is that the surrounding lowlands are so low: The entrance is at 1,700 feet, and the highest point on the road, Thoroughfare Pass, is just under 4,000 feet. The base of Mount McKinley is at 2,000 feet, and the north face rises at a 60-degree angle straight up to 20,000 feet—the highest vertical rise in the world.

Weather patterns here differ between the south side of the range (wetter and cooler) and the north. During the summer, the prevailing winds come from the south, carrying warm moisture from the Pacific. When they run smack into the icy rock wall of the Alaska Range, they climb, the moisture condenses,

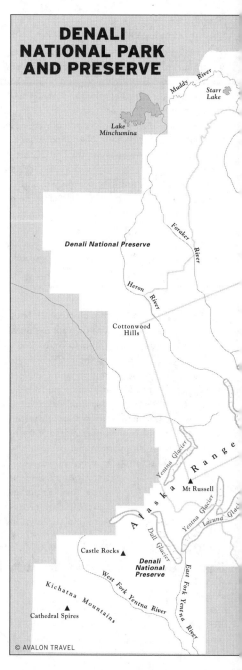

DENALI NATIONAL PARK

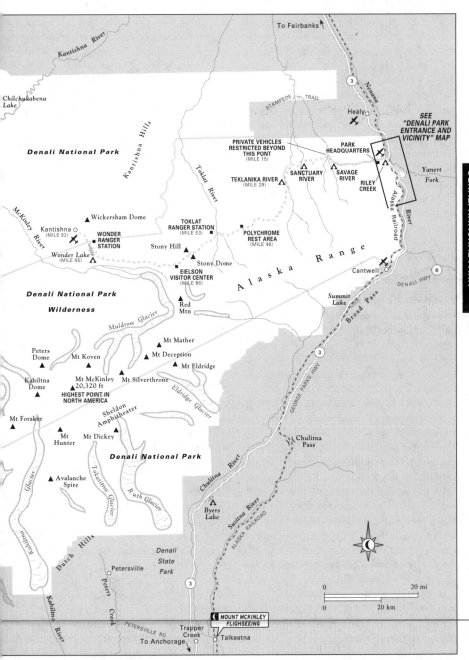

To Fairbanks

Kantishna River

Chilchukabena Lake

Denali National Park

Kantishna Hills

STAMPEDE TRAIL

Healy

SEE "DENALI PARK ENTRANCE AND VICINITY" MAP

PRIVATE VEHICLES RESTRICTED BEYOND THIS POINT (MILE 15)

PARK HEADQUARTERS

Toklat River

SANCTUARY RIVER

SAVAGE RIVER

RILEY CREEK

Yanert Fork

Nenana River

TEKLANIKA RIVER (MILE 29)

Wickersham Dome

Kantishna (MILE 92)

McKinley River

WONDER RANGER STATION

TOKLAT RANGER STATION (MILE 53)

POLYCHROME REST AREA (MILE 46)

Stony Hill

Wonder Lake (MILE 85)

Stony Dome

EIELSON VISITOR CENTER (MILE 66)

Alaska Range

Alaska Railroad

Cantwell

DENALI HWY

8

Denali National Park Wilderness

Muldrow Glacier

Red Mtn

Summit Lake

Broad Pass

Mt Mather

Mt Deception

Mt Koven

Mt Eldridge

Peters Dome

GEORGE PARKS HWY

3

Kahiltna Dome

Mt McKinley 20,320 ft HIGHEST POINT IN NORTH AMERICA

Mt Silverthrone

Eldridge Glacier

Mt Foraker

Sheldon Amphitheater

Chulitna Pass

Mt Hunter

Mt Dickey

Denali National Park

Chulitna River

Avalanche Spire

Tokositna Glacier

Ruth Glacier

Susitna River

ALASKA RAILROAD

Glacier

Byers Lake

Dutch Hills

Denali State Park

Kahiltna River

Petersville

Peters Creek

3

20 mi

20 km

PETERSVILLE RD

Trapper Creek

To Anchorage

MOUNT McKINLEY FLIGHSEEING

Talkeetna

DENALI NATIONAL PARK

and depending on the amount of moisture and altitude, it either rains or snows—a lot. On top of that whole system sits mighty Mount McKinley, high, cold, and alone; it's so alone that the mountain has its own relationship to the weather. The combination of wind, wet, cold, and height creates extremely localized— and often violent—weather around Mount McKinley. Storms can blow in within an hour and last a week or more, dumping 10 feet of snow. Winds scream in at up to 80 mph. The mercury drops below zero in mid-July. Some of the worst weather in the world swirls around up there. But when the mountain emerges bright white against bright blue, and you're craning your neck to see the top, it's an unforgettable sight worth waiting around for—even in the rain.

Flora and Fauna

From sea level to around 2,300 feet is the habitat for the **boreal forest,** in which the black spruce, with its somber foliage and clusters of tawny cones, is the climax tree. Younger white spruce, along with deciduous aspen, birch, and cottonwood, grow near the streams and the road and in recently burned areas.

Climbing out of the forest above 2,300 feet you enter the **taiga,** a Russian word meaning "land of twigs." This transition zone (between the forest below and tundra above) accommodates no deciduous trees; the spruce are thinned out and runty (though they can be over 60 years old), and a green shag carpet of bush, mostly dwarf willow, layers the floor. Sitka spruce is the state tree because of its size, grandeur, and commercial value, but it's the willow that vegetates Alaska. And it has endless uses: Before synthetics like nylon, the willow bark was stripped, split, and braided and made into rope, bows, wicker baskets, snowshoes, fishnets, and small game and bird snares and traps. The inner bark is sweet; the sap is very sweet. Young buds and shoots are edible and

nourishing, and willows are the nearly exclusive staple of the moose diet. The taiga also hosts a variety of berries: blueberries and low-bush cranberries by the ton, crowberries, bearberries, soap and salmon berries, and raspberries.

Above 2,500 feet is the **tundra,** its name a Lapp word meaning "vast, rolling, treeless plain." There are two types of tundra: The moist, or Alaskan, tundra is characterized by the taiga's dwarf shrubbery, high grasses, and berries, but no trees; the alpine tundra, the highest zone, has grasses, moss, lichens, and small hardy wildflowers, including the stunning forget-me-not, Alaska's state flower.

The animal life varies with the vegetation. In the forest, look for moose, porcupine, snowshoe hare, marten, lynx, two kinds of weasels, red or tree squirrels, and several varieties of small rodents. On the taiga—or in both the forest and the tundra—you might see coyotes, wolves, foxes, grizzlies, and ground squirrels. In the tundra, keep an eye out for caribou, wolverines, Dall sheep, marmots, voles, lemmings, and shrews.

HISTORY

In 1896 a prospector named Bill Dickey was tramping around Interior Alaska looking for gold. Like everyone who sees it, Dickey was captivated by the size and magnificence of the mountain that was then variously known as Tenada, Denali, Densmore's Mountain, Traleika, and Bulshaia. Dickey was from Ohio, William McKinley's home state, and a Princeton graduate in economics. When he came out of the bush and heard that McKinley had been nominated for president, he promptly renamed the mountain "McKinley," wrote numerous articles for stateside magazines, and lobbied in Washington, D.C., in support of adoption of the name, which finally caught on after President McKinley was assassinated in 1901. The name has been something of a sore point with Alaskans ever

Dall sheep

since, for McKinley had absolutely nothing to do with the mountain, and the more lyrical Native Alaskan names were completely ignored. Many in Alaska support renaming the peak Denali ("the high one"), a term used by Native Alaskans of the lower Yukon and Kuskokwim Rivers. Unfortunately, any move to eliminate "McKinley" from maps is inevitably met by howls of protest from Ohio's congressional delegation.

Creating a Park

Harry Karstens reached the Klondike in 1898 when he was 19, bored by Chicago and attracted by adventure and gold. Within a year he'd crossed over into U.S. territory and wound up at Seventymile, 20 miles south of Eagle. When the local mail carrier lost everything one night in a card game and committed suicide, Karstens took his place. He became proficient at dog mushing and trailblazing and within a few years was delivering mail on a primitive trail between Eagle and Valdez, a 900-mile round-trip every month (the Richardson Highway follows the same route). Later he moved on to Fairbanks and began delivering mail to Kantishna, the mining town on what is now the west end of the park, growing very fond of and familiar with the north side of the Alaska Range. So when a naturalist from the East Coast, Charles Sheldon, arrived in 1906 to study Dall sheep in the area, Karstens guided him around Mount McKinley's northern foothills, delineating the habitat of the sheep. Karstens was also the co-leader of the four-man expedition that was the first party to successfully climb the true peak of Mount McKinley, the south summit, in 1913.

Meanwhile, Charles Sheldon was back in Washington, lobbying for national-park status for the Dall sheep habitat, and when Mount McKinley National Park was created in 1917, Karstens was the obvious choice to become the first park superintendent. He held that post in 1921-1928, patrolling the park boundaries by dogsled.

Woodrow Wilson signed the bill that created Mount McKinley National Park, Alaska's first, in 1917. The Park Road, begun five years later, was completed to Kantishna in 1940. In 1980, with the passage of the Alaska National Interest Lands Conservation Act, McKinley Park was renamed Denali National Park and Preserve and expanded to nearly six million acres, roughly the size of Vermont.

Pioneer Climbs

Many pioneers and prospectors had seen the mountain and approached it, but Alfred Brooks, a member of the first U.S. Geological Survey expedition in Alaska in 1902, was the first to set foot on it. He approached it from the south and reached an elevation of 7,500 feet before running out of time. He published an article in the January 1903 issue of *National Geographic* in which he recommended approaching the mountain from the north. Following that suggestion, the next attempt was from the north, led by James Wickersham, U.S. district judge for Alaska. Judge Wickersham was sent from Seattle to bring law and order to Eagle in 1900; he moved to Fairbanks in 1903. That summer, he had a spare couple of months and set out to climb the mountain, traveling more than 100 miles overland and reaching the 7,000-foot level of the north face, later named Wickersham Wall in honor of His Honor.

That same summer, Dr. Frederick Cook, who'd been with Peary's first party to attempt to reach the north pole in 1891 and Amundsen's Antarctic expedition of 1897, also attempted to climb the mountain from the north and reached 11,300 feet. In 1906, Cook returned to attempt Mount McKinley from the south, but he failed to get near it. His party broke up and went their separate directions, and a month later, Cook sent a telegram

to New York claiming he'd reached the peak. This was immediately doubted by the members of his party, who challenged his photographic and cartographic "evidence." But through public lectures and articles, Cook's reputation as the first man to reach the peak grew. Two years later, he claimed to have reached the North Pole several months ahead of another Peary expedition, and Cook began to enjoy a cult status in the public consciousness. Simultaneously, however, his credibility among fellow explorers rapidly declined, and Cook vanished from sight. This further fueled the controversy and led to the Sourdough Expedition of 1910.

Four sourdoughs in Fairbanks simply decided to climb the mountain to validate or eviscerate Cook's published description of his route. They left town in December and climbed to the north peak in early April. The three members who'd actually reached the peak stayed in Kantishna to take care of business, while the fourth member, Tom Lloyd, who hadn't reached the peak, returned to Fairbanks and lied that he had. By the time the other three returned to town in June, Lloyd's story had already been published and widely discredited. So nobody believed the other three—*especially* when they claimed they'd climbed up to the north peak and down to their base camp at 11,000 feet in 18 hours, with a thermos of hot chocolate, four doughnuts, and dragging a 14-foot spruce log that they planted up top and claimed was still there. Finally, in 1913, the Hudson Stuck-Harry Karstens expedition reached the true summit, the south peak, and could prove that they'd done so beyond a shadow of a doubt. Only then was the Sourdough Expedition vindicated: All four members of the Stuck party saw the spruce pole still standing on the north peak!

Today more than 1,000 mountaineers attempt the summit of Mount McKinley each year, and approximately half of them actually reach the top. The youngest climbers ever to summit, a girl and a boy, were 12; the oldest man was 71, and the oldest woman 62.

PARK ENTRANCE

Pay the park admission ($10 pp) or buy a National Park Pass ($40 per year)—good for all national parks. A Senior Pass ($10) for all national parks is available to anyone over age 62 for a one-time fee, and people with disabilities can get a free Access Pass that covers all the parks. Get additional park information (907/683-2294, www.nps.gov/dena) by phone or online.

Planning Your Time

Denali National Park is open year-round, though most facilities only operate mid-May through mid-September. Plowing of the Park Road generally starts in early May, but only the first 30 miles are open before late May, when the shuttle buses begin running. Th arrive before this date will not be able the best vantage points for Mount McKinley.

The wildflowers peak around summer solstice—as do the mosquitoes. The berries, rose hips, and mushrooms are best in mid-August—as are the no-see-ums. The fall colors on the tundra are gorgeous around Labor Day weekend, when the crowds start to thin out and the northern lights start to appear, but it can get very cold. A skeleton winter Park Service crew patrols the park by dogsled. After the first heavy snowfall, the Park Road is plowed only to headquarters.

Visitor Centers

The **Denali Visitor Center** (Mile 1.2 Park Rd., daily 8am-6pm mid-May-mid-Sept.) is right across from the railroad depot. Step inside to explore the exhibits, get oriented from

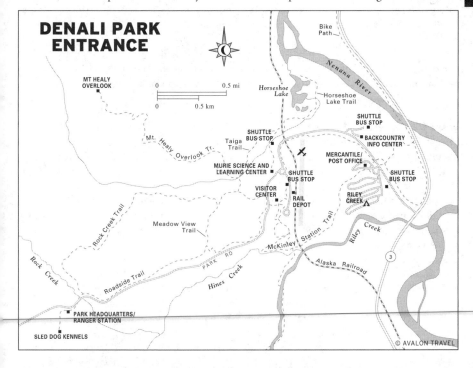

© AVALON TRAVEL

the enormous relief map of the park, talk with the rangers, and view an extraordinary 20-minute film, *Heartbeats of Denali.* Pick up a copy of *Denali Alpenglow,* the park newspaper, and check the bulletin board for a schedule of today's guided walks, talks, and kids' programs. Adjacent are an Alaska Natural History Association gift shop and Morino Grill, serving sandwiches, burgers, fish and chips, and pizzas.

On the other side of the traffic circle, the **Murie Science and Learning Center** (907/683-1269 or 888/688-1269, www.murieslc.org) promotes scientific research and education through youth camps, field seminars, and courses in the summer. In the off-season—when other facilities are closed—the Murie building becomes the **winter park visitor center** (daily 9am-4pm winter). Check out the dinosaur track here that was found in the park.

Get park shuttle bus tickets and campground information at the **Wilderness Access Center** (daily 5am-8pm mid-May to mid-Sept.), located a half-mile up the Park Road. The reservations desk opens at 7am. While here you could also watch an 18-minute film about the park or buy snacks. This facility is run by the park concessionaire, Aramark.

Sled Dog Demonstrations

One of the highlights of the park is the sled dog demonstration (daily 10am, 2pm, and 4pm in peak season) at the kennels behind headquarters. The dogs are beautiful and accessible (the ones not behind fences are chosen for friendliness and patience with people), and the anxious collective howl they orchestrate when the lucky six dogs are selected to run is something to hear. Naturalists give a talk about the current and historical uses of dogs in the park, their breeding and training, different commands for controlling them, and the challenge of maintaining a working kennel in a national park. Then dogs are hitched up to a wheel sled and run around a gravel track. The enthusiasm of the dogs to

get off the chain and into the harness is an eyebrow-raising glimpse into the consciousness of Alaskan sled dogs—they live to run.

A free shuttle bus leaves the Denali Visitor Center and the Riley Creek bus shelter 40 minutes before the demonstrations. Don't miss this one!

GETTING AROUND DENALI

In 1971, before the George Parks Highway connected McKinley National Park to Fairbanks (125 miles) and Anchorage (245 miles), you had to take the train, or from Fairbanks you had to drive down to Delta Junction, take the Richardson Highway to Paxson, the Denali Highway to Cantwell, then the Parks Highway up to the park entrance, for a grand total of 340 miles. From Anchorage you had to drive to Glennallen, then up the Richardson to Paxson, over to Cantwell and beyond, for 440 miles. That year, nearly 45,000 visitors passed through the park. In 1972, when the George Parks Highway radically reduced driving times from both main urban centers, almost 90,000 visitors came. In anticipation of the huge jump in tourism, the Park Service initiated the shuttle system of school buses running a regularly scheduled service along the Park Road. Today, the park sees 400,000 visitors annually.

◖ Denali Shuttle Bus Tours

There's no question that the shuttle system is highly beneficial to the park experience: The road is tricky and dangerous, crowds are much more easily controlled, there's much less impact on the wildlife (which take the buses for granted), and it's much easier to see wildlife when 40 passengers have eyeballs, binoculars, spotting scopes, and telephotos trained on the tundra. The excellent *Denali Road Guide,* available in park bookstores, has detailed information on sights along the road.

Green buses (daily mid-May-mid-Sept.) depart from the Wilderness Access Center, with some continuing all the way to the Kantishna, an exhausting 89-mile 13-hour round-trip ride. Most visitors don't go that far (or certainly not in one day), turning around instead at Polychrome Pass, Eielson, Wonder Lake, or other places along the way. Buses for Eielson begin departing from the Wilderness Access Center at 5am and continue roughly every 30 minutes through 3:30pm. Other buses depart during the day for Polychrome/Toklat and Wonder Lake.

You can reserve tickets in advance (907/272-7275 or 800/622-7275, www.reservedenali. com), starting in mid-February over the phone or on December 1 online, and up to the day before you travel. Sixty-five percent of the available tickets go on sale December 1; the other 35 percent are made available just two days ahead of the travel date. Adults pay $27 to Polychrome/Toklat (6 hours round-trip), $34 to Eielson (8 hours round-trip), $46 to Wonder Lake (11 hours round-trip), and $50 to Kantishna (12 hours round-trip). Kids under 15 ride free, and fares are half the adult price for children ages 15-17. Fares do not include park entrance fees ($10). Wheelchair-accessible shuttle buses are available. Backpackers pay $34 round-trip to anywhere in the park on the special **camper bus.**

It's recommended that you try to get on an early-morning bus into the park: There is a better chance to see wildlife and the mountain in the cool of the morning, and more time to get off the bus and fool around in the backcountry.

Schedules are readily available at the visitor centers and hotels. Take everything you need, as nothing (except books and postcards) is for sale once you get into the park. You can get off the bus and flag it down to get back on (if there's room; the buses leave with a few seats empty to pick up day-hikers in the park) anywhere along the road. Many riders never get off the bus at all and just stay on it for the entire exhausting round-trip.

Local Shuttles

A **Riley Creek Loop Bus** (5am-7pm mid-May-mid-Sept., free) provides service connecting the Riley Creek Campground, Wilderness Access Center, and train depot every half hour. In addition, a free bus connects the Wilderness Access Center with the dogsled demonstrations at park headquarters, and the free **Savage River Shuttle** provides service as far as Savage River Bridge at mile 15.

Private shuttle buses ($1-5) run among the train depot, Wilderness Access Center, and the larger hotels, including Denali Bluffs Hotel, Grande Denali Lodge, McKinley Village Lodge, McKinley Chalet Resort, and Denali Princess Lodge. **Denali Salmon Bake** (www. denaliparksalmonbake.com, $1 each way, $2 to the Wilderness Access Center) provides a 24-hour shuttle that operates every 1.5 hours, stopping at the Wilderness Access Center, train depot, Denali Park/Canyon hotels and restaurants, and Healy businesses. The shuttle also stops at Riley Creek Campground upon request (call 907/683-2733 for a campground pickup).

Tour Buses

The park's **tan nature tour buses** (907/272-7275 or 800/622-7275, www.reservedenali. com) leave from the Wilderness Access Center throughout the day. For a good introduction, take a five-hour **Denali Natural History Tour** ($67 adults, $33 under age 15) to Primrose Ridge (17 miles each way), or for a better look, join the seven-hour **Tundra Wilderness Tour** ($113 adults, $57 under age 15, includes a box lunch) to Toklat, a distance of 53 miles each way. A shorter **Teklanika Tundra Wilderness Tour** ($74 adults, $37 kids) to Mile 30 may be offered in mid-May and mid-September if snow prevents access farther out the Park Road. **Kantishna Experience** ($159 adults, $80 under age 15, includes lunch) is a 12-hour tour that focuses both on wildlife and the history of this old gold mining town. All these tours are extremely popular, and fill up fast, so you need to make your reservations as far in advance as possible.

Kantishna Wilderness Trails (907/683-8002 or 800/230-7275, www.denaliwildlifetour.com, $169 pp) provides private all-day bus tours that leave Denali Park hotels at 6:30am. These take you to Kantishna Roadhouse near the end of the road for a lunch, gold panning, and sled dog demonstration before heading back out, arriving at the hotels by 8pm.

Denali Backcountry Adventure (866/900-1992, www.alaskadenalitours.com, $169 pp) provides all-day bus tours to Denali Backcountry Lodge in Kantishna. These 13-hour trips include lunch. Make it a fly/drive trip by flying back out on Kantishna Air (an additional $150).

Driving

For most of the summer, only the first 15 miles (to Savage River) of the Park Road are open to private vehicles. This portion is paved and makes for an excellent day trip. From early May, when the road is plowed, to late May, when the shuttle buses start running, it is possible to drive as far as the Teklanika River rest area at Mile 30. The road beyond this doesn't open until late May, so early park arrivals will not be able to see many of the sights for which it is famous.

At the end of summer, the Park Road is opened to auto traffic for four days in mid-September. Only 400 vehicles are allowed per day, and passes are selected by a lottery. In a typical year, you may be competing with 10,000 other entries for these passes! You'll need to apply during June; contact the **Park Service** (907/683-2294, www.nps.gov/dena) for details.

A handful of professional photographers are allowed vehicular access to the park during the summer, but these slots are highly sought after.

HEADING OUT ON THE PARK ROAD

A few miles beyond headquarters the road climbs out of the boreal forest, levels off, and

travels due west through a good example of taiga. The ridgeline to the north (right) of the road is known as the **Outer Range**, foothills of the massive Alaska Range to the south (left). The Outer Range is much older, of different geological origins, and much more rounded and eroded than the jagged Alaska Range. The first view of the mountain comes up at Mile 9; look southwest. The day has to be nearly perfectly clear to see Mount McKinley from here: You're at around 2,400 feet, and the mountain is at 20,000 feet, which leaves nearly an 18-grand spread over 70-odd miles of potential cloud cover. That's a lot of potential.

Next you pass the Savage River Campground, then wind down to the river valley and cross the bridge that marks the end of road access for those in private vehicles. The "Checkpoint Charlie" kiosk at Mile 15 has a park employee to turn back private vehicles; they're prohibited beyond this point. From the bridge, look upriver (left) and notice the broad, U-shaped, glacial valley with large gravel deposits forming braids or channels, then look right to compare the V-shaped valley obviously cut by running water. The Savage Glacier petered out right where the bridge is now around 15,000 years ago during the last ice age. Here you also kiss the pavement good-bye, then start climbing Primrose Ridge, which offers excellent hiking, especially in June-early July when the wildflowers are in full bloom. Turn around and look back at the Savage Bridge; the stark rock outcropping just up from it has a distinct resemblance to an Indian's facial bone structure, which is how the Savage got its politically incorrect name. Just up the road is a pullout—if the mountain's out, the driver should stop for the clear shot.

Savage River to Igloo Canyon

Mount McKinley disappears behind jagged lower peaks as the road descends into the broad, glacial **Sanctuary River** valley at Mile

23. Watch for moose, caribou, foxes, lynx, waterfowl, and eagles along here. Right on the other side of the Sanctuary is a good view down at a "drunken forest," one effect that permafrost has on the vegetation. Notice how many of the trees are leaning at bizarre and precarious angles, with some of them down entirely. As an adaptation to the permafrost, these spruce trees have evolved a root system that spreads horizontally across the surface soil; there's no taproot to speak of. So the taller a tree grows around here, the less support it maintains, and the more susceptible it is to falling over. When the surface soil becomes saturated (because of lack of absorption over the permafrost), it sometimes shifts, either spontaneously or because of slight tremors (a major fault runs through here), taking the trees with it.

Next you descend into the broad **Teklanika River** valley, with a good view across the river of the three vegetation zones on the mountain slopes: forest, taiga, and tundra. You pass a number of small ponds in this area, known as "kettles," usually formed when a retreating glacier drops off a large block of ice, which melts, leaves a depression, and fills with rainwater. The stagnant water is rich in nutrients and provides excellent hatching grounds for Alaska's famous mosquitoes, and as such the ponds are good feeding spots for ducks and shorebirds. Look for mergansers, goldeneyes, sandpipers, buffleheads, and phalaropes in these ponds. And in some of the higher, smaller, more private kettles, look for hikers and park employees with no clothes on... maybe even join them, if you care to brave the skeeters, which have been known to show up on Park Service radar screens.

Cross the river and enter **Igloo Canyon,** where you turn almost due south. The mountain on the right is Igloo (4,800 ft.); the one on the left is Cathedral (4,905 ft.). Igloo is in the Outer Range, Cathedral in the Alaska Range. At the closest distance between the two ranges,

the canyon is right on the migration route of the Dall sheep and a great place to view them as white dots on the slopes; or climb either mountain to get closer.

Sable Pass (3,900 ft.) is next at Mile 38, the second-highest point on the road. This area is closed to hiking and photography because of the large grizzly population. Keep your eyes peeled. The next good views of the mountain are from these highlands.

Over Polychrome Pass to Eielson

Once you cross the **East Fork River** at Mile 44 (there is great hiking out onto the flats from here), you begin your ascent of Polychrome Pass, one of the most spectacular and fear-inducing sections of the road. If you're scared of heights or become frightened at the 1,000-foot drop-offs, just do what the driver does—close your eyes. These rocks have a high iron content; the rate of oxidation and the combination of the iron with other minerals determine the different shades of rust, orange, red, and purple. Look and listen for hoary marmots in the nearby rocks, and, from here almost the rest of the way to Eielson Visitor Center, watch for caribou and wolves; these are the Murie flats, where wildlife biologist Adolph Murie studied the lifestyle of *Canis lupus.*

Descend to the **Toklat River** at Mile 53, the last and largest you cross before Eielson. This is the terminus of the wildlife tour, but the shuttle buses continue on to Eielson and Wonder Lake. The Toklat's source is the Sunrise Glacier, just around the bend upriver (left). You can see from the size of the river how big the glacier was 20,000 years ago. There is great hiking up into the Alaska Range from here. Next you climb up **Stony Hill** and, if the weather is cooperating, when you crest the ridge you're in for the thrill of a lifetime: Denali, The Great One, in all its immense majestic glory. It's hard to believe that the mountain is still 40 miles away! But wait, you get another five miles closer, crossing

Thorofare Pass (3,950 ft.), the highest elevation on the road, at Mile 62.

🄲 Eielson Visitor Center

Eielson Visitor Center (daily 9am-7pm June-mid-Sept.) is four hours and 66 miles from the park entrance. The view from here—weather cooperating—is unforgettable. Even if you can only see the bottom 12,000-14,000 feet, have a naturalist or your driver point to where the top of Mount McKinley is, and visualize it in your mind's eye. Also, things change fast around here, so keep an eye out for the peak popping out of the clouds as a surprise just for you.

The earth-friendly visitor center at Eielson opened in 2008, featuring exhibits, tall windows facing McKinley, short-term lockers, an outdoor deck, 24-hour bathrooms, and space to enjoy your lunch or relax. Check out the interlocked moose antlers out front; the two bulls died when they sparred and their antlers became locked together.

Naturalists lead 45-minute walks (daily 1pm). The excellent backpacking zones in this area are usually the first to fill up. There's nothing for sale at Eielson, so be sure to bring food and any needed maps or books.

🄲 Wonder Lake

Beyond Eielson, the road comes within 25 miles of the mountain, passing **Muldrow Glacier,** which is covered by a thick black layer of glacial till and vegetation. From Wonder Lake, the **Wickersham Wall** rises magnificently above the intervening plains, with the whole Alaska Range stretching out on each side. In addition, the reflection from the lake doubles your pleasure and doubles your fun, from which even the mosquitoes here, some of the most savage, bloodthirsty, insatiable beasts of the realm, cannot detract.

There's a popular campground at Wonder Lake (Mile 85), and a nearby pond is where those postcard-perfect moose-in-the-lake-with-Mount-McKinley photos are taken. Many buses turn around at Wonder Lake, but a few continue to Kantishna.

Kantishna

The town of Kantishna, 92 miles from the park entrance at the western end of the Park Road, has five roadhouses. The area was first settled in 1905, when several thousand miners rushed to the foothills just north of Mount McKinley to mine gold, silver, lead, zinc, and antimony. After 1980 and the Alaska National Interest Lands Conservation Act, which expanded Denali National Park's boundaries, Kantishna found itself inside the park, and in 1985 mining was halted by court order. The road ends at the last lodge, where buses turn around to return to the park entrance. An air taxi is based here, and most Kantishna lodges have their own shuttle buses and tours.

DAY HIKES

Ranger-led walks are available daily all summer at both the Denali Visitor Center and Eielson Visitor Center. More ambitious are the half-day **Discovery Hikes** ($34 adults, free kids under 15) led by rangers to more remote areas. These include several hours on the bus en route to your starting point; reserve a day or two in advance at the Wilderness Access Center (daily 5am-8pm mid-May to mid-Sept.).

Note: Guns are now legally permitted within Denali National Park, but they aren't allowed on most shuttle and tour buses. Research indicates that hikers carrying guns are more likely to be injured in bear attacks than those who carry pepper-based bear sprays such as Counter Assault. There has only been one fatal bear attack in the park (in 2012), but bears certainly are a potential hazard. Be sure to carry bear spray, and have it accessible.

Entrance Area Hikes

Several paths take off from the Denali Visitor

Mount McKinley vista from Wonder Lake

Center, including two easy ones: the **Spruce Forest Trail** (15 minutes) and a slightly longer **Murie Science and Learning Center Trail** (20 minutes). **Horseshoe Lake Trail** (three miles round-trip) starts at the shuttle bus stop and then descends to the lake, where you might see waterfowl and beavers.

Hiking the five-mile round-trip **Mount Healy Overlook Trail** is a great way to get the lay of the land, see the mountain if it's out, quickly leave the crowds behind, and get your heart pumping. Once at the overlook (one mile in), keep climbing the ridges for another several hours to get to the peak of Mount Healy (5,200 ft.).

The 2.3-mile **Rock Creek Trail** starts near the post office and climbs to park headquarters, gaining 400 feet along the way. You can then loop back along the road via the 1.8-mile **Roadside Trail.** The **Taiga Trail** is an easy 1.3-mile loop that also begins near the post office.

Eielson Hikes

The Eielson Visitor Center at Mile 66 is located in open tundra, with Mount McKinley and other Alaska Range peaks dominating southern vistas. Just downhill from Eielson is the 0.8-miles **Tundra Loop Trail,** a good place to stretch your legs after the four-hour bus ride from the park entrance. Look for wildflowers and arctic ground squirrels along the way. A spur leads to a knoll overlooking the valley, and across the road from Eielson is an even shorter loop path for a quick jaunt before settling back into your bus.

The **Alpine Trail** is considerably more strenuous, climbing steeply up Thorofare Ridge, which looms above Eielson Visitor Center. It's 2.2 miles each way, with a gain of 1,000 feet in elevation as you hike a series of switchbacks and rock steps. Stop along the way to take in the view. The summit (almost 5,000 feet in elevation) is wide and flat with views in all directions. Grizzly bears and caribou are often

DENALI NATIONAL PARK

COEXISTING WITH BEARS

© DON PITCHER

Bears seem to bring out conflicting emotions in people. The first is an almost gut reaction of fear and trepidation: What if the bear attacks me? But then comes that other urge: What will my friends say when they see these *incredible* bear photos? Both of these reactions can lead to problems in bear country. "Bearanoia" is a justifiable fear, but it can easily be taken to such an extreme that one avoids going outdoors at all for fear of running into a bear. The "I want to get close-up shots of that bear and her cubs" attitude can lead to a bear attack. The middle ground incorporates a knowledge of and respect for bears with a sense of caution that keeps you alert for danger without letting fear rule your wilderness travels. Nothing is ever completely safe in this world, but with care you can avoid most of the common pitfalls that lead to bear encounters.

Both brown (grizzly) and black bears occur throughout Southcentral Alaska. Old-timers joke that bears are easy to differentiate: A black bear climbs up the tree after you, while a griz-

zly snaps the tree off at the base. Both grizzlies and black bears pose potential threats to back-country travelers.

Enter bear country with respect but not fear. Bears rarely attack humans; you're a thousand times more likely to be injured in a highway accident than by a bear. In fact, more people in Alaska are hurt each year by moose or dogs than by bears. Contrary to the stories you often hear, bears have good eyesight, but they depend more upon their excellent senses of smell and hearing. A bear can tell who has walked through an area, and how recently, with just a quick sniff of the air. Most bears hear or smell you long before you realize their presence, and they hightail it away.

Bears are beautiful, eminently fascinating, and surprisingly intelligent animals. They can be funny, playful and inquisitive, vicious or protective, and unpredictable. The more you watch bears in the wild, the more complex their lives seem, and the more they become individual animals, not simply the big and bad.

spotted along the way. Return the same way, and plan on two hours round-trip. This hike is one of the popular ranger-led Discovery Hikes offered daily at noon in the summer. Make reservations at Eielson (daily 9am-7pm June-mid-Sept.), but get here early to reserve your place for this memorable hike (maximum of 11 people).

Wonder Lake Hikes

The open country around Wonder Lake Campground provides relatively easy hiking, or walk up the road to Reflection Pond and the outlet to Wonder Lake. The only trail in the area is the **McKinley Bar Trail,** an easy five-mile round-trip hike from the campground. The trail passes through open country with small ponds, bogs, and creeks before cutting through spruce forests to the McKinley River. The braided river changes channels constantly, with easy hiking opportunities on the open mile-wide river bar with Denali providing a magnificent backdrop. Do not attempt to cross this large glacier-fed river with deep, fast-flowing water. The area is plagued by mosquitos much of the summer, so bring a head net and bug dope.

Guided Hikes

Denali Backcountry Guides (907/683-4453, www.walkdenali.com, mid-May-mid-Sept.) offers two unique ways to explore the country just outside the park. Seven-hour pack rafting trips ($199 pp) are tailored to your abilities, providing time on a local river plus hiking; cost includes dry suits and transport. Also popular are four-hour heli-hiking wildlife walks ($475 pp) that include a helicopter flight to the high country followed by a hike. The company also leads three-hour natural history walks ($109 pp) in the Healy area for cruise ship folks.

BACKCOUNTRY TRIPS

For details on backcountry hikes and camping, head to the **Backcountry Information Center**

(across the parking lot from the Access Center, 907/683-9510, daily May 20-Sept. 20).

Popular backpacking areas includ₍ ᵤp the Savage River toward Fang Mountain; down the far side of Cathedral Mountain toward Calico Creek (get off the bus just before the Sable Pass closure); up Tatler Creek a little past Igloo Mountain; anywhere on the East Fork flats below Polychrome toward the Alaska Range; anywhere around Stony Hill; and the circumnavigation of Mount Eielson (get off 5-6 miles past the visitor center, cross the 100 braids of the Thorofare River, and walk around the mountain, coming back up to the visitor center). There are backcountry description guides at the backcountry desk, or you can find the same info online, with photos.

On all these hikes, you can get off the outbound bus, explore to your heart's content, then get back on an inbound bus, if space is available. Consult with the driver and study the bus schedule closely; the camper buses may have space coming back.

Large as it is, it's hard to get lost in Denali—you're either north or south of the road. And since the road travels mostly through open alpine tundra, there aren't any artificial trails to follow—just pick a direction and go. Usually you'll want to make for higher ground in order to get out of the knee- to hip-high dwarf shrubbery of the moist tundra and onto the easy hiking of the alpine area, get to where the breeze will keep the skeeters at bay, and see more. Or walk along the river gravel bars into the mountains, although depending on the size of the gravel, it can be ankle-twisting. Hiking boots are a must, and carry food, water, a compass, binoculars, maps, rain gear, and a bear-proof food canister. Keep your eyes and ears wide open for wildlife that you don't want to get close to, sneak up on, or be surprised by.

© DON PITCHER

ranger giving a talk at Wonder Lake

Backcountry Permits

You need a free permit to spend the night in the backcountry. Permits are issued 24 hours in advance from the Backcountry Information Center, and reservations are not accepted. Check the big maps and look over descriptions of the 43 units, where a limited number of backpackers are allowed. (The same information can be found online at www.nps.gov/dena to help you plan prior to your trip.) Now check the board to find the vacancies in the units. Make sure the unit is open (some are always closed; others periodically close because of overcrowding or bears) and that there are enough vacancies to accommodate your whole party. Watch the 30-minute backcountry video that describes bear safety, river crossings, minimum-impact camping, emergencies, and other topics; listen to a 10-minute safety talk; and finally get a permit from the ranger. You might have to wait a few days for openings in your chosen area, or have a plan B or C in mind. The park loans out free bear-proof food storage containers; be sure to get one for your hike. Finally, reserve a seat on one of the camper buses ($33) to get you and your gear into the park.

OTHER RECREATION
Mountain Biking

An excellent way to explore Denali at your own pace is by mountain bike. Bikes are allowed on the Park Road, and can be transported aboard the camper shuttle bus, but be sure to mention the bike when you make a reservation. Note that only camper buses carry bikes and that they only carry two at a time, so it is possible to get far out on the Park Road and then find yourself unable to catch a bus back. Be sure to pick up a "rules of the road" handout at the visitor center before heading out.

Denali Outdoor Center (907/683-1925 or 888/303-1925, www.denalioutdoorcenter.com, bike rental: $25/half-day, $40 for 24 hours) has mountain bike rentals and tours. Two-hour

PROTECTING YOURSELF DURING A BEAR ENCOUNTER

If you happen to encounter a bear, stay calm and don't make any sudden moves. Do not run: Bears can exceed 40 miles per hour for short distances. Don't climb a tree, as it may actually incite an attack. Instead, make yourself visible by moving into the open so the bear will identify you as a human and not something to eat. Never stare directly at a bear. Dropping an item such as a hat or jacket may distract the bear, and talking calmly also seems to have some value in convincing bears that you're a human. If the bear sniffs the air or stands on its hind legs, it is probably trying to identify you. When it does, it will usually run away. If a bear woofs and postures, don't imitate—this is a challenge. Keep retreating. Most bear charges are also bluffs; the bear will often stop short and amble off.

If a **grizzly bear** attacks, freeze. It may well be a bluff charge, with the bear halting at the last second. If the bear does not stop its attack, use bear spray immediately. If the bear is going to make contact, curl up facedown on the ground in a fetal position with your hands wrapped behind your neck and your elbows tucked over your face. Your backpack may help protect you. Remain still even if you are attacked, because sudden movements may incite further attacks. Often a bear will only sniff or nip you and leave. The injury you might sustain would be far less than if you tried to resist. After the attack, prevent further attacks by staying down on the ground until the grizzly has left the area. Do not play dead if the bear is at a distance or is leaving the area.

Bear authorities recommend against dropping to the ground if you are attacked by a **black bear**, because they tend to be more aggressive in such situations and are more likely to prey on humans. If a black bear attacks, use bear spray immediately. If you don't have the spray, fight back with whatever weapons are at hand; large rocks and branches can be effective deterrents, as can yelling and shouting. Aim for sensitive areas such as the bear's eyes or nose. Have a park ranger explain the difference between brown and black bears before you head into the backcountry.

Nighttime bear attacks could happen to even the most seasoned adventurer. In the rare event of a night attack in your tent, defend yourself *very* aggressively. Never play dead under such circumstances. Before going to bed, try to plan escape routes, and be sure to have a flashlight and pepper spray handy. Keeping your sleeping bag partly unzipped also allows the chance to escape should a bear attempt to drag you away. There are advantages to having multiple tents in case one person is attacked, and if someone is attacked in a tent near you, yelling and throwing rocks or sticks may drive the bear away.

A relatively recent development for campers in bear country is the use of portable **electric fences** made by Electro Bear Guard (907/562-2331, www.electrobearguard.com) to surround your campsite; a backpacker unit runs on two AA batteries, weighs just 2.5 pounds, and costs $395.

Cayenne pepper sprays ($35-50) such as Counter Assault (800/695-3394, www.counter-assault.com) can be useful in fending off bear attacks, and experts recommend that hikers in bear country carry a can. They're sold in most Alaskan camping supply stores.

These sprays are effective only at close range (10-30 feet), particularly in tundra areas, where winds quickly disperse the spray. When you carry pepper spray, make sure it is readily available by carrying it in a holster on your belt or across your chest. Be sure to test-fire it to make sure you are comfortable using it. If you use the spray to drive a bear away, immediately leave the area since the bear may return. When carrying the spray, be sure the safety clip remains in place so it doesn't accidentally discharge.

Detailed bear safety brochures are available at the Alaska Public Lands Information Center (www.alaskacenters.gov) in Anchorage, or on the Alaska Department of Fish and Game's website (www.adfg.state.ak.us). Two good bear safety books are *Bear Attacks: Their Causes and Avoidance* by Stephen Herrero and *Bear Aware: Hiking and Camping in Bear Country* by Bill Schneider.

mountain bikers in Denali National Park

bike tours (from $50 pp) have a minimum of four riders. Their office is eight miles north of Denali Park and two miles south of Healy, with a free shuttle provided.

Rafting

Three raft companies run the Nenana River along the eastern margin of the park, including two-hour Class II-IV white-water trips or Class II-III float trips ($90): **Denali Outdoor Center** (907/683-1925 or 888/303-1925, www.denalioutdoorcenter.com), **Denali Raft Adventures** (907/683-2234 or 888/683-2234, www.denaliraft.com), and **Nenana Raft Adventures** (907/683-7238 or 800/789-7238, www.raftdenali.com). All provide rain gear, boots, and life jackets, plus transportation to and from local hotels. Denali Raft Adventures and Denali Outdoor Center also offer trips that combine both segments for a four-hour trip ($122) that includes both the rapids and easy sections of the river.

Other Denali Raft Adventures options

include a four-hour scenic float ($142) and an all-day trip that includes floating and rapids ($183). Denali Outdoor Center has five-hour whitewater and scenic trips ($117 adults, $57 kids) and all-day 30-mile trips down the Nenana River ($173 adults, $153 kids). Float trips are okay for children, but only adults can do the white-water runs. Denali Outdoor Center would be my first choice, and they also provide inflatable kayak tours for those who want to paddle on their own.

Flightseeing

If the mountain is out and there's room on the plane, this is the time to pull out the credit card. These one-hour flights around Mount McKinley will leave you flying high for days.

Denali Air (Mile 229 Parks Hwy., 907/683-2261, www.denaliair.com, one-hour trip $375) operates from a private airstrip (eight miles south of the park entrance). Their one-hour trip over the mountain is in a twin-engine plane.

DENALI NATIONAL PARK

© DON PITCHER

Mount McKinley, as seen from a flightseeing trip over the park

Operating from Healy—12 miles north of the park entrance—**Fly Denali** (a.k.a. Talkeetna Aero Services, Healy River State Airport, 907/683-2899 or 888/733-2899, www.talkeetnaaero.com, $449 pp) has 2.5-hour flights that include a glacier landing.

Based in Kantishna at the center of the park, **Kantishna Air Taxi** (907/644-8222, www.katair.com) provides charter air service to end-of-the-road Kantishna lodges, and flightseeing trips within the park. Quite a few other flightseeing companies operate out of Talkeetna and Anchorage.

You can go for a helicopter ride on **Era Helicopters** (907/683-2574 or 800/843-1947, www.eraflightseeing.com), based along the river in Denali Park. Tour options include a 60-minute flight over the park ($339 pp), a 75-minute trip that includes a 20-minute glacier landing ($439), and a heli-hiking adventure that includes a 15-minute flight plus 3.5 hours of hiking ($475).

Mountaineering

Mount McKinley—the tallest peak in North America—is a major destination for mountaineers from around the globe. Over 1,000 climbers attempt to summit Mount McKinley each year, with three-quarters of these attempts via the West Buttress. The primary climbing season is May-July. From the south side of Mount McKinley, the usual approach is by ski plane from Talkeetna to the Southeast Fork of the Kahiltna Glacier or to the Ruth Glacier in the Don Sheldon Amphitheater. From the north, the approach for Denali and other peaks is by foot, ski, or dogsled. Specific route information can be obtained from the Talkeetna Ranger Station. Climbers on Mount McKinley and Mount Foraker are charged a special use fee ($350 per climber). Call the ranger in Talkeetna (907/733-2231), or visit the Park Service website (www.nps.gov/dena) for additional mountaineering information.

Six companies are authorized to lead guided

mountaineering climbs of Mount McKinley and other peaks in the Alaska Range; contact the Park Service for specifics. One of the finest is **Alaska Mountaineering School** (headquarters at 3rd St. and D St., Talkeetna, 907/733-1016, www.climbalaska.org, late Apr.-mid-July, 21-day climb $6,400 pp). The company guides 21-day climbs of the West Buttress with six climbers and two or three guides. These depart every week (or more often). The school also teaches intensive mountaineering courses, skills workshops, wilderness first responder classes, glacier treks, and wilderness backpacking. Another recommended climbing program is **NOLS** (907/745-4047, www.nols.edu), based in Palmer.

Dog Mushing

Visitors whose appetite is whetted by the daily dogsledding demonstrations at park headquarters may want to return when the snow flies for the real thing. **Earth Song Lodge** (Stampede Rd., 907/683-2863, www.earthsonglodge.com) offers wintertime dogsled adventure tours into Denali National Park. These range from an easy overnight trip to ones lasting 10 days.

Four-time Iditarod winner Jeff King lives with his family at Goose Lake near Denali, and his staff offers summertime tours of his state-of-the-art **Husky Homestead** (907/683-2904, www.huskyhomestead.com, 2.5 hour tours $59 adults, $39 children) kennels and training area. Tours and demonstrations depart from local hotels. It's by far the most tourist-oriented dog tour you'll ever see, handling almost 100 people at a time on busy summer days.

ENTERTAINMENT AND EVENTS

All the Denali Park hotels have lounges, but if you want to hang out with the young working crowd, head to **Denali Salmon Bake** (Mile 238.5 Parks Hwy., 907/683-2733, www.denaliparksalmonbake.com, daily 7am-11pm

mid-May-late Sept.). For frivolity, check out **Alaska Cabin Nite Dinner Theater** (McKinley Chalet Resort, 907/276-7234 or 800/276-7234, www.denaliparkresorts.com) or the **Music of Denali Dinner Theater** (Denali Princess Lodge, 907/683-2282 or 800/426-0500, www.princesslodges.com).

Park Service rangers give talks, walks, and kid programs. For specifics, check the bulletin boards at the Denali Visitor Center or the free park newspaper, *Denali Alpenglow*.

SHOPPING

Denali Park's "Glitter Gulch" area is filled with gift shops, most of which are completely forgettable. Two good seasonal places for Alaskan art on the boardwalk are **Denali Glass Studio** (Mile 238.5 Parks Hwy., 907/683-2787) and **Three Bears Gallery** (Mile 238 Parks Hwy., 907/683-3343). Get quality outdoor gear, freeze dried food, and clothing at **Denali Mountain Works** (907/683-1542, www.akrivers.com), where you'll also find rental tents, packs, sleeping pads, stoves, and binoculars. It's a good place for that last-minute item you forgot.

There's a seasonal **farmers market** (parking lot of 229 Parks Restaurant, Mile 229 Parks Hwy., Sat. 10am-2pm) with local crafts and produce.

ACCOMMODATIONS

Most of the local lodging action centers around busy Denali Park, though other lodges and B&Bs are a few miles south of the park entrance, or 10 miles north in the town of Healy. Denali area lodging options are expensive, so those on a tight budget will either need to camp or head to the hostel 13 miles south at Carlo Creek.

Denali Park Lodging

If you've been driving the Parks Highway north from Anchorage, soaking up the wild Alaskan wilderness, you're in for a rude awakening

© DON PITCHER

DENALI NATIONAL PARK

"Glitter Gulch" shops near the entrance to Denali National Park

when you reach the unincorporated settlement called—take your pick—**"The Canyon," Denali, Denali Park,** or **"Glitter Gulch."** Just a mile north of the Denali National Park turnoff, it's impossible to miss: an ugly hodgepodge of giant hotels, restaurants, RV parks, rafting companies, and gift shops crammed between the highway and the Nenana River to the west, and climbing the steep hillside to the east. The area is packed with tour buses, tottering tourists, and rumbling RVs.

Most lodging choices start well over $200 per night, but one place offers a less-expensive option: **Denali Salmon Bake Cabins** (Mile 238.5 Parks Hwy., 907/683-2733, www.denali-nationalparklodging.net, early May-late Sept., $64 d shared bath, $145 d private bath, suite $269). For the full-on Alaskan experience, stay in a "hostel style cabin" consisting of insulated tent-like structures with two double beds and a shared bath. There are also four standard cabins with two full beds, private baths, cable TV,

fridges, and air-conditioning. It's not for everyone, but the "Bake" is right there in the thick of things near the park entrance, with free Wi-Fi. Also available is a large luxury suite that sleeps up to six and has a king bed, two futons, two TVs, a full kitchen, and bath. It's located atop Sled Dog Market. Reservations are advised.

Denali Bluffs Hotel (Mile 238 Parks Hwy., 907/683-8500 or 866/683-8500, www.denalialaska.com, late May-mid-Sept., $199 d) is a pleasant hillside place where 112 rooms all contain two doubles or one king bed. Request a room with a private balcony. High atop the bluff sits **Grande Denali Lodge** (Mile 238 Parks Hwy., 907/683-8500 or 866/683-8500, www.denalialaska.com, late May-mid-Sept., guest rooms $279 d, cabins $329 for up to four), a 166-room hotel accessed by a steep switchbacking road marked by amusing signs. Guests stay in spacious rooms or family style cabins. Both Denali Bluffs and Grande Denali have the same Native Alaskan management. There is a free shuttle to the park visitor center or a ride ($4) to the train depot.

Also managed by Aramark, **McKinley Chalet Resort** (Mile 236 Parks Hwy., 907/276-7234 or 800/276-7234, www.denaliparkresorts.com, mid-May–mid-Sept., $299–334 d, rooms with a view $369 d) is a 345-room hotel along the Nenana River. Most rooms are set aside for Holland America passengers, so call well ahead of your visit. Standard rooms are very overpriced.

Though primarily for cruise ship passengers, the sprawling **Denali Princess Lodge** (Mile 238 Parks Hwy., 907/683-2282 or 800/426-0500, www.princesslodges.com, mid-May–mid-Sept., $299 d) is also open to independent travelers if they don't mind the corporate feeling and constant parade of tour buses. There are 656 rooms, and so many buildings here that you'll need a map to find your way around. Amenities include outdoor hot tubs overlooking the Nenana River, a fitness center, restaurants and cafés, a dinner theater, and a bar.

On the east side of the road, **Denali Rainbow Village** (Mile 238.6 Parks Hwy., 907/683-7777, www.denalirv.com, mid-May–mid-Sept., $125 d) has a handful of motel rooms, each with a queen bed, kitchenette, private bath, and Wi-Fi.

Carlo Creek Area Lodging

A number of lodging places are in the Carlo Creek area near Mile 224 of the Parks Highway, 14 miles south of the park entrance. The least expensive is the friendly **Denali Mountain Morning Hostel and Lodge** (Mile 224.1 Parks Hwy., 907/683-7503, www.denalihostel.com, early May–late Sept.), with a variety of earthy creek-side accommodations: coed bunk cabins ($32 pp), a private room ($85 d), two-person cabins ($80-95 d; add $15 pp for additional adults), family cabins ($128-160 for up to five), and wall tents ($32 s, $55 d). There's a two-night minimum

stay in the private accommodations. A shower house and bathrooms are separate, and guests can use the central kitchen, computer, laundry, free Wi-Fi, and lounge. Rent bear spray and binoculars if you're heading into the park. Two good restaurants—Pizza Panorama and McKinley Creekside Café—are directly across the highway. The hostel provides a free four-times-daily shuttle to Denali's Wilderness Access Center.

Denali Perch Resort (Mile 224 Parks Hwy., 907/683-2523 or 888/322-2523, www.denaliperchresort.com, mid-May–mid-Sept., $85 d shared bath, $125 d private bath) has 20 tiny hillside cabins with a shared bathhouse or with Lilliputian private baths and Wi-Fi. There are no phones or TVs, but a good restaurant is on the premises, with two more just down the way.

Nearby is **Carlo Creek Lodge** (Mile 224 Parks Hwy., 907/683-2576, www.denaliparklodging.com, late May–early Sept., $84-90 d shared bath, $120-140 d private bath, motel rooms $120-130 d), which has 10 attractive cabins near the creek; some contain kitchens. In addition to cabins, there are a half-dozen motel rooms with queen beds. All units include microwaves, fridges, Wi-Fi, and guest computers.

Best known for its popular café, **McKinley Creekside Cabins & Café** (Mile 224 Parks Hwy., 907/683-2277 or 888/533-6254, www.mckinleycabins.com, $139-189 d, house $449) has a variety of rooms and cabins, along with a custom three-bedroom house. Wi-Fi is available.

Denali Cabins (907/683-2643 or 800/808-8068, www.denali-cabins.com, $159 d one double bed, $189 d two double beds, add $20 pp for extra guests) consists of 45 basic cedar cabins seven miles south of the park entrance. There is no Wi-Fi, but the cabins—connected by boardwalks—include phones, TVs, and private baths. A free shuttle to the park train station is provided, and guests can use the two hot tubs. Also here is restaurant (Prey Bar &

© DON PITCHER

Grande Denali Lodge, near the entrance to Denali National Park

Eatery) with pub fare. Alaska Denali Tours owns these cabins, and offers park day trips on their buses.

Across the highway is **Denali Grizzly Bear Resort** (Mile 231.1 Parks Hwy., 907/683-2696 or 866/583-2696, www.denaligrizzlybear.com, mid-May–mid-Sept.), with a range of lodging choices sprawling up the hillside. These include simple little cabins ($69-109 d), some of which use a central shower house, and attractive log cabins with private baths and kitchens ($199-269 for up to six people). Traffic noise can be an annoyance. Four new hotel buildings ($199 d) each have a private deck overlooking the Nenana River, private baths, and a continental breakfast. There is free Wi-Fi throughout the resort, and a guest laundry is available.

McKinley Village Lodge (Mile 231 Parks Hwy., 907/276-7234 or 800/276-7234, www. denaliparkresorts.com, $293-373 d) is along the Nenana River. Here you'll find 150 comfortable—and overpriced—hotel rooms, a café,

and lounge. It's run by Denali Park Resorts (Aramark), the park concessionaire.

Kantishna Lodges

This private inholding is deep within Denali, 92 miles out the Park Road. Originally a gold mining settlement, it now has several lodges and an air taxi operator. These upscale lodges are definitely not for budget travelers, and it's a long bus ride to Kantishna, so most guests stay at least three nights in this very scenic area. All five of the lodges are open only early June–mid-September. Private buses transport visitors to the lodges at Kantishna, or you can fly out on Kantishna Air Taxi (907/644-8222, www. katair.com). There is no cell phone service in the Kantishna area.

At **Kantishna Roadhouse** (907/683-8003 summer or 800/942-7420, www.kantishnaroadhouse.com, June–mid-Sept., $910 d per day) the all-inclusive rate includes lodging in cabins or duplex rooms, meals, bus

© DON PITCHER

Denali Mountain Morning Hostel and Lodge

transportation from the park entrance, dogsled demonstrations, mountain bikes, gold panning, guided hikes, and interpretive programs. A bar and restaurant are on the premises. A two-night minimum stay is required.

Two wonderful Kantishna lodges—Camp Denali and North Face Lodge—have the same management and contacts. At both places, the emphasis is on the natural world, with guided hikes, mountain biking, canoeing, fishing, evening programs, and delicious meals, and the rates are all-inclusive. Established in 1952, **《 Camp Denali** (907/683-2290, www.campdenali.com, early June-mid-Sept., three nights: $1,635 adults, $1,226 children under 12; four nights: $2,180 adults, $1,635 children under) has spectacular views of Mount McKinley, and is operated as a low-key wilderness retreat for a maximum of 40 guests. International experts lead special programs throughout the summer, focusing on such topics as bird conservation, nature photography, mountaineering, photography, northern lights, and environmental issues. Lodging is in 18 cozy cabins with woodstoves, propane

lights, an outhouse, and a shower building. If you can't handle an outhouse, book a room at North Face Lodge instead.

One mile from Camp Denali is **《 North Face Lodge** (907/683-2290, www.campdenali.com, early June-mid-Sept., three nights: $1,635 adults, $1,226 children under 12; four nights: $2,180 adults, $1,635 children under), which is operated more like a country inn, with 15 guest rooms, all containing private baths. The all-inclusive price includes lodging, food, bus transportation to and from Kantishna, lectures, guided hikes, and other activities. Guests must stay at least three nights, with fixed arrival and departure dates.

Denali Backcountry Lodge (907/644-9980 or 877/233-6254, www.denalilodge.com, early June-mid-Sept., $930-1,070 d per day) has cabins and a main lodge at the end of the road. The cabins—all with private baths and one or two beds—range from basic units with no view to nicer ones with decks along the creek. The all-inclusive rates are for two people per day. Rates includes round-trip transport by bus into the park, meals, bikes, fishing, and naturalist presentations. There are no TVs, Wi-Fi, or cell phone coverage. It's a long ride, so some guests opt to ride the bus in and fly back out on Kantishna Air (an extra $150 pp).

Operated by the owners of Kantishna Air Taxi, **Skyline Lodge** (Mile 92 Park Rd., 907/644-8222, www.katair.com, June-Sept., $265 d, $384 for two people including lodging and meals) provides the least expensive accommodations in Kantishna. The solar-powered lodge can accommodate up to 10 guests in four cabins, each with a queen bed downstairs plus a sleeping loft with double bed. The bathroom and showers are in the main lodge, and phone and Internet are very limited.

Park Campgrounds

Inside Denali National Park are six campgrounds, four of which have evening nature programs throughout the summer. Riley Creek, Savage River, Teklanika River, and Wonder Lake campgrounds can be reserved in advance through **Doyan/Aramark** (907/272-7275 or 800/622-7275, www.reservedenali.com, $5 reservation fee) starting in mid-February. You can also reserve campsites at the visitor centers if they aren't already full, but this is definitely *not* a wise move if you want any choice of where you stay.

You can drive to Riley Creek, Savage River, and Teklanika River campgrounds, so they fill up fast. Otherwise, campground access is via the **camper buses** (adults $33, kids free).

RILEY CREEK CAMPGROUND

Largest and most accessible campground in the park, Riley Creek Campground ($22-28 pull-in sites, $14 walk-in sites, free in winter) has 146 sites just a quarter-mile off the Parks Highway. It's open year-round, with bear-proof food lockers, running water, and flush toilets, but limited facilities and no water September-May. This campground is very popular with RVers and car campers, but suffers somewhat from highway noise. Park rangers provide evening nature programs, and the adjacent **Riley Creek Mercantile** provides firewood, a few supplies, a dump station, coin laundry, $5 showers, and free Wi-Fi.

SAVAGE RIVER CAMPGROUND

Near the end of the paved, publicly accessible portion of the Park Road, Savage River Campground (Mile 13 Park Rd., late May-mid-Sept., $22, $28 pull-through sites, $40 group sites) has 33 wooded sites for vehicles and tents, with bear-proof lockers and flush and vault toilets. Two group sites (tents only) are available. You'll need to bring firewood for campfires.

SANCTUARY RIVER CAMPGROUND

Remote and tranquil, Sanctuary River Campground (Mile 23 Park Rd., late May-mid-Sept., $9) contains seven heavily forested tent sites. The campground has vault toilets and bear-proof lockers, but no potable water. You'll need to bring water or filter it from the silty river, and campfires aren't allowed. Unlike most Denali campgrounds, reservations aren't taken for Sanctuary River; check at the Wilderness Access Center or Riley Creek Mercantile to see if sites are available. No vehicles are allowed here, so access is only via the camper bus.

TEKLANIKA RIVER CAMPGROUND

Teklanika River Campground (Mile 29 Park Rd., late May-mid-Sept., $16) provides 53 forested sites for tents and vehicles. The braided Teklanika River provides an easy gravel surface for day hikes from the campground, and this is the farthest point RVs can drive into the park. Vault toilets and running water are provided, along with bear-proof food storage, but bring firewood with you (available at Riley Creek Mercantile) if you want a campfire, since none is available for sale.

There's a three-night minimum stay for vehicular campers at Tek, and your vehicle must stay at your campsite for the duration of your stay. It can only leave when you're driving back out of the park. There is no minimum stay requirement for campers arriving on the camper bus since they don't have a private vehicle.

Campers at Teklanika should purchase a **"Tek Pass"** for each member of your party. This allows you to use the park shuttle buses throughout your stay at Teklanika Campground for the price of just one trip; it's only available for travel farther into the park, not back to the park entrance.

IGLOO CREEK CAMPGROUND

Hemmed in by the mountains, little Igloo Creek Campground (Mile 35 Park Rd., late May-mid-Sept., $9) features seven wooded tent-only sites. The campground has pit vault toilets, but you'll need to bring plenty of water or a filter. Fires are not permitted and vehicles aren't allowed, so you'll need to arrive via the camper bus. Reservations aren't taken for Igloo Creek Campground, so stop by the Wilderness Access Center or Riley Creek Mercantile to see if sites are available. There's great hiking around Igloo Creek, with relatively easy access to the high country.

WONDER LAKE CAMPGROUND

Wonder Lake Campground (Mile 85 Park Rd., early June-mid-Sept., $16) has 28 tent-only sites in one of the most dramatic settings anywhere on the planet. The country is rolling tundra, with a few trees and the potential to see Mount McKinley in all its glory (if the weather cooperates). The lake—2.7 miles long by 0.5 miles wide—is a short walk away. Wonder Lake Campground has running water, flush toilets, cooking shelters, and bear storage lockers. Because of its location, Wonder Lake doesn't open until early June. Make reservations well ahead for campsites here, especially when fall colors peak in late August and early September.

RV Parks

Denali Rainbow Village (907/683-7777, www.

denalirv.com, mid-May-mid-Sept., RVs $38-42, tents $25) is in the heart of the Denali Park/Glitter Gulch action, with a big lot behind the row of buildings on the east side of the road. It has a laundry, Wi-Fi, and cable TV. Showers are $5 if you aren't camping here.

Eight miles south of the park entrance is **Denali Grizzly Bear Resort** (907/683-2696 or 866/583-2696, www.denaligrizzlybear.com, RVs $38, tents $25, tent cabins $38). Showers, laundry, a central cooking shelter, and Wi-Fi (fee) are available.

Fourteen miles south of the park is **Denali Mountain Morning Hostel and Lodge** (907/683-7503, www.denalihostel.com, early May-late Sept., wall tents $32 s, $55 d). There is no camping, but it does have creekside wall tents, with sleeping bags, cots, a bathhouse, central kitchen, computer, laundry, free Wi-Fi, and free park shuttle. Additional RV parks are in Healy, 11 miles north of the park entrance.

FOOD

A number of places offer pricey summertime eats just north of the park entrance at the packed settlement of businesses called The Canyon, Denali Park, Denali, or Glitter Gulch; most are shuttered when the tourists flee south after mid-September.

Cafés and Diners

Begin your day at **Black Bear Coffee House** (Mile 238 Parks Hwy., 907/683-1656, daily 6:30am-10pm mid-May-mid-Sept., $5-10) with eggy breakfasts, bagels, espresso, sandwiches, and muffins, plus "$5 after 5" deal with burritos and grilled cheese in the evening. The café also has Wi-Fi, a free guest computer, and a loaner iPad ($3 for 30 minutes), along with occasional live music on the deck. Expect a long wait most mornings.

If you're just hankering for that old standby, head over to **Great Alaska Fish & Chips Co.** (Mile 238.9 Parks Hwy., 907/683-3474, www.

alaskafishandchip.com, daily 10:30am-9pm mid-May-mid-Sept., $15-17) for a big serving of halibut or cod fish and chips. There's a salad bar and a handful of other choices too, including burgers, sandwiches, and cold pitchers of Alaskan Amber.

One of the better restaurants in the Denali area is 11 miles south of the park entrance: **McKinley Creekside Café** (Mile 224 Parks Hwy., 907/683-2277 or 888/533-6254, www. mckinleycabins.com, daily 6am-10pm mid-May-mid-Sept., $15-23). You'll find good breakfasts (including gigantic half-pound cinnamon rolls), homemade soups, sandwiches, and gyros for lunch, plus meatloaf, pasta specials, and fresh chicken pot pie in the evening, along with Friday night prime rib and filling box lunches ($13). The little deck is perfect for mid-summer dining. Pop open your laptop for free Wi-Fi.

Bar and Grills

In business for more than 25 years, **Denali Salmon Bake** (Mile 238.5 Parks Hwy., 907/683-2733, www.denaliparksalmonbake. com, daily 7am-11pm mid-May-late Sept., $20-29) is extremely popular and quite reasonable for breakfast, lunch, and dinner. When you step into this rustic old building the slanting floors are immediate evidence of the melting permafrost beneath the structure; the slope increases by an inch or two each year! The Bake's diverse menu stars apple stuffed waffles and stampede scramble skillet for breakfast, sourdough grilled cheese sandwiches and Alaska buffalo burgers for lunch, plus baby back ribs, halibut and chips, or king salmon for dinner. The restaurant has Wi-Fi and a **free shuttle** to local hotels, campgrounds, and the Wilderness Access Center. A sprawling upstairs no-smoking bar comes alive with bluegrass and folk bands four nights a week, and has 21 beers on tap, along with an enormous frozen blue concoction called the McKinley margarita. Join all the Bulgarian, Serbian, and Slavic seasonal workers for Wednesday-night "J-1" dance parties. Heading into the park? Have the "Bake" make a big box lunch ($13). Hungry late? Halibut tacos are available till the bar closes at 4am. The Salmon Bake's owners seem to have half the local businesses, with seven different places at last count, including Prospectors Pizza, 49th State Brewing Co., and Miners Market & Deli.

Pizza

On the north end of the Glitter Gulch action, **Prospectors Pizzeria & Alehouse** (Mile 238.9 Parks Hwy., 907/683-7437, www.prospectorspizza.com, daily 11am-10 or later mid-May-late Sept., pizzas $20-29 for a 17-incher) gets packed with folks most summer evenings, so be ready for a 45-minute wait. In addition to wood stone brick oven pizzas, the menu includes salads, pastas, sandwiches, and a locally famous baked tomato soup. There's outside seating and 49 beers on tap.

Right across the creek is **Panorama Pizza Pub** (Mile 224 Parks Hwy., 907/683-2623, www.panoramapizzapub.com, food daily until 11pm mid-May-mid-Sept., $21-32), with excellent pizzas and live bluegrass music Wednesday-Saturday nights. The Denali pizza is topped with pepperoni, sausage, olives, mushrooms, and green peppers. Slices only are available after 11pm, and the bar stays open till 3am. The pub provides a free shuttle from Denali Park.

Steak and Seafood

High atop the bluff behind Denali Park, **Alpenglow Restaurant** (Grande Denali Lodge, Mile 238 Parks Hwy., 907/683-8500 or 866/683-8500, www.denalialaska.com, daily 5am-10pm mid-May-mid-Sept., breakfast buffet $12-16, $19-31) has the most extraordinary vistas in the area. Wraparound windows face Denali National Park, and the high ceilings are accented by a beautiful timber-frame design. In addition to a good steak and seafood selection, there's a lighter bar menu with burgers, salads, and BBQ

DENALI NATIONAL PARK

sliders. Call to reserve a window table for dinner. Breakfast buffets are a good stuff-yourself deal.

At ◖ **229 Parks Restaurant** (Mile 229 Parks Hwy., 907/683-2567, www.229parks. com, Fri.-Sat. 9am-9pm and Sun. 9am-1pm Jan.-late Apr., Tues.-Sun. 5pm-10pm late May-Sept., closed late Apr.-late May and Oct.-Dec., $24-36) the name is also the location: Mile 229 on the Parks Highway. Housed within a bright timber-frame building nine miles south of Denali Park, the restaurant serves a bistro-style menu that changes frequently. Organic locally-grown vegetables and free-range meats are used whenever possible. Dinner entrées include steak au poivre and wild Alaskan scallops. "Tavern fare" options ($10-16) such as Caesar salads, Parmesan aioli flatbreads, or bison burgers offer a less expensive option. Save room for their ice cream sandwich with homemade ice cream between dark chocolate cookies. In addition to dinner, the restaurant serves pastries and espresso for brunch. Don't come here in a hurry; service can be slow since everything is made fresh. Reservations are highly recommended since the restaurant fills most nights; call several days ahead. The restaurant doesn't provide a shuttle, so you'll need your own wheels or a taxi ride from Denali Park.

Sweets

Denali Glacier Scoops (Mile 238 Parks Hwy., 907/683-6002, daily 11am-10pm mid-May-mid-Sept.) offers a double scoop of ice cream at Alaskan prices ($6). Also available are shakes, sundaes, soft serve, and smoothies.

Markets

Canyon Market and Cafe (Mile 238.4 Parks Hwy., 907/683-7467, www.canyonmarketcafe. com, daily 6am-1:30am) makes deli sandwiches and pastries, and offers a decent selection of groceries and produce. There is free Wi-Fi here, too.

In the heart of the action, **Lynx Creek Store/The Park Mart** (Mile 238.6 Parks Hwy., 907/683-2548, 8am-10pm summer) is a quickie-mart with some of the most expensive gas on the road system, along with such essentials as soda, sweets, and limited food items. The store also rents mountain and hybrid bikes ($20 for a half-day, $30 for all day).

INFORMATION AND SERVICES

The large Denali Park hotels all have **ATMs,** as does the Lynx Creek Store (Mile 238.6 Parks Hwy., 907/683-2548, 8am-10pm summer). A **post office** is adjacent to the Riley Creek Campground inside the park.

For medical help, head to **Canyon Clinic at Denali** (Parks Hwy., close to Denali Princess Lodge, 907/683-4433, daily in the summer). The nearest hospital is in Fairbanks.

GETTING THERE

The **Alaska Railroad's *Denali Star*** (907/265-2494 or 800/544-0552, www.alaskarailroad. com) leaves Fairbanks at 8:15am and arrives at Denali at noon ($51 one way); it departs Anchorage at 8:15am, arriving at Denali at 3:45pm ($117 one way).

Several companies have van transportation to Denali from Anchorage, Talkeetna, or Fairbanks. **Alaska/Yukon Trails** (907/479-2277 or 888/770-7275, www.alaskashuttle. com, daily Apr.-Sept.) connects Denali with Anchorage ($75 pp one-way), Talkeetna ($65 pp one-way), and Fairbanks ($55 pp one-way).

The **Alaska Bus Guy** (907/720-6541, www. alaskabusguy.com, daily in summer, twice-weekly in winter, $67 one way) operates an environmentally friendly hydrogen-hybrid van with runs between Anchorage (or Talkeetna) and Denali.

Park Connection (907/245-0200 or 800/266-8625, www.alaskacoach.com, mid-May-mid-Sept.) provides daily service connecting Denali with Talkeetna ($65), Anchorage ($80-90), Whittier ($155), and Seward ($155).

Local air taxis include **Denali Air** (Mile 229 Parks Hwy., 907/683-2261, www.denaliair.com), which operates from eight miles south of the park entrance, **Fly Denali** (a.k.a. Talkeetna Aero Services, 907/683-2899 or 888/733-2899, www.talkeetnaaero.com) from Healy, and **Kantishna Air Taxi** (907/644-8222, www.katair.com) from Kantishna deep inside the park. **Era Helicopters** (907/683-2574 or 800/843-1947, www.eraflightseeing.com) is based next to the river in Denali Park.

GETTING AROUND

Call **Denali Transportation** (907/683-4765, www.denalitaxishuttle.com) for taxi service in the Healy/Denali Park area.

The Park Service's **Riley Creek Loop Bus** (5am-7pm mid-May-mid-Sept., free) provides service connecting the Riley Creek Campground, Wilderness Access Center, and train depot every half hour. In addition, a second free bus connects the Wilderness Access Center with the dogsled demonstrations at park headquarters, and the free Savage River Shuttle continues to Savage River Bridge at Mile 15.

Private shuttle buses are provided by local hotels. **Denali Salmon Bake** (Mile 238.5 Parks Hwy., 907/683-2733, www.denaliparksalmonbake.com, $1-2 one-way) provides a 24-hour shuttle that stops at the Wilderness Access Center, train depot, Denali Park/Canyon hotels and restaurants, and Healy businesses. The shuttle also stops at Riley Creek Campground upon request (call for a campground pickup).

HEALY AND VICINITY

Located 11 miles north of the turnoff to Denali National Park at Mile 249 of the Parks Highway, the town of Healy (pop. 640) has most of the necessities of life, including gas stations (considerably cheaper than at Denali Park), convenience stores, restaurants, a coin laundry, and a medical clinic.

Healy has grown up around the coal mining

that has operated here since the 1930s. **Usibelli Coal Mine** (907/683-2226, www.usibelli.com) is the largest in Alaska, which isn't saying much, since it's Alaska's *only* commercial coal mine. However, its 1.5 million tons of subbituminous coal mined each year does say something: a 4-million-pound "walking dragline" digs 1,000 cubic yards of overburden every hour, exposing the seams. The coal is shipped to Korea or used at an adjacent power plant that supplies the Tanana Valley and Fairbanks. Coal burning is a big factor in the earth's rapid warming. There's a certain irony in Alaska as the source of the coal that is leading to drastic changes across the state. Healy also benefits greatly from tourism to nearby Denali National Park.

Two miles south of town, play a round of golf at the nine-hole **Black Diamond Golf Course** (Otto Lake Rd., 907/683-4653, www.blackdiamondgolf.com, wagon ride: $89 adults, $39 kids) or take a three-hour covered wagon ride.

Accommodations

Add a seven percent tax to all Healy lodging rates.

◖ **Earth Song Lodge** (Stampede Rd., 907/683-2863, www.earthsonglodge.com, year-round, small cabins $155 d, family-size cabins $185 d, two-bedroom cabins $215 d, add $10 pp for extra adult guests) rents 12 cozy cabins, all with private baths. The cabins are all very clean and well-maintained. Earth Song is four miles down Stampede Road off the Parks Highway at Mile 251. Earth Song is open all year, with a nightly slide show at the coffeehouse, Wi-Fi in the lodge, and guided winter dogsledding into Denali National Park. Co-owner Jon Nierenberg is a former Denali park ranger and his wife Karin is an accomplished author.

Three miles south of Healy is **Denali RV Park and Motel** (Mile 245.1 Parks Hwy., 907/683-1500 or 800/478-1501, www.denalirvpark.com, late May-early Sept., $79 d, family units $139), with tiny motel rooms with private baths and family units with kitchens for four people. Units have cable TV, and there is Wi-Fi in the office.

White Moose Lodge (Mile 248 Parks Hwy., 907/683-1231 or 800/481-1232, www.whitemooselodge.com, early May-late Sept., $105 d) has 15 reasonably priced no-frills motel rooms with two double beds, satellite TVs, breakfast pastries and juice, and Wi-Fi.

Denali Park Hotel (Mile 247 Parks Hwy., 907/683-1800 or 866/683-1800, www.denaliparkhotel.com, $119-139 d, add $10 pp for extra guests) is something of a misnomer. This 12-room motel has parking right outside your door and spacious older rooms with queen or king beds, fridges, microwaves, satellite TVs, and Wi-Fi. The motel lobby is a World War II-era Alaska Railroad railcar, and a complimentary shuttle is provided for visitors arriving by train.

Park's Edge Log Cabin Accommodations (Hilltop Ln., 907/683-4343, www.parksedge.com, late May-early Sept., cabins $100-125 d, add $10 pp for extra guests, maximum of six) has modern economical cabins and a larger cabin. The cabins are adjacent to Black Diamond Golf Course. All include private baths and Wi-Fi.

Open all year, **Motel Nord Haven** (Mile 249 Parks Hwy., 907/683-4500 or 800/683-4501, www.motelnordhaven.com, year-round, $152 one queen bed, $170 two queen beds, $180 kitchenette unit) has nicely appointed rooms, hot breakfasts, a guest computer, and Wi-Fi. Request a room in the quieter annex building if possible. Rose's Café is next door.

It's hard to miss the geodesic-shaped **Denali Dome Home B&B** (Healy Spur Rd., 907/683-1239 or 800/683-1239, www.denalidomehome.com, year-round, $180 d), where lodging is available in a unique 7,000-square-foot house with rock fireplaces and seven guest rooms, all with king or queen beds, flat screen TV, and

private baths. Two rooms contain jetted tubs, and guests appreciate the sauna, seven acres of parklike grounds and flower gardens, Wi-Fi, extensive art collection, and traditional cook-to-order breakfasts.

Touch of Wilderness B&B (2.9 Stampede Rd., 907/683-2459 or 800/683-2459, www.touchofwildernessbb.com, year-round, $165-198 d) is a 7,000-square-foot home in a quiet location 5 miles north of Healy along Stampede Road and 16 miles north of the park entrance. The nine guest rooms—one handicap accessible—have a variety of configurations and beds, plus private baths, self-serve breakfasts, comfortable common areas with fireplaces and TVs, and Wi-Fi.

Denali Lakeview Inn (Otto Lake Rd., 907/683-4035, www.denalilakeviewinn.com, $139-209 d) is a large place right on Otto Lake with 20 bright guest rooms and suites, plus in-room continental breakfast and Wi-Fi. The main attraction here is the spectacular lake-and-mountains view from the deck.

An immaculate modern home in a quiet neighborhood, ◖ **Denali Primrose B&B** (1 Stoney Creek Dr., Healy, 907/683-1234, www.denaliprimrose.com, one-bedroom suite $126 d, three-bedroom suite $172 d, add $15 pp for extra guests) has two suites. Lodging options are a downstairs one-bedroom suite and a three-bedroom upstairs suite with a whirlpool tub. Amenities include private baths, TVs, Wi-Fi, continental breakfasts, and a gracious owner.

Aspen Haus B&B (907/683-2004, www.aspenhaus.com, late May-early Sept., cabins $129-179 d, suites $145 d) has a quiet in-the-trees setting and four spacious cabins, the largest with room for six people, plus two upstairs suites. Each unit includes private baths, queen beds, a fridge, a microwave, Wi-Fi, and breakfast ingredients.

Operated by the Denali Outdoor Center, **Otto Lake Cabins & Camping** (Otto Lake Rd., 907/683-1925 or 888/303-1925, www.

INTO THE WILD PHOTO-OP

© DON PITCHER

bus from the film *Into the Wild* in front of 49th State Brewery

A few miles north of Healy is the turnoff for the Stampede Road, made infamous in the book and movie *Into the Wild*. Access to the old bus where Chris McCandless died is very difficult. Here's what the locals tell folks trying to get there: "This is where you turn off the highway; this is where you park the car; this is where you get eaten to death by mosquitoes; this is where you might drown; this is where the bear mauls you; and this is where you starve to death and die." At least one person has died attempting to reach the bus, so don't take the chance. An identical replica of the Magic Bus—it was used in the movie—sits out front of 49th State Brewery in Healy. Take your photo there instead of risking your life!

denalioutdoorcenter.com, $92 d, $112 for four people) has economy cabins on the shore of this lake just two miles south of Healy. The cabins share a shower house, laundry, and kitchen facility.

Camping

Three miles south of Healy, **Denali RV Park and Motel** (Mile 245.1 Parks Hwy., 907/683-1500 or 800/478-1501, www.denalirvpark.com, late May-early Sept., RVs $40, showers $3) has nicely maintained RV spaces and clean showers. There is free Wi-Fi and cable TV.

McKinley RV and Campground (Mile 248.5 Parks Hwy., 907/683-1418 or 800/478-2562, www.mckinleyrv.com, May-Sept., RVs $38, tents $15) occupies a somewhat wooded area just off the highway. The campground gets complaints about cleanliness and maintenance, so you may want to check it out first, but there's free Wi-Fi and a shuttle to the park. It's adjacent to 49th State Brewing Co. and the Chevron gas station with its 24-hour convenience store, deli, ATM, espresso, laundry, and liquor store.

Two miles south of Healy, **Otto Lake Cabins & Camping** (Otto Lake Rd., 907/683-1925 or 888/303-1925, www.denalioutdoor-center.com, mid-May-mid-Sept., $8 pp) has lakeside campsites. Potable water is provided and outhouses are available, along with showers ($5), a laundry ($5), and canoe and bike rentals ($8/hour).

Food

Healy's main attraction is **49th State Brewery** (Mile 248.5 Parks Hwy., 907/683-2739, www.49statebrewing.com, daily noon-1:30am mid-Mar.-Oct., $16-33), a cavernous industrial-style building with a pub menu of burgers, sandwiches, pizzas, and munchies served all day, plus such dinner entrées as alderwood smoked ribs, beer battered shrimp tacos, and Alaskan ribeye steak. There's a pig roast every Thursday, and all-you-can-eat pork on Fridays. The brewery produces seven or so beers, including the popular Baked Blonde Ale, and also has a good choice of cocktails, wine, and more than 130 whiskeys. Food is served till 1:30am, with a limited menu after 11pm. The pub provides a free shuttle van to Denali Park, and has live music on the patio most summer weekends. Parked out front is the bus used in the *Into the Wild* movie; it's a replica of the real one a few miles away.

Find a lounge and a 24-hour restaurant with family fare and pizzas at **Totem Inn** (Mile 249 Parks Hwy., 907/683-6500, www.thetoteminn.com, daily 7am-10pm).

Try the bacon cheeseburgers and other home-cooked food at friendly **Rose's Café** (Mile 249.5 Parks Hwy., 907/683-7673, www.roses-cafealaska.com, daily 6:30am-9:30pm Mar.-late Oct., $11-16), open for three meals a day. There's a "Grizzly Wall of Fame" for anyone who eats Rose's infamous one-pound grizzly burger (topped with an egg and a slice of ham) plus the side order of fires and potato salad.

Henry's Coffeehouse at Earth Song Lodge (Stampede Rd., 907/683-2863, www.earthsonglodge.com, breakfast and dinner in summer) serves bagels, baked goods, soups, sandwiches, salads, pizzas, and espresso.

The **Black Diamond Grill** (Otto Lake Rd., 907/683-4653, www.blackdiamondgolf.com, daily 11am-11pm, $18-36) serves a menu of prime rib sandwiches, steaks, and halibut. The restaurant has a free shuttle bus if you're staying in Healy or Denali Park hotels. It's owned by the Usibelli family, which also operates the coal mine in Healy and Usibelli Vineyards in Napa Valley.

Information and Services

There is no local visitor center, but the **Denali Chamber of Commerce** (907/683-4636, www.denalichamber.com) will send you local brochures. For medical care, head to **Interior Community Health Center** (Usibelli Spur Rd., 907/683-2211, www.myhealthclinic.org); a physician's assistant and nurse are on call.

Getting There and Around

Denali Salmon Bake shuttle (Mile 238.5 Parks Hwy., 907/683-2733, www.denaliparksalmonbake.com, $1 one way, $2 to Wilderness Access Center) provides a 24-hour summertime shuttle that operates every 1.5 hours, stopping at the Wilderness Access Center, train depot, Denali Park/Canyon hotels and restaurants, 49th State Brewing, Miners Market, and McKinley RV in Healy. The shuttle also stops at Riley Creek Campground upon request (call for a campground pickup).

Call **Denali Transportation** (907/683-4765, www.denalitaxishuttle.com) for taxi service in the Healy/Denali Park area.

The owners of Denali Dome Home B&B provide rental cars through **Keys to Denali** (907/683-5397 or 800/683-1239, www.denalidomehome.com, $110-150/day), and provide pick ups and drop offs anywhere in the area, including the Denali train station. This is a great way to explore the area without having to drive all the way from Anchorage.

THE KENAI PENINSULA

The Kenai Peninsula is like a mini-Alaska, compressing all of the state's features into an area roughly three percent the size of the state. You'll find mountains, icefields and glaciers, fjords and offshore islands, large fish-filled rivers and lakes, swampy plains, varied climate and precipitation, and a smattering of interesting towns. The Kenai is a major playground for both Anchorage residents and travelers from outside, and it's possibly the most popular all-around destination for all Alaskans. The outdoor recreational opportunities are practically inexhaustible—from charter fishing and kiteboarding to river rafting and dog sledding. Nearly 300,000 Anchorageites live just up the road, so you probably won't be the only one on that fishing stream. But don't let the possibility of crowds deter you. The resources are abundant, well developed, and often isolated. And besides, what's wrong with a little company along the trail or under sail?

At 16,056 square miles, Kenai Peninsula is a little smaller than Vermont and New Hampshire combined. The Kenai Mountains form the peninsula's backbone, with massive Harding Icefield dominating the lower lumbar. The east side, facing Prince William Sound, hosts a spur of the Kenai Mountains, with the glimmering Sargent Icefields; the west side, facing Cook Inlet, is outwash plain, sparkling with low-lying swamp, lakes, and rivers. The icefields, glaciers, and plains are

© DON PITCHER

HIGHLIGHTS

LOOK FOR ◖ TO FIND RECOMMENDED SIGHTS, ACTIVITIES, DINING, AND LODGING.

◖ **Hope:** This once-booming mining town is the place that time forgot. Several fine hikes head out from here (page 170).

◖ **Alaska SeaLife Center:** The touch tanks and fascinating exhibits are great, but seals and sea lions steal the show at this popular marine science center (page 176).

◖ **Resurrection Bay Tours:** Several Seward companies offer wildlife and glacier tours by boat. Half-day excursions tour the bay; all-day versions make it into Kenai Fjords National Park (page 178).

◖ **Exit Glacier:** This glacier is part of Kenai Fjords National Park and has camping, hiking trails, and glacier tours (page 195).

◖ **Combat Fishing:** The Kenai and Russian Rivers are major destinations for anglers in search of red salmon. It's an elbow-to-elbow frenzy at the midsummer peak (page 200).

◖ **The Homer Spit:** Jutting four miles into Kachemak Bay, this narrow sandy peninsula provides a great base for halibut charters, sea kayaking, bird-watching, cycling, dining, and shopping (page 226).

◖ **Islands and Ocean Visitor Center:** Modern and slick, this free center has exhibits on the Alaska Maritime National Wildlife Refuge (page 227).

◖ **Pratt Museum:** One of the finest small museums in Alaska, the Pratt always has something interesting, including a touch tank with tidepool animals (page 228).

◖ **Kachemak Bay and Gull Island:** Glimpse thousands of nesting seabirds on Gull Island (page 252).

all a result of ice sculpting over the million-year course of the Pleistocene, with its five major glacial periods. During the last, the Wisconsin Period, Portage Glacier filled the entire Turnagain Arm, 50 miles long and a half-mile high. Ten thousand years ago Portage stopped just short of carving a fjord between Prince William Sound and Turnagain Arm; otherwise, Kenai Peninsula would've been Kenai Island. Still, this peninsula has more than 1,000 miles of coastline. The land is almost completely controlled by the federal government: Chugach National Forest, Kenai National Wildlife Refuge, and

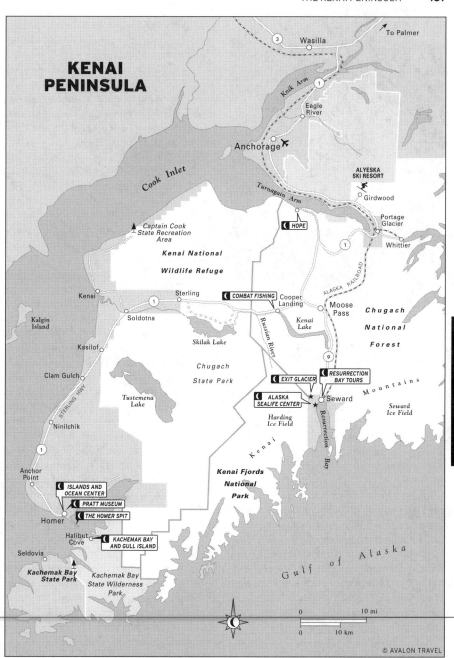

THE KENAI PENINSULA

© AVALON TRAVEL

© DON PITCHER

Kenai Mountains

Kenai Fjords National Park account for nearly 85 percent of the peninsula.

Two roads provide the primary access to the Kenai. The 127-mile **Seward Highway** connects Anchorage with Seward on the southwest end of the peninsula, and the 143-mile **Sterling Highway** cuts across the Kenai, leading west and south from Tern Lake (where it meets the Seward Highway) to Soldotna and Homer.

The off-the-beaten-path settlement of **Hope** has a picture-perfect collection of gold rush-era buildings along Turnagain Arm. A very scenic three-hour drive south from Anchorage, the town of Seward is home to the **Alaska SeaLife Center** (great for kids), along with **Kenai Fjords National Park,** where visitors can take guided hikes across **Exit Glacier,** join Resurrection Bay boat tours, or take longer day (or multiple-night) trips into the park.

Kenai National Wildlife Refuge is home to the Kenai and Russian Rivers, the scene of **combat fishing,** where hundreds of anglers crowd the banks when the salmon are running.

The **Homer Spit,** a sandy strip of land extending four miles into the bay, is the primary visitor attraction in Homer, with charter halibut fishing, sea kayaking, Kachemak Bay tours to Gull Island or the remote villages of Halibut Cove and Seldovia, and some of the finest restaurants and lodging in Alaska.

Every Kenai Peninsula town of any size has its own chamber of commerce and website; they're listed under the individual towns. A good overall information source is the **Kenai Peninsula Tourism Marketing Council** (907/262-5229 or 800/535-3624, www.kenaipeninsula.org), which produces a detailed annual travel publication.

HISTORY

You begin to feel the Russian influence strongly in this neck of the woods. Alexander Baranov's first shipyard was somewhere along Resurrection Bay down from present-day Seward. Russians built a stockade near Kasilof in 1786 and a fort at Kenai in 1791. Other than these brief incursions, the land belonged to the Kenai Natives Alaskans: part of the great Athabascan tribe on the north half of the peninsula, while the Alutiiqs occupied the southern half.

During the gold rush, color was uncovered around Hope and Sunrise on Turnagain Arm, and at Moose Creek, halfway to Seward. At first, trails ran between the mining communities, then wagon roads, and finally the railroad pushed from Seward through Anchorage to Fairbanks in the early 1920s. The Seward and Sterling Highways were completed in 1952, opening the Kenai's western frontier. When Atlantic Richfield tapped into oil (1957) and gas (1962) off the west coast, the peninsula's economic star began to twinkle. Oil and gas production has dropped steadily since the peak in the 1970s as the reserves are depleted, but new gas deposits have been discovered in recent years and exploration continues.

Today, the Kenai Peninsula Borough's 55,000 residents are occupied with fishing, oil and gas, tourism, and services.

PLANNING YOUR TIME
The Kenai Peninsula is readily accessible by car, bus, plane, or train from Anchorage, making it perfect if you have a few days, but adventurers could easily spend considerably longer exploring backcountry areas or playing in the scenic towns.

Driving distances between (relatively) larger towns like Seward and Homer tend to be significant. You can feasibly cover 200-plus miles in a day, but if you have the time to slow down and stop in the smaller villages along the way, you'll get more out of your visit to Kenai Peninsula. Plan on stopping frequently as you drive, for the picturesque views and wildlife sightings are best appreciated outside of the car. This will affect your travel time, so plan your overnights accordingly.

Eastern Kenai Peninsula

THE SEWARD HIGHWAY
The 127-mile Seward Highway—a National Scenic Byway—connects Anchorage with Seward on the Kenai Peninsula. Mileposts are numbered from the Seward end; subtract these numbers from 127 for the distance to Anchorage. The Seward Highway has passing lanes, wide shoulders, and a 65 mph speed limit much of the way, but take the time to enjoy the scenery. Keep your headlights on at all times, and watch for moose.

Near Portage at Mile 48, the Seward Highway banks sharply to the west along Turnagain Arm before turning again southward as it climbs into the Kenai Mountains. At **Turnagain Pass** (Mile 69, elev. 988 ft.), the west side of the road has a big pullout with portable toilets. Stop and stretch in this pretty alpine area where the snow remains until late June. In the winter the snow is often 10 feet deep. The west side is popular with snowmobilers, while the east side is reserved for those on skis or snowshoes. Turnagain Pass can be deadly at certain times of the winter, and a number of snowmobilers have died in avalanches here while riding on the dangerous upper slopes.

At Mile 64 is the northern trailhead for the **Johnson Pass Trail,** which goes 23 miles

over relatively level terrain (with some short, steep sections) and emerges at Mile 33 of the Seward Highway. Two in-the-trees Forest Service campgrounds are nearby: **Bertha Creek Campground** (Mile 65 Seward Hwy., no phone, $14) and **Granite Creek Campground** (Mile 63, 518/885-3639 or 877/444-6777, www.recreation.gov, $14, add $9 for campsite reservation). The paved **Sixmile Bike Trail** parallels the highway from the Johnson Pass Trailhead south to the junction with the Hope Highway.

Sixmile Creek
At Mile 59 the highway crosses a staging area along Granite Creek for rafters and kayakers down Granite Creek and on to Sixmile Creek. This is one of Alaska's premier white-water areas. Check out the action from the footbridge that crosses Sixmile Creek, accessible via a short path from the parking area just east of the Canyon Creek bridge. Two companies lead white-water trips here: **Chugach Outdoor Center** (907/277-7238 or 866/277-7238, www.chugachoutdoorcenter.com) and **Nova Riverrunners** (907/745-5753 or 800/746-5753, www.novalaska.com). Three-hour trips ($99) are in Class IV water, while the five-hour trips ($149) include some intense Class V sections of the narrowly constricted lower canyon.

Nova is the original company on the river, but Chugach Outdoor is more established, with a permanent office at Mile 7.5 of the Hope Road; rafters appreciate the hot tub to warm up after the adventure. You must be age 12 to run the canyon, or 15 for the Class V section. Chugach also offers family-friendly 2.5-hour Turnagain Pass float trips ($80) on the scenic East Fork of Sixmile Creek.

◖ HOPE

Now almost a ghost town, Hope (www.hope-alaska.info) is a charming step into the past, with winding dirt roads, weathered log buildings with piles of firewood on the side, a little museum, a couple of eateries and lodging places, quiet waterside campsites, and great hiking. Bring your bike to ride the back roads of this town that time forgot.

The Hope Highway begins at Mile 56 of the Seward Highway, just west of the towering bridge over Canyon Creek. This sparsely trafficked road follows Sixmile Creek north back up to Turnagain Arm; pan for gold along the first five miles of the creek. The entire 17 miles to Hope is paved.

Gold was discovered on Resurrection Creek in 1888, and by 1896 there were 3,000 people inhabiting this boom neighborhood between Hope and Sunrise on Sixmile Creek. Many came by way of the Passage Canal where Whittier now squats, portaging their watercraft over the Chugach glacial pass to Turnagain Arm, which is how Portage Glacier got its name. Large-scale mining prospered into the 1940s, but then Sunrise was abandoned and left to the ghosts. Hope hangs on today primarily as a place where recreation and tourism support the town's 135 people.

Sights

Downtown Hope is marked by a cluster of old buildings, some over a century old. Stop here to walk the dirt street past photogenic **Social Hall**—the original Alaska Commercial Co. store—and down to the tidal flats (caused by the earth sinking seven feet in the 1964 quake). They're dangerous; don't walk on them! Go back and turn left for new Hope, with its post office, red schoolhouse, and beautiful new and old log cabins.

Hope & Sunrise Historical and Mining Museum (907/782-3740, Fri.-Mon. noon-4pm late May-early Sept., free) is a collection of log buildings housing historical photos and artifacts from the Turnagain Arm gold rush of 1894-1899. The grounds contain the original Canyon Creek Mining buildings, including the town's original school (1904), a blacksmith shop, historic barn, and a classic 1947 Dodge Power Wagon.

Recreation
HIKING

Gull Rock Trail begins from Porcupine Campground and parallels the shoreline of Turnagain Arm. It's a fairly easy stroll out to Gull Rock (five miles), making this a popular family hike or overnight camping trip.

Hope Point Trail starts at the campground and climbs steeply into the alpine for 2.5 miles, passing a microwave tower before reaching the peak. From here you can hike forever along the ridgeline. It's a wonderful day hike, but you're starting at sea level and ending at 3,630-foot Hope Point, so be prepared for a real workout. The trail isn't well maintained, but affords a good chance to see mountain goats, bears, and moose.

RESURRECTION PASS TRAIL

A half-mile east of Hope on the Hope Highway is the junction with Palmer Creek Road. Follow it 0.75 miles to a fork. Turn left and continue six long miles to **Coeur D'Alene Campground,** which has six free spots with fire rings and bear boxes.

Beyond the campground, go right on

FOLLOWING THE RESURRECTION PASS TRAIL

The Resurrection Pass Trail covers 38 miles between the towns of Hope and Cooper Landing, with two side routes leading off to trailheads along the Seward Highway. You'll gain and lose 2,000 feet in elevation along the way. A series of Forest Service cabins make this one of the most popular hiking destinations in Southcentral Alaska. The trail winds through spruce forests and tops out in tundra, affording opportunities to see a variety of habitats. Wildlife, wildflowers, and wild fish in the lakes and streams add to the trail's appeal.

The trail begins four rough miles from Hope up Resurrection Pass Road, where a trailhead has parking, an information signboard, and a fun bridge across the creek. Eight cabins (reservations: www.recreation.gov, $35-45 per night) along the trail, one of which can only be reached via a floatplane, provide a welcome respite from the often inclement weather. The cabins are basic, each consisting of wooden bunks, a table and benches, a countertop for cooking, an outhouse, and a heating stove for warmth, but without running water, cooking utensils, or bedding. The farther in advance you can make plans for these very popular cabins, the more likely you are to secure a reservation.

If you can't secure a cabin, there are plenty of spots to camp for the night. Be very careful with campfires, or better yet, use a camp stove for cooking. Also filter or boil all drinking water.

Local wildlife includes moose, black and brown bears, wolves, mountain goats, Dall sheep, and even a local caribou herd. The caribou are scattered and often hard to spot in the summer, but if you look up high in the Resurrection Pass and Devil's Pass areas, maybe you'll get lucky. They often like to bed down in snow patches during the heat of the day, so look for dark spots in the snow near ridgelines.

Loop trips are possible, and you can do the Devil's Pass trailhead-Devil's Pass cabin-Cooper Landing trip (27 miles) in three or four days, though hard-core mountain bikers often do it in one day. Hitchhiking to pick up your car is possible, but the Hope trailhead is well off the beaten path for most car traffic.

The high point of the main trail is Resurrection Pass at 2,600 feet. However, even at this comparatively low elevation, the snows of winter can linger well into June. Postholing through thigh-deep snow can dampen the enthusiasm of even the jolliest of hikers. If you're thinking of an early-season hike, check with the Forest Service office in Anchorage (907/271-2500) or the Seward Ranger District (907/224-3374, www.fs.fed.us/r10/chugach) for trail conditions.

At the southern end of the Resurrection Pass Trail at Cooper Landing, you can continue south on the 16-mile **Russian Lakes Trail,** which connects with the 16-mile **Resurrection River Trail** all the way to Exit Glacier near Seward. Together, these three trails make it possible to hike 74 miles, a 12-day trek that covers the Kenai Peninsula from head to toe.

Resurrection Pass Road six miles to the Resurrection Pass trailhead, with parking, an information signboard, and a fun bridge across the creek. This popular backpack or mountain bike trip leads 38 miles down to Cooper Landing on the Sterling Highway, or you can cut across on the 10-mile **Devil's Pass Trail** to Mile 39 on the Seward Highway.

Accommodations

Clustered around a tiny pond, **Bowman's Bear Creek Lodge** (Mile 16, Hope Hwy., 907/782-3141, www.bowmansbearcreeklodge.com, Tues.-Sun. year-round, cabins $210 d with dinner, cottage $310 d with dinner, add $40 pp for extra guests) provides unique dinner-and-lodging in a peaceful setting. Five log cabins contain woodstoves and a shared bathhouse. Also available is a lovely cottage with separate bedroom, full kitchen, and private bath. One cabin sleeps six. Several units are wheelchair accessible, and guests appreciate the cozy cedar sauna, paddleboat, and canoe. Relaxing four-course dinners are included, with a gourmet menu that focuses on steak, local seafood, pasta, and vegetarian options.

Discovery Cabins (on the edge of Bear Creek, 907/782-3730 or 800/365-7057, www.adventurealaskatours.com, mid-May-Sept., $90 d, add $15 pp for extra guests, up to four) has five modern cabins in Hope (near the school). The cabins share a bathhouse and an outdoor hot tub (but this may not be available). The owners also operate Adventure Alaska, a tour company with a guided adventure for small groups.

You'll find a convenience store, laundry, showers, and RV spaces at **Alaska Dacha** (19842 Hope Hwy., 907/782-3223, www.alaskadacha.com, mid-May-mid-Sept., $35 RVs with full hookups, $15 tents, motel rooms $100-120 d, cabin $155, hostel unit $70) along the road as you come into town. The second level has motel rooms, each with a private bath, fridge, microwave, satellite TV, and Wi-Fi. The most expensive of the motel rooms has a whirlpool tub. A separate cabin sleeps up to eight and contains a kitchen and bath. Also available is a hostel-style unit with two sets of bunk beds, fridge, and microwave, but the shared bath and shower are outside.

Adjacent to Alaska Dacha, **Hope's Hideaway** (19796 Hope Hwy., 907/252-1044, www.hopeshideaway.com, $160 d, add $10 pp for extra guests) is a duplex cabin where each side contains a full kitchen, private bath, and two bedrooms. A door connects the two units for large groups. There's a hot tub inside and the owners are hospitable.

Three miles from Hope along secluded Middle Creek, **■ Black Bear B&B** (63640 Resurrection Creek Rd., 907/782-2202, www.alaskablackbearbnb.com, May-Sept., $145 d, add $20 pp for extra guests) is a delightful cabin with a comfortable log bed, private bath, wood burning stove, screened-in back porch, and BBQ grill. Breakfast ingredients are stocked in the kitchenette. Owner Maggie Holeman has a lifetime of knowledge about the area.

Camping

At the end of Hope Highway is the Forest Service's delightful **Porcupine Campground** (Mile 17.8 Hope Hwy., www.fs.usda.gov/chugach, $18), featuring fine views across Turnagain Arm, plenty of shade, and red raspberries as hors d'oeuvres in late summer. The 34-site campground makes an excellent base to explore the area, just a short distance from town and with tall trees and fine hiking opportunities.

Park RVs or pitch a tent in town at **Seaview RV Park** (end of Main St., 907/782-3300, www.seaviewcafealaska.com, $6 tents, $18 RVs with electricity, cabin $60 d). Sites are along the creek, which is a popular spot to catch pink salmon (humpies) or to pan for gold. There are also rustic cabins with outhouses available. Get water at adjacent Seaview Café.

Food

Built in 1896, picturesque **Seaview Café** (end of Main St., 907/782-3300, www.seaviewcafealaska.com, Sun.-Wed. noon-9pm, Thurs.-Sat. noon-11pm mid-May-mid-Sept., $20) serves giant burgers, seafood chowder, Reubens, and the house specialty—halibut fish and chips. There's live music of the roots-Americana type Thursday-Saturday evenings in the bar or on the front deck when the weather cooperates, plus Alaska beers on draught.

The best local restaurant is **Discovery Café** (907/782-3274, Thurs.-Mon. 7am-9pm, Tues.-Wed. 7am-3pm late May-early Sept.; Thurs.-Mon. 9am-7pm May and Sept., $15-20), serving three meals a day. Dinners include blackened halibut, wraps, teriyaki burgers, stir-fried veggies, and daily specials, along with homemade pies and soup.

Bowman's Bear Creek Lodge (Mile 16 Hope Hwy., 907/782-3141, www.bowmansbearcreeklodge.com, Tues.-Sun. dinner year-round, $35 pp for non-guests) serves four-course dinners; reservations are required.

Co-owner of Bowman's Bear Creek Lodge,

© DON PITCHER

historic Seaview Café in Hope

Melanie Bowman also operates **Sweet Mo's** (2nd St., 907/782-3141, daily noon-6pm late May-mid-Sept.), serving scoops of Alaska Supreme ice cream and pizza slices. The shop also has a few gifts, and is across from the museum in town. Credit cards are not accepted. **Grounds for Hope** (2nd St. and A St., 907/947-9037, Thurs.-Mon. 8am-2pm summer, closed winter), next to the library, has espresso to go.

Information and Services

Stop by the **Hope Library** (2nd St. and A St., 907/782-3121, Mon.-Sat. noon-4pm, Sun. 11am-2pm) which has Wi-Fi, computers, and an adjacent gift shop.

SOUTH TO SEWARD

Beyond the Hope Highway junction, the Seward Highway climbs to scenic Summit Lake at Mile 46 (80 miles south of Anchorage). Surrounded by high mountains, the lake makes a great place for summertime photos. Signs warn against stopping in winter when avalanches have been known to slide across the highway.

Cozy and well placed **Summit Lake Lodge**
(51826 Seward Hwy., 907/244-2031, www.summitlakelodge.com, May-mid-Sept., motel rooms $125 d, cabins $165 d) overlooks the lake. The original lodge was built in 1953, but the big fireplace and chimney are the only parts of the building that survived the 1964 quake. The restaurant (daily 11am-8pm, $18-28) serves seafood and Alaskana fare, along with a memorable Fruit of the Forest pie. A separate ice cream shop serves 16 flavors, plus espresso and homemade pizza by the slice or pie. Walk out the door for a lovely picnic along the lake. There's also a small motel (no TVs) and six spacious waterside cabins with private baths and flat-screen TVs. There are no phones, and your cell phone may not work, but Wi-Fi is available in the lodge. Overnight guests are served a made-to-order breakfast.

Just a half-mile down the highway from the lodge is the turnoff to **Tenderfoot Creek Campground** (Mile 46 Seward Hwy., 518/885-3639 or 877/444-6777, www.recreation.gov, $14, plus $9 reservation fee), a beautiful area with 36 campsites on the shores of this alpine lake. Sites can be reserved in advance.

Perfect for a late-summer day hike or an extended backcountry trip, **Summit Creek Trail** is a hidden gem that gets you into the alpine area in less than an hour. The trailhead isn't signposted, so look for the small parking area on the west side near Mile 44; it is just above the avalanche gates. The trail gains 2,600 feet in elevation over eight beautiful miles to a junction with Resurrection Trail.

Just after Mile 40 and a mile before the Seward-Sterling junction is **Devil's Creek Trailhead;** this trail leads 10 miles to the pass, then another mile to where it joins the Resurrection Pass Trail. An **alpine cabin** (518/885-3639 or 877/444-6777, www.recreation.gov, $45) sits on the pass. (A great overnight hike takes Summit Creek Trail to Resurrection Pass Trail, then back down via Devils Creek Trail to the highway.)

The **Carter Lake Trail** leaves the highway at Mile 33, climbs nearly 1,000 feet in just over two miles to Carter Lake, and continues another mile around Carter Lake to Crescent Lake. This route gets you into the alpine fast and can be used to loop back to the highway on the Crescent Lake and Crescent Creek Trails. There's a **Forest Service cabin** (518/885-3639 or 877/444-6777, www.recreation.gov, $45) on the south shore of Crescent Lake.

A half-mile beyond the Carter Lake Trailhead is the southern trailhead to **Johnson Pass Trail** (whose northern trailhead is at Mile 64). And just beyond that is **Trail Lakes Fish Hatchery** (907/288-3688, www.ciaanet.org, daily 8am-4:30pm), which has a fascinating display about spawning and stocking salmon. Tours are often available (10am and 2pm), but depend upon staffing. The facility produces millions of sockeye and coho salmon fry and smolt for lakes across the Kenai Peninsula.

MOOSE PASS

Nestled on the shore of Trail Lake, tiny Moose Pass (pop. 200, www.moosepassalaska.com)

is 30 miles north of Seward. Here since 1928, the classic **Estes Brothers Grocery** (Mile 29.5 Seward Hwy., 907/288-3151, Mon.-Sat. 8am-7pm, Sun. 10am-6pm in summer, closed Tues. in winter) has a limited selection of groceries, along with sandwiches and espresso. Don't miss the 10-foot-high **Estes waterwheel** just up from the store. Pull out your pocketknife to give it an edge on the grindstone; the sign proclaims, "Moose Pass is a peaceful little town. If you have an axe to grind, do it here."

The main event comes on the **summer solstice** (June), when the town springs to life with music, food, and games.

Scenic Mountain Air (907/288-3646 or 800/478-1449, www.scenicmountainair.com, floatplane $129 pp) offers 30-minute floatplane trips from Trail Lake. If it's a clear day, the views are stunning. The company can also provide wilderness fishing trips and drop-offs at Forest Service cabins.

Accommodations

A large and exquisite B&B, **⬛ Inn at Tern Lake** (Mile 36 Seward Hwy., 907/288-3667, www.ternlakeinn.com, $175-200 d) has a mountain-rimmed setting that encompasses muskeg ponds, forests, a putting green, tennis courts, and even a private airstrip. The inn is six miles north of Moose Pass and just south of pretty Tern Lake. Guests stay in four luxuriously appointed suites, with access to a hot tub, a sauna, and a high-ceilinged great room. A delicious full breakfast is included. The inn is a great place for summer weddings, but isn't really set up for young children.

Set atop a hill along Trail Lake, **Alpenglow Cottage** (36215 Seward Hwy., 907/288-3142, www.alpenglowcottage.com, $135 d, add $25 pp for extra guests) is a fine choice for families or two couples traveling together. Inside are two bedrooms with double beds, a full kitchen, private bath, and deck.

Jewel of the North B&B (31087 Seward

Hwy., 907/288-3166 or 877/317-7378, www. jewelofthenorth.net, $125 d) is a private and woodsy haven overlooking Trail River. The single suite has a king bed and the kitchenette is stocked with breakfast fixings. There is a two-night minimum stay.

On a hillside, **Spruce Moose Chalets** (36035 Seward Hwy., Mile 29.9, 907/677-7543, www. sprucemoosealaska.com, $349-399) consists of three very comfortable chalets; one sleeps up to seven for the same rate. Each has bedrooms, kitchens, and baths. A three-night minimum is required.

Right in the heart of town, **Trail Lake Lodge** (Mile 29.5 Seward Hwy., 907/288-3103 or 800/865-0201, www.traillakelodge.com, motel rooms $109 d, lodge units $126 d) is the least expensive place to stay at Moose Pass, with basic motel rooms and larger lodge units; there is also a restaurant and a lounge.

Teddy's Inn the Woods B&B (29792 Seward Hwy., 907/288-3126, www.seward.net/teddys, $150 d, $180 for four) is a charming upstairs apartment with a bedroom, full kitchen and bath, outside decks, and space for up to four guests. Owner Teddy Berglund serves warm cookies in the evening, plus homemade scones and fresh fruit for breakfast. The place is perfect for couples looking for quiet, but also has bunks for kids. Teddy's is five miles south of Moose Pass, and 23 miles north of Seward. Credit cards are not accepted.

Renfro's Lakeside Retreat (Seward Hwy., 907/288-5059 or 877/288-5059, www.renfroslakesideretreat.com, mid-Apr.-mid-Oct., lakeside cabins $150, woods cabins $125-135, $30 RV hookups) is 8 miles south of Moose Pass—and 20 miles north of Seward—along the shore of Kenai Lake. Here you'll find eight cabins, all with private baths and kitchenettes. Five are right on the beautiful lake and three are back in the woods; all of these sleep 4-5 people. Full RV hookups are also available, along with Wi-Fi, paddleboats, and a playground. There are no TVs or phones.

South from Moose Pass

Six miles south of Moose Pass is the turn-off for **Trail River Campground** (Trail River Rd., 518/885-3639 or 877/444-6777, www. recreation.gov, $18, plus $9 reservation fee), a quiet wooded campground just over a mile off Seward Highway, with some choice sites on the lakeshore loop. Next up on the left is **Ptarmigan Creek Campground** (Mile 23 Seward Hwy., 518/885-3639 or 877/444-6777, www.recreation.gov, $14, plus $9 reservation fee). **Ptarmigan Creek Trail** climbs from the campground for 3.5 miles along the creek to Ptarmigan Lake, where there's good fishing for grayling. The trail continues another four miles to the east end of the lake.

Magnificent **Kenai Lake** comes into view just south of here: huge, beautiful, blue-green, with snowcapped peaks all around. Three-mile **Victor Creek Trail** starts at Mile 20. Three miles south on the Seward Highway is the turn-off to little **Primrose Campground** (Mile 17 Seward Hwy., $14). It's right on the shore of Kenai Lake, a mile up the road.

Eight-mile long **Primrose Trail** takes off from Primrose Campground, climbing 1,500 feet to Lost Lake, where you can hook up to **Lost Lake Trail** and come out at Mile 5 near Seward. This 15-mile hike is one of the most popular loop trails in the area. If you planned far enough ahead and made a reservation, you can stay at the **Dale Clemens cabin** (Lost Lake Trail, 518/885-3639 or 877/444-6777, www.recreation.gov, $45, plus $9 reservation fee). On clear days, you get a magnificent view of Resurrection Bay and beyond, out to the Gulf of Alaska.

Beautiful **Porcupine Creek Falls** is three miles in on the Primrose Trail and is a favorite day-hike destination. Above the lake are dramatic alpine views and the chance to explore this high and mighty landscape.

Seward

Seward is a pocket-sized port town (pop. 3,000) on a sparkling bay surrounded by snowcapped peaks, and is the only large settlement on the east side of the Kenai Peninsula. It's connected by bus, ferry, and plane and has a maritime climate and a seafood industry, just like a half-dozen other places you've visited so far, but with a difference: Seward is right on the doorstep of Kenai Fjords National Park. This park contains some of the most inhospitable visitable country in the state. Boat tours into the park are a major attraction, with a wide variety of day-tour options. Harding Icefield—a prehistoric frozen giant with three-dozen frigid fingers—rivals Glacier Bay for scenery and wildlife but is decidedly less expensive to visit. Combine this with Seward's Alaska SeaLife Center, convenient camping, good food, and excellent access by public transportation, and you've got all the elements for a great time in this old town.

Today, Seward has a diverse economy supported by tourism, commercial fishing and sportfishing, fish processing, and other activities. The Alaska SeaLife Center is the main focal point for travelers and has excellent exhibits. The Alaska Vocational Technical Center (AVTEC, www.avtec.edu) trains 1,600 students each year in such fields as welding, diesel repair, and marine sciences, and a maximum security prison on the east side of Resurrection Bay houses another 450 folks in less academic conditions.

A towering coal-shipping facility dominates the harbor; the Alaska Railroad hauls coal here from the Usibelli Coal Mine in Healy for shipment to South Korea. Some cruise ships also dock in Seward, but most companies have shifted their ships to Whittier. It's too bad for them, since they miss one of the most enjoyable towns in Southcentral Alaska.

HISTORY

In 1791, Alexander Baranov, on a return voyage to Kodiak from around his Alaskan domain, waited out a storm in this bay on the Sunday of Resurrection, a Russian holiday. The sheltered waters of Resurrection Bay prompted Baranov to install a small shipyard. In 1903 surveyors for the Alaska Central Railroad laid out the town site for their port. This private enterprise, financed by Seattle businessmen, established Seward, laid 50 miles of track, and went broke. In 1911, Alaska Northern Railroad extended the track almost to present-day Girdwood. In 1912 the U.S. government began financing the completion of this line, which reached Fairbanks, 470 miles north, in 1923. From then, Seward's history parallels Valdez's as one of the two year-round ice-free ports with shipping access to Interior Alaska—Seward's is by rail, Valdez's is by road. And like Valdez, Seward was almost completely destroyed by 1964's Good Friday earthquake.

SIGHTS
◖ Alaska SeaLife Center

Seward's most enjoyable attraction, the SeaLife Center (Mile 0 Seward Hwy., 907/224-7908 or 888/378-2525, www.alaskasealife.org, Mon.-Thurs. 9am-6:30pm, Fri.-Sun. 8am-6:30pm mid-May-mid-Sept.; daily 10am-5pm mid-Sept.-mid-May, $20 adults, $15 ages 12-17, $10 ages 4-11, younger children free) sits on the south edge of town facing Resurrection Bay. This impressive facility provides visitors with a wonderful way to learn about marine wildlife up close. There are informative exhibits about commercial fishing and the impacts of ocean acidification, aquariums filled with crabs, sea jellies, and octopuses, tide-pool touch tanks, and a big gift shop, but the main attractions are three gigantic tanks, each with two-story

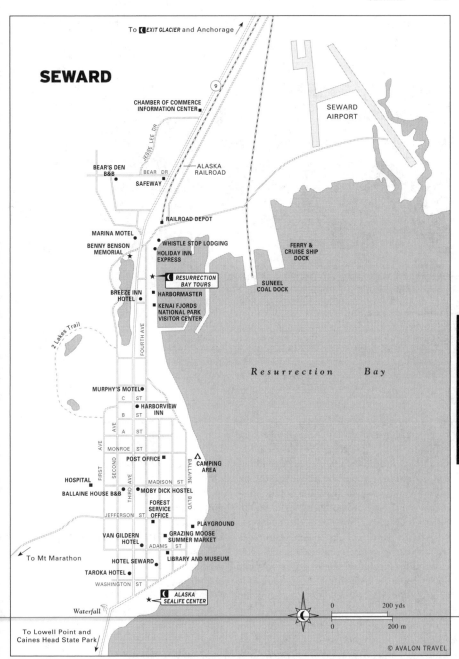

SEWARD

To ◖ *EXIT GLACIER* and Anchorage

CHAMBER OF COMMERCE
INFORMATION CENTER

SEWARD
AIRPORT

JESSE LEE DR

9

BEAR'S DEN
B&B
BEAR DR
— ALASKA
RAILROAD

SAFEWAY

RAILROAD DEPOT

MARINA MOTEL

WHISTLE STOP LODGING

BENNY BENSON
MEMORIAL
★
HOLIDAY INN
EXPRESS

FERRY &
CRUISE SHIP
DOCK

★ ◖ *RESURRECTION
BAY TOURS*

BREEZE INN
HOTEL ●
■ HARBORMASTER

SUNEEL
COAL DOCK

■ KENAI FJORDS
NATIONAL PARK
VISITOR CENTER

2 Lakes Trail

FOURTH AVE

R e s u r r e c t i o n   B a y

MURPHY'S MOTEL ●

C   ST

● HARBORVIEW
INN

B   ST

A   ST

AVE

MONROE   ST

POST OFFICE ■

⌂ CAMPING
AREA

BALLAINE

HOSPITAL ■

FIRST

SECOND

THIRD AVE

MADISON   ST

BALLAINE HOUSE B&B ■

● MOBY DICK HOSTEL

FOREST
SERVICE
OFFICE

JEFFERSON   ST

BALLAINE   BLVD

■ PLAYGROUND

VAN GILDERN
HOTEL ■

■ GRAZING MOOSE
SUMMER MARKET

ADAMS   ST

To Mt Marathon

HOTEL SEWARD ●

■ LIBRARY AND MUSEUM

TAROKA HOTEL ●

WASHINGTON   ST

Waterfall

★ ◖ *ALASKA
SEALIFE CENTER*

To Lowell Point and
Caines Head State Park

0   200 yds

0   200 m

© AVALON TRAVEL

© DON PITCHER

downtown Seward

windows where visitors can take in the under-sea world.

The seabird tank houses puffins and other birds whose ability to fly underwater delights all, and the harbor seals' playful personality shows through in their amusing interactions with people. Most extraordinary of all are the Steller sea lions that circle their tanks, coming up to check out children next to their windows. They're amazingly agile, even though the big male (Woody) weighs over 2,000 pounds—more than a small car! For visitors, the SeaLife Center is a place to learn about the marine environment, but this is also an important center for marine research and the rehabilitation of wildlife, including pigeon guillemots and Steller sea lions. Behind-the-scenes tours ($15 adults, $10 students) provide an excellent hour-long look at the center's facilities, research programs, and wildlife rehabilitation efforts. For a hands-on experience with puffins, marine mammals, and a giant Pacific octopus, take

a personalized one-hour encounter tour ($79 adults, $59 students, $39 kids); a maximum of four people can join this one. Another hour-long tour option—puffin experience ($25)—provides an opportunity to help feed the puffins. Groups are much larger on the puffin tour. Reservations are required for all the tours, so call ahead of your visit. In addition, Kenai Fjords National Park rangers offer 45-minute slideshows all summer at the SeaLife Center, with a morning talk about glaciers and an afternoon program on archaeology.

◖ Resurrection Bay Tours

The most exciting thing to do in Seward is to get on a tour boat out into Resurrection Bay or into some nearby fjords. This is *the* cruise for seeing marine wildlife. On a good day, you could see humpbacks and orcas, plus porpoises, seals, sea otters, sea lions, hundreds of puffins, kittiwakes, auklets, and the occasional bald eagle and oystercatcher. Half-day trips take you around nearby Resurrection Bay and out as far as Rugged Island, while longer voyages include Aialik Bay, Holgate Glacier (with calving icebergs), and the Chiswell Islands (with a Steller sea lion rookery and nesting seabirds—most notably puffins). The latter is a far more interesting trip and actually goes inside Kenai Fjords National Park rather than to its edge, but the waters are often rough, so take your seasickness pills.

Tour boats operate daily throughout the season, with gray whale trips from early April to mid-May, and a multitude of other tour options mid-May through September. Visit early or late in the season and you're likely to find lower prices and fewer people on board. Binoculars and telephoto lenses are handy, and a light jacket is wise. These trips are guaranteed to be a highlight of your Alaskan visit.

Seward's largest tour company, **Kenai Fjords Tours** (907/224-8068 or 888/478-3346, www.kenaifjords.com) primarily operates big 95-foot vessels that hold up to 150 people. They offer a wide variety of cruises, starting with a too-quick 3.5-hour dinner trip to Fox Island ($64). Better options are a 4.5-hour Resurrection Bay tour ($94) that includes a lunch stop on Fox Island; a six-hour trip with time in Kenai Fjords National Park plus lunch ($144); or a nine-hour sail to Northwestern Fjord ($174) that includes breakfast and lunch. Their most popular voyage—and my favorite—is an 8.5-hour trip ($164) to Aialik Bay that includes lunch plus an hour-long stop on Fox Island for a big salmon and prime rib buffet dinner at Kenai Fjords Wilderness Lodge. Rates for children are half the adult prices.

For a more intimate sailing, book a trip aboard the company's 22-passenger boat. These "Captain's choice" nine-hour trips (adults or children $214) focus on birds and wildlife, and include a morning snack and lunch. The destination varies depending upon the interest of passengers, but may include the Chiswell Islands, Aialik Glacier, and Northwestern Fjord. Kenai Fjords Tours is owned by CIRI, an Anchorage-based Native Alaskan corporation. Spring trips (early Apr.-mid-May) follow the gray whale migration (four-hour tour $84).

Major Marine Tours (907/224-8030 or 800/764-7300, www.majormarine.com) offers half-day cruises to Resurrection Bay ($69-79) and all-day trips to Holgate or Aialik Glacier in Aialik Bay ($149-159). Guests are treated to an all-you-can-eat salmon and prime rib buffet ($19 extra). Boats heading to Aialik Bay are speedy and stable catamarans, helpful when seas are rough. These are large vessels, holding up to 250 passengers. Early in the year (Apr.-mid-May), Major Marine offers four-hour gray whale watching trips ($79). On all Major Marine Tours, rates for children under 12 are half the adult rate. A National Park Service ranger provides expert narration and commentary on all Major Marine tours.

For a more personalized adventure, **Alaska Saltwater Lodge** (907/224-5271, www.alaskasaltwaterlodge.com) has customized small-group trips ($209) into the park, with a maximum of 15 passengers. (The larger operators sometimes have more than 150 people onboard.)

Some Seward B&Bs and hostels offer 10 percent discounts on Resurrection Bay tours; ask your lodging place if these are available before booking a tour.

Seward Museum

The new library building houses the Seward Museum (6th Ave. and Adams St., 907/224-3902, Mon. 11am-6pm, Tues.-Thurs. 11am-8pm, Fri.-Sat. 11am-6pm summer, by appointment in winter, $3 adults, $0.50 children). The museum's collection includes Native Alaskan baskets and carved ivory, equipment from the original Brown & Hawkins store, the cross-section of a 350-year-old Sitka spruce, and photographs from the 1964 earthquake that dropped parts of this country by six feet.

THE KENAI PENINSULA

Also here is Alaska's original flag, designed by a local boy—Benny Benson—in 1927.

Other Sights

Find a small memorial to **Benny Benson** (corner of Seward Hwy. and Dairy Hill Ln.), the 13-year-old orphan who designed Alaska's state flag, on the north side of town next to the lagoon. There's also a bust of **William H. Seward** (Adams St.) next to the Van Gilder Hotel. Far more imposing statues of Seward are in New York and Seattle.

An ever-expanding collection of murals graces the sides of many Seward buildings. Pick up a brochure showing the locations at the visitors center, or check out www.seward-muralsociety.com.

Lowell Point Road extends 2.5 miles south of Seward, hugging the shoreline of Resurrection Bay. Just south of the SeaLife Center is a much-photographed waterfall on Lowell Creek, and the road ends in a cluster of homes, campgrounds, and businesses at **Lowell Point.** Park at Lowell Point State Recreation Site, where a trail leads to the beach. Time your visit with the tides to explore nearby tidepools for sea stars, sea anemones, and other creatures. The 4.5-mile Coastal Trail leads to Caines Head.

Seven miles north on the Seward Highway, turn onto Bear Lake Road and continue a half-mile to **Bear Creek Weir.** The weir is used to count fish returning to Bear Lake, with upwards of 20,000 sockeye and coho salmon swimming up this creek to spawn. See the spawning sockeye in June and July, followed by coho late July into September. While here, keep your eyes open for dippers, unusual birds with the ability to walk underwater.

ENTERTAINMENT AND EVENTS

Downtown Seward has several popular drinking establishments with pool tables and occasional live music. **Liberty Theater** (305 Adams St., 907/224-5418) is the local movie house.

The year kicks off in Seward with the **Polar Bear Jump-Off** (third weekend in Jan.), a leap of faith into the frigid 39°F water of Resurrection Bay. All sorts of goofy-costumed jumpers join the fray. It's all for a good cause, however, since jumpers collect pledges for contributions to the American Cancer Society.

Every July 4th the **Mount Marathon Race** (www.seward.com) attracts 960 runners who race up and back down the steep slopes of this 3,022-foot summit that rises behind Seward. Some slots are held open to the highest bidder, and folks have been known to bid $1,000 for the privilege to race! Many runners do it in under an hour, but they end up with bruises and bloody knees to show for the torture—the record is 43 minutes and 23 seconds. The race has been run annually since 1915. This event is a major Alaskan institution, filling the bars and campgrounds with runners and 40,000 or so spectators. In addition to the Mount Marathon race, other Fourth of July events include a parade, food and crafts booths, live music, and midnight fireworks. Make lodging or camping reservations far ahead.

The end of summer brings another event that draws the crowds, the **Silver Salmon Derby** (Aug., $10 per day), where the prizes total over $100,000. This is one of Alaska's richest fishing derbies, and it's been going on since 1956.

SHOPPING

Seward has a number of interesting studios scattered around town, including the **Resurrect Art Coffeehouse Gallery** (320 3rd Ave., 907/224-7161, www.resurrectart.com, daily 7am-7pm summer, daily 8am-5pm the rest of the year). Also worth a look is **Ranting Raven** (224 4th Ave., 907/224-2228, open seasonally), with art and gifts, pastries, and light lunches.

Cover to Cover (215 4th Ave., 907/224-2525, daily 9am-10pm summer) is the local bookshop.

Downtown's **Brown & Hawkins Store** (204 4th Ave., 907/224-3011, www.brownandhawkins.com) is Alaska's oldest family-owned business. It's been here since 1900 and still houses the old bank vault and cash register. The store houses a good selection of outerwear, but the main draw is Sweet Darlings Candies, with homemade gelato, fudge, and other treats.

Downtown's **Grazing Moose Summer Market** (312 5th Ave., 907/491-1076, www.thegrazingmoose.com, Thurs.-Sun. 10am-4pm June-Sept.) has local artists, organic produce, food (tasty veggie nachos or reindeer sausages), and gifts.

RECREATION

If you have kids along, give everyone a break at **Seward Community Playground** (just south of the campground at Ballaine Boulevard and Adams Street).

Day Hikes

For an enjoyable one-mile walk on a winding trail through the forest and around the creatively named First Lake and Second Lake, look for the **Two Lakes Trail** behind the AVTEC Center (2nd Ave. and C St.). There's a picnic area at the trailhead.

The high bare slope hanging over Seward is **Mount Marathon,** featured attraction for the 4th of July Mountain Marathon Race. It generally takes nonrunners at least four hours to get up and back. Follow Jefferson Street due west up Lowell Canyon and look for the trailhead to the right just beyond a pair of large water tanks. You can run all the way back down the mountain on a steep gravel incline if your legs and nerves are good, but beware of slipping on the solid rock face near the bottom. The trail does not actually reach the summit of Mount Marathon (4,560 ft.) but rather the broad east shoulder (3,022 ft.), which offers a spectacular view of Seward and the entire surrounding country.

State Parks

Two popular state parks (907/262-5581, www.alaskastateparks.org) are close to Seward on the shores of Resurrection Bay: Caines Head State Recreation Area and Thumb Cove State Marine Park.

Caines Head State Recreation Area (accessible via the Coastal Trail) was the site of a World War II military base, Fort McGilvray, and the old command post still stands atop a massive 650-foot headland. There are dramatic views of Resurrection Bay and the surrounding country. The 4.5-mile Coastal Trail leads to the old fort from **Lowell Point State Recreation Site** (Mile 2 Lowell Point Rd.), three miles south of Seward. Parts of the trail follow the shoreline and can only be hiked at low tide; be sure to check the tide charts before heading out. Take a flashlight to explore the maze of underground passages and rooms at Fort McGilvray. Also here are ammunition magazines and firing platforms for the six-inch guns that guarded Seward. This area makes a fine overnight trip, and a walk-in campground complete with three-sided shelter is available at **Tonsina Point,** a mile in. Caines Head is very popular with sea kayakers who paddle here from Seward to hang out with the sea otters and seals. Also within the park are often-booked hike-in **public use cabins** ($65) at Derby Cove and Callisto Canyon.

Thumb Cove State Marine Park is on the east side of Resurrection Bay, seven miles from Seward, and accessible only by boat. The park includes a long sandy beach, forested uplands, and the waters of Thumb Cove. Porcupine Glacier towers behind. Thumb Cove is a favorite stop for recreational boaters, and camping is popular along its beaches. Two cozy cabins ($65) are in the park, each sleeping up to eight people.

THE KENAI PENINSULA

Fishing

Fishing is one of Seward's most popular activities, and in midsummer dozens of boats dot the waters while hundreds of anglers cast from the shore. Salmon are the main attraction, made all the more enticing by a summer-long fishing derby. Your odds of catching one increase if you can get away from the shore, and many charter boats are available. Halibut fishing is another favorite, but you'll need to get quite far out—sometimes all the way to Montague Island in Prince William Sound—to catch one.

Get a complete list of charter operators from the Visitors Information Center, or contact a booking agency. The oldest and largest (it represents 30 or so boats) is **The Fish House** (across from the harbormaster's office, 907/224-3674 or 800/257-7760, www.thefishhouse.net). If you aren't fishing, drop by the harbor in the late afternoon when charter operators hang up the day's catch for photos. It's quite a sight. **Miller's Landing** (907/224-5739 or 866/541-5739, www.millerslandingak.com) has fishing charters and also rents 16-foot skiffs ($120 for four hours) for do-it-yourselfers. In addition, they rent fishing equipment, from rods and reels to dry bags, waders, and VHF marine radios. Miller's Landing is on Lowell Point, 2.5 miles south of Seward.

Sea Kayaking and Water Taxis

Most Resurrection Bay sea kayaking originates from the scenic Lowell Point area, three miles south of Seward. Five companies—Adventure 60 North, Backcountry Safaris, Kayak Adventures, Liquid Adventures, and Sunny Cove Sea Kayaking-offer an all-day trip to Caines Head ($130-165), along with trips that combine a boat tour to Aialik Bay within Kenai Fjords National Park, followed by a glacier paddle and return to town ($400). In addition, all five companies offer multiday trips to Northwestern Fjords and Aialik Bay within Kenai Fjords National Park.

Kayak trips are generally offered mid-May to early September.

Kayak Adventures (907/224-3960, www.kayakak.com) has a kayak-and-sailing day trip ($230) that combines both of these activities, plus a Kayakers Cove day trip ($200) that adds a water taxi for kayaking along the eastern shoreline near Fox Island.

Sunny Cove Sea Kayaking (907/224-4426 or 800/770-9119, www.sunnycove.com) has day trips ($179-189) to Fox Island aboard a Kenai Fjords tour boat followed by a paddle, salmon bake, and wildlife cruise back to town. The company also offers three-hour sunset paddles ($65).

For something completely different, **Liquid Adventures** (907/224-9225 or 888/325-2925, www.liquid-adventures.com) leads stand up paddling day trips to Bear Glacier ($500). These trips include a helicopter flight from Seward and several hours on stable, inflatable paddle boards. Clients wear dry suits, and are able to paddle around the lagoon and up to icebergs. Liquid Adventures also has three-hour paddles to Tonsina Creek, a good place to view spawning salmon.

Based along Exit Glacier Road, **Adventure 60 North** (907/224-2600, www.adventure60.com) also rents kayaks, outdoor gear such as tents, sleeping pads, bear spray, and even rubber boots. Adventure 60's most unique offerings combines a scenic helicopter flight to Bear Glacier followed by sea kayaking on the lake ($550 for five hours, $675 for eight hours). A full 10-hour trip ($814) includes a helicopter to Bear Glacier, kayaking, and a hike onto the glacier. Overnight camping trips to the glacier are also available. In winter, the company provides snow cat trips to Exit Glacier.

Kayak rentals are available from **Backcountry Safaris** (907/222-1632 or 877/812-2159, www.alaskakayak.com), which also has kayak rentals and water taxi services. **Miller's Landing** (Lowell Point, 907/224-5739 or 866/541-5739, www.millerslandingak.com) rents kayaks for experienced do-it-yourselfers, and provides kayaking day trips and instruction, along with water-taxi service to transport kayaks into remote parts of Kenai Fjords.

Other water taxis with landing crafts are **Weather Permitting/Alaska Wildland Adventures** (907/224-6595 or 877/907-3677, www.watertaxiak.com) and **Seward Water Taxi** (907/362-4101, www.sewardwatertaxi. com). These water taxis go to Fox Island ($70 round-trip), Bear Glacier ($220 round-trip), and Aialik Bay ($300 round-trip).

Kayakers Cove (907/224-8662, www.kayakerscove.com) is a unique and well-run operation a dozen miles from Seward. Reasonably priced hostel-type lodging and kayak rentals are available, with access by water taxi from Miller's Landing.

In the summer, **Chugach Outdoor Center** (907/277-7238 or 866/277-7238, www.chugachoutdoorcenter.com, $80 adults, $60 ages 5-10) has an easy eight-mile (2.5-hour) float down the Resurrection River from Exit Glacier.

Sailing

Sailors say Resurrection Bay contains some of the finest sailing waters north of San Francisco Bay, with windy conditions almost every day. Because of this, there are two local yacht clubs, **Kenai Fjords Yacht Club** (www.kfyc.org) and **William H. Seward Yacht Club** (www.whsyc. org), plus dozens of sailboats berthed in the Small Boat Harbor.

In business since 1975, **Sailing, Inc.** (907/224-3160, www.sailinginc.com, May-mid-Sept., two-hour trip $425 for up to six people) has personalized two-hour sailing trips on a 32-47-foot boat. Guests can help hoist sails and take a turn at the helm but won't be forced to walk the plank if they mess up. The company's American Sailing Association classes for both novices and experts include a four-day intensive learn-to-sail class ($895).

THE KENAI PENINSULA

© DON PITCHER

Seward boat harbor

Their six-day basic-to-bareboat sailing package ($1,450) is especially popular with travelers since it includes three days living onboard the boat. Sailing Inc. also has bareboat charters for experienced sailors.

Dogsledding and Glacier Tours

Seward Helicopter Tours (907/362-4354 or 888/476-5589, www.sewardhelicopters.com, late May-early Sept.) has on-the-snow summertime dogsledding trips. The action begins from Seward Airport, where you climb aboard a helicopter for a 10-minute flight to a world of snow, ice, and rocky peaks on crevice-free Godwin Glacier. The base camp here has 30 dogs and their handlers, including experienced musher Joe Holod. Guests are given a tour of the operation, an introduction to mushing, a fun ride behind a team of dogs, and a bundle of cute puppies. The entire trip lasts 1.5 hours ($419 pp). A shorter option ($179 pp) is a helicopter ride to the glacier and 15 minutes on the ice (without a sled ride). There are similar one-hour trips that land on magnificent Bear Glacier ($249 pp).

Veteran musher—and 2004 Iditarod winner—Mitch Seavey operates **IdidaRide Sled Dog Tours** (Mile 1.1 Old Exit Glacier Rd., 907/224-8607, www.ididaride.com, $69 adults, $35 children) from his home off Exit Glacier Road. Summertime visitors are pulled on a wheeled cart along a two-mile route. These 1.5-hour tours include an introduction to the Iditarod and a chance to play with adorable husky puppies. Mitch's son, Dallas Seavey, won the 2012 Iditarod. At only 25 years old, he was the youngest person ever to win the race.

Exit Glacier Guides (405 4th Ave., 907/224-5569, www.exitglacierguides.com) offers helicopter ice hikes that include a round-trip flight to Godwin Glacier and a guided glacier hike with options for 1.5 or 2.5 hours on the ice ($350 and $415, respectively). They also provide a shuttle service to Exit Glacier ($10) and guided hikes on this very accessible glacier ($130).

Flightseeing

Scenic Mountain Air (907/224-9152 or 800/478-1449, www.scenicmountainair.com) provides flightseeing and charter trips from the airport.

Horseback Riding

Bardy's Trail Rides (Old Nash Rd., 907/224-7863, www.sewardhorses.com, $95) leads two-hour horseback rides twice daily throughout the summer. This is a fun way to explore the scenic country at the head of Resurrection Bay, with good chances to see bald eagles, moose, and spawning salmon.

Biking

Karl Mechtenberg of **Seward Bike Tours** (907/362-7433, www.sewardbiketours.com) leads mountain biking trips of all lengths, from three-hour rides to Exit Glacier ($80) to week-long all-inclusive backcountry adventures on Chugach National Forest trails. He also offers unique wintertime fat bike rentals, along with rides to Exit Glacier and along nearby beaches.

Rent mountain bikes, beach cruisers, and baby joggers from **Seward Bike Shop** (411 Port Ave., 907/224-2448, Apr.-Oct., mountain bikes $38/day, $21/half day) in the collection of "Train Wreck" Alaska railcars.

ACCOMMODATIONS

Seward has plenty of indoor lodging options, but be sure to book ahead in the summer, especially any weekend in August when the Silver Salmon Derby attracts throngs of visitors and fills every room for miles around. The city of Seward hits travelers with a 10 percent lodging tax.

A great first stop when looking for lodging is **Alaska's Point of View Reservation Service** (907/224-2323, www.alaskasview.com), where owner Debra Hafemeister makes bookings (no extra charge) for more than 100 local places at a wide range of prices.

Hostels

Right downtown, **Moby Dick Hostel** (432 3rd Ave., 907/224-7072, www.mobydick-hostel.com, May-Sept., $25 pp dorm rooms, $70 d, $80-85 larger units) has clean dorm-style rooms with kitchen facilities and showers. There are basic private rooms with a queen bed as well as two nicer units with kitchenettes and a double and twin bed.

Six miles north of town, **Nauti Otter** (13609 Seward Hwy., 907/491-2255, www.nautiotter-inn.com, $30 pp hostel, $65 d, cabins $80-90) has clean private rooms, cabins, and a six-bed hostel room. All guests have access to two fully stocked kitchens, stocked with ingredients for a filling breakfast, along with freshly baked muffins. There's a bathhouse with showers outside, plus a flushable outhouse. A paved bike path provides access to town, and bike rentals are available. Owner Heather Callen has a strong knowledge of the area and will be happy to direct you to off-the-beaten-path sights.

Snow River Hostel (Mile 15.5 Seward Hwy., 907/440-1907, $20 pp dorm rooms, $65 d, add $10 pp for extra guests, $10 for sauna), 16 miles north of Seward, is a quiet creekside place convenient to hikers coming off the Lost Lake Trail. Inside are dorm rooms with baths, a kitchen, and a common room. There are also private rooms and cabins. A sauna is also available. The hostel is open summers and may remain open through the winter months.

Adventurous travelers should check out **Kayakers Cove** (907/224-8662, www.kay-akerscove.com, late May-early Sept., $20 pp hostel, $60 cabin for up to three people), on a small bay near Fox Island, 12 water miles from Seward. There is rustic wilderness hostel-type lodging and a private cabin. There are no showers, and you'll need a sleeping bag, but

a kitchen and a wood-fired sauna are on the grounds. Kayakers Cove is accessible by water taxi ($60 pp round-trip) and rents kayaks (doubles $30/day, singles $20/day) for guests.

Hotels and Motels

Located in the center of town and decked out with stuffed critters, the **Hotel Seward** (221 5th Ave., 907/224-2378 or 800/655-8785, www.hotelsewardalaska.com, $109 d shared bath, $159 d private bath, $229-279 d deluxe rooms) has a variety of rooms for all budgets. The historic section (no elevator) contains economy guest rooms with two single beds and a bath down the hall. Standard guest rooms with private baths are in the older section. Deluxe rooms in the modern Alaska wing of the hotel are large and nicely appointed. Breakfast is not included in the room price, but there is a restaurant and lounge on the premises. There is free Wi-Fi here, too.

An old-time 1970s-era downtown place, **Taroka Motel** (233 3rd Ave., 907/224-8975, www.alaskaone.com/taroka, $125 d or $135 for four guests) has simple, clean (but dark) rooms with separate bedrooms and full kitchens. It's not the least bit fancy, but it is conveniently located and reasonably priced.

Just two blocks from the boat harbor, **Murphy's Alaskan Inn** (909 4th Ave., 907/224-8090 or 800/686-8191, www.murphysmotel.com, $139 d, $179 d larger units) provides a no-frills mix of older guest rooms and larger units with harbor views and balconies. All rooms contain fridges, microwaves, and Wi-Fi, and a continental breakfast is available in the lobby.

Opened in 1916, and now on the National Register of Historic Places, the **Van Gilder Hotel** (308 Adams St., 907/224-3525 or 800/204-6835, www.vangilderhotel.com, $119 d shared bath, $169-189 d private bath, $229 suites) is a classic hotel just two blocks from the Alaska SeaLife Center. The immaculate small rooms feature brass beds and antiques, along with Wi-Fi, a continental breakfast, and budget-saving community kitchen, but the lack of an elevator can be a challenge in this three-story structure. There are standard rooms with a queen bed and three budget "pension rooms" with a bath down the hall. Families appreciate the four suites, each featuring a main room with a queen bed plus a connecting room with a queen bed and twin murphy bed; suites accommodate up to five guests. Guests sometimes report hearing or seeing the ghostly apparition of Fannie Guthry-Baehm; she died in room 209 after being shot by her husband in 1950.

Directly across the street from the small boat harbor, clean and comfortable 100-room **Breeze Inn Hotel** (1306 3rd Ave., 907/224-5237 or 888/224-5237, www.breezeinn.com, $159 d, $209-259 d newer units, $279 suites) has two-double-bed standard rooms (no view) and newer units with limited harbor or mountain views. Two-room suites accommodate up to four guests. There is free Wi-Fi and in-room fridges, plus a spacious lobby and summer-only shuttle service.

It's hard to beat the harbor-side location of **Holiday Inn Express** (1412 4th Ave., 907/224-2550 or 800/465-4329, www.holidayinn.com, $219-229 d, $269-279 d waterside units), which also offers a small indoor pool (the only one in town), a hot tub, a breakfast buffet, a business center, limited Wi-Fi, and balconies on some units. The hotel has predictable chain-motel guest rooms (each with two queen or one king bed) with units facing the mountains or the water.

Fittingly located across from the railroad station, **Whistle Stop Lodging** (411 Port Ave., 907/224-5050, www.sewardak.net/ws, June-mid-Sept., $150 d, $180 for four people) provides a fun opportunity to overnight in a vintage Alaska Railroad car from the World War II era. Originally used as a sleeping car, it was converted into a two-room lodging place with baths, microwaves, and fridges. Windows

look out on the harbor. Also in the railroad cars is Smoke Shack—famous for mouth-watering ribs.

Bed-and-Breakfasts

Seward has dozens of bed-and-breakfasts. The Visitors Information Center has rack cards from most of these, and its website (www.seward.com) provides links; or give the **Point of View Reservation Service** (907/224-2323, www.alaskasview.com) a call to book a good B&B.

Blending Asian and Scandinavian sensibilities, **Soo's B&B** (810 2nd Ave., 907/224-3207 or 888/967-7667, www.soosbandb.com, $145 d) was designed by owner Soo Kang's architect son. Four bright guest rooms are available and include a full breakfast, private baths, Wi-Fi, and freezer space for your fish.

Centrally located in a quaint 1905 home, **Ballaine House B&B** (437 3rd Ave., 907/224-2362, www.superpage.com/ballaine, mid-May-mid-Sept., $86 s, $122 d) gets raves from guests who appreciate the cozy Grandma's-house setting, reasonable rates, and Wi-Fi. The home—now on the National Register of Historic Places—was built by Frank Ballaine. Frank and his brother John were the founders of Seward. Friendly owner Marilee Koszewski crafts a made-to-order breakfast each morning and is a great source for information on local sights and attractions. Guests have access to the kitchen and laundry service, along with booking discounts and Wi-Fi. Five guest rooms share two baths (one bath for each floor).

One of the finest local places, **Bear Paw Lodge** (Bear Paw Dr., 907/224-3960, www.sewardbearpawlodge.com, mid-May-early Sept., $125 d shared bath, $185 d suite, $125 family bunk room) is a beautiful hand-built log home just north of town. The energetic owners are local kayak guides—they also run Kayak Adventures—who will happily provide an introduction to the area. Two downstairs guest rooms share a bath, and the master suite fills the loft. There's also a bunk room for families, along with such amenities as a full kitchen, gas fireplace, large hot tub on the deck, Wi-Fi, and filling continental breakfasts. The kitchen is stocked if you want to cook dinners on your own. There is a two-night minimum stay.

Located at Lowell Point 2.5 miles south of town, **Alaska Saltwater Lodge** (Lowell Point, 907/224-5271, www.alaskasaltwaterlodge.com, mid-May-mid-Sept., $109-189 d, $269-309 d suites, $229 cottage, add $20 pp for extra guests) is right on Resurrection Bay. There are stunning vistas from the common room, and just out the door is a quiet sandy beach. All units have private baths, and guests are served a filling breakfast. There are small rooms, larger units with windows on the bay, spacious 2-3-bedroom suites with private kitchens, and a cottage that sleeps six comfortably. The owners also operate a water taxi and a kayak rental business, with customized small-group whale watching tours.

Six miles north of Seward along Bear Lake, with impressive glacier vistas, **Kim's Forest B&B** (33780 Bear Lake Rd., 907/224-7632 or 888/512-7632, www.sewardalaskabnb.com, $138 d shared bath, $168-200 d private bath) is a luxurious home with six guest rooms, an attentive owner, queen beds, Wi-Fi, and great breakfasts. The master suite contains a big whirlpool tub, and the setting is relaxing. Bear Creek weir is a quarter mile walk. No kids under age 11 are allowed.

◖ **Bear Lake Lodgings B&B** (33820 Bear Lake Rd., 907/224-2288, www.bearlakelodgings.com, $150 d shared bath, $205 d suites) is six miles north of town along this quiet and pristine lake. Two guest rooms share a bath, while the two suites have private baths. A big breakfast is served in the second floor dining room, and the owners are famous for their hand-dipped ice cream bars, served each evening. (Co-owner Pat Perry runs the popular

Original Gourmet Ice Cream Bar stand at the Alaska State Fair each summer.) Guests can borrow a canoe or kayak to explore the lake, or listen to the loons calling each evening. In the winter, the lake is groomed for cross-country skiing right out your door. Wireless Internet is available.

A modern home across from the beach at Lowell Point, ◖ **Alaska Paddle Inn** (13745 Beach Dr., 907/362-2628, www.alaskapaddleinn.com, $209-219 d), has two very nice rooms with a good view of the bay. Owners Alan and Alison Heavirland are former kayaking guides with an affinity and strong knowledge of the outdoors. Alan's carpentry skills are exhibited in the artistically designed rooms, and Alison (a licensed massage therapist) offers massage services at the inn. Both units include kitchenettes stocked with breakfast ingredients, gas fireplaces, private baths, and Wi-Fi. The upstairs suite has a king bed, and the downstairs unit has a separate bedroom with queen bed, plus a futon couch. There is a two-night minimum on weekends.

Just a few blocks from the harbor, **Bear's Den B&B** (221 Bear Dr., 907/224-3788 or 800/232-7099, www.bearsdenalaska.com, May-Oct., $155-185 d) has three lodging options, all with private baths, decks or patios, TV, and Wi-Fi. The largest unit sleeps six, and includes a full kitchen and private entrance.

Other recommended Seward B&Bs include: **Raven's Haven B&B** (211 Lowell Canyon Rd., 907/224-3637, www.ravenshavenbandb.com, $145 d), **Sourdough Sunrise B&B** (Old Exit Glacier Rd., 907/224-3600, www.sourdoughsunrise.com, $139 d), **Steller B&B** (11952 Old Exit Glacier Rd., 907/224-7294, www.stellerbandb.com, $139 d), **A Swan Nest Inn** (504 Adams St., 907/224-3080 or 866/224-7461, www.sewardvacationproperties.com, $125-135 d), and **Brass Lantern B&B** (331 2nd Ave., 907/224-3419, www.brasslanternbandb.com, $150 d).

Cabins and Suites

◀ **Alaska Creekside Cabins** (Old Exit Glacier Rd., 907/224-1996, www.welovealaska.com, mid-May-mid-Sept., $110-150 d) consists of eight in-the-woods cabins north of town on the road to Exit Glacier. All contain fridges, microwaves, TVs, Wi-Fi, and a fire pit out front; the largest has space for five. The cabins share a modern bathhouse with showers. Clear Creek flows through the property, providing spawning habitat for chum salmon, and they in turn often attract brown bears. The cabins are rustic, but clean and authentically Alaskan, with a super friendly owner. Dogs are welcome.

Situated up the hill behind Seward, the appropriately named **A Cabin on the Cliff** (1104 Hulm Ln., 907/224-2411 or 800/440-2444, www.acabinonthecliff.com, $389 d) provides a unique perspective of Resurrection Bay. Originally a trapper's cabin, this adorable log cabin has an antique brass bed, fireplace, kitchenette, and a large private deck where the hot tub is enclosed by a gazebo.

A quarter-mile off Seward Highway, **Exit Glacier Lodge** (Exit Glacier Rd., 907/224-6040, www.sewardalaskalodging.com, $149-169 d, $219 d suite, $119 cabins) provides modern hotel rooms in a Victorian-style false-front building. Fifteen guest rooms have private baths, fridges, TV, and Wi-Fi, with a light breakfast in the lobby each morning. The second floor suite has its own balcony, king and queen beds, and a leather sofa. Nearby are four private cabins, each with a queen and bunk bed, plus a bath, microwave, fridge, and TV. These sleep four guests. There is no breakfast, and Wi-Fi is available only in the lodge lobby.

A beautifully appointed cedar home six miles north of town, **Havenwood Guest House** (13670 Oakwood St., 907/224-3261, www.havenwoodak.com, $149 for two, add $15 for extra guests) provides a private escape. The spacious master bedroom has a queen bed, and the loft contains twin beds, making this perfect for families. On the deck is a hot tub and BBQ grill, and the guesthouse has a well-stocked kitchen, laundry, and Wi-Fi.

Located in a secluded forest setting a mile from Seward Highway, **Box Canyon Cabins** (Old Exit Glacier Rd., 907/224-5046, www.boxcanyoncabin.com, $155 d one bedroom, $249-279 two bedrooms, add $15 pp for extra guests) consists of six very nice log cabins, each with full kitchens (stocked with breakfast ingredients), private baths, TVs, and Wi-Fi. There are one-bedroom and two-bedroom cabins; the latter sleep four. A laundromat is on the premises.

Located on Fox Island and accessible only by boat, **Kenai Fjords Wilderness Lodge** (Fox Island, 907/224-8068 or 877/777-4053, www.kenaifjordslodge.com, June-early Sept., $454 pp, $349 pp shorter tour) sits in the heart of Resurrection Bay. Guests stay in modern private cabins (but no electricity, phones, or Wi-Fi) and enjoy hearty family-style meals at the lodge. Get there on board a Kenai Fjords Tours boat, and spend a night and two days on the island. The excursion includes meals, guided kayaking, and an all-day boat tour into Northwestern Fjord. There is a lower rate if you opt for a much shorter Resurrection Bay tour with your stay.

Angel's Rest on Resurrection Bay (Beach Dr., Lowell Point, 907/224-7378 or 866/904-7378, www.angelsrest.com, $199 d, $251-261 d cabins, $229 d suites) encompasses a variety of delightful lodging options in the Lowell Point area south of town. They include three modern waterfront cabins, two guest rooms, and two mini-suites, all with queen beds, private baths, kitchenettes, BBQ grills, and Wi-Fi. A newly constructed retreat center here provides space for gatherings of all types, from family reunions and weddings to business meetings.

Yurts

Yurts have become a popular lodging option around Seward, with three very different options available. Six miles north of town near Bear Lake, **Sourdough Sue's Bear Lake Lodging** (33910 Tressler Ave., 907/362-2454, www.sourdoughsue.com, May-Sept., $149 d, add $15 for extra guests; larger yurt: $200 for four guests, $225 for six, $250 for eight) has three modern yurts, each with heat, private bath, queen and futon beds, and a covered porch with gas grill. Two sleep up to six and have kitchenettes, while a third larger yurt encloses two private bedrooms and a full kitchen. It sleeps 4-8 people. There are no TV or phones, but your cell phone probably works here and Wi-Fi is available.

Close to the beach at Lowell Point is another yurt at **Alaska Base Camp** (14000 Beach Dr., 907/224-4692, www.alaskabasecamp.com, mid-Apr.-Sept., $175 d). Inside the large yurt are three beds, a futon, kitchenette, private bath, deck with BBQ grill, and Wi-Fi. Otters and bald eagles are a common sight from the deck, and Liquid Adventures kayaking is adjacent.

Nine miles southeast of town in Humpy Cove, **Orca Island Cabins** (Orca Island, 907/224-5846, www.orcaislandcabins.com, May-Sept., $398 d, add $125 pp for extra guests) provides a great way to get in touch with your wild side. Three surprisingly comfortable 20-foot yurts are perched along the shore of this small island, with two new ones on the mainland across an 80-foot arched footbridge. Each yurt has a waterside deck with Adirondack chairs, queen bed and futon, kitchenette, private bath, heater, and grill. The owners emphasize an eco-friendly experience, with on-demand hot showers, composting toilets, and other features. The cost includes round-trip water taxi from Seward. Rates drop if you stay extra days, and guests have access to kayaks (plenty for everyone), a rowing skiff, firewood, and fishing gear. Kids under age 10 are not allowed for safety reasons.

Camping
City officials provide a long stretch of crowded year-round camping at **Waterfront Park** (Ballaine Blvd., 907/224-4055, www.cityofseward.us, tents $10, RVs $15, with hookups $30) along the shore, with toilets, showers ($2), picnic shelters, beautiful views, and lots of company—there are 450 sites. You can also camp at the city's **Forest Acres Campground** (Mile 2 Seward Hwy., 907/224-4055, $10), where there are large trees and some highway noise.

Six miles north of town, **Stoney Creek RV Park** (off Stoney Creek Ave., 907/224-6465 or 877/437-6366, www.stoneycreekrvpark.com, late May-early Sept., $35-40) is a full-service RV campground with Wi-Fi, satellite TV, showers, and laundry. Tent camping is discouraged here.

Silver Derby Campground (Lowell Point Rd., 907/224-4711, www.resres.net/silverderby, mid-May-mid-Sept., $12 tents, $20 RVs) is near Miller's Landing, with wooded sites for tents and RVs. There is no running water, but outhouses are available and potable water is available nearby. (Water may be added by 2014.) The bay is just a few steps away.

Miller's Landing Campground (Lowell Point, 907/224-5739 or 866/541-5739, www.millerslandingak.com, May-mid-Sept., $26 tents, $36 RVs) has RV and tent spaces. In the Lowell Point area, the rough-around-the-edges campground contains coin-op showers, oceanfront and wooded sites, laundry facilities, Wi-Fi, a fish cleaning area, and a small store. Fishing charters, kayak rentals, and water taxi services are available through Miller's Landing.

FOOD
Breakfast
On summer mornings, the fishing crowd crowds into **Bakery at the Harbor** (across from the Small Boat Harbor, 907/224-6091, daily 5am-7pm June-Aug., Thurs.-Mon. 7am-1pm Sept.-May, $5-13) for espresso and fresh-baked

THE KENAI PENINSULA

© DON PITCHER

You can camp at Waterfront Park in Seward.

pastries (gigantic cinnamon rolls). Pastries sell out, so get here early. The bakery has decent lunch sandwiches, burgers, and soups too, but the prices are high.

Housed within an old Lutheran church, **Resurrect Art Coffeehouse Gallery** (320 3rd Ave., 907/224-7161, www.resurrectart.com, daily 7am-7pm summer, daily 8am-5pm winter, under $5) is a wonderful place to hang out over an espresso on a rainy day, play a game of chess, check your email (free Wi-Fi), or listen to occasional live music. It's also the best Seward spot to buy Alaskan art, pottery, and jewelry.

Sea Bean Café (225 4th Ave., 907/224-6623, www.seabeancafe.com, daily 7am-9pm summer, Mon.-Sat. 7am-5pm winter) is a pleasant downtown coffeehouse with their own blend of coffee, cushy couches, street-side bay windows, free Wi-Fi, and rental computers ($2 for 15 minutes).

Crepes
◖ **Le Barn Appetit** (11786 Old Exit Glacier Rd., 907/224-8706, www.lebarnappetit.com, daily 7am-4pm May-Dec., by appointment only the rest of the year, $10-18) is locally famous for authentic Belgian waffles and enormous crepes from friendly chef Yvon van Driessche. The creperie isn't much from the outside, but Yvon's savory and dessert crepes will win you over. Try his crepe du-jour with spinach, egg, cheese, and reindeer sausage. The café also serves quiche, éclairs, and espresso.

Chinese
Two places serve Chinese food in Seward, both with lunch buffets and Korean American owners: **Peking Chinese Cuisine** (338 4th Ave., 907/224-5444, daily 11am-10pm, $14-21) and **Oriental Garden** (311 4th Ave., 907/224-7677, daily 11am-10pm, lunch buffet $10, dinner $14-21), just up the street. Of the two, I'd probably pick Oriental Garden, but Peking has a decent view of the bay.

Mexican

Get a fast taco, burrito, or quesadilla from **Railway Cantina** (1401 4th Ave., 907/224-8226, www.railwaycantina.com, daily 10am-midnight summer; daily 10am-8pm spring and fall, closed Nov.-Feb., $9-10), directly across from the boat harbor. Check the blackboard for all the options—including Alaskan halibut, reindeer, smoked salmon, and rockfish—and top them off with a selection of hot sauces and a draught of beer. The owners are big hockey fans, as you'll quickly learn from the decor.

Barbecue

It isn't the least bit pretentious, but you'll find great barbecue ribs, burgers, smoked green chili burritos, creole shrimp tacos, memorable smoked Reuben sandwiches, and other "food for the soul" at ◖ **Smoke Shack** (411 Port Ave., 907/224-7427, daily 7am-8pm May-Sept., daily 7am-3pm the rest of the year, $11-22), located in the collection of vintage Alaska Railroad cars on Port Avenue. Portobello mushroom sandwiches and a few other vegetarian options are also available, along with an amazing crab cakes eggs Benedict for breakfast. Owner and chef Steve Miller makes everything entirely from scratch; his corned beef hash is a three-day process—and it's worth it. The railcar has 24 often-full seats inside, but you can also take food outside to the picnic tables.

Pizza

Just across the street from the SeaLife Center is busy **Christo's Palace** (133 4th Ave., 907/224-5255, www.christospalace.com, daily 9am-11pm late May-Christmas, Wed.-Sun. 11am-5pm the rest of the year, $16-29). Pizzas are available all day, including several no-red-sauce variations and a Mama Mia thick-crust pizza with pepperoni, Canadian bacon, sausage, hamburger, and veggies. Local seafood is a specialty; try the smoked salmon fettuccine, king crab legs, or the house specialty, tequila honey shrimp over jasmine rice. Lunch features charbroiled burgers, gyros, and sandwiches. Belly up to the gorgeous mahogany back bar—constructed in 1887—for a beer (nine Alaskan brews on draught). The restaurant is noisy enough that your kids won't even be heard.

Seafood

The food better be good when the sign out front of **Thorn's Showcase Lounge** (208 4th Ave., 907/224-3700, 11am-midnight, $24-30) proclaims "Home of the Bucket of But" and the interior is filled with ancient velvet furniture, big TVs, and dense cigarette smoke. The "but" in question is, of course, halibut, and this old bar—probably not remodeled since it's 1971 opening—really does serve the best fish and chips in town. Get a big bowl of deep fried halibut chunks with fries ($28) or a basket ($17). Bacon cheeseburgers, French dip sandwiches, steamer clams, and other pub fare are also available, along with full dinners of steak or halibut. The smoke can be pretty bad in the lounge, so order your meal to go. It's hard to miss the lounge's amazing collection of 525 historic Jim Beam bottles covering the walls (with hundreds more in the basement); it's said to be one of the largest in existence.

Ray's Waterfront (1316 4th Ave., 907/224-5606, www.rayswaterfrontak.com, daily 11am-10pm mid-Apr.-Sept., $24-40), at the Small Boat Harbor, is especially convenient for grabbing a bite while you wait for your tour boat (or for a hot toddy when you get back). The walls of Ray's are lined with trophy fish, and picture windows look out over the harbor. House specialties include seafood such as crab cakes, Cioppino, and cedar planked salmon, but steaks are also popular. Ray's main problem is its popularity, so reservations are highly recommended—especially on summer weekends.

A few doors up the street is **Chinooks Waterfront Grill** (907/224-2207, www.chinookswaterfront.com, daily 11am-11pm

CHUGACH NATIONAL FOREST

© DON PITCHER

Tern Lake near Moose Pass, Chugach National Forest

Much of the eastern Kenai Peninsula lies within Chugach National Forest, the second-largest national forest in the country after the Tongass. Covering 5.5 million acres—bigger than Massachusetts—the Chugach not only encompasses this part of the Kenai but also continues eastward across all of Prince William Sound well beyond the Copper River. Developments and logging are relatively minor on the Chugach, but all this wild country provides incredible opportunities for recreation, with good fishing, hiking, mountain biking, river rafting, skiing, kayaking, wildlife-watching, glacier-gazing, and a host of other outdoor adventures. The forest headquarters (3301 C. St., 907/743-9500, www.fs.usda.gov/chugach) are in Anchorage, with district offices in Seward (907/224-3374), Girdwood (907/783-3242), and Cordova (907/424-7661).

CABINS AND CAMPING

The Kenai Peninsula has 18 Forest Service public-use cabins (518/885-3639 or 877/444-6777, www.recreation.gov, $45 per night, $9 reservation fee). These are mostly Pan-Abode log structures that sleep four and have wood or oil stoves. Most of these are along hiking trails—including eight cabins on the Resurrection Pass Trail—but a few are accessible only by floatplane. The Chugach website has cabin details, or you can get brochures from the Alaska Public Lands Information Center in Anchorage. Because of their high popularity, it's wise to reserve cabins well ahead of your visit. Additional public cabins can be found within Kenai Fjords National Park and Kachemak Bay State Park.

Six Forest Service campgrounds are located along the Seward Highway south of Portage, with another four along the Sterling Highway, and two more off the Hope Highway.

HIKING

A number of very popular hiking trails cover the eastern half of the Kenai Peninsula, and it's possible to hike (or mountain bike) all the way from the town of Hope to Exit Glacier near Seward, a distance of 74 miles. Contact the Forest Service for details on various hiking options within the Chugach.

year-round, $24-28), with two levels fronting the harbor and a menu of local seafood, including the house specialty, pan roasted halibut, along with rockfish and chips ($18), hand-crafted burgers ($12), and steaks.

North of town, **Exit Glacier Salmon Bake** (Exit Glacier Rd., 907/224-2204, www.sewardalaskacabins.com, daily 5pm-10pm mid-May-mid-Sept., $10-28) is exceptionally popular with locals, serving good baked salmon dinners, along with halibut, prawns, steaks, and burgers in a wooded, family-friendly setting.

Brewpub

Seward's newest and most exciting restaurant is ◖ **Seward Brewing Company** (139 4th Ave., 907/422-0337, www.sewardbrewingcompany.com, daily 4pm-10pm, $15-37), with an enormous two-level space, large windows looking across Resurrection Bay, and a friendly waitstaff. Check out the brewery and bar menu on the main floor or fine dining upstairs. The menu changes often, but typically includes grilled halibut with pesto, black and blue burgers, crab cakes with Basmati rice, BBQ ribs, and tasty appetizers such as house fried crispy potato chips, or Portobello mushroom strips with ginger aioli. The brewery produces several beers—available on tap or in growlers to go, including SBC White and SBC Red Ale; get a four-beer sampler ($7).

Sweets

Housed within the historic Brown & Hawkins Store, **Sweet Darlings** (209 4th Ave., 907/351-2107, www.sweetdarlings.com, daily 9am-9pm, gelato $4/two scoops) will be a hit with your sweet tooth, featuring wonderful homemade gelato, truffles, fudge, and other treats.

INFORMATION AND SERVICES

Soap and rinse your entire body at the **Harbormaster Building** (907/224-3138). Additional showers are in the city campground at the foot of Madison Street. There's a **swimming pool** at the high school (2001 Swetmann Ave., 907/224-3900) where they throw in a free swim with your shower. Wash your clothes at **Suds-N-Swirl** (335 3rd Ave., 907/224-3111) in town, or **Box Canyon Cabins** (907/224-5046, www.boxcanyoncabin.com) north of Seward, a mile out Old Exit Glacier Road. Suds-N-Swirl also houses a coffee shop (aptly named the Sip-N-Spin), so you can tank up while washing your duds.

For medical emergencies, head to **Providence Seward Medical Center** (417 1st Ave., 907/224-5205, www.providence.org).

Brand new in 2012, the **Seward Community Library** (6th Ave. and Adams St., 907/224-4082, www.cityofseward.net/library, Mon. 11am-6pm, Tues.-Thurs. 11am-8pm, Fri.-Sat. 11am-6pm) provides a welcome escape on a rainy (or snowy) day. Free computers and Wi-Fi are available.

Parking is often a challenge in Seward, particularly near the harbor, where you'll need to pay $5 per day at the pay station. If you're heading out for the day, boat tour companies provide free lots with shuttle buses back to the harbor.

Visitor Centers

For Seward maps and brochures, start out at the **Seward Chamber of Commerce** (907/224-8051, www.seward.com, Mon.-Fri. 9am-6pm, Sat. 9am-5pm, Sun. 9am-4pm mid-May-mid-Sept.; Mon.-Fri. 9am-5pm mid-Sept.-mid-May), located two miles north of town. It's one of the first places you pass as you're driving into Seward from Anchorage.

Adjacent to the harbor, **Kenai Fjords National Park Information Center** (1212 4th Ave., 907/422-0500, www.nps.gov/kefj, daily 8:30am-7pm late May-early Sept.; daily 9am-5pm the rest of May and most of Sept.; closed late Sept.-Apr.) has videos of the park, along with maps and publications of local interest. Park rangers provide daily talks at the SeaLife

Center downtown, and daily hikes from the Exit Glacier Visitor Center, just north of town out Exit Glacier Road.

The staff at **Chugach National Forest Seward Ranger District** office (334 4th Ave., 907/224-3374, www.fs.usda.gov/chugach, Mon.-Fri. 8am-5pm) can tell you about all regional hikes, campgrounds, and cabins.

GETTING THERE

The Alaska Marine Highway ferry doesn't stop in Seward; the closest ports are Whittier and Homer.

Train

An **Alaska Railroad** *Coastal Classic* **train** (907/265-2494 or 800/544-0552, www.alaskarailroad.com, $79 one way, $125 round-trip; kids half-price) leaves Anchorage daily during the summer at 6:45am and arrives in Seward at 11am, then returns to Anchorage at 6pm, arriving at 10:15pm. For the deluxe version, **GoldStar** double-decker coaches (mid-May-mid-Sept., $134 one way) include open-air viewing platforms for an old-fashioned luxury rail experience.

Bus

Seward Bus Lines (907/224-3608 or 888/420-7788, www.sewardbuslines.net, daily in summer, six times a week in winter, $40) has year-round bus service to and from Anchorage.

The Stage Line (907/235-2252, www.stagelineinhomer.com, Mon.-Fri. May-early Sept.) runs vans connecting Seward with Homer ($80) and Soldotna ($50). Drivers can stop almost anywhere along the route to pick up or drop off passengers. Vans stop at the Seward Chamber of Commerce office.

Park Connection (907/245-0200 or 800/266-8625, www.alaskacoach.com, mid-May-mid-Sept.) has buses connecting Seward with Anchorage ($55-65), Talkeetna ($130), and Denali ($155). Park Connection buses only stop in Seward on days when cruise ships are in port.

GETTING AROUND

Rent a car from **Hertz** (907/224-4378 or 800/654-3131, www.rentacaralaska.com) or catch a ride from **PJ's Taxi** (907/224-5555, www.pjstaxi.com), **Glacier Taxi** (907/224-5678, www.glaciertaxicab.com), **Alaska Mike's Taxi** (907/224-6453, www.alaskamikestaxi.com), or **Seward Taxi & Tours** (907/362-8000). It costs $5 around town or $10 from the harbor to Lowell Point.

Kenai Fjords National Park

Kenai Fjords National Park covers 580,000 acres of ice, rock, and rugged coastline on the southern end of the Kenai Peninsula. The centerpiece of this magnificent national park is the Harding Icefield, a massive expanse of ice and snow broken only by "nunataks"—the peaks of high rocky mountains. The icefield pushes out in all directions in the form of more than 30 named glaciers. Along the coast, eight of these glaciers reach the sea, creating a thundering display of calving icebergs. Kenai Fjords has only been a national park since 1980, but today it is one of the most popular attractions in Alaska. Many visitors come to ride the tour boats past teeming bird colonies or up to tidewater glaciers; many others hike to scenic Exit Glacier or up a steep path to the edge of Harding Icefield itself.

Next to the Seward harbor is **Kenai Fjords National Park Information Center** (907/422-0500, www.nps.gov/kefj, daily 8:30am-7pm late May-early Sept.; daily 9am-5pm the rest of May and most of Sept.; closed late Sept.-Apr.). Inside are exhibits on Harding Icefield and little-known sights within the park.

© DON PITCHER

touring Kenai Fjords National Park

The best way to see Kenai Fjords National Park is onboard one of the tour boats that depart from Seward harbor throughout the summer.

◖ EXIT GLACIER

One of Alaska's most accessible glaciers, Exit Glacier has a pretty setting, plus a mix of hiking trails, nearby campsites, and guided glacier hikes. This is the only part of the park that is accessible by road. Get to Exit Glacier by driving four miles north from Seward and turning left at the sign. The road ends nine miles later at a big parking lot. The glacier has been retreating rather dramatically in recent years, and areas that were under ice just a decade ago are now a hundred feet from the terminus.

Exit Glacier Nature Center (907/422-0500, www.nps.gov/kefj, daily 9am-8pm Memorial Day-Labor Day, closed the rest of the year)—the only one in Alaska powered by fuel cells—houses interpretive displays and a natural history bookstore. Rangers give programs and lead one-hour nature walks three times daily, along with very popular all-day hikes to Harding Icefield on Saturdays in July and August.

Exit Glacier Guides (405 4th Ave., 907/224-5569, www.exitglacierguides.com) lead five-hour excursions onto the glacier ($130 pp) as well as more adventurous ice-climbing trips ($185). For a bit more excitement, join a helicopter ice hike: a flight to Godwin Glacier followed by the chance to hike on the glacier with your guide before flying back over the mountains to Seward ($350 with 1.5 hours on the ice, $415 with 2.5 hours). Exit Glacier Guides also provide a shuttle service ($10 round-trip) from town that runs hourly all summer.

Hiking

A one-mile round-trip **nature trail** provides an easy, quiet forest walk. Two paths break off from it: **Glacier's Edge Trail** climbs a steep 0.25 miles up to the 150-foot face of Exit

THE KENAI PENINSULA

© DON PITCHER

Exit Glacier Nature Center

Glacier; a second path, **Toe of the Glacier Trail,** crosses the rocky outwash plain where you'll probably need to wade an icy-cold creek or two (use caution) to reach the end of the glacier. Don't get too close since the glacier can calve without warning.

Harding Icefield Trail, seven miles round-trip, forks off just after the bridge over the creek and climbs to 3,500 feet and to the icefield. Plan on at least six hours for this far more difficult hike, and check at the ranger station for current trail conditions since deep snow may block this route until midsummer. In the winter, the road into Exit Glacier is not plowed but is very popular with skiers and snowmobilers.

The 16-mile **Resurrection River Trail** starts at Mile 8 of the Exit Glacier Road. This is the southern end of the 74-mile three-trail system from Kenai's top to bottom. Resurrection River Trail leads to the 16-mile Russian Lakes Trail, which hooks up near Cooper Landing to the 38-mile Resurrection

Pass Trail to Hope. A **Forest Service cabin** (518/885-3639 or 877/444-6777, www.rec-reation.gov, $45) is six miles from the trailhead. Note that the Resurrection River Trail can become quite a quagmire when it rains, and it may be poorly maintained beyond the cabin; most folks simply hike to the cabin and then turn around. The trail is popular with cross-country skiers in wintertime because of its relatively low avalanche danger; it doesn't go into the alpine at all.

CAMPING AND CABINS

The excellent **Exit Glacier Campground** (907/422-0500, free) has a dozen walk-in tent sites just a short distance from the glacier. There's also a bear-proof food locker and modern cooking shelter. There is no cell phone coverage here.

The Park Service maintains two exceptionally popular public-use cabins within Kenai Fjords. **Aialik Bay Cabin** (907/644-3661 or

866/869-6887, www.alaskacenters.gov, mid-May-mid-Sept., $50/night, three-night maximum stay) sits along a long cobblestone beach with direct views across to Aialik Glacier. It's a fine base for kayaking expeditions. **Holgate Arm Cabin** (907/644-3661 or 866/869-6887, www.alaskacenters.gov, mid-May-mid-Sept., $50/night, three-night maximum stay) sits on a small bluff where you can watch the thunderous calving of Holgate Glacier or kayak to Pedersen Lagoon. Each cabin sleeps four, with a heating stove, but no outhouse. You'll need to use "Wag Bags" for human waste; yes, *everything* has to be packed out! Access to the cabins is primarily by charter boat from Seward. Be sure to reserve far ahead of time for these extremely popular cabins by contacting the **Alaska Public Lands Information Center** (907/644-3661 or 866/869-6887, www.alaskacenters.gov) in Anchorage. Bookings are available in early January for the summer season, and nearly all the spaces for the cabins fill up by the end of April.

During the winter, the Park Service rents the **Willow Cabin** (907/422-0500, near Exit Glacier, $35). To get to this cabin, ski the eight easy miles from the highway along unplowed Exit Glacier Road, or get a snowcat ride through Adventure 60 North. There is also a second enclosed winter-use structure nearby that is used as a warming shelter.

Kenai Fjords Glacier Lodge (907/283-2928 or 877/907-3677, www.kenaifjordsglacierlodge.com, June-mid-Sept., one night and two days $675 pp, two night and three days $1,095 pp) is tucked into a spectacular spot close to Pedersen Glacier along remote Aialik Bay. Located on and inholding of Native Alaskan land, this is the only lodge inside the park. There's a main lodge, 16 cabins (two double beds, private baths, and a small porch), plus guided kayak trips and beach hikes. Guests are treated to striking views of Pedersen Glacier and Pedersen Lagoon from the cabins and the lodge deck. Family style meals are served in the main lodge, and all meals are included, along with round-trip boat transport from Seward. Though shorter visits are possible, to really enjoy the remarkable setting book a three-day, two-night visit. There is no cell phone coverage or Wi-Fi in this remote spot. This is a wonderful place to splurge!

Backcountry Safaris (907/222-1632 or 877/812-2159, www.alaskakayak.com, one day and night $432 pp) has a less ostentatious operation on state land adjacent to Bear Glacier. Camp lodging (in sturdy WeatherPorts), water taxi to and from Seward, meals, kayaks, and guides are all included in the cost. You can stay for only one night, but rates drop substantially for multi-night stays. If you don't mind hostel-style accommodations, one WeatherPort is set up with three bunk beds ($40 pp). Lodging includes a covered kitchen and dining area. Rental kayaks are available, and access to the camp is extra ($220 pp round-trip by water taxi, $450 pp by helicopter). Day trips are also offered, but you'll probably want more time to explore this beautiful spot with towering icebergs.

Northwestern Kenai Peninsula

The northwestern end of the Kenai Peninsula is accessible via the **Sterling Highway,** which joins the Seward Highway 37 miles north of Seward and 90 miles south of Anchorage. The mileposts along the Sterling also start counting at 37 from this point. The Sterling Highway heads west through Cooper Landing and Soldotna, then south all the way to Homer, a total of 142 miles from the junction.

Pretty **Tern Lake** sits at the junction of the

THE KENAI PENINSULA

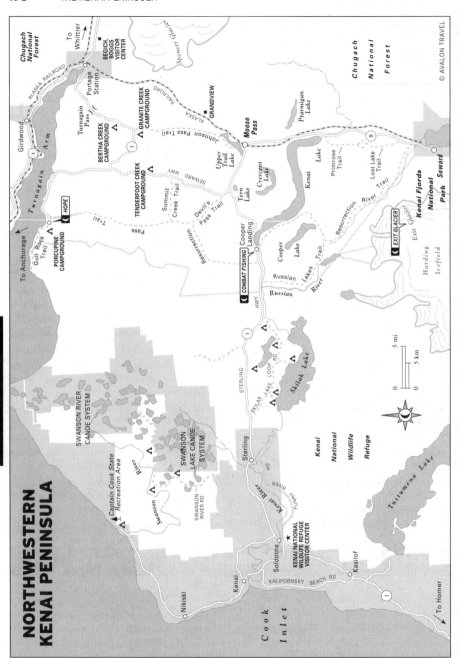

NORTHWESTERN KENAI PENINSULA

© AVALON TRAVEL

Seward and Sterling Highways. Pull off to watch the arctic terns, beavers, muskrats, and other critters.

EAST TO COOPER LANDING

Sunrise Inn (eight miles west of the junction at Mile 45 Sterling Hwy., 907/595-1222, www.alaskasunriseinn.com, year-round, $110 d, larger units $160 d, add $10 pp for extra guests) is a classic Alaskan roadhouse that's been here since 1952. The inn houses a popular café (daily 7am-10pm May-Oct., daily 8:30am-8pm winter, $10-15) with 1950s fare three meals a day: big breakfasts (great homefries), tasty burgers, homemade meatloaf, fresh soups and buffalo chili, and even a Rudolph reindeer sandwich. The smoke-free bar—decorated with memorabilia—has live bands every other weekend all summer. A 10-unit motel contains standard rooms with microwaves, fridges, TV, and Wi-Fi. There's also an RV park ($28 with electricity but no showers) and gas pumps.

Atop a hill near Sunrise Inn, **Cozy Bear Cabins** (Mile 45 Sterling Hwy., 907/440-1923, www.cozybearcabinsalaska.com, $150 d) is a modern house with three comfortable guest rooms, a shared bath, private entrances, and complimentary breakfast. The back patio has a gas fireplace and views of the surrounding mountains.

The turnoff for Quartz Creek Road is adjacent to Sunrise Inn. A half-mile down the road is **Quartz Creek Campground** (Quartz Creek Rd., 518/885-3639 or 877/444-6777, www.recreation.gov, tents $18, RVs $28; add $9 for reservations). It's a beautiful setting right on Kenai Lake. **Crescent Creek Campground** (Quartz Creek Rd., no phone, $14) is three miles down Quartz Creek Road. A 6.5-mile trail climbs 1,000 feet from the Crescent Creek parking lot to Crescent Lake.

COOPER LANDING

A dozen miles west of the Seward Highway junction is Cooper Landing (www.

cooperlandingchamber.com), with a scattering of businesses—lodges, river guides, restaurants, gas stations, and tackle shops—on both sides of the Sterling Highway.

The little **Cooper Landing Historical Society Museum** (Mile 49 Sterling Hwy., 907/598-1042, www.cooperlandingmuseum.com, Wed.-Mon. noon-5pm mid-May-mid-Sept., free) houses the articulated skeleton of a brown bear, historical items, and other items in two old cabins.

Managed by the Kenaitze Indian Tribe, **K'Beq' Interpretive Site** (Mile 53 Sterling Hwy., 907/283-6423, www.kenaitze.org, Thurs.-Mon. 11am-5pm June and Aug.-early Sept., daily 11am-5pm July, free) offers cultural tours to a pre-historic Dena'ina house site several times a day. A gift shop sells local Native Alaskan crafts. It's across from the entrance to the Russian River Campground.

Recreation

Cooper Landing's main attractions are Kenai River fishing and float trips. The river flows out of Kenai Lake at Cooper Landing, heading 80 miles west to the town of Kenai, where it meets Cook Inlet. Many businesses provide guided fishing trips on the river; see the Cooper Landing Chamber of Commerce website (www.cooperlandingchamber.com), or find a multitude of guided fishing brochures in the Soldotna Visitor Center.

On the river side just after the bridge, **Alaska Troutfitters Fly Shop** (907/595-1212, www.aktroutfitters.com) offers fly-fishing instruction and rents fishing gear and waders.

You can also buy or rent fishing gear, including poles and hip waders and even rental bear spray at **Gwin's Lodge** (907/595-1266, www.gwinslodge.biz, daily 6am-10pm late May-late Oct.). Drop off your catch to have them freeze it and process for shipping.

Several raft companies offer a 14-mile ride to Jim's Landing, which includes some Class

THE KENAI PENINSULA

II rapids at Schooner Bend. There are three-hour float trips ($55) and all-day Kenai trips ($140-150) from **Alaska River Adventures** (907/595-2000 or 888/836-9027, www.alaskariveradventures.com), **Alaska Rivers Co.** (907/595-1226 or 888/595-1226, www.alaskariverscompany.com), and **Alaska Wildland Adventures** (907/595-1279 or 800/478-4100, www.alaskarivertrips.com). These companies also guide all-day fishing trips aboard drift boats ($220-275 pp with lunch; $120 for a half-day trip).

Alaskan Horsemen Trail Adventures (behind Sunrise Inn at Mile 45 Sterling Hwy., 907/595-1806 or 800/595-1806, www.alaskahorsemen.com) leads trail rides into the scenic country around Resurrection Trail and Cooper Landing. Take a short one-hour ride ($60), or join an all-day horseback trip ($300) into the Chugach National Forest backcountry. Wilderness pack trips are also available.

◖ COMBAT FISHING

Alaska's most famous salmon-fishing area is near the junction of the Russian and Kenai Rivers. The **Russian River Ferry** (Mile 55 Sterling Hwy., $9 adults, $5 kids) is a cable-guided, current-powered ferry that shuttles anglers across the Kenai River to the sockeye-rich opposite bank. Come in July to learn the true meaning of "combat fishing" as hundreds of folks fight for space, hooking both sockeye salmon and fellow anglers in the process. You'll need hip waders, and you can only use flies, not lures. Local fishing shops have the correct flies and often rent out poles and boots. Nonfishers are bemused by the oddity of such crowds, but for anglers the salmon fishing is the attraction, since many folks get their limit despite the hordes. A real fly-fishing angler wouldn't be caught dead here, but this is all about catching fish, not enjoying a wilderness or purist experience. Limited roadside parking

rafting on the Kenai River near Cooper Landing

is available around the ferry, or you can park in the big lot ($10).

Accommodations

Cooper Landing spreads out over a five-mile stretch that centers around Mile 50 of the Sterling Highway. Lodging options are listed from east to west.

Primarily for cruise passengers, **Kenai Princess Lodge** (Mile 48 Sterling Hwy., 907/595-1425 or 800/426-0500, www.princesslodges.com, mid-May-mid-Sept., $249 d), near the Kenai River bridge, overlooks the roiling turquoise water of the river and features a restaurant and lounge, a half-mile nature trail, and a gift shop. Bungalow-style guest rooms include a sitting area, wood-burning stove, TV, phone, Wi-Fi, and a small private deck. Two large hot tubs and saunas add to the appeal.

Alpine Motel (Mile 48 Sterling Hwy., 907/595-1557, www.alpinemotelak.com, June-Sept., $115-135 d) has a dozen kitchenette units with dishes, TVs, private baths, and Wi-Fi.

Just up the road is **Drifters Lodge** (Mile 48.3 Sterling Hwy., 907907/595-5555 or 866/595-5959, www.drifterslodge.com, Apr.-mid-Oct., cabins $275-375 d, guest rooms $150-225 d shared bath), with chalet-style cabins, containing fridges and microwaves, along with shared-bath guest rooms in the lodge. A big breakfast, sauna access, and Wi-Fi are included in the rates. The lodge is right on the river.

Appropriately named **[** **Alaska Heavenly Lodge** (near Mile 49 Sterling Hwy., 907/595-2012 or 866/595-2012, www.alaskaheavenly.com, closed Dec.-Jan., guest rooms $175 d, lodge $1,000 for up to 10 people) has a fantastic hillside spot. Set on an 18-acre spread, this homey lodge overlooks the Kenai River and surrounding mountains. The Mount Cecil cabin has three guest rooms, each with two beds, a bath, kitchenette, and grill. A historic homestead serves as the main lodge, with four bedrooms, three baths, a full kitchen, open

layout, stone fireplace, and big deck. A third cabin—open to all guests—houses a pool table, sauna, flat-screen TV, and a seven-person hot tub on the deck. The location, lush grounds, friendly owners, and lovely accommodations make this a popular spot for weddings and family reunions. Wi-Fi is available.

A three-story hotel/B&B with wrap-around porches, **The Hutch B&B** (Mile 49 Sterling Hwy., 907/595-1270, www.arctic.net/~hutch, late Apr.-Oct., guest rooms $89-119 d, cabin $225 for up to four) has a dozen guest rooms with private baths, plus a two-bedroom cabin with a full kitchen and bath. A hearty continental breakfast is included, and The Hutch has Wi-Fi, a communal room with TV, and evening campfires.

In the heart of Cooper Landing, **Upper Kenai River Inn** (Mile 49 Sterling Hwy., 907/595-3333, www.upperkenairiverinn.com, $200 d) is a spacious and modern riverside home with four guest rooms. Breakfast is included, and there's a two-night minimum stay.

Located on the western edge of "town," **Gwin's Lodge** (Mile 52 Sterling Hwy., 907/595-1266, www.gwinslodge.biz, late May-late Oct., $150-250 d) has a wide variety of newly remodeled lodging choices, including 15 cabins and two full houses; the largest can accommodate eight guests.

Alaska Wildland Adventures operates two Kenai Peninsula lodges. Located on the river in Cooper Landing, **Kenai River Sportfishing Lodge** (907/595-1279 or 800/478-4100, www.alaskawildland.com, three-night stay $1,625 pp) has a variety of all-inclusive fishing, food, and lodging packages. More unique is **Kenai Backcountry Lodge** (907/783-2928 or 800/334-8730, www.alaskawildland.com, two nights from $1,050 pp), hidden away on Skilak Lake and accessible only by boat. Accommodations are comfortably-rustic tent cabins and log cabins, with a central bathhouse and historic lodge. All-inclusive stays include kayaking and hiking.

THE KENAI PENINSULA

Camping

Just west of Cooper Landing is the Forest Service's **Cooper Creek Campground** (Mile 50 Sterling Hwy., 518/885-3639 or 877/444-6777, www.recreation.gov, tents $18, RVs $28, no hookups, $9 reservation fee), with sites on both sides of the road.

The large **Russian River Campground** (Mile 51.5 Sterling Hwy., 518/885-3639 or 877/444-6777, www.recreation.gov, tents $18, RVs $28, no hookups, $9 reservation fee) is one of the best places in the state to catch sockeye salmon when they're running (generally mid-June and mid-July). Campsites are strung along the two-mile paved road, and the sites are large and well spaced. Campground reservations (518/885-3639 or 877/444-6777, www.recreation.gov) are strongly recommended for July visits to Cooper Creek and Russian River Campgrounds.

Kenai Princess RV Park (Mile 48 Sterling Hwy., 907/595-1425, mid-May-mid-Sept., full hookups $40, no tents) is located at Kenai Princess Lodge near the Kenai River bridge. Guests have access to hot tubs at the lodge, plus Wi-Fi, cable TV, and pay showers (open to the public for just $1).

Kenai Riverside Campground and RV Park (Mile 50 Sterling Hwy., 888/536-2478, www.kenairv.com, late May-early Sept., tents $18, RVs $35, guest rooms $69 d) has RVs sites and tent spaces, plus guest rooms with continental breakfast and shared baths. The campground is owned by Alaska Wildland Adventures, which also offers Kenai River fishing and float trips.

Food

Popular with anglers, rafters, and locals, **Sackett's Kenai Grill** (Mile 50 Sterling Hwy., daily 11am-10pm, 907/595-1827, $11-20) is next to Cooper Creek North and South Campgrounds. Owner Glenn Sackett and his chef/son Trevalyan welcome everyone with a menu that stars pulled pork BBQ sandwiches,

handmade pizzas, burgers, and smoked prime rib—served in plastic baskets. The bar stays open later than the restaurant (until 2am) with occasional live music; pizza by the slice is available after 10pm. Surprisingly, Sackett's even has Wi-Fi.

◖**Kingfisher Roadhouse** (Mile 47 Sterling Hwy., 907/595-2861, www.letseat.at/kingfisherak, daily 4:30pm-10:30pm May-mid-Oct., closed in winter, $25-30) serves Alaskan cuisine in a unique setting on the shore of Kenai Lake. Dining is rustic and relaxed, with friendly service, an enclosed deck, and big windows affording views across the lake. House specialties include calamari, bleu burger, and Bellavista pasta. Owner Dominic Bauer emphasizes local seafood and uses organic burgers and produce as much as possible. Beer and wine are available, and the bar comes alive with music several nights a week.

Gwin's Lodge (907/595-1266, www.gwinslodge.biz, daily 6am-10pm late May-late Oct., $16-30) is a classic Alaskan eatery. In business since 1952, this is a great place to pick up tips from the anglers while enjoying down-home cooking, especially the smoked salmon chowder ($7), burgers ($6-10), and famous pies. The restaurant opens early for the fishing crowd. The country store sells groceries, sodas, beer, gifts, ice, and fishing licenses.

Cooper Landing Grocery (Mile 48 Sterling Hwy., 907/595-1677) has supplies, ice cream, pizza by the slice, videos, and rocking chairs on the front porch to watch the world go by.

Practicalities

Cooper Landing Chamber of Commerce Visitor Center (Mile 47 Sterling Hwy., 907/595-8888, www.cooperlandingchamber.com, daily 8am-8pm late May-mid-Sept., staffed Fri.-Sun. noon-4pm, closed winter) is next to Wildman's. Public outhouses are next to the boat launch on the south side of the Kenai River bridge.

A quarter mile before the bridge over the Kenai River, **Wildman's** (Mile 48 Sterling Hwy., 907/595-1456, www.wildmans.org, 6am-11pm late May-early Sept., 8am-10pm winter) is the local everything store. The convenience store here has basic supplies and gifts, and serves breakfast items, local pastries, freshly made sandwiches, hot dogs, espresso, ice cream cones, and liquor. Laundry and shower facilities are available, and you can check email using the free Wi-Fi. RV spaces are available out back.

Operating out of an RV next to Wildman's, **Cooper Landing Medical Clinic** (Mile 48 Sterling Hwy., 907/262-3119 or 855/262-3119, www.pchsak.org) provides seasonal medical care.

Getting There and Around

The Stage Line (907/235-2252, www.stagelineinhomer.com, Mon.-Fri. summer, once a week in winter) has van service connecting Cooper Landing with Anchorage ($54), Homer ($50), and Seward ($42). Drivers can stop almost anywhere along the route to pick up or drop off passengers. There are no winter runs to Seward.

Wildman's (Mile 48 Sterling Hwy., 907/595-1456 or 866/595-1456, www.wildmans.org, 6am-11pm late May-early Sept., 8am-10pm winter) offers a shuttle service for bikers, hikers, and boaters.

KENAI NATIONAL WILDLIFE REFUGE

This large habitat (907/262-7021 or 877/285-5628, http://kenai.fws.gov) supports so many moose, bears, salmon, and other wildlife that it was designated a refuge by President Roosevelt in 1941. The Alaska National Interest Lands Act of 1980 changed the name from Kenai National Moose Range and expanded the refuge to its present 1.9 million acres, managed by the federal Fish and Wildlife Service. A **visitors center** (Ski Hill Rd., Soldotna, 907/262-7021

THE KENAI PENINSULA

© DON PITCHER

Kenai National Wildlife Refuge

or 877/285-5628, http://kenai.fws.gov, Mon.-Fri. 8am-4:30pm, Sat.-Sun. 10am-5pm late May-early Sept.; Mon.-Fri. 8am-4:30pm, Sat. 10am-5pm winter) is at the refuge headquarters in Soldotna. Stop here to pick up a copy of *Reflections,* the refuge's annual newspaper, with details on day hikes, wildlife viewing, fishing, canoeing, picnicking, and camping.

Hiking

The **Resurrection Pass Trail** crosses the Sterling Highway just west of Cooper Landing, and is accessible from a trailhead at Mile 52. More challenging is the three-mile **Fuller Lakes Trail.** It takes off from a parking area at Mile 57 and climbs sharply to a pair of small lakes filled with small Dolly Varden (bring your pole).

Skilak Lake Loop Road

Located in the heart of Kenai National Wildlife Refuge, this very scenic—but dusty—17-mile gravel road meets the Sterling Highway at two places: Mile 58 on the east end and Mile 75 on the west end. Five campgrounds, several trails, and two public use cabins are located off this popular side road; it's a very popular recreation area throughout the summer.

Beginning at the east end (Mile 58 Sterling Hwy.), Skilak Lake Loop Road immediately passes **Jim's Landing** on the Kenai River, a busy picnic area and boat ramp for rafting and drift boats. Look for bald eagles in the trees and fly fishermen along the shore. **Hidden Lake Campground** ($10) has 44 campsites, with campfire programs on summer weekends. It's the largest and most developed campground on the refuge.

A pair of overlooks near Mile 5 provide a great view over Skilak Lake. The **Skilak Lookout Trail** at Mile 5.5 climbs to a high hillside above the lake, with good crops of berries in the fall. It's 2.5 miles each way. A short distance up the road at Mile 6.0 is the **Bear Mountain Trail,** a quick one-mile hike with a rocky promontory affording dramatic views across Skilak Lake.

At Mile 8, turn left and drive two miles to popular **Upper Skilak Lake Campground** (tents and RVs $5-10), with 25 campsites for both tents and RVs (no hookups), and access to the three-mile **Vista Trail.** There's another campground at nearby Lower Ohmer Lake (Mile 8.5 Skilak Lake Loop Rd., free), and a couple more sites at Engineer Lake (Mile 9.4, free). The nearly level **Seven Lakes Trail** begins at Engineer Lake, connecting to three more lakes before ending at Kelly Lake Campground off the Sterling Highway. **Lower Skilak Lake Campground** (free) is on a side road at Mile 13.6 of Skilak Lake Loop.

Two popular public use cabins are readily accessible off Skilak Lake Loop. **Engineer Lake Cabin** (518/885-3639 or 877/444-6777, www.recreation.gov, $45/night, $9 reservation fee) is on the north shore of this lake, a one-mile hike from the trailhead. The **Upper Ohmer Cabin** (518/885-3639 or 877/444-6777, www.recreation.gov, $45/night, $9 reservation fee) is an easy 0.25-mile hike off Skilak Lake Loop Road at Mile 8. Fourteen more **public cabins** are scattered around the refuge, but most of these require boat or canoe access.

In addition to those along Skilak Lake, three other Fish and Wildlife Service campgrounds are on the Sterling Highway between Cooper Landing and Sterling.

Swanson River Area

Oil was discovered in 1957 in the northern wilderness near the Swanson River, and the 18-mile gravel **Swanson River Road** built to the oilfields also opened up this lake-studded lowlands. The road turns north off the Sterling Highway at Mile 84. Approximately 13 miles in is **Dolly Varden Lake Campground** (Swanson River Rd., no phone, free). It is not crowded, has nice views, is right on the lake, and has frequent moose visits.

© DON PITCHER

Skilak Lake from Bear Mountain Trail

CANOEING

Two canoe routes—the Swanson River Route and the Swan Lake Route—are accessible by Swanson River Road. Both offer a wonderful way to explore the refuge and to see wildlife up close. Pick up the Fish and Wildlife Service brochure *Canoeing in the Kenai National Wildlife Refuge* for detailed information, or find it at http://kenai.fws.gov.

Mark Weigner of **Weigner's Guided Canoeing** (907/262-7840, www.alaska. net/~weigner, canoe rental $40/day, day trips $185 pp, overnight trips $230 pp per day) leads customized all-inclusive canoe trips for two or more people. Mark personally guides all trips, providing Old Town canoes, tents, sleeping bags, food, and other gear for the trips. Shuttle services are also available, or you can rent a canoe and head out on your own.

Alaska Canoe & Campground (Mile 84 Sterling Hwy., 907/262-2331, www.alaskacanoetrips.com) has canoe, kayak, and drift boat rentals. It's close to the turnoff for Swan Lake Canoe Route, and guided trips may be available. *Kenai Canoe Trails* by Daniel L. Quick is a useful guidebook for anyone heading out on the refuge's lakes.

Located on the northern Kenai Peninsula, **Swan Lake Canoe Route** is the most popular canoeing area within Kenai National Wildlife Refuge. This 60-mile route encompasses 30 lakes that are connected by fairly short portages (the longest is under 1 mile). The entire 60-mile route can be traversed in less than a week. In addition, the route provides access to a 17-mile float down the gentle Moose River. Canoeing on this system offers not only scenic beauty but also excellent wildlife viewing and good rainbow trout fishing.

The **Swanson River Canoe Route** links 40 small lakes on the northern Kenai Peninsula, and also includes a 46-mile stretch of the Swanson River. The lakes are connected by portages of varying lengths and conditions, but they are more difficult than those on the nearby Swan Lake Canoe Route. Traveling from the Paddle Lake entrance (at Mile 12 on Swan Lake Rd.), trips can stretch from a long weekend to over a week. In remote lake areas of the Swanson River Route east of Pepper Lake, travel is difficult and the routes and portages are often indistinct. This is true wilderness and can be challenging. Bring a compass, an accurate map, a pair of hip waders, and a lot of patience.

STERLING

The unincorporated settlement of Sterling (pop. 6,000)—spread over a wide area around Mile 83—is mainly notable for the four-lane highway that cuts across this part of the northern Kenai Peninsula; it seems totally out of place in such a spot. The Sterling Highway crosses the Moose River in Sterling, where the Moose joins the widening Kenai River and the fishhook frenzy pervades all your senses.

The 13-mile stretch of highway from Sterling to Soldotna bristles with guides and outfitters, fish camps, bait and tackle shops, charters, fish smokehouses, boat and canoe rentals, boat engine sales and repairs, and so forth—essential infrastructure in the eternal struggle between sport anglers and salmon.

Recreation

Ken Marlow, co-owner of Marlow's on the Kenai cabins, operates **Alaska Birding Tours** (www.alaskabirdingtours.com), with personalized bird-watching trips throughout the Kenai. Pelagic birding out of Seward is a favorite, but he also leads trips to Nome and other parts of Alaska.

Accommodations

Marlow's on the Kenai (halfway between Sterling and Soldotna, 907/262-5218 or 800/725-3327, www.marlowsonthekenai. com, from $1,300 for a six-night trip) consists of three spacious cabins (one has three bedrooms) just 50 feet from the Kenai River. All three include full kitchens, baths, Wi-Fi, TVs, outdoor grills, and decks. Most guests book for multi-night fishing packages.

One of the most popular places in Sterling, **Alaska Red Fish Lodge** (El Dorado Way, 907/262-7080 or 888/335-4490, www.alaskaredfishlodge.com, mid-May-mid-Sept., $159 d, $183 for four) has 14 modern cedar cabins with a main lodge and dock right on the Kenai River. Each cabin contains space for four guests, a kitchenette, private bath, TV, picnic table, and patio with gas grill. Nightly campfires are a highlight, and the hosts offer twice-a-week communal dinners around the fire. The lodge is popular with anglers, but also caters to families, even offering a gated play area for children. The main lodge has a common area with couches and a guest computer and Wi-Fi (not available in the cabins), plus a walk-in freezer. Access is from Mile 81 of the Sterling Highway.

Great Alaska Adventure Lodge (Mile 87 Sterling Hwy., 907/262-4515 or 800/544-2261, www.greatalaska.com) has a wide range of expensive all-inclusive fishing and adventure packages, from 1-night quick getaways to the 11-night bucket-list version.

Alaska Canoe & Campground (Mile 84 Sterling Hwy., 907/262-2331, www.alaskacanoetrips.com, tents $13, RVs $28 with full hookups; cabin $150 d, add $10 pp for extra guests) has a small RV park. The campground shop rents canoes, kayaks, drift boats, and mountain bikes. A three-bedroom cabin is also available with a private bath and full kitchen.

Izaak Walton State Recreation Site (907/262-5581, campsites $10) on the east side of the river is a pretty campground with toilets and water. Archaeological excavations conducted here indicate that Native Alaskans occupied this fish-rich confluence up to 2,000 years ago.

Food

If kids are in your vehicle, pull into the **Cook's Corner Tesoro** gas station (Mile 82 Sterling Hwy., 907/262-6021) for a soft-serve ice cream cone or outsized cinnamon roll. **Susie's Café** (Mile 83 Sterling Hwy., 907/260-5751) serves bacon cheeseburgers, clam chowder, and other fare.

Services

Wash Out Laundry (Mile 83 Sterling Hwy., 907/262-7666) has drop-off service, showers, a kids' play area, and even tanning beds.

SOLDOTNA

Soldotna was established in the late 1940s, as World War II veterans filed for homestead lands along Soldotna Creek. Today this town of 4,000 is the seat of the Kenai Borough government and serves as a busy stopping point for travelers, anglers, and locals. "Slowdotna" has all the charm of Wasilla, another place disparaged by anyone not living there. Fast food joints, strip malls, fishing supply stores, shopping centers, and a jumble of signs greet your arrival in this sprawling suburban burg with no real downtown—unless you count the big Fred Meyer store. The latter's parking lot also serves as a de facto free RV campground all summer.

Sights

Follow the 0.25-mi **Kenai River Fish Walk** from the Visitors Information Center to the **Soldotna Homestead Museum** (1 Centennial Park Rd., 907/262-3832, Tues.-Sat. 10am-4pm, Sun. noon-4pm mid-May-mid-Sept., free), or drive there by turning up Kalifornsky Beach Road, followed by an immediate right onto Centennial Park Road. This collection of a half-dozen log cabins contains the usual settlers' items, stuffed critters, and Native artifacts. The real treat is that this surprisingly quiet spot is just a short distance from the bustling Sterling Highway.

Festivals and Events

Soldotna's biggest event, **Progress Days** (fourth weekend of July), arrives with a parade, car races, art and craft booths, live music, and more. The **Kenai River Festival** (www.kenai-watershed.org, early June) is another fun family celebration, with live bands, food and art vendors, a beer garden, and the Run for the River race. The **Peninsula Winter Games** (late Jan.) features ice carving, hockey games, fireworks, and games.

Shopping

Far more down-home than the big Fred Meyer store, **Beemun's Variety Store** (35277 Kenai Spur Hwy., 907/262-1234) has an upstairs bike shop that becomes a ski and snowboard shop in winter, plus outdoor clothing, art supplies, sporting goods, and other gear downstairs.

If you're heading out on the water, be sure to stop at **Soldotna Hardware & Fishing** (44648 Sterling Hwy., 907/262-4655, www.soldotna-hardware.com) for fishing gear. The store is packed with hardware oddities and critter heads.

A quarter mile out Funny River Road, **Birch Tree Gallery** (Funny River Rd., 907/262-4048, www.alaska.net/~birchtre) has Alaskan art, pottery, and knit wear. Also well worth visiting is **Art Works Gallery** (35210 Kenai Spur Hwy., 907/262-1777).

River City Books (43977 Sterling Hwy., 907/260-7722, Sun. 11am-4pm, Mon.-Sat. 9am-5pm) has a decent collection of books, plus a popular café.

For fresh veggies and fruits, head to the **Kenai Peninsula Farmers' Market** (intersection of Kenai Spur Hwy. and Corral Ave., 907/262-5463, Sat. 10am-2pm mid-June-mid-Sept.). A second market takes place at **Soldotna Creek Park** (Wed.).

Recreation

Home to one of the best playgrounds on the peninsula, **Soldotna Creek Park** (States Ave.

behind Don Jose's Mexican Restaurant) provides a great break for the kids. It's a great place for running, jumping, and general mayhem. Just a short distance off busy Sterling Highway in the heart of town, this 13-acre park also has picnic tables, a pavilion, and 2,250 feet of elevated boardwalk along the Kenai River.

There are two nine-hole golf courses to choose from in Soldotna. **Birch Ridge Golf Course** (907/262-5270, www.birchridgegolf.com, $19) is a private resort three miles east of town, and **Bird Homestead Golf Course** (Funny River Rd., 907/260-4653, www.alaska-golf.com, $15) is 12 miles up Funny River Road. The Homestead's driving range is certainly different; golfers drive floating balls onto a pond!

For a break from fishing and shopping, take a spin on the **Go Cart Race Track** (corner of Sterling Hwy. and Funny River Rd., 907/262-1562).

Skyview High School (325 W. Marydale Ave., 907/262-7419) has an Olympic size pool with open swim times. Adjacent to the high school are the **Tsalteshi Trails** with 10 miles of biking and running paths. Come winter, these are some of the best cross-country ski trails in the area.

Accommodations

More than 100 lodging options crowd the Sterling-Soldotna-Kenai area, from rustic cabins to riverside wilderness lodges. Visitors center racks are crammed with descriptive flyers, and the chamber's website (www.soldotnachamber.com) has links to many lodging places. Many local lodges provide freezers for your freshly caught fish.

MOTELS

Aspen Hotel (326 Binkley Circle, 907/260-7736 or 888/308-7848, www.aspenhotelsak.com, $189-209 d) is a large and modern place with an indoor pool and hot tub, exercise facility, Wi-Fi, and breakfast with waffles. All rooms include fridges and microwaves, and five suites (add $20) provide room to spread out. The hotel is right on the river and across the street from fast food places and a Safeway store.

Not far away is another sprawling motel, **Kenai River Lodge** (393 Riverside Dr., 907/262-4292 or 800/977-4292, www.kenairiverlodge.com, $189-209 d) with rooms facing the river. The lodge has a private shoreline for fishing, with cleaning tables, freezer space, and a BBQ grill once you pull one in. Rooms have one or two queen beds, fridges, microwaves, and Wi-Fi.

Best Western King Salmon Motel (35545 Kenai Spur Hwy., 907/262-5857 or 888/262-5857, www.bestwestern.com, $199-209 d) has large rooms with two queen beds, fridges, microwaves, and Wi-Fi. Rates include a full breakfast at the adjacent restaurant.

BED-AND-BREAKFASTS

The **Kenai Peninsula B&B Association** website (www.kenaipeninsulabba.com) provides links to Soldotna B&Bs.

A 16-room European-style place on the river, **Soldotna B&B Lodge** (399 Lovers Ln., 907/262-4779 or 877/262-4779, www.soldotnalodge.com, $199 d shared bath) is a favorite of both anglers and families. A dozen of the rooms share four baths, while the other four have private baths. A filling breakfast is included, and the hosts speak German, Japanese, and French.

Right on the river in Soldotna, **Kenai River Raven Lodge** (48630 Funny River Rd., 907/262-5818 or 888/262-5818, www.kenairiverraven.com, $200-250 d, includes breakfast) is open year-round. Eight guest rooms are available, all with private bath and TV; some contain kitchenettes. Most folks visit as part of a fishing package. Kenai River Raven is also popular for summer weddings.

If you're looking for a romantic getaway,

be sure to check out **Escape for Two** (49300 Charlie Brown Dr., 907/262-1493, www.escapefortwo.com, $195 d), on a small pond five miles south of Soldotna. Two quaint and very private cabins are lovingly decorated, each with a forest setting, king bed, kitchenette, Wi-Fi, and breakfast basket. One has a large jetted tub in the bath, along with its own dock with a central fire pit. The other cabin has heated floors, a hot tub on the outside deck, and a lovely gazebo with fire pit. Two canoes await for a paddle around the pond. These cabins aren't for kids or anglers, just couples looking to escape.

Longmere Lake Lodge B&B (35955 Ryan Ln., 907/262-9799, www.longmerelakelodge.com, June-Aug., $300 for four guests) is six miles east of Soldotna. The home sits right on the lake, with a dock, canoes, and fishing poles if you want to try your luck with the rainbow trout. There's a big walk-in freezer if you've come back with salmon from the river, and the two apartment-style units each contain two bedrooms, two baths, full kitchens, and private entrances. The kitchens are stocked with breakfast items, and the B&B has Wi-Fi, a fire pit, and a fish cleaning area.

CABINS

A Cabin by the Pond (Airport Heights Rd., 907/262-4728, www.acabinbythepond.com, cabins $150-200 d, log house $653 per night, three-night minimum) provides a relaxing setting just minutes from downtown Soldotna. Five delightful cabins cluster around a tiny pond frequented by moose (hence their alternative name, Munch Moose Cabins). Each has a kitchenette, private bath, and porch; the largest has a gas fireplace and accommodates five guests. Larger groups will love the classic 1970s-era Alaskan log house with two bedrooms, a full kitchen, living room, and bath. Wi-Fi is available in all units. Also here is a picture-perfect log wedding chapel with space for up to 50 guests.

Halfway between Kenai and Soldotna, **Caribou Crossings Cabins** (Ollie St., 907/262-7783 or 888/268-9464, www.cariboux.com, late May-mid-Sept., $175-200 d, add $25 pp for extra guests) consists of four log cabins, each with a kitchenette, private bath, and space for 4-6 people. There is no Wi-Fi here. Befitting the name, caribou are often seen in the field out front.

FISHING LODGES

Fishing is the main attraction for most Soldotna visitors, with many lodges catering to the hip-waders and tackle crowd. Each lodge has its own packages, but most include a minimum of four nights lodging and three days of charter salmon and halibut fishing with river float trips and ocean charter boats.

Two popular lodges are **Kenai River Raven Lodge** (48630 Funny River Rd., 907/262-5818 or 888/262-5818, www.kenairiverraven.com, $200-250 d, includes breakfast) and **Soldotna B&B Lodge** (399 Lovers Ln., 907/262-4779 or 877/262-4779, www.soldotnalodge.com, $199 d shared bath).

Soldotna has an abundance of high-end fishing lodges where seven-night trips start around $1,800 per person. A great one is **All Alaska Outdoors Lodge** (35905 Ryan Ln., 907/262-6001 or 800/646-4868, www.allalaska.com), where the owner is also a pilot, providing floatplane trips to remote lakes and rivers.

Also highly recommended is luxurious **Tower Rock Lodge** (38156 Woods Dr., 907/283-3662 or 800/284-3474, www.towerrocklodge.com). On pretty Denise Lake just east of town, **Alaska Serenity Lodge** (41598 Aksala Ln., 907/260-7647 or 877/260-7647, www.alaskaserenitylodge.com) has a log home and three cabins.

Other fishing lodges well worth checking out include **Kenai Riverbend Resort** (45525 Porter Rd., 907/283-9489 or 800/625-2324, www.kenairiverbend.com) and **King Salmondeaux**

Lodge (33126 Johnson Dr., 907/360-3474 or 866/651-3474, www.kingsalmondeauxlodge.com). **Funny Moose Lodge** (Funny Moose Ln., 907/262-3701 or 800/770-3701, www.funnymoose.com, $995 pp for seven nights) provides the economy version for those whose primary goal is slaying fish.

CAMPING

Two Soldotna city parks provide excellent camping close to town, with picnic tables, water, fire pits, and elevated riverbank boardwalks. Get to **Centennial Park Campground** (Kalifornsky Beach Rd., 907/262-5299, www.ci.soldotna.ak.us, $17, no reservations) by crossing the bridge on the Sterling, taking a right at the light onto Kalifornsky Beach Road, then another immediate right into the campground. This is a big city park with 190 wooded sites (some right on the river) and boat-launching ramps. Equally attractive is **Swiftwater Campground** (off East Redoubt St., 907/262-5299, www.ci.soldotna.ak.us, $17, no reservations), just past Fred Meyer, with 40 quiet campsites. Take **showers** at Central Peninsula Sports Center (538 Arena Ave., 907/262-3151, Tues.-Fri. noon-4pm, $4), close to Centennial Park.

Find RV parking in the **Fred Meyer** parking lot (43843 Sterling Hwy., 907/260-2200, www.fredmeyer.com, two-night limit, free). Right in town, **River Terrace RV Park** (44755 Sterling Hwy., 907/262-5593, $40-50 RVs) has full hookup sites with Wi-Fi, including some right on the river. The campground is open year-round.

Two RV parks are near each other on Funny River Road. **Klondike RV Park & Cabins** (48665 Funny River Rd., 907/262-6035 or 800/980-6035, www.klondikervpark.com, $44 RVs) has free Wi-Fi and showers, but no tents. You're just a short walk to fishing sites along the Kenai River. **Kenai River Fishing and RV Camp** (48748 Funny River Rd., 907/262-5818 or 888/262-5818, www.krrfishingrv.wordpress.com, late May-early Sept., $40 RVs) has its own dock on the river with 200 feet of shoreline, making it a favorite of anglers. There are just 10 sites and no showers or laundry, but guests are welcome to use the facilities at the adjacent Klondike RV Park.

Food
BREAKFAST

Moose is Loose (44278 Sterling Hwy., 907/260-3036, Tues.-Sat. 6am-6pm, under $5) makes—without a doubt—the best donuts, apple fritters, and maple bars on the Kenai Peninsula. Doughy, sweet, and fattening, these are the perfect match for a mug of coffee. Gargantuan 6-inch donut rings are famous, and the back room is a locals' hangout. Make a stop here to stock up on calories before heading out for a day of fishing.

Hidden away on a side-street near the Safeway store, **Kaladi Bros. Coffee** (315 S. Kobuk St., 907/262-5890, www.kaladi.com, Mon.-Fri. 6am-6pm, Sat. 7am-7pm, Sun. 8am-6pm, $4-7) serves good espresso and features art on the walls as well as occasional live music. Be sure to check out the unique ceiling tiles. There's a second Kaladi Bros. shop along the highway next to Subway.

SANDWICHES

Located at the Soldotna Y inside River City Books, **Fine Thyme Café** (43977 Sterling Hwy., 907/260-6620, Sun. 11am-4pm, Mon.-Sat. 9am-5pm, sandwiches $11) provides an escape from the ubiquitous fast-food joints and anglers in hip waders. You'll find both a fair selection of new books and a café serving sandwiches, daily soups, quiche, salads, fresh-baked breads, cookies, homemade desserts, and espresso.

Find the best sandwiches in Soldotna at **Odie's Deli** (44315 Sterling Hwy., 907/260-3255, Mon.-Tues., Thurs., and Sat. 8am-6pm, Wed. and Fri. 8am-9pm, closed Sun., $6-12), where the bread—including a jalapeno cheddar variety—is made on the premises. Fresh soups are made daily, along with espresso and sweets. Sandwiches are enormous, so go for a half if you aren't really hungry. You'll probably recognize the Odie's building as on old Burger King.

In the Blazy Mall, **Mugz's Café** (44539 Sterling Hwy., 907/260-9113, Mon.-Fri. 8am-4pm, Sat. 11am-3pm, $5-11) has a relaxing, homey atmosphere of cushy chairs and tables, with free Wi-Fi and good lunches. The breads are made on the premises, and specialties includes prime rib Phillys and stout kraut Reubens, along with chipotle chicken wraps, apple pecan salads, and the usual assortment of espresso, teas, and smoothies.

BREWPUBS

It's easy to miss 🄲 **St. Elias Brewing Co.** (434 Sharkathmi Ave., 907/260-7837, www.steliasbrewingco.com, Sun.-Thurs. noon-10pm, Fri.-Sat. noon-11pm May-Aug., closes one hour earlier in winter, pizzas $14, sandwiches and salads $11), located on a side road just east of the Fred Meyer store. The food is consistently flavorful, with rustic pizzas emerging from the wood stone oven, plus salads and baked sandwiches. The Brewhouse pizza is a favorite, topped with bacon, sausage, pepperoni, marinated mushrooms, caramelized onions, and cheese. A central fireplace adds to the allure, and local musicians show up for Thursday night performances. Several of the brewery's beers are on tap, or get a growler to go of Farmer's Friend Ale. St. Elias crafts a tasty root beer and cream soda for teetotalers.

AMERICAN

Alaska Reel Café (44847 Sterling Hwy., 907/262-1254, www.alaskareelcafe.com, daily 5:30am-6:30pm mid-June-mid-Aug., Mon.-Fri. 6:30am-6:30pm mid-Aug.-mid-June, $6-11) is one of those don't-judge-a-book-by-its-cover places. The bland exterior and busy

intersection location belies a good little restaurant. Lots of reasonable breakfast and lunch choices on the menu, including paninis, burgers, salads, and more. Favorites such as BBQ ribs, fish and chips are a bit more expensive ($16-18) than most items on the menu and there's always a before-6:30pm special for just $8. They also offer filling gourmet boxed lunches ($16).

Open for lunch and dinner, **Mykel's Restaurant & Lounge** (35041 Kenai Spur Hwy., 907/262-4305, www.mykels.com, Sun.-Thurs. 11am-9pm, Fri.-Sat. 11am-10pm, $23-30) is just up Kenai Spur Highway from the Sterling Highway and features fresh salads, pasta, seafood, rack of lamb, steaks, and fine wines. The atmosphere is quiet and upscale. There is free Wi-Fi and a smoke-free bar, too.

MEXICAN

There's nothing great on the international food scene in Soldotna, but **Acapulco Restaurant** (44758 Sterling Hwy., 907/260-4999, daily 11am-9pm, $12-17) is your best bet for Mexican food. Local favorites include the halibut burrito and tacos al pastor.

Information and Services

The **Soldotna Visitors Information Center** (Sterling Hwy., 907/262-9814, www.visitsoldotna.com, daily 9am-7pm June-Sept., Mon.-Fri. 9am-5pm Oct.-Apr.) is on Sterling Highway just south of the bridge over the Kenai River. Stop by to sift through several hundred pamphlets describing B&Bs, fishing charters, RV parks, restaurants, and other businesses. The walls are lined with photos, and be sure to see the 97-pound king salmon that was caught nearby in 1984; it's the largest ever caught by a sport angler. Just out the door, a short path leads to a dock on the Kenai River, where you can try your luck at catching an even bigger one.

For the **Kenai National Wildlife Refuge Visitors Center** (Ski Hill Rd., 907/262-7021 or

877/285-5628, http://kenai.fws.gov, Mon.-Fri. 8am-4:30pm, Sat.-Sun. 10am-5pm late May-early Sept.; Mon.-Fri. 8am-4:30pm, Sat. 10am-5pm winter), take a left at Funny River Road, then an immediate right, and go a mile up Ski Hill Road. You can buy books, see the free wildlife videos, or stroll the mile-long nature trail. The staff leads nature walks and talks weekly.

The largest hospital on the Kenai Peninsula, **Central Peninsula Hospital** (250 Hospital Pl., 907/714-4404, www.cpgh.org), is especially adept at removing fishhooks from all parts of the body; in a typical year they pull out 100 of them! Be sure to wear shatterproof eyewear to protect your eyes while rubbing shoulders with the Kenai River fishing crowds. The hospital has some of the most experienced surgeons in the state, able to even repair bilateral quadriceps tendon ruptures if you trip while carrying a canoe (speaking from personal experience here).

KDLL (91.9 FM, www.kdllradio.org) is the local public radio station.

The **Soldotna Public Library** (235 N. Binkley St., 907/262-4227, www.ci.soldotna.ak.us, Mon.-Thurs. and Sat. 9am-6pm, Fri. noon-6pm) has Internet access and Wi-Fi, plus a free fishing pole loaner program for kids.

Grab a shower at **Soldotna Wash-N-Dry** (121 Smiths Way, 907/262-8495, daily 24 hours mid-June-mid-Aug.).

Getting There

Air taxis offering charters (as well as bear viewing trips, fly-in fishing, and flightseeing) from the Soldotna Airport include **Talon Air Service** (907/262-8899, www.talonair.com), **Natron Air** (907/262-8440 or 877/520-8440, www.natronair.com), and **High Adventure Air** (907/262-5237, www.highadventureair.com).

Get a ride from **Alaska Cab** (907/283-6000, www.akcab.com).

The Stage Line (907/235-2252, www.stagelineinhomer.com) runs vans connecting Soldotna with Anchorage ($70), Homer ($50), and Seward ($80). Service is Monday-Friday to Anchorage, Seward, and Homer in the summer. Winter service is once a week to Homer or Anchorage, and there are no winter runs to Seward.

KENAI

The town of Kenai sits on a bluff above the mouth of the Kenai River overlooking Cook Inlet. With over 7,000 residents, it's the largest town on the Kenai Peninsula. Across the inlet to the southwest rise Redoubt and Iliamna, active volcanoes at the head of the Aleutian Range. The Alaska Range is visible to the northwest. Beluga whales sometimes enter the mouth of the river on the incoming tides to look for fish.

History

Kenai is the second-oldest permanent settlement in Alaska, founded by Russian fur traders who built St. Nicholas Redoubt in 1791. The U.S. Army built its own fort—Kenay—in 1869, two years after the Great Land changed hands. Oil was discovered at Swanson River in 1957, followed by natural gas two years later, and now Kenai is the largest and most industrialized town on the peninsula. Several of the 15 Cook Inlet platforms are visible from shore, but production has declined in recent years, forcing the closure of a fertilizer plant and an LNG plant. A Tesoro refinery still operates in nearby Nikiski, along with a power plant. The rich past has been buried by Kenai's rather uneventful present in which the town isn't much more than a series of intersections and gas stations.

Sights

The Kenai Visitors and Cultural Center's **museum** (11471 Kenai Spur Rd., 907/283-1991, www.visitkenai.com, Mon.-Fri. 9am-6pm, Sat. 10am-6pm, Sun. 10am-5pm late May-early Sept.; Mon.-Fri. 9am-5pm, Sat. 10am-4pm in

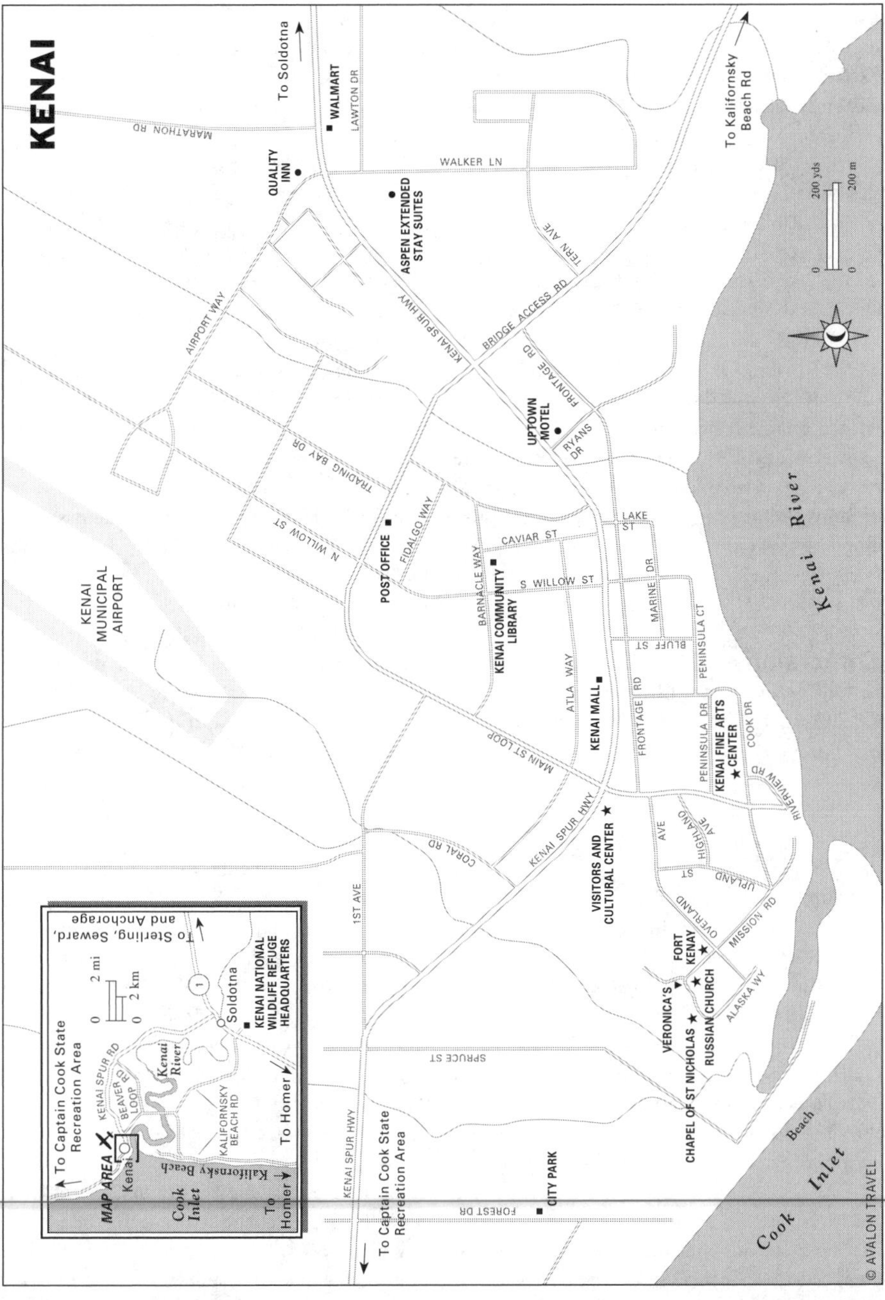
KENAI
To Soldotna
WALMART
LAWTON DR
MARATHON RD
QUALITY INN
WALKER LN
ASPEN EXTENDED STAY SUITES
TERN AVE
To Kalifornsky Beach Rd
200 yds
200 m
BRIDGE ACCESS RD
KENAI SPUR HWY
AIRPORT WAY
FRONTAGE RD
UPTOWN MOTEL
RYANS DR
TRADING BAY DR
N WILLOW ST
FIDALGO WAY
POST OFFICE
LAKE ST
CAVIAR ST
BARNACLE WAY
KENAI COMMUNITY LIBRARY
S WILLOW ST
MARINE DR
PENINSULA CT
BLUFF ST
KENAI MUNICIPAL AIRPORT
Kenai River
ATLA WAY
KENAI MALL
FRONTAGE RD
PENINSULA DR
COOK DR
KENAI FINE ARTS CENTER
MAIN ST LOOP
RIVERVIEW RD
KENAI SPUR HWY
VISITORS AND CULTURAL CENTER
CORAL RD
HIGHLAND AVE
AVE
ST
UPLAND
OVERLAND
MISSION RD
1ST AVE
FORT KENAY
VERONICA'S
RUSSIAN CHURCH
ALASKA WY
CHAPEL OF ST NICHOLAS
SPRUCE ST
KENAI SPUR HWY
To Captain Cook State Recreation Area
CITY PARK
FOREST DR
Beach
Cook Inlet
© AVALON TRAVEL
To Captain Cook State Recreation Area
MAP AREA
Kenai
KENAI SPUR RD
BEAVER LOOP RD
Kenai River
KALIFORNSKY BEACH RD
Kalifornsky Beach
Cook Inlet
To Homer
To Homer
Soldotna
KENAI NATIONAL WILDLIFE REFUGE HEADQUARTERS
0 2 mi
0 2 km
To Sterling, Seward, and Anchorage

winter, $5 adults, $3 seniors, free for kids) is impressive, with gorgeous cultural artifacts from Kenaitze Native peoples, a permanent exhibit of local historical lore and natural history, temporary art exhibits, and a gift shop.

From the museum, walk down toward the bluff on Overland Avenue to the replica of **Fort Kenay,** built in 1967 for the Alaska Centennial. It isn't open to the public. Just up the way is **Holy Assumption of the Virgin Mary Orthodox Church** (1106 Mission Ave., 907/283-4122), built in 1895 and the second-oldest Russian Orthodox Church in the state (the oldest is on Kodiak). It's a working church with regular services; tours are available on request, or peek through the windows at the painted altar and brass chandelier. The **Chapel of Saint Nicholas** (1906) across the street, built atop the grave of Kenai's first priest, also reflects the traditional Russian Orthodox architectural style.

Entertainment and Events

In Old Town, **Kenai Fine Arts Center** (816 Cook Ave., 907/283-7040, www.kenaifinearts. com) provides gallery space for local artists and serves as home to regional art organizations.

The **Kenai Birding Festival** (907/260-5449, www.kenaibirdfest.com, mid-May) encompasses bird and nature photography walks, an art show, birding raft trips, and more. Most activities take place around Kenai.

The **Kenai River Marathon** (www.kenairivermarathon.org, late Sept.) is one of the state's top marathon races.

The grounds of the Kenai Visitors and Cultural Center are transformed into the **Kenai Saturday Market** (11471 Kenai Spur Rd., 907/283-1991, www.visitkenai.com, Sat. in summer), with arts, crafts, and fresh produce.

Recreation

My favorite destination in Kenai is **Kenai Beach** (end of Spruce St. on the north side of the river) near the mouth of the Kenai River and just a short distance from the Russian Orthodox Church; it's one of the best and most easily accessible beaches in Alaska. A line of low dunes backs the fine sand.

The Kenai River mouth gets crowded with hundreds of dipnetters when salmon are running each July. Dipnetting is only open to Alaskan residents, but makes a great spectator sport for all. Special nets with long metal handles are used to snag fish as they head up the river to spawn.

Captain Cook State Recreation Area (end of North Kenai Rd., 907/262-5581, www.alaskastateparks.org, $5 day use) is 25 miles from Kenai. This is a delightful place to camp ($12), hike the rocky shoreline, look for colorful agates on the beach, enjoy the views across Cook Inlet, or simply relax. On summer weekends locals come here to swim in the surprisingly warm waters of Stormy Lake.

Families will love spending an afternoon at the North Peninsula Recreation Area's dome-covered **Nikiski Pool** (Mile 23 Spur Hwy., 907/776-8472, www.northpenrec.com, daily, $9 with waterslide), where the featured attractions are a corkscrew waterslide, a "rain umbrella," hot tub, and a large pool for lap swimming.

The **Kenai Peninsula Oilers** (corner of Cook Ave. and Main St., 907/283-7133, www.oilersbaseball.com) play semiprofessional baseball at Coral Seymour Memorial Park. Always fun to watch, the team has won several National Baseball Congress World Series championships over the years. It's one of six teams within the nation's top collegiate summer league, the Alaska Baseball League.

Kenai Golf Course (1420 Lawton Dr., 907/283-7500, www.kenaigolfcourse.com) is an 18-hole public course. **Kenai Central High School** (9583 Kenai Spur Hwy., 907/283-2100, www.kpbsd.k12.ak.us) has an Olympic size pool with open swim times.

© DON PITCHER

Holy Assumption of the Virgin Mary Orthodox Church, Kenai

Accommodations

HOTELS

The Kenai Visitors and Cultural Center has a complete listing of local lodging places, along with their brochures. In the middle of Kenai town, **Uptown Motel** (47 Spur View Dr., 907/283-3660 or 800/777-3650, www.up-townmotel.com, $155-165 d) has fridges, microwaves, and Wi-Fi in all the guest rooms, plus Louie's Restaurant and Back Door Lounge. There is free airport transportation, and freezer space is available to store your catch. Check out the 100-year-old gold-plated cash register behind the front desk.

Close to WalMart and Home Depot, **Quality Inn** (10352 Kenai Spur Hwy., 907/283-6060 or 877/883-6060, www.qualityinn.com, $189 d) has updated guest rooms, microwaves, fridges, flat-screen TVs, an indoor pool, a hot tub, and an exercise facility, plus Wi-Fi and a hot breakfast buffet.

Not far away is the newest Kenai lodging place, **Aspen Extended Stay Suites** (10431 Kenai Spur Hwy., 907/283-2272, www.aspen-hotelsak.com, $189-199 d), with generously sized rooms, small kitchens, an exercise room, and Wi-Fi. Rates drop if you're staying for more than a day or two.

CABINS AND BED-AND-BREAKFASTS

On a small pond with a view of the river, **Log Cabin Inn** (49860 Eider Dr., 907/283-3653 or 877/834-2912, www.alaskalogcabininn.com, cabins $159, guest rooms $135-145 d) has three cabins and a main lodge. The small cabins sleep three and have a microwave, fridge, and tiny bathroom. The lodge contains seven guest rooms, each with a private bath. A filling breakfast is included for all guests, who will also appreciate the enclosed hot tub and Wi-Fi.

For homey accommodations just a 10-minute drive from Kenai, stay at **Blonde Bear B&B** (47004 Emery St., 907/776-8957 or 888/776-8956, www.blondebear.com,

$159-169 d). This comfortably Alaskan lodge contains six guest rooms, private or shared baths, Wi-Fi, and full hot breakfasts. It's just a short walk from Kidney Lake, where you can paddle around in their canoe. No children under age eight are allowed.

On the shore of Carol Lake between Kenai and Soldotna, **The Potter's House B&B** (43880 Supreme Ct., 907/252-4579, www. pottershouselodge.com, two-bedroom unit $200 for up to four, guest room $100 d) is a quiet home where guests can borrow the canoe, kayak, or paddleboat to explore this 12-acre lake. Downstairs, find a spacious two-bedroom unit with a full kitchen, bath, continental breakfast, and laundry. Upstairs is a queen bedroom overlooking the lake, with private bath and a full breakfast. Wi-Fi is available in the B&B, and pets are accepted.

Daniels Lake Lodge B&B (Mile 29.7 Kenai Spur Hwy., 907/776-5578 or 800/774-5578, www.danielslakelodge.com, guest rooms $98-128 d, cabins $155-260) includes three rooms in the main house and three log cabins that are perfect for families. This is a fine get-away-from-it-all place set on 10 acres of lakeshore. Amenities include a waterside hot tub, private baths, Wi-Fi, and self-serve breakfasts. A canoe, paddleboat, and motorboat are available to explore this quiet two-mile-long lake. Friendly owners Karen and Jim Burris have a well-behaved golden doodle dog and pet ducks, and the lodge is 5 miles east of Nikiski and 21 miles north of Kenai. It's near the Swanson River, a good place for fishing without the crowds. There's a two-night minimum in the cabins and on weekends for all units.

Located in Old Town Kenai, **Harborside Cottages** (813 Riverview Dr., 907/283-6162 or 888/283-6162, www.harborsidecottages.com, 150-195 d) are cute kitchenette units overlooking the Kenai River beach, with private baths and Wi-Fi.

FISHING LODGES

Kenai is home to several fishing lodges, offering packages to please anglers of all types. An excellent choice is **Jimmie Jack Fishing** (36065 Reef Dr., 907/262-5561 or 866/553-4744, www.jimmiejackfishing.com, seven days $2,700 pp), with a beachfront location, good food, modern boats, and pleasant accommodations. Most guests stay for seven days, providing time to fish for kings, halibut, and silvers while also exploring the area.

CAMPING

The nearest public camping places are in Soldotna. Twenty-five miles north of Kenai is quiet Captain Cook State Recreation Area, where **Discovery Campground** (39 Kenai Spur Hwy., 907/262-5581, www.alaskastateparks. org, mid-May-Sept., $12) has 53 campsites with water and pit toilets. The beach here is an outstanding place to find agates.

Five miles south of Kenai, **Diamond M Ranch** (Kalifornsky Beach Rd., 907/283-9424, www. diamondmranch.com, RVs $48-56, tents $42 d, suites $159-169 d, B&B rooms $129 d, cabin $115 d) is a full service resort with laundry facilities, fish cleaning stations, freezer space, and Wi-Fi. The site overlooks the Kenai River estuary, a good place to watch for moose, caribou, and bald eagles. Paved walking and biking trails continue all the way to Soldotna. Located on an 80-acre spread, the RV park centers around a "Main Street" cluster of Gold Rush style buildings that house suites with private baths, kitchens, and decks. Other lodging options include everything from B&B rooms to an authentic homestead cabin with a sod roof and outhouse.

Beluga RV Park (929 Mission Ave., 907/283-5999 or 800/745-5999, www.beluga-lookout.com, RVs $55-65) has full hookups along Cook Inlet. It's near the Kenai River mouth, making it especially popular with anglers, and has a fish cleaning station, cable TV, and Wi-Fi.

Close to the Kenai Visitors Center, **Kenai RV Park** (507 Upland Ave., 907/335-5400, www.kenairvpark.com, RVs $40) has RV sites.

Food

Cozy **Veronica's Café** (602 Petersen Way, 907/283-2725, Tues.-Thurs. 10am-3pm, Fri.-Sat. 10am-9:30pm, $6-12) is *the* place in the Kenai-Soldotna area. Hidden in a historic log cabin across the street from the Russian Orthodox Church in Old Town Kenai, the café serves breakfast blintzes with reindeer sausage, polenta-crust quiche specials, fresh salads, soups, sandwiches (try the chicken cashew), espresso, and wonderful desserts. Friday clam chowder is a locals' favorite, and the café features acoustic musical accompaniment on Friday and Saturday evenings.

Housed within the Uptown Motel near Bridge Access Road, **Louie's Steak & Seafood** (47 Spur View Dr., 907/283-3660, www.uptownmotel.com, Mon.-Fri. 5am-10pm, Sat.-Sun. 5am-11pm, $23-45) is the local surf-and-turf restaurant with rustic Alaskan decor accented by trophy animal mounts. They serve good steaks, king crab, beef stroganoff, and seafood fettuccine. Eggs Benedict breakfasts are popular on weekends. The lounge attracts the sports crowd with 16 TVs and complimentary hors d'oeuvres.

The aptly named **Burger Bus** (912 Highland Ave., 907/283-9611, Mon.-Sat. 11am-6pm, $7-9) is just up the street from the visitors center. Try the Kenai killer burger, a mushroom Swiss burger, green chili chicken, or fish and chips. It's all made while you wait and surprisingly tasty. These are easily the best burgers in the area.

For the best local pizza you'll need to drive north to Nikiski, where **Charlie's Pizza** (51400 Kenai Spur Hwy., 907/776-8778, Tues.-Fri. 11am-9pm, $12-24) gets raves from locals and folks passing through. The mozzarella cheese bread and bread sticks are popular, along with a variety of specialty pizzas. Get a Bulldog pizza with extra thick crust and loads of meat, or the Bombdiggity, topped with alfredo sauce, parmesan, mozzarella, ground beef, minced garlic, and jalapeno peppers. Pizzas by the slice ($3 for one, $5 for two) are offered Tuesday-Friday 11am-2pm. There is no alcohol here.

Information and Services

For information, start at the **Kenai Visitors and Cultural Center** (11471 Kenai Spur Rd., 907/283-1991, www.visitkenai.com, Mon.-Fri. 9am-6pm, Sat. 10am-6pm, Sun. 10am-5pm late May-early Sept.; Mon.-Fri. 9am-5pm, Sat. 10am-4pm in winter), where you'll find a big rack of brochures about the area and a helpful staff.

Kenai Wash-N-Dry (502 Lake St., 907/283-8473, daily 8am-10pm) has laundry and showers.

Kenai Public Library (163 Main St. Loop, 907/283-4378, www.kenailibrary.org, Sun. 1pm-4pm, Mon.-Thurs. 9am-7pm, Fri. 9am-6pm, Sat. 9am-5pm) has a large collection of Alaskan titles, plus computers and Wi-Fi.

The **WalMart** (intersection of Kenai Spur Hwy. and Marathon Rd., 907/395-0971, www.walmart.com) is the largest store on the Kenai Peninsula.

Getting There and Around

Both **Era Alaska** (907/266-8394 or 800/866-8394, www.flyera.com) and **Grant Aviation** (907/283-6012 or 888/359-4726, www.fly-grant.com) offer flights between Kenai Airport and Anchorage. Service is almost hourly throughout the day. Based on Island Lake between Kenai and Nikiski, **Alaska West Air** (907/776-5147, www.alaskawestair.com) has charters (along with flightseeing, bear viewing trips, and sportfishing). Call **Alaska Cab** (907/283-6000) for rides into town.

Rent cars and vans at the Kenai Airport (www.kenaiairport.com) from **Avis**

(907/283-7900 or 800/331-1212, www.avis. com) or **Budget** (907/283-4506 or 800/527- 0770, www.budget.com).

SOUTH TO HOMER

South of Soldotna, the Sterling Highway hugs the coastline all the way to Homer, a distance of 75 miles. The view across the Cook Inlet is of the Aleutian volcanic crown, **Mount Redoubt** (10,197 ft.) to the north and **Mount Iliamna** (10,016 ft.) to the south—both within Lake Clark National Park. On a very clear day you can also see **Mount Augustine,** a solitary volcanic island with a well-defined cone at the bottom of the Inlet. They're all very active; Augustine last erupted in 2006, followed by Redoubt in 2009. See www.avo.alaska.edu to check current activity levels.

Travelers will be dismayed to find that many of the larger spruce trees in this area were killed by spruce bark beetles in the 1990s, leaving behind the brown skeletons of a once-healthy forest. Fortunately, the youngest spruce trees generally survived the onslaught, and other species, such as birch and alder, were unaffected. The dead spruce forests extend well south of Homer and across Kachemak Bay into Kachemak Bay State Park. Unfortunately, the infestation that began near here spread eastward across the Kenai Peninsula and all the way to Yukon in Canada, so this isn't the only place you'll find dead trees.

KASILOF

Tiny Kasilof (ka-SEE-loff, pop. 600) is 15 miles south of Soldotna along the Kasilof River. Kalifornsky Beach (a.k.a. K-Beach) Road meets the Sterling Highway here. The road continues north to Kenai and Soldotna. Kasilof is home to four-time Iditarod champion Lance Mackey. There's a post office, but no visitor center; get details on local businesses at www.visitkasilofalaska.com.

The **Kasilof Regional Historical Association Museum** (Kalifornsky Beach Rd., 907/262-2999, www.kasilofhistoricalsociety. org, daily 1pm-4pm late May-early Sept.) has a collection of restored historic cabins from early day fox farmers and trappers. Find it a half-mile up K-Beach Road.

At Mile 5 of K-Beach Road, turn left on Kasilof Beach Road for access to the north side of the Kasilof River mouth. Access to the south side is via North Cohoe Loop Road, which turns off the Sterling Highway at Mile 110. During the height of the silver salmon run in July, hundreds of Alaskan dipnetters descend upon this area, camping on the dunes and tramping down to the water with giant nets as the incoming tide brings a rush of salmon up the river. Dipnetting is only open to Alaskan residents, but nonresidents can try their luck with a rod and reel.

At Mile 110, look for the big metal T and follow the road to pretty **Johnson Lake,** stocked with rainbow trout. The state recreation area here has picnic shelters and campsites ($10) with water and toilets. Continue five miles out the road to a free boat launch that serves as an access point for **Tustumena Lake** within Kenai National Wildlife Refuge. This huge lake is infamous for sudden weather changes that can swamp unprepared boaters.

Kasilof is the starting point for the **Tustumena 200 Sled Dog Race** (www.tustumena200.com, last Sat. in Jan.). It's a qualifying race for the Iditarod, and a great place to meet mushers and dogs up close.

Kasilof Mercantile (Mile 109 Sterling Hwy., 907/262-4809, www.kasilofmercantile.com) has a café, groceries, video rentals, ice cream, and espresso.

Accommodations

Right on the banks of the Kasilof River, **Gallery Lodge** (Terrace Dr., 907/229-2999, www.gallerylodge.com, house $250 for four guests, rooms and suites $130-190 d) has a two-bedroom house with a full kitchen, plus a variety of suites and rooms. Fishing packages are also offered, and the facility is popular for weddings.

Friendly and clean, **Kasilof River Lodge and Cabins** (Cohoe Loop Rd., 907/262-6348 or 888/262-7075, www.kasilofriverlodge. com, guest rooms $50-100 d, yurt $75 d, cabins $100-150 d) has a variety of accommodations, including lodge rooms, a yurt, and cabins. Some units have private baths and kitchens, while others share a bathhouse and cooking area. A hearty continental breakfast is included for all guests, and the owners have 20 acres of land with river access for fishing. Located near the mouth of the Kasilof River, the lodge is a good place to hang out with local commercial anglers and serves as the de facto community center for the settlement of Cohoe.

Crooked Creek Retreat (59325 Sterling Hwy., 907/260-9014, www.crookedcreekretreat.com, $180 pp) is a good choice for multinight fishing packages based in Kasilof.

On a bluff overlooking Cook Inlet and Mount Redoubt, **Alaskan Sunset Cabins** (Mile 6 Kalifornsky Beach Rd., 907/283-9246 or 866/286-6946, www.alaskansunset. com, May-Sept., smaller units $170 d, $190 for four; larger units $300 d, add $10 pp for extra guests) consists of seven modern cabins that are popular with families and anglers. All include full kitchens, private baths, decks, grills, Wi-Fi, and scenic vistas. The smaller units have a bedroom and sleeping loft, while the larger house-size units have three bedrooms and two baths, with room for six.

Alaska Riverview Lodge (Amber Dr., 907/260-5432, www.alaskariverview.com, May-Sept., kitchenette rooms $125 d, house $300, add $25 pp for extra guests) has an array of lodging options: two cabins, an apartment suite, kitchenette rooms, a master suite, and even a four-bedroom house. Rates include breakfast in the main lodge. This is the only

local lodge with its own dock on the Kasilof River, and guests can borrow fishing or clamming gear. There's a fish cleaning station, Wi-Fi, picnic tables, and an observation deck. All rooms contain freezers to store your catch. The lodge is off K-Beach Road, a mile north of the junction with Sterling Highway.

Camping

At the confluence of Crooked Creek and the Kasilof River, **Crooked Creek RV Park** (907/262-1299, www.crookedcreekrv.com, RVs $39) is a good base for fishing. Access is from North Cohoe Loop Road at Mile 111 of the Sterling Highway.

Kasilof RV Park (21377 Crooked Creek Rd., 907/262-0418 summer or 785/657-1465 winter, www.kasilofrvpark.com, RVs $35) is close to Johnson Lake.

CLAM GULCH

Another wide spot in the road, appropriately-named Clam Gulch has a few businesses and a whole lot of clams.

At Mile 117 is the turnoff for **Clam Gulch State Recreation Area** (day use $5/vehicle, campsites $10) and a two-mile gravel road down to the campground and clamming grounds. Make sure you have a sportfishing license (required for clam diggers over age 16), a shovel, a bucket, and gloves before you dig in the cold sand for the razor-sharp clams. Clamming is best during a low tide in early summer but is possible anytime April-September. Contact the Alaska Department of Fish and Game (www.adfg.alaska.gov) for regulations.

Clam Gulch Lodge B&B (Mile 119 Sterling Hwy., 907/260-3778 or 800/700-9555, www. clamgulch.com, guest rooms $130 d, cabin $270) is a modern place with a hearty breakfast and shared baths. A spacious cabin has a loft, full kitchen, and private bath. It sleeps up to six and has a three-night minimum.

Located on a high bluff facing Cook Inlet, the lodge also offers a variety of fishing and adventure packages.

Another especially nice option is **Alaska Log Haven** (66486 Sterling Hwy., 907/262-5563, www.alaskaloghaven.com, $175-200 d), with a gorgeous bluff-top setting, full breakfasts, private baths, and a hot tub on the deck. The family room has two queen beds.

NINILCHIK

This small town of 700 is halfway between Soldotna and Homer. Located where the Ninilchik River empties into the Inlet, it was settled in the early 1800s by retired Russian-American Company workers who took Native Alaskan wives. You'll find classic water's-edge houses and weathered structures at the old village, down a short side road off Sterling Highway. Follow the road that parallels the Ninilchik River around toward the "spit"; you wind up on the other side of the river and village on the hardpan inlet beach.

Ninilchik's beloved **Transfiguration of Our Lord Russian Orthodox Church** was built on a hilltop in 1900. Access is via Orthodox Avenue (look for the sign at Mile 134 Sterling Hwy.), or by a footpath from Ninilchik Village. Fireweed fills the adjacent graveyard in midsummer, providing a colorful foreground for photos of the church with a backdrop of Cook Inlet and the volcanic summit of Mount Iliamna. The main town of Ninilchik is a mile south of the church, with a smattering of businesses along the highway.

Many charter boats put in at Deep Creek State Recreation Area, where large tractors pull boat trailers down the beach and launch boats out beyond the waves. Don't miss this unique scene on a summer weekend morning, with the action generally taking place an hour or two before high tide. **Deep Creek Custom Packing** (Mile 137 Sterling Hwy., 907/567-3395 or 800/764-0078, www.

deepcreekcustompacking.com) sells quality fresh and smoked fish and is open for tours.

Festivals and Events

Ninilchik hosts the **Kenai Peninsula Fair** (16200 Sterling Hwy., www.kenaipeninsulafair.com, third weekend in Aug.) with games, livestock, pig races, and food booths. It's decidedly small-town fun, and perfect if you have kids with you.

Don't miss **Salmonstock** (16200 Sterling Hwy., www.salmonstock.org, early Aug.)—three days of fish, fun, and live music at the fairgrounds. Past festivals have included such bands as Ozomatli, Robert Randolph, Bill Kreutzmann, Todd Snider, Tim Easton, and Clinton Fearon, plus—of course—the jam band Leftover Salmon. Since it's debut in 2011, Salmonstock has quickly become Alaska's biggest summertime concert venue, attracting several thousand people.

Accommodations and Food

A completely unexpected find, **🄲 Great House Lodge** (64316 Elizabeth Ave., 907/299-0984, www.aksupperclub.com, $200-350 d) crowns a high bluff three miles north of Ninilchik. The deck affords panoramic vistas of Cook Inlet and the sometimes-steaming summits of three volcanoes. Owners Paul and Angela Warner opened this lodge and restaurant in 2011, quickly gaining a loyal following. Inside the lodge are three luxuriously appointed guest rooms. The lodge's restaurant, **aksupperclub** (four-course meal $45 pp, add $25 for wine pairings), is open nightly, with a single seating at 6pm. There's space for 12 guests around a large table, and the menu changes every day, reflecting the seasons. Fresh and local is the theme; the owners managed a local seafood company for years and use produce from their own garden. Don't miss the award-winning burgundy chocolate tart. Meals are a leisurely affair, so be ready

Transfiguration of Our Lord Russian Orthodox Church, Ninilchik

for three or four relaxing hours to enjoy the food and intimate setting. Reservations are required. Weekly cooking classes ($25) take place on summer Saturdays.

Budget travelers should check out **The Eagle Watch** (Oilwell Rd., 907/567-3905, www.theeaglewatchhostel.com, mid-May-mid-Sept., dorm beds $15 adults, $8 kids; $40 d). A full kitchen is available, along with dorm beds and two private rooms. The hostel is closed 10am-5pm and credit cards are not accepted. The hostel is on the banks of the Ninilchik River three miles out Oilwell Road. Friendly hosts Frank and Roswitha will gladly provide info on local attractions.

One mile out Oilwell Road is **Drift-In B&B** (Oilwell Rd., 907/567-3448 or 800/567-0249, www.driftin.com, $95 d shared bath, $105 d private bath), where three rooms share two baths and a fourth room has its own bath. The house has a lounge and small kitchen with freezer space. Rates include a full breakfast, or

a continental breakfast and sack lunch if you're leaving early on a fishing charter.

In the heart of historic Ninilchik village and just steps from the river, **Alaska Adventure Suites** (66710 Mission Ave., 907/277-1800, www.alaskaadventuresuites.com, $165-195 d, add $25 pp for extra guests, maximum seven) has two luxurious, nicely decorated apartment suites, each with a full kitchen, living room, and bath. The larger 1,200-square-foot unit has two bedrooms, panoramic views of Cook Inlet and three active volcanoes, hardwood floors, and a fireplace. Most guests stay several days to take advantage of local fishing charters.

On the north edge of town, **The Buzz Café** (15555 Sterling Hwy., 907/567-3307, daily 6am-4:30pm) serves Kaladi Bros. lattes and mochas; it's the best espresso buzz spot for 20 miles in either direction.

Camping

Three very popular state campgrounds

(907/235-7024, www.alaskastateparks.org, $10) are scattered around town: **Ninilchik River Campground** is big, woodsy, and un-crowded, **Ninilchik View Campground** is atop a high bluff, and **Ninilchik Beach Campground** has undeveloped sites. **Deep Creek State Recreation Area** (day-use parking $5, camp-sites $10) is just two miles to the south.

Park RVs at **Heavenly Sights Camping** (13295 Sterling Hwy., 907/567-7371 or 800/479-7371, www.heavenlysights.com, RVs $35 with electricity, tents $20) atop the bluff four miles north of Ninilchik.

Aptly named **Scenic View RV Park** (Mile 127 Sterling Hwy., 907/567-3909, www.sce-nicviewrv.com, RVs $35 with full hookups) is eight miles north of town on a 200-foot bluff that fronts on Cook Inlet.

Located on an eight-acre spread right in town, **Alaskan Angler RV Resort** (15640 Kingsley Rd., 907/567-3393 or 800/347-4114, www.afishunt.com, RVs $43-49, tents $15) has RV sites and tent spaces. Simple cabins are also available.

Country Boy Campground (Mile 3.1 Oilwell Rd., 907/567-3396, www.country-boycampground.com, May-Sept., RVs $30 with full hookups, tents $10) has full hookup sites and tent spaces. In addition to laundry, fish processing, and other showers, the RV park has a café rather disturbingly called Up-Chuck Restaurant.

Information and Services

Contact the **Ninilchik Chamber of Commerce** (907/567-3571, www.ninilchikchamber.com) for information on local places. Stock up at **Ninilchik General Store** (Mile 135.7 Sterling Hwy., 907/567-3378), or talk with folks at the charter fishing companies.

ANCHOR POINT

This no-frills town of 2,000 people is another sportfishing destination, with the Anchor River attracting anglers in pursuit of king salmon, silver salmon, Dolly Varden, and steelhead. Anchor Point is the most westerly highway point in North America (or, more precisely, the most westerly town on a road system con-nected with the Lower 48). The point of land was named by Captain James Cook after his ship lost an anchor here in 1787.

Shopping
ART GALLERIES

Four miles south of Anchor Point is the turn-off to **Norman Lowell Gallery** (Mile 160.9 Sterling Hwy., 907/235-7344, www.norman-lowellgallery.net, Sun. 1pm-5pm, Mon.-Sat. 9am-5pm May-mid-Sept., free). A half-mile gravel road leads steeply uphill to this 10,000 square-foot gallery that exhibits more than 300 of Norman Lowell's paintings in a vari-ety of mediums. Norman and Libby Lowell homesteaded here in 1958, and he built a reputation as a painter of traditional Alaskan landscapes. Many of his paintings are large, with one stretching 7 by 14 feet! The sales gallery has both prints (starting at $150) and originals (some for $30,000) for sale. Saunter the grounds to see the family homestead.

Across the road from the turnoff to Norman Lowell Gallery is the **Ben Firth Studio** (Mile 161 Sterling Hwy., 907/226-2009, www.ben-firthstudio.com, Mon.-Sat. 10am-5pm mid-May-mid-Sept.), showcasing art by the entire Firth family—including award-winning bird paintings by their children.

Recreation

If you aren't into fishing, Anchor Point's most popular attraction is the long sandy beach at the mouth of the Anchor River. Get here by heading downhill from town on the Old Sterling Highway. Turn right after the bridge and continue a mile down Beach Road. Watch tractors launching fishing boats on the beach most summer mornings or head up the beach in either direction for a long hike. This entire area is part of the **Anchor River State Recreation Area,** with five popular campgrounds ($12) between town and the beach.

Fireweed Meadows Golf Course (72749 Milo Fritz Ave., 907/226-2582, www.fireweed-meadowsgolf.com, $18) is a nine-hole course for golf enthusiasts.

Accommodations

Anchor River Inn (34358 Old Sterling Hwy., 907/235-8531 or 800/435-8531, www.anchor-riverinn.com, $99 d, "fishermen's special" $65-70 d) has standard rooms with two queen beds, microwaves, and fridges. There are aging and tiny "fishermen's special" rates, but these are often booked months ahead for midsummer. Rooms have Wi-Fi and guests can use the small fitness center. Also here are a full-service restaurant and lounge.

Alaska Lakefront Cabin (69180 Karen Circle, 907/235-8881, www.alaskalakefront-cabin.com, $145 d) is situated along a private lake eight miles south of Anchor Point and eight miles north of Homer. The cabin has a kitchen, loft, and private bath, with space for four. Moose are a common sight in this peaceful spot.

Other good lodging choices include **Sleepy Bear Cabins** (North Fork Rd., 907/235-5625 or 866/235-5630, www.sleepybearalaska.com, $110 d), **Bear Essentials Lodging** (Mile 149.5 Sterling Hwy., 907/235-4175, www.bearessen-tialslodging.com, $75-85 d), and **Northwood Cabins** (73405 Twin Peaks Loop, 907/235-8454, www.northwoodcabins.com, $55-150 d).

Camping

Four miles north of Anchor Point, **Stariski State Recreation Site** (Mile 152 Sterling Hwy., day-use parking $5, campsites $10) has one of the best views of any state campground. A steep road—not recommended for RVs—provides access off the highway.

Kyllonen RV Park (Beach Rd., 907/235-7762 or 888/848-2589, www.kyllonensrvpark.com, RVs $38) has view sites near the end of Beach Road and close to the Anchor River. Amenities include laundry, showers, Wi-Fi, and charter bookings.

Food

Anchor Point dining options are very limited, and the dominant theme seems to be converted old buses and Quonset huts. The best of these is **Ramiro's** (33840 Sterling Hwy., 907/235-9694, Tues.-Sat. 11am-7pm, $9-14), an authentic family run Mexican-American eatery housed in a little red bus. (This is not to be confused with The Blue Bus restaurant directly across the street.) There are a couple of picnic tables out front, or you can head down to the beach for a better vista. Get two enchiladas, rice, and beans; it's finger-licking good. The priciest item is shrimp fajitas. Other menu items include a half-pound burger with fries. Breakfast items are served all day, and a kids' menu is available.

Information

The Anchor Point Chamber of Commerce **Visitors Information Center** (34175 Sterling Hwy., 907/235-2600, www.anchorpointchamber.org, daily 10am-2pm late May-early Sept., limited winter hours) maintains a mini-museum with historical photos and memorabilia. The office is right next to the school.

NIKOLAEVSK

The Russian Old Believer village of Nikolaevsk is nine miles east of Anchor Point via North Fork Road and Nikolaevsk Road. This isolated community of 300 is one of several on the Kenai Peninsula where these traditional people live; nearly all speak both Russian and English. Three Russian villages (Kachemak Selo, Razdolna, and Voznesenka) are 25 miles east of Homer, and other Old Believer

© DON PITCHER

St. Nicholas Church in Nikolaevsk

settlements are in Delta Junction, Kodiak Island, and Sterling. Many Old Believers fled from Russia following tsarist persecution and the Bolshevik Revolution, settling in such far-flung places as Brazil, Australia, Alberta, Minnesota, and Oregon.

There's a picturesque church in Nikolaevsk, and the women and girls wear scarves and ankle-length dresses. But they also have all the modern conveniences, including big pickup trucks, satellite dishes, and computers. Villagers are not particularly welcoming to voyeurs, so don't go around pointing your camera at folks.

One ultra-friendly local is Nina Fefelov, the owner of the **Samovar Café** (907/235-6867, www.russiangiftsnina.com, Apr.-Sept., closed Sun. and Russian holidays). The café serves such traditional dishes as borscht, pelmeni, piroshki, and Russian tea, and sells traditional Russian gifts. The hours are a bit hit or miss, so call ahead to make sure she's open. Credit cards are not accepted. Nina is quite the entrepreneur, and visitors may find themselves pushed into dressing in Old Believer garb to have their photo taken (for cash of course). Overnight stays at her B&B ($69 d) include a Russian breakfast. You may also park RVs here ($29, no hookups, but showers are available).

Homer

Homer has a dazzling reputation for some of the finest scenery, the mildest climate, heaviest halibut, biggest bays, longest spits, coolest people, and best quality of life in the state. And the truth is, Homer is one of Alaska's peerless towns. It has an undeniably beautiful setting, with the unruly coastline, undulating fjords, and cavalcading Kenai Mountains across magnificent Kachemak Bay. The temperatures are generally mild—for Alaska. The halibut sometimes tip the scales at over 200 pounds, and you can try your luck at salmon fishing for the cost of a fishing license. An abundance of fine artists and craftspeople call Homer home, selling their wares at small galleries full of rare and tempting stuff. And some of the state's best fishing, boating, hiking, kayaking, natural history, wildlife, and photo ops revolve around Homer in Kachemak Bay. So the bottom line is: Homer distinctly deserves its reputation. Welcome to Homer, Cosmic Hamlet by the Sea.

HISTORY

The Russians knew of the limitless coal in this area in the early 1800s, and Americans were mining the seams only a decade after the Alaska Purchase. The gold rush began delivering people and supplies to the small port at the end of the sandy spit on their way to the

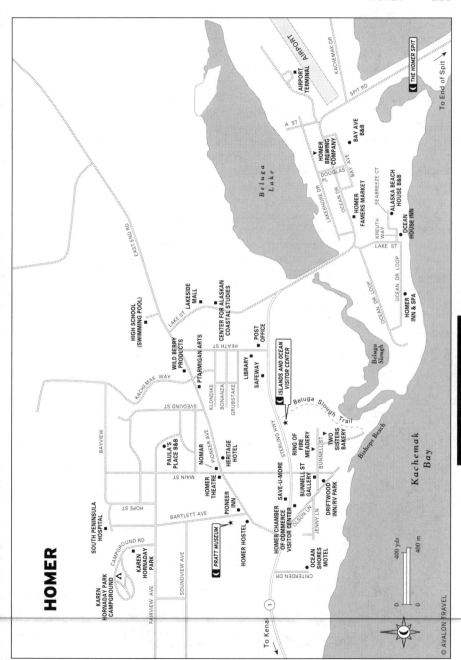

HOMER

THE KENAI PENINSULA

Beluga Lake

Beluga Slough

Beluga Slough Trail

Kachemak Bay

Bishops Beach

AIRPORT

THE HOMER SPIT

To End of Spit

AIRPORT TERMINAL

KACHEMAK DR

SPIT RD

A ST

BAY AVE B&B

HOMER BREWING COMPANY

BAY AVE

DOUGLAS PL

SEABREEZE CT

ALASKA BEACH HOUSE B&B

OCEAN DR

LAKESHORE DR

HOMER FARMERS MARKET

KREUTH WAY

OCEAN HOUSE INN

LAKE ST

OCEAN DR LOOP

OCEAN DR LOOP

HOMER INN & SPA

EAST END RD

LAKESIDE MALL

CENTER FOR ALASKAN COASTAL STUDIES

HIGH SCHOOL (SWIMMING POOL)

LAKE ST

WILD BERRY PRODUCTS

PTARMIGAN ARTS

HEATH ST

POST OFFICE

KACHEMAK WAY

LIBRARY

SAFEWAY

ISLANDS AND OCEAN VISITOR CENTER

KLONDIKE

BONANZA

GRUBSTAKE

SVEDLUND ST

STERLING HWY

RING OF FIRE MEADERY

TWO SISTERS BAKERY

BAYVIEW

PAULA'S PLACE B&B

NOMAR

PIONEER AVE

HERITAGE HOTEL

MAIN ST

HOMER THEATRE

PIONEER INN

SAVE-U-MORE

BUNNELL ST GALLERY

BUNNELL ST

HOPE ST

BARTLETT AVE

SOUTH PENINSULA HOSPITAL

OLSON LN

DRIFTWOOD INN/RV PARK

JENNY LN

CAMPGROUND RD

KAREN HORNADAY PARK

KAREN HORNADAY PARK CAMPGROUND

FAIRVIEW AVE

SOUNDVIEW AVE

PRATT MUSEUM

HOMER HOSTEL

HOMER CHAMBER OF COMMERCE VISITOR CENTER

CRITERDEN DR

OCEAN SHORES MOTEL

1

To Kenai

0   400 yds

0   400 m

© AVALON TRAVEL

gold fields at Hope and Sunrise up the Inlet in the mid-1890s. One of the most flamboyant prospectors to pass through, Homer Pennock left his name on the settlement. Mining the hundreds of millions of tons of accessible bituminous fuel continued until 1907, when a combination of fire in Homer, federal policy, and falling prices burned out the market. Slowly and inevitably, the fishers and homesteaders began settling in during the 1920s, and they found a lifetime supply of home-heating fuel free for the taking right on the beach; it's still collected by some locals.

Homer remained a small fishing and canning port until the early 1950s, when the Sterling Highway finally connected the town with the rest of the continent. Since then, the population has grown to over 4,000 today, with commercial fishing and tourism the primary economic pillars. Homer has an interesting mix of people. Drop by the docks and you'll encounter both the long-haired Rasta crowd and Russian Old Believers whose women wear prim and proper long dresses while the men sport long beards.

SIGHTS
Overlook

Homer is the end of the line. After the five-hour drive south from Anchorage, travelers crest a high hill to a stunning view as they come into Homer. Pull off the Sterling Highway at Mile 170 where a big overlook looks over Kachemak Bay, the Homer Spit, and a line of snowy mountains, glaciers, and volcanoes. Don't arrive on a clear summer afternoon or you're next stop will be a real estate office in downtown Homer! But do stop for a photo or two to show you've made it to one of the prettiest places in Alaska.

◖ The Homer Spit

This four-mile finger of real estate jutting boldly into Kachemak Bay hosts the Small

© DON PITCHER

There are breathtaking views of Kachemak Bay from Homer's overlook.

© DON PITCHER

Homer Harbor and the Homer Spit

Boat Harbor, touristy boardwalks, a famous Fishing Hole, infamous Salty Dawg Saloon, Land's End Resort, public camping, charter halibut and salmon fishing, a ferry terminal, and lazy beachcombing with an incomparable view. It is Homer's main attraction, and a wonderfully busy place in midsummer. You could easily spend several days just exploring the shops, walking the beaches, flying kites, fishing for salmon in the Hole, renting a sea kayak to paddle around, soaking up the mountain vistas, and sitting around a campfire as the midsummer sun heads down around midnight. Day breezes kick up most afternoons, making for fine sailing and ideal conditions for an increasing number of kiteboarders. And when the wind really blows, the waves roll in, attracting surfers and kayakers. No wonder so many folks love Homer! The Pratt Museum's **Historic Harbor Walking Tours** (4380 Homer Spit Rd., 907/235-8635, Fri. and Sat. 3pm summer, $5) depart from the Salty Dawg Saloon.

A paved two-mile **bike path** starts at the base of the Spit and continues to the Fishing Hole; it's great for bikes and inline skates, but the traffic is constant and noisy. Come out early in the morning before the cars and wind pick up. Bike rentals are available from **Cycle Logical** (3585 East End Rd., 907/226-2925, www.cyclelogicalhomer.com), **Homer Saw and Cycle** (1532 Ocean Dr., 907/235-8406), and **Land's End Resort** (4786 Homer Spit Rd., 907/235-2500, www.lands-end-resort.com).

Islands and Ocean Visitor Center

Located on the edge of Homer, this extraordinary, free (!) facility (95 Sterling Hwy., 907/235-6961, www.islandsandocean.org, daily 9am-5pm early May-early Sept.; Tues.-Sat. noon-5pm Sept.; Tues.-Sat. noon-5pm Oct.-early May, free) provides an introduction to the 4.9-million-acre **Alaska Maritime National Wildlife Refuge,** some 2,500 islands, spires, and coastal headlands scattered from Southeast Alaska to the Arctic. These remote islands provide the largest seabird refuge in the United States, with millions of them nesting on rugged cliffs. Inside the Alaska Islands and Ocean Visitor Center a grand two-story glass lobby faces Kachemak Bay, and visitors can take a stunning voyage to the islands via a 14-minute award-winning video. After viewing the video, step into a room that recreates the sights, sounds, and smells of a bird rookery in the Pribilofs, and learn about the birds and marine mammals that inhabit these remote places, and the researchers that work there, through interactive exhibits. Guided birdwatching, beach walks, and estuary walks are offered daily at 11pm mid-June through mid-August. The building also houses **Kachemak Bay Research Reserve** (907/235-4799, www.kbayrr.org, Discovery Lab: Mon., Wed., and Sat. 1pm-3pm mid-June-mid-Aug.), whose hands-on Discovery Lab is open to the public for kid-friendly events.

Bishops Beach

A short trail leads from the Islands and Ocean Visitor Center past Beluga Slough to Bishops Beach, which is also accessible by car from Bunnell Avenue; turn right on Beluga Avenue and follow it to the beach. This is a delightful spot for a low-tide walk, with extraordinary views of mountains, volcanoes, and glaciers lining the bay. Pieces of coal wash ashore from nearby outcrops, and intrepid hikers can follow the beach north seven miles to the Diamond Creek Trail, which heads uphill to the Sterling Highway. Leave a car at the Diamond Creek trailhead off the highway to make your return easier. You'll need to time this hike with the tides to avoid getting trapped against the cliffs.

Diamond Creek Trail is an easy and fun path, even if you don't do the long beach walk. The trailhead is directly across the Sterling Highway from Diamond Ridge Road. A narrow dirt road—small cars only—takes you a half-mile in, or you can park along the highway and walk in. The trail drops down to the gorgeous, remote beach in a fun and scenic mile.

◖ Pratt Museum

Be sure to visit the Pratt Museum (3779 Bartlett St., 907/235-8635, www.prattmuseum.org, daily 10am-6pm mid-May-mid-Sept.; Tues.-Sun. noon-5pm winter, closed Jan., $8 adults, $6 seniors, $4 ages 6-18, free for younger children, $25 for families), just up from Pioneer Avenue. This is one of the finest small museums in Alaska, with interesting historical and cultural pieces, artwork, and wildlife displays. The beaked whale skeleton extends nearly the length of one room; follow the story of how it was shot and washed up onto a Homer beach, then was taken apart and put back together piece by piece. A gift shop sells Alaskan-made crafts, and you can control the museum's webcams of McNeil River bears and Gull Island (also broadcast live on the Internet). Help feed the sea critters Tuesdays and Fridays at 4pm.

Scenic Drives and Hikes

Head back out the Sterling Highway and take a right on West Hill Road; just after the pavement ends, go right at the fork (a left puts you on Diamond Ridge Rd., which drops you back down to the Sterling) onto **Skyline Drive.** You climb along a high ridge among expensive homes and B&Bs until you see the famous view of the Spit, the bay, and the march of mountains on the southern coast, all framed by fireweed late in the summer.

Continue on Skyline Drive to the turnoff for **East Hill Road,** which takes you steeply downhill to Homer, or continue out East Skyline Drive 1.5 miles to **Carl E. Wynn Nature Center** (East Skyline Dr., 907/235-5266, www.akcoastalstudies.org, daily 10am-6pm mid-June-early Sept., guided walks: $7

© DON PITCHER

Bishops Beach and Kachemak Bay

families. Singer Jewel Kilcher is the best-known member of this talented family, but not the only star. The Discovery Channel show *Alaska: The Last Frontier* features a reality-show take on Atz, Otto, Eiven, Atz Lee, and other Kilcher family members. Tours of the homestead are available, and the annual Kilcher Homestead Games in mid-July are a fun step back in time. Tours of this amazingly beautiful homestead are by appointment only.

East End Road ends 20 miles from town, but you can walk down a steep dirt road from here to the shore and past the Russian Old Believer village of **Kachemak Selo** along the beach at the head of Kachemak Bay. Not many folks get this far from Homer, but those who do are well rewarded for the effort. If you don't want to drive all that way, take a hard right onto Kachemak Drive three miles out of Homer, and head back down to the Spit.

adults, $6 seniors, $5 for children under 18, $20 for families). Here you'll find nature trails and a learning center.

Keep going out on East Skyline Drive and turn left on remote Ohlson Mountain Road (gravel) until it ends at **Ohlson Peak** (1,513 ft.). Return to town via East Hill Road, which meets East End Road on—you guessed it—the east side of town.

Pioneer Avenue through town turns into **East End Road,** which also has beautiful homes and great views of the Spit and the bay. Nine miles out are the down-home Fritz Creek General Store (great lunches) and the Homestead Restaurant (wonderful dinners), along with increasingly jaw-dropping views of the Kachemak Bay and the glaciers.

Farther out East End Road, the **Kilcher Homestead Living Museum** (East End Rd., 907/235-8713, www.kilcheronline.com, by appointment only) is a 600-acre homestead established by one of Homer's homesteading

Tours

The Pratt Museum (3779 Bartlett St., 907/235-8635, www.prattmuseum.org) operates excellent 1.5-hour **Historic Harbor Walking Tours** (Fri. and Sat. at 3pm June-Aug., $5), which include local history and lots of detail on commercial fishing and sportfishing. Get tickets at the Pratt or in the little booth next to the Salty Dawg Saloon on the Spit.

Shelly Erickson of **Homer Tours** (907/235-6200, www.ptialaska.net/~ericson) leads custom van tours of the Homer area.

Cooking Classes

Kirsten Dixon, a Cordon Bleu-trained chef and nationally recognized cookbook author, operates **The Cooking School at Tutka Bay** (907/274-2710, www.withinthewild.com, Fri.-Sun. afternoon, five-hour session $225 pp), where five-hour sessions including a 25-minute water taxi ride from Homer. Courses have an emphasis on local seafood and produce, recipes from Tutka Bay Lodge, and international

© DON PITCHER

Kilcher Homestead Living Museum can be found on a scenic drive on East End Road.

cuisine. Cooking classes take place on the *Widgeon II,* an old crabbing boat that has been moored to shore, with a two-story addition atop the deck. This now-landlocked boat provides a completely unique setting to learn the culinary arts.

ENTERTAINMENT AND EVENTS
Nightlife

Homer's old favorite, **Alice's Champagne Palace** (195 E. Pioneer Ave., 907/235-6909) has music and events on a regular basis, and also serves surprisingly good burgers, fish and chips, and buffalo wings. A few blocks away is **The Alibi** (453 E. Pioneer Ave., 907/235-9199, www.wlibi-homer.com), another smoke-free bar with pool tables and frequent live music.

Five miles out East End Road, **Fusion at Wasabi's** (57219 East End Rd., 907/226-3663, www.wasabisrestaurant.com) is downstairs from Wasabi's restaurant, with pool tables,

darts, five huge flat screen TVs, a digital jukebox, and live music or DJs on weekends. Dark and spacious, it feels like a classy cave.

Packed with smokers, **Down East Saloon** (Mile 3 East End Rd., 907/235-6002, www. downeastsaloon.com) has a large dance floor, colorful paintings on the walls, and bands play most weekends. There's a big deck out back, with horseshoes and occasional barbeques.

The **Salty Dawg Saloon** (4380 Homer Spit Rd., 907/235-6718, www.saltydawgsaloon. com, daily 11am-closing), out near the end of the Spit, is Homer's most famous landmark. The original building dates from 1897, the second building from 1909, and the tower from the mid-1960s. Each building housed different companies in eight different locations before settling down here on the Spit. The Salty Dawg is open until the last patron staggers out the door; have a beer for the (now smoke-free) experience and leave your business card or signed bra with the thousands of others. And don't

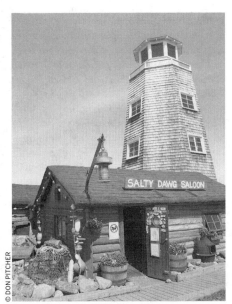

Homer's famous Salty Dawg Saloon

© DON PITCHER

for popcorn and get free refills. Every Thursday the theater screens something special—from documentaries to opera performances.

Festivals and Events

More than 100,000 shorebirds migrate through Kachemak Bay each spring, stopping to rest and feed at critical places, including the Homer Spit. More than 100 species have been recorded in one day during the festival. The first weekend of May brings Homer's biggest annual event, the **Kachemak Bay Shorebird Festival** (907/235-7740, www.homeralaska. org/shorebird.htm, May). Dozens of events await, including bird walks, bay tours, an arts fair, speakers, nature writing, and kid activities, all in celebration of the great northward migration of shorebirds. The keynote speaker is usually an internationally renowned naturalist.

The annual **Kachemak Bay Writers' Conference** (Land's End Resort, end of Homer Spit, http://writersconference.homer.alaska. edu, early June) encompasses workshops, readings, manuscript reviews, agent consultations, and an array of other activities, including keynote speeches by such writers as Barry Lopez, Russel Banks, Amy Tan, Anne Lemott, and Billy Collins.

Public radio station KBBI's **Concert on the Lawn** (907/235-7721, www.kbbi.org, last weekend in July) is the biggest summer event, attracting musicians from around the state for two days of partying. KBBI is one of Alaska's best and most eclectic radio stations; find it at 890 AM.

If you're in town at the right time, don't miss the **Kachemak Bay Wooden Boat Festival** (www.kbwbs.org, second weekend in Sept.), where it's practically illegal for men to not have a beard. Check out the classic wooden boats on display, watch old-time high seas films, sing sea chanteys, and watch the kids building and painting their own wooden boats.

For an entirely different musical experience,

forget to buy one of their famous T-shirts to impress your friends back home.

Performing Arts

Homer has an extraordinary level of talent, and some of the performers have gotten together to do **Pier One Theater** (Homer Spit, 907/235-7333, www.pieronetheatre.org, Thurs.-Sun. nights May-early Sept.) on the Spit. The frumpy red building next to the fishing hole houses a few dozen utilitarian seats, but whatever is playing, this is guaranteed to be one of the finest theater experiences in the state. You might see a youth musical, an old classic, or a controversial play that's definitely not for kids.

Movies

Catch a flick at little **Homer Theatre** (Pioneer Ave. and Main St., 907/235-6728, www.homer-theatre.com). Get there early to snag one of the comfy couches up front. It's Alaska's longest-running movie house. Bring your own bowl

Quiet Cove Lodge in Halibut Cove hosts **Jazz in the Cove** (907/235-1800, www.halibutcovelive.com) several times each summer. Guests are treated to round-trip transport from Homer, a gourmet meal, and a day of jazz. Guests sit beneath canopies on the deck, with a floating amphitheater for the musicians. Limited to just 60 people, this is an intimate way to enjoy an evening of jazz in a beautiful setting.

If you happen to be around for this, do not miss performances of the **Nutcracker ballet** (Homer High School Mariner Theater, 600 E. Fairview Ave., early Dec.). Not at all what you might expect from a small town, these productions have a cast of more than a hundred.

SHOPPING

Gift shops, restaurants, art galleries, charter fishing shops, bear viewing operations, and other businesses are located in several clusters near the end of the Spit. Nearly all of these are only open late May-early September, though a few places such as Coal Point Seafood and Land's End Resort remain open year-round.

In business since 1946, **Alaska Wild Berry Products** (528 E. Pioneer Ave., 907/235-8858 or 800/280-2927, www.alaskawildberryproduct.com) specializes in Alaska-made wild berry jams, jellies, chocolates, and sauces, some of which are fashioned on the premises. The counter usually has free samples, but it's hard to resist buying some before you leave. The company started in Homer, but is now based in Anchorage, where it operates a far larger facility.

Downtown near the movie theater, **Nomar** (104 E. Pioneer Ave., 907/235-8363 or 800/478-8364, www.nomaralaska.com) sells high-quality handmade clothing and outdoor gear. Some of its most popular items are specifically designed for commercial fishers, but Nomar also has warm and windproof outerwear, kids' garb, hats, rain gear, purses, duffel bags, and more. This is the real deal: tough,

well-made Alaskan gear. It's also a great place for repairs of all types, from that broken zipper on your daypack to the torn sail on your boat.

Three miles out on East End Road is **Redden Marine** (a.k.a. Kachemak Gear Shed, 3625 East End Rd., 907/235-8612 or 800/478-8612, www.reddenmarine.com/homer), selling quality clothing, rubber boots, and outerwear for anyone heading out on the water, not to mention freezer boxes if you're shipping fish home. It's a great place to check out the commercial fishing supplies, too. The back wall has a rather unusual souvenir from the *Exxon Valdez* spill.

Homer Bookstore (332 E. Pioneer Ave., 907/235-7496, www.homerbookstore.com) is a true book lover's shop, with works by local authors, a big Alaskana section, field guides, kids' books, and espresso in the back. You'll find humorous titles by Tom Bodett, known to most Americans as the folksy "We'll leave the light on for you" voice in the Motel 6 commercials. Like fellow celebrity Jewel, Bodett no longer lives in Homer. But another author, Dana Stabenow, still resides in the town. Many of her crime fiction novels starring Kate Shugak have landed on *The New York Times* bestseller list.

Old Inlet Bookshop (3487 Main St., 907/235-7984, www.oldinletbookshop.com) is a packed used bookstore with a café in the back and lodging upstairs. This beautifully restored (and expanded) log cabin was originally part of a 1905 fox farm on Yukon Island.

Fans of *Deadliest Catch,* the ever-popular Discovery Channel show won't want to miss **Time Bandit Store** (451 Sterling Hwy., 907/226-2722, www.timebandit.tv, daily in summer, Mon.-Sat. in winter), where sweatshirts, hats, flags, books, and kid stuff emblazoned with the boat's distinctive pirate emblem are sold. Captains Andy and Johnathan Hillstrand and the crew of the *Time Bandit* have become minor celebrities wherever they go, and you might encounter them and the boat during your time in Homer.

The ever-popular **Homer Farmers Market** (Ocean Dr., 907/299-7540, www.homerfarmersmarket.org, Sat. 10am-3pm and Wed. 3pm-6pm late May-Sept.) takes place along Ocean Drive. Booths carry local produce, arts and crafts, jewelry, seafood, fresh produce, and more. The back tent has live music and games for kids. It's a great way to find a sampling of work by local artists, gardeners, and chefs.

Art Galleries

Homer has a statewide reputation as an arts center, and local showcases are must-sees on any Homer itinerary. Pick up a map of local galleries at the visitor center or find it online (www.homerartgalleries.com). The **Homer Council on the Arts** (355 W. Pioneer Ave., 907/235-4288, www.homerart.org) houses a small gallery and collaborates with local art events. If you're around on the first Friday of the month, don't miss the aptly named **First Friday,** when new exhibitions open at local galleries and the hors d'oeuvres come out.

Homer's most innovative gallery, the nonprofit **Bunnell Street Arts Center** (106 W. Bunnell Ave., 907/235-2662, www.bunnellstreetgallery.org), presents new exhibits monthly, and has a choice selection of works for sale. It's in the old Inlet Trading Post, built in 1937, and just up from Bishops Beach. Although small, Bunnell attracts nationally known artists. Don't miss their First Friday openings, often with informative talks by the artists (not to mention amazing treats provided by Maura's Café).

One of Alaska's oldest cooperative galleries, **Ptarmigan Arts** (471 E. Pioneer Ave., 907/235-5345, www.ptarmiganarts.com) has a diversity of artists, all of whom also work here one day a month. Here you'll find everything from handmade hats to ceramics, beaded jewelry, wildlife and landscape photos (including those of the author), and watercolors.

Several other excellent galleries are within walking distance. Next door is **Fireweed Gallery** (475 E. Pioneer Ave., 907/235-3411, www.fireweedgallery.com), and **Picture Alaska** (448 E. Pioneer Ave., 907/235-2300 or 800/770-2300, www.picturealaska.com) is across the street. It's just two blocks to **Art Shop Gallery** (202 W. Pioneer Ave., 907/235-7076 or 800/478-7076, www.artshopgallery.com), and **Jars of Clay Pottery** (behind the movie theater at Main St. and Pioneer Ave., 907/235-8533) is nearby.

Quality art galleries on the Spit include **High Tide Arts** (907/226-2600, www.leslieklaar.com), **Sea Lion Gallery** (907/235-3400, www.sealiongallery.com), **Local Showcase** (907/235-8415, www.local-showcase.com), and **Homer Clay Works** (907/235-6118). Spit galleries are only open seasonally, typically mid-May-mid-September.

Wine, Beer, and Mead

Spend any time in Homer and you'll encounter a bumper sticker that proclaims, "Homer: a quaint drinking town with a fishing problem." The town has its share of bars, and locals also craft a diversity of spirits. Find more than 1,500 different wines in a temperature-controlled room at **Grog Shop** (369 E. Pioneer Ave., 907/235-5101).

A must-see for beer aficionados is **Homer Brewing Company** (1411 Lakeshore Dr., 907/235-3626, www.homerbrew.com, daily noon-5pm or later), where you can sample the China Poot Porter, Old Inlet Pale Ale, Red Knot Scottish, and other specialties—including seasonal brews—before buying a half-gallon growler to go. The brewery also crafts Zen Chai and Alaska Chai teas. During the summer, the Brat Shop parks adjacent to the brewery, providing the perfect bratwurst compliment to their beers.

Three miles east of town, **Bear Creek Winery** (Bear Creek Dr., 907/235-8484, www.bearcreekwinery.com, daily 10am-6pm summer, noon-6pm winter) produces distinctive wines from local raspberries, rhubarb, blueberries, apples, and other fruits. If chocolate raspberry port is in stock, you'll want to buy several bottles of this decadent dessert wine. Taste a few of the award-wining wines (no charge) or just take a ride on the four-person rope swing out front. The production building is just up the road, with tours by appointment.

Homer is also home to **Ring of Fire Meadery** (178 E. Bunnell Ave., 907/235-2656, www.ringoffiremeadery.com, daily in summer), where you can sample honey wines crafted from local fruits, along with seasonal specialty meads. In existence for only a few years, the meadery has quickly gained a national following, winning an array of international gold medals. The black current mead and apple cyser are especially popular. The meadery is just up the street from Two Sisters Bakery.

RECREATION

Homer High School houses the local **swimming pool** (600 E. Fairview Ave., 907/235-7416, www.homerpool.org, $5 adults, $2.50 kids), open daily for lap swimming.

For a beautiful view of Kachemak Bay while you work out, head to **The Bay Club** (2395 Kachemak Dr., 907/235-2582, www.homerbayclub.com, day pass $18), a fine private facility with a pool, racquetball courts, workout equipment, yoga classes, saunas, and a climbing wall.

Seven miles out on East End Road, **Kachemak Bay Lynx Golf Course** (56910 East End Rd., 907/235-0606, daily mid-Apr.-mid-Oct.) is a par-three course with fine views of the bay. The little clubhouse rents clubs.

Located three miles out on East End Road next to Redden Marine, **Cycle Logical** (3585 East End Rd., 907/226-2925, www.cyclelogicalhomer.com) is the local bike shop. Owner Derek Reynolds rents bikes and knows how to repair your two-wheeler. In the winter, he sells fat bikes for on-the-snow riding.

At the base of the Spit, **Homer Saw and Cycle** (1532 Ocean Dr., 907/235-8406, bike rental $25/day) has mountain bikes, cruisers, hybrids, trail bikes, and kid bikes. **Land's End Resort** (4786 Homer Spit Rd., 907/235-2500, www.lands-end-resort.com) also has a few mountain bikes for rent. Local water taxis will transport your bikes across the bay at no extra charge; Red Mountain is an especially enjoyable backcountry ride.

Mark Marette of **Trails End Horse Adventures** (907/235-6393, $90 pp for four hours, two-person minimum) leads horseback rides in the very scenic Fox River area at the head of Kachemak Bay. It's a remote and fascinating area, with lots to see along the way. One of a handful of real-life cowboys in the Homer area, Mark spends a lot of time "off the grid" so he can be hard to reach.

If you have kids in tow, drive uphill on Bartlett Street, then left on Fairview Avenue to **Karen Hornaday Park** (629 Fairview Ave., 907/235-3170, www.cityofhomer-ak.gov), where the playground has all sorts of fun adventures.

For a great introduction to the amazing invertebrate life of Kachemak Bay, join a one-hour **Creatures of the Dock tour** (www.akcoastalstudies.org, tours daily 1pm and 4pm June-Aug., $5), offered by the Center for Alaskan Coastal Studies. Tours—great for all ages—depart from the CACS yurt on the Spit next to Ramp 2.

Better known by it's acronym HOWL, **Homer Wilderness Leaders** (907/399-4695, www.howlalaska.org) leads a range of outdoor activities for young people age eight and up. Many of these are multi-night trips, but kids can join a fun HOWL day trip on Sundays and Tuesdays noon-4pm in the summer. Call or check the website for details. HOWL's office is in the yurt village across from Fat Olive's on the Homer Bypass.

Across the Bay Tent & Breakfast Adventure Company (907/235-3633 summer or 907/345-2571 winter, www.tentandbreak-fastalaska.com, late May-early Sept., lodging and all meals $110 pp/day, tent and breakfast $75 pp) has a distinctive operation that's perfect for adventurous travelers on a budget. The lodge is located along Kasitsna Bay, with access by water taxi from Homer ($75 round-trip) or via an eight-mile gravel road from Seldovia (taxis available). Kasitsna Bay Lab, a NOAA marine research facility, is just up the bay, but is not open to the general public. Guests stay in simple cabins or furnished canvas wall-tents set atop wooden platforms with showers, and "two of the most beautiful outhouses in Alaska." Bring your own sleeping bag or borrow one of theirs. Meals have a seafood focus. While here, you can rent a mountain bike to ride the back roads, take a guided sea kayak tour, or join a boat tour of Kachemak Bay. Across the Bay often fills with adventure tour groups and workshops, so call ahead for reservations.

Kayaking

A number of local companies lead seasonal guided sea kayak trips within Kachemak Bay, or you can rent kayaks to do it on your own. Based on protected Yukon Island near Kachemak Bay State Park, **True North Kayak Adventures** (907/235-0708, www.truenorthkayak.com, half-day paddle $105, full-day trip $150, kayak rental $205 for two people) offers a range of guided trips, from half-day paddles to multiple-night packages. The all-day trip (includes lunch) is especially popular. All trips include a round-trip water-taxi ride to peaceful Yukon Island, sea kayaks, and a guide. Kayak rentals (with water taxi) are available for experienced paddlers; the kayaks are based on Yukon Island.

St. Augustine's Kayak & Tours (907/299-1894 or 800/770-6126, www.homerkayaking.com, mid-May-mid-Sept., half-day trip $100, full-day trip $140, combination trip $170) has a base in Peterson Bay, adjacent to the Center

for Alaskan Coastal Studies field station, with half-day and full-day trips, plus a combination version that includes a morning with naturalists at CACS and an afternoon of paddling. Several other options exist, all the way up to multi-night adventures. Many people book through the Inlet Charters and other booking agencies on the Spit. All trips include round-trip transportation by water taxi from Homer.

A Seaside Adventure (907/235-6672, www.seasideadventure.com, May-mid-Oct., half-day trip $110, full-day trip $150) operates out of Little Tutka Bay, a lovely wooded spot surrounded by Kachemak Bay State Park. Tours include a water-taxi ride from the Spit, knowledgeable guides, a slow-paced natural history paddle in this protected cove (lots of eagles and otters), and a distinctive lunch that includes "beach soup" made from mussels and clams collected along the way. It's a real taste of Alaska, but call ahead since group sizes are small and the tours fill quickly.

Local **water taxi** companies book kayak trips (package for two: double kayak $190 d, add $50 extra for each additional day) through the companies listed in this section and offer rental kayaks for experienced kayakers. A package for two people includes round-trip water taxi to the park.

Surfing, Kiteboarding, and SUPs

In addition to more traditional sports, Homer is gaining recognition for unique wind and water adventures. Surfing can be quite good during storms, particularly in the winter months. Day breezes kick up most afternoons, providing ideal conditions for kiteboarders. On a summer afternoon you'll see kiteboarders skimming waves along the base of the Spit.

Scott Dickerson of **Surf Alaska** (907/399-7873, www.surfalaska.net) rents surfboards and wetsuits, and has a good knowledge of local conditions. Rent one of Surf Alaska's stand up paddleboards (SUPs) at the office of **Ashore**

Water Taxi (on the Spit, 907/399-2340, www.ashorewatertaxi.com, $35 for three hours, $60 for six hours). The shop is directly across from the beach, so you can grab an SUP and head out for a paddle. Scott is also captain of the *Milo* (907/235-1478, www.oceanswellventures.com), a 58-foot former fishing vessel that serves as a base for surfing safaris, cinematography, wildlife viewing, sea kayaking, and SUP trips.

Charter Fishing and Boating

Homer calls itself the halibut fishing capital of the world, with commercial fishers often landing more halibut here than at any other port. Sportfishing attracts droves of enthusiasts every day of the summer, not only for halibut but also for king and silver salmon. Wear warm, layered clothing topped by rain gear, and soft-soled shoes. Binoculars are a definite plus, since seabirds and marine mammals are usually viewable. You can have your catch vacuum-packed, frozen, and shipped home for additional fees, but they add up quickly. Half-day fishing charters typically cost $105 per person, with all-day charters for $250. Rates are a bit lower on the larger boats that carry up to 18 people (versus 6 on most boats), and during the shoulder seasons. Add $40 or so for a trip that combines halibut and salmon fishing.

Whatever you do, don't forget to enter the summerlong **Homer Jackpot Halibut Derby** (www.homerhalibutderby.com) if you go fishing. In existence since 1986, this has long been the most lucrative halibut fishing derby in the state. Because of decreasing stocks of halibut, the derby was dramatically changed in 2012 to deemphasize keeping the largest halibut. (Those giant 200-plus pound halibuts are almost always females, and killing them negatively impacts the population.) Today the first prize is $10,000 for the largest halibut of the season (down from $40,000 before). Winners for tagged fish or released fish might also win up to $10,000, and everyone is entered in the $5,000 end-of-season drawing—even if you didn't catch anything. Sob stories abound of people who saved $10 by not entering, then caught potential prizewinners. Don't let this happen to you!

Halibut populations have been dropping throughout the Gulf Coast of Alaska in recent years. As of 2012, the sport-caught quota was still two halibut of any size, but this may drop to one fish if halibut stocks continue to decline.

Homer has dozens of fishing charter boats to help you go out and bag a big halibut. An easy way to find one is through **Central Charters & Tours** (907/235-7847 or 800/478-7847, www.centralcharter.com), **Homer Ocean Charters** (907/235-6212 or 800/426-6212, www.homer-ocean.com), **Inlet Charters** (907/235-6126 or 800/770-6126, www.halibutcharters.com), or **North Country Charters** (907/235-7620 or 800/770-7620, www.northcountrycharters.com). In addition to charter fishing, all of these can set up sea kayaking, water-taxi service, flightseeing, bear-viewing, and lodging for the area.

Hackle Shack Flyshop (near the end of the Spit, 907/399-4542, www.kgbalaska.com, mid-May-mid-Oct.) guides fly-fishing trips to local rivers, and fly-in fly-fishing at Lake Clark and Katmai National Parks. Bike rentals are available out front. Owner Brian Saunders guides trips in Zihuatanejo, Mexico all winter.

Do-it-yourselfers can rent a 22-foot boat from **Homer Boat Rentals** (Homer Boat Harbor, 907/299-6065, www.homerboatrentals.com, $550/day).

Once you do catch a big halibut or salmon, how do you get it back home? **Coal Point Seafood** (4306 Homer Spit, 907/235-3877 or 800/325-3877, www.welovefish.com) offers processing and flash-freezing, and will FedEx the fish to your home. If you're going to be flying out and can take the fish with you, be sure to get the specially coated cardboard box (sold in grocery stores and at Redden Marine) and pack it with blue ice. Freezer space ($15/day) is available at the Anchorage airport, and many hotels provide freezer space for guests.

The Fishing Hole

If you simply want to drive into town and cast a line in the water, head out to the Fishing Hole on the Spit, across from Glacier Drive-In and Sportsman's Supply. The Alaska Department of Fish and Game stocks this little bight with king and silver salmon smolt, but returns have diminished in recent years as sediment filled the basin. The crowds of anglers that formerly lined the Fishing Hole all summer have mostly disappeared, but there are plans to fix the problems through dredging. Hopefully, things will have improved by the time you read this, so ask at the visitor center for the latest.

Get fishing licenses or rent a pole from **Sport Shed** (3815 Homer Spit, 907/235-5562) across from the Hole or **Sportsman's Supply** (1114 Freight Dock Rd., 907/235-2617) near the boat launch.

Bear Viewing and Flightseeing

Homer is a popular base for flightseeing trips and bear-viewing flights to **Katmai National Park** (mid-May-mid-Sept., $600-700 pp for 6-7 hour trips), primarily the coastal stretch between Geographic Harbor and Swikshak Lagoon (some trips go to Brooks Camp or Lake Clark National Park). Call well ahead for reservations during July and August, but walk-ins may be available one day before if you get lucky. Floatplane operations are based at Beluga Lake next to the airport.

Operated by lifelong Alaskans Gary and Jeanne Porter, **Bald Mountain Air Service** (907/235-7969 or 800/478-7969, www.baldmountainair.com) is a long-established company with a fine reputation. Another company with a very experienced pilot, **Emerald Air Service** (907/235-4160 or 877/235-9600, www.emeraldairservice.com) flies to Brooks Camp.

crowds at the Fishing Hole on the Homer Spit

© DON PITCHER

Jose de Creeft of **Northwind Aviation** (907/235-7482, www.northwindak.com)—one of the finest bush pilots around—offers flightseeing and bear-viewing trips to Brooks Camp or McNeil River.

Other companies with floatplane bear-viewing trips from Beluga Lake include **Steller Air** (907/299-0284, www.stellerairservice.com), **Alaska Bear Adventures** (907/299-5229 or 877/522-9247, www.alaskabearviewing.com), **Homer Flyout Adventures** (800/219-1592, www.homerflyoutadventures.com), and **AK Adventures** (907/235-1805 or 888/233-1805, www.goseebears.com).

Hallo Bay Bear Lodge (Katmai National Park, 907/235-2237, www.hallobay.com, full-day trips $675 pp, two-night tour $2,000) is a unique camp setting in the heart of Katmai National Park with access by Homer air taxis. To really appreciate this remarkable place you'll want to stay several nights. A two-night tour is expensive and worth every penny!

© DON PITCHER

Homer is a popular base for bear-viewing flights to Katmai National Park.

Homer Air (907/235-8591, www.homerair. com), **Smokey Bay Air** (907/235-1511 or 888/482-1511, www.smokeybayair.com), and **Adventure Airways** (907/299-7999, www. adventureairways.com) all provide flightseeing and air charters, along with bear-viewing trips to Katmai National Park or Lake Clark National Park. All three operate wheeled planes from the airport.

Pilot Zack Tappen of **Sasquatch Alaska Adventure Company** (907/299-7272 or 888/662-0999, www.sasquatchalaska.com) provides fly-out bear-viewing day trips to Katmai, multi-night stays in a comfortable tent camp, fly-out kayaking, and glacier landings.

Maritime Helicopters (907/235-7771, www.maritimehelicopters.com) guides eagle-eye tours of the region's glaciers, islands, and mountains on a charter basis.

Bird-Watching

Kachemak Bay provides an outstanding opportunity for birders, especially during the spring migration when thousands of sandpipers and other species crowd the tide flats. The **Kachemak Bay Shorebird Festival** (907/235-7740, www.homeralaska.org/shorebird.htm, early May) brings guest speakers and bird experts to town for one of Homer's most popular events. The **Kachemak Bay Birders** (www. kachemakbaybirders.org) is a very active local group of birders with birding trips and monthly meetings. Call their **Kachemak Bay Bird Alert** (907/235-7337) for a recording of recent bird sightings; the same info is also posted on their website. Also check out **A Birders Guide to Kachemak Bay** at www.birdinghomeralaska. org, maintained by the Shorebird Festival. The Chamber of Commerce has a weekly sheet listing unusual birds.

Dog Mushing

Howling Husky Homestead (14 miles out East End Rd., 907/235-1922, www.howlinghusky-homestead.com, tours: Fri.-Mon. summer, $32 pp, two-person minimum) is owned by author and scientist Linda Chamberlain. Two-hour private tours include kennel tours, harnessing the sled dogs, and a visit to her mushing museum. Dr. Chamberlain also uses the dogs in her leadership and teamwork courses.

Sailing

Kachemak Bay is a great place for sailing, and the **Homer Yacht Club** (www.homeryachtclub.org) holds semi-competitive races on weekends all summer, with the Land's End Regatta the last weekend of June. Crewmembers are often needed; contact the club if you're interested in joining the fun—no experience necessary.

Daily four-hour sailing trips are available on-board the 26-foot *Kiana*. Book these through **Central Charters & Tours** (907/235-7847 or 800/478-7847, www.centralcharter.com, $75 pp, two-person minimum).

Winter Sports

Homer is just above sea level, and it might even rain in January, but surrounding hills often pile high with snow. **Kachemak Nordic Ski Club** (www.kachemaknordicskiclub.org) maintains over 40 miles of groomed cross-country trails near McNeil Canyon (13 miles east of town), at Baycrest (just west of town off Sterling Hwy.), and at Lookout Mountain (out on Ohlson Mountain Rd.). The last of these has the best snow and most adventurous trails. Check the website for current conditions and the grooming status. Also popular in the winter are snowmobiling and ice skating on Beluga Lake. Located halfway out on the Spit, the **Kevin Bell Ice Arena** (907/235-2647, www.homerhockey.org) is open for skaters and hockey players throughout the fall and winter.

ACCOMMODATIONS

The Homer Chamber of Commerce website (www.homeralaska.org) has links to most local lodging places. Many people come to Homer to fish, and this typically means very early

sailboats in Kachemak Bay

departures. Because of this you may be subjected to noise at 5am as folks head out for the one day when you just wanted to sleep in.

Hostels

Homer's old-time favorite is **Seaside Farm Hostel** (40904 Seaside Farm Rd., 907/235-7850, www.seasidealaska.com, mid-May–mid-Sept., dorm beds $20 pp or $30 pp with bedding, guest rooms and cabins $65-95 d, tent spaces $10 d), five miles out on East End Road. It's a great rural location with horses in the pasture below, an organic garden, beach access, campfire cookouts, and killer views across Kachemak Bay. There are accommodations in an eight-bed coed dorm, which include cooking facilities and showers; private rooms in the lodge; and four simple cabins (showers are in the lodge). Scenic tent spaces have access to a cooking pavilion and outdoor cold showers. Wi-Fi is available throughout the property. Seaside Farm is owned by Mossy Kilcher, an avid birder and organic farmer. Her internationally known niece is the singer Jewel Kilcher, better known as simply Jewel. Homer's most famous former resident now lives in Texas.

Housed within the historic Pratt House (built in 1939), the **Homer Hostel** (304 W. Pioneer Ave., 907/235-1463, www.homerhostel.com, May–Sept., dorm beds $25 pp, guest rooms $55 s or $68 d) has bunks in three dorm rooms and rudimentary private rooms. The hostel has a kitchen, four bathrooms, a lounge, a guest computer, Wi-Fi, a convenient downtown location, friendly owner, and no curfew. The hostel gets complaints about cleanliness, and is somewhat rundown.

Hotels

[C] Driftwood Inn (135 W. Bunnell Ave., 907/235-8019 or 800/478-8019, www.thedriftwoodinn.com, $95-110 d shared bath, $105-110 d small with private bath, $145-180 d standard with private bath) is an unexpected gem in the rough. The historic main building has a wonderful common room with a stone fireplace, comfortable chairs for relaxing, a playground for kids, a Keurig coffee pot, Wi-Fi, and inexpensive breakfast and snack items. Across the street is AJ's Oldtown Steakhouse (same owners) and Maura's Café. Several budget guest rooms—cute but basic—have shared baths, and a half-dozen "shipquarter rooms" provide only slightly more space than a ship's bunk but come with private baths and a charming cedar-paneled nautical interior; they're not for anyone with claustrophobia. There are also more standard units with private baths. Across the street is **Seaside Lodge** (owned by Driftwood Inn, $175-245 d), a modern home overlooking Bishops Beach and Kachemak Bay with five guest rooms, private baths, and a full kitchen. Adjacent are two modern places also rented by Driftwood: **Bluffview Lodge** ($147-245 d), with space for up to 17 people, and **Kachemak Cottage** ($295 for four), a two-bedroom cottage that sleeps four. Together, these three places provide a very popular setup for weddings, with the big lawn and amazing vistas from Seaside Lodge, plus plenty of space for family and friends right next door.

It's hard to miss the **Heritage Hotel** (147 E. Pioneer Ave., 907/235-7787 or 800/380-7787, www.alaskaheritagehotel.com, $99-109 d, suites $155 d). Built in 1948, this rambling log building has heart-of-town rooms and large, apartment-style suites. This is a love-it-or-hate-it place; some folks rave about the quirky guest rooms, while others prefer something more modern and complain of thin walls, noise, and the older furnishings. All guests have access to a shared kitchen, and Wi-Fi is available.

Pioneer Inn (244 W. Pioneer Ave., 907/235-5670 or 800/782-9655, www.pioneerinnhomerak.com, $119 d, suites $139 d or $164 for four guests) is an unpretentious downtown motel with standard guest rooms and five large apartment-style units with full kitchens.

The TVs are miniscule, but there's Wi-Fi, and the rooms are very clean and the super-friendly owners make you feel at home.

Popular with anglers are three units over the **Sport Shed** (Homer Spit, 907/235-5562, mid-May-Sept., $129 d, add $5 pp for extra guests), a fishing shop. These studio units come with full kitchens and water views.

Ocean House Inn (1065 Krueth Way, 907/235-3294 or 888/353-3294, www.homer-oceanhouse.com, rooms and suites $149-189 d, condos $299-450 d, add $25 pp for extra guests) sits atop a low cliff facing the Homer Spit, with beach access, private entrances, a large hot tub, Wi-Fi, and a guest computer. Accommodations encompass rooms and suites with microwaves and fridges, along with condos containing full kitchens.

Spread across four buildings on a gentle slope, **Ocean Shores Motel** (451 Sterling Hwy., 907/235-7775 or 800/770-7775, www.akoceanshores.com, May-Sept., $159-209 d) has an old-fashioned plain-vanilla exterior, but the rooms are large and well-maintained, with comfortable beds, fridges, microwaves, and Wi-Fi. Rooms face Kachemak Bay, with prices matching your proximity to the water. A few cheaper units ($139) are popular with anglers who don't care as much about where they sleep.

Advertised as Alaska's only beachfront hotel, **Land's End Resort** (4786 Homer Spit Rd., 907/235-0400 or 800/478-0400, www.lands-end-resort.com, $159-269 d) occupies the very tip of Homer Spit, with bay-and-mountain views from some rooms, a waterside hot tub, and a tiny exercise pool (not for kids). The 84 rooms range greatly in price and quality, from an economy unit facing the parking lot to luxurious two-room suites in the new building. The in-house restaurant features a big back deck on the water and an upstairs reception hall that's popular for summer weddings. Also available are a number of totally luxurious condos (Land's End Lodges, downstairs studios

$200-250 d, upstairs apartments $375-500 d) right on the beach and a short walk from dining and shopping on the Spit. There are downstairs studio units in the condos (with no kitchens) and the far more impressive upstairs apartments. The latter have two or three bedrooms, large kitchens and living rooms with enormous picture windows, and decks to take in the sunset vistas. Wi-Fi is available throughout Land's End Resort, including the condo units.

On the crest of the hill as you enter Homer, ◖ **Alaskan Suites** (3255 Sterling Hwy., 907/235-1972 or 888/239-1972, www.alaskansuites.com, $285 for up to five people) consists of five modern cabins on the west side of town, each containing two queen beds, a Murphy single bed, fridge, microwave, flat-screen TV, private bath, kitchenette, grills, and Wi-Fi. Outside are two hot tubs. The panoramic views include Kachemak Bay and an array of snowy mountains, glaciers, and volcanoes.

Bed-and-Breakfasts

Homer probably has more B&Bs per capita than any town its size anywhere, with several dozen places—many with jaw-dropping vistas. A pair of bed-and-breakfast organizations provide one-stop shopping: **Homer B&B Association** (907/226-1114 or 877/296-1114, www.homerbedbreakfast.com) and the much smaller **Homer's Finest B&B Network** (907/235-4983 or 800/764-3211, www.homer-accommodations.com). You'll also find links to 30 or so B&Bs on the Chamber's website (www.homeralaska.org).

◖ **Old Town B&B** (106 W. Bunnell St., 907/235-7558, www.oldtownbandb.com, $110 d shared bath, $130 d private bath) is owned by renowned artist Asia Freeman, who also manages Bunnell Street Arts Center downstairs. The three immaculate rooms have period pieces in this renovated 1936 building with a false-front exterior. A full breakfast is served in the parlor, and Asia's paintings hang in the rooms. Narrow stairs may make the B&B challenging for older travelers.

A block up the hill is **Mermaid B&B** (3487 Main St., 907/235-7984, www.vrbo. com/122901, $185 d summer, add $20 pp for extra guests, maximum of five), a pleasant little apartment over Old Inlet Bookshop. It has a hot tub on the deck, along with a full kitchen and private bath. The craftsmanship of builder and bookstore-owner Andy Wills shows in all the little details.

One of Homer's oldest—and finest—B&Bs, ◖Halcyon Heights B&B (1200 Mission Rd., 907/235-2148, www.homerbb.com, $165-215 d, two-room suites $315 for up to five people) has a beautiful East Hill location with panoramic views of Kachemak Bay from the deck. Amenities include an outdoor hot tub, private entrances and baths, full breakfasts, and Wi-Fi. Three upstairs rooms open onto the deck, and families appreciate the garden-level suites with a shared kitchen. Halcyon has a two-night minimum stay. Co-owner Juxia is fluent in Mandarin and also operates an itinerary planning service, Alaska Private Lodgings (www. alaskabandb.com).

Alaska Beach House B&B (1121 Seabreeze Ct., 907/235-3232, www.alaskabeachhouse. com, mid-May-early Sept., $119-234 d, cottage $264 d) is a favorite of travelers, with four guest rooms and a modern cottage, private entrances and baths, a beach-side hot tub and fire pit, Wi-Fi, microwaves, fridges, and continental breakfasts brought to your room the evening before.

Whalesong B&B (4002 Kachemak Way, 907/235-2564, www.thewhalesong.com, $125 d) is a reasonably priced option just a block from the downtown galleries and restaurants. Two rooms have private entrances and guests are served a continental breakfast.

High atop the bluff overlooking Kachemak Bay, ◖Cozy Cove Inn B&B (205 Cozy Cove Dr., 907/399-6277, www.cozycoveinn.com,

$155 d, $195 for four) is one of Homer's premier B&Bs. Two units are available, both with private baths and Wi-Fi. The upstairs studio apartment has its own entrance, with a queen bed, pull-down Murphy queen bed, full kitchen, and breakfast ingredients and baked goods. The downstairs suite includes a king bed, Amish furnishings, large screen TV, bath with jetted tub, and a full organic breakfast. The B&B is run by Marcella Suydam, who spent many years as a commercial fisher on the Alaska Peninsula.

On a quiet side street just two blocks up from Pioneer Avenue, **Paula's Place B&B** (4067 Calhoun St., 907/435-3983, www.paulasplacebandb.com, $140 d, add $15 pp for extra guests, maximum of six) consists of a 900-square-foot two-bedroom lower-level with private entrance, queen beds, bath, flat screen TV, BBQ grill, Wi-Fi, microwave, and fridge. Owner Paula Riley cooks a delicious breakfast each morning, and her friendly corgi dog greets guests. The B&B is set up for just one couple or group at a time. Plan your stay early since Paula's fills quickly in the peak summer season.

A fine option is **Bay Avenue B&B** (1393 Bay Ave., 907/235-3757 or 800/371-2095, www. bayavebb.com, late May-early Sept., $135-145 d), with seven rooms in the main house. A big breakfast is included and there is Wi-Fi. A separate vacation rental ($150 d, add $25 pp for extra guests, maximum of six) has two bedrooms, two baths, and a full kitchen. The marsh below is a good place to spot shorebirds and bald eagles.

A Room with a View (840 Rosebud Ct., 907/235-3706, www.aroomwithaviewhomer. com, $135 d) is a large hillside home off West Hill Road with two guest rooms, private baths, a big deck, and filling breakfasts. The owners speak German, and their decades as florists show in the immaculately landscaped grounds. No children under age eight are allowed.

Aptly named **Majestic View B&B** (1660

© DON PITCHER

A Room with a View B&B in Homer

THE KENAI PENINSULA

Race Rd., 907/235-6413 or 888/246-6413, www.majesticviewbb.com, $135-150 d; cabin suites $185 d, add $10 pp for extra guests) is a very comfortable home with three guest rooms, all with private baths. The deluxe room includes a whirlpool tub, private balcony, and tall windows. Two cabin suites offer more privacy. Each has a queen and twin beds, kitchenette, and bath. All guests appreciate the big deck with unobstructed bay vistas, outdoor hot tub, Wi-Fi, and wonderful homemade breakfasts served family style.

Aloha B&B (62209 Glacier View Ct., 907/235-0607 or 877/355-0607, www.alohabb.com, May-Oct., $114 d shared bath and kitchen, $129 d private bath and kitchen) has one of Homer's famous "million-dollar" views—a 180-degree panorama of bay, mountains, and glacier. The owners are natives of Hawaii, and a Hawaiian theme carries throughout the B&B. Two guest rooms share a bath and kitchen, while the other two apartment-style rooms have private entrances, baths, and full kitchens. Breakfast ingredients are provided, and the B&B has Wi-Fi and flatscreen TVs.

A delightful log home six miles out on East End Road, **Good Karma Inn** (57480 Taku Ave., 907/235-4728 or 866/435-2762, www.goodkarmainn.com, $165 d) fits Homer to a T, mixing functionality and comfort with a fine bay and mountain view, plus distinctive local artwork on the walls. Kindly owner Michael LeMay will fill you in on local attractions, and he stocks the kitchen with a full range of breakfast ingredients. Three guest rooms (with private baths and Wi-Fi) are available; one is completely accessible for disabled travelers.

Three miles east of town, **Bear Creek Winery and Lodging** (60203 Bear Creek Dr., 907/235-8484 or 888/649-2176, www.bearcreekwinery.com, $275 d) has two lovely log cottages with kitchenettes, private baths, and Wi-Fi. Guests are provided a bottle of wine and can unwind in the cedar hot tub or steam bath. A breakfast voucher ($15) can be used at local restaurants. The winery here crafts distinctive fruit wines, and the unique four-person rope swing out front is always fun. A two-night minimum stay is required and no kids under 12 are allowed.

A modern timber frame home, **Timber Bay B&B** (Timber Bay Ct., Fitz Creek, 907/235-3785, www.timber-bay.com, $130-150 d, apartment $190 d, two-night minimum) sits atop a ridge 15 miles east of Homer. Inside are four guest rooms, along with a separate apartment over the garage. A filling breakfast is served, and other amenities include a seasonal outdoor hot tub, Wi-Fi, private baths, and decks providing a panoramic view of Kachemak Bay.

Cabins and Guesthouses

Cabins and guest houses provide the perfect option for families looking for a place to call their own, and Homer has a multitude of choices; find them on the chamber website (www.homeralaska.org) or visit **Homer Cabins & Cottages Network** (907/235-0191 or 888/364-0191, www.cabinsinhomer.com), with 15 or so rental cabins in the Homer area.

Sea Lion Cove (near the end of Homer Spit, 907/235-3400 summer or 907/235-8767 winter, www.sealiongallery.com, mid-May-mid-Sept., $135-145 d) is operated by artist Gary Lion, whose gallery is downstairs. The two rooms are right in the heart of the summertime fishing action. Each has a kitchenette, TV, and a shared deck, delivering full-on bay vistas.

Easily the most unique lodging in Homer, **⟨ Kenai Peninsula Suites** (3685 Sterling Hwy., 907/235-1866 or 877/635-1866, www.kenaipeninsulasuites.com, $245-285 for up to four guests) has five newly built units, all with kitchenettes, private baths, large plasma TVs, Wi-Fi, and gas grills. There's a circular two-story log yurt, a private cottage, a two-level loft house, and two dome-shaped subterranean units that are literally tucked into the hillside facing the bay. Access to these is via a spiral staircase from a circular tower. Most units have king beds, and guests can take in a panoramic view from the hot tub. Winter visitors will appreciate the ski trails that begin right across the highway.

A fine waterfront place, **Homer Inn & Spa** (895 Ocean Dr. Loop, 907/235-1000 or 800/294-7823, www.homerinn.com, suites $179-199 d, villa $229 d, add $20 pp for extra guests), has a wonderful beachside hot tub, garden swing, day spa facilities (including side-by-side massage), plush king-size beds, fridges, microwaves, continental breakfasts, Wi-Fi, decks, and complimentary wine. There are three mini-suites as well as a separate villa perfect for families. To emphasize relaxation the inn is "TV free" (though flat screens are available for videos). There's a two-night minimum stay in the summer.

Situated atop a high bluff on the west side as the highway drops into Homer, **Alaska Adventure Cabins** (2525 Sterling Hwy., 907/223-6681 or 866/287-1530, www.alaskaadventurecabins.com, $245-425 for up to 4 people) has a fun mélange of lodging: two gorgeous cabins, a timber frame guesthouse, a newly built log cabin, a restored Alaska Railroad caboose, and a landlocked boat called the *Double Eagle* that began life as a Gulf Coast shrimper. Each unit contains a full kitchen, private bath, space for four guests, Wi-Fi, and a large deck with all-encompassing views of volcanoes, glaciers, Kachemak Bay, and the Spit.

Ten miles out East End Road from Homer, **Moose Creek Cabins** (Middleton, Fritz Creek, 907/235-6406, www.moosecreekcabins3.com, suite and cabin $115 d, chalet $165 d, add $20 pp for extra guests) consists of a studio suite in the main house, a cabin, and a secluded log chalet. The last of these has a deck with grill, stocked kitchen, private bath, wood stove, hot tub, sauna, and space for five. There is a two-night minimum stay in all units. Befitting the name, moose are often seen near the cabins.

A charming New England style cottage in the heart of town, **Spyglass Inn** (385 W. Fairview Ave., 907/235-6075 or 866/535-6075, www.homerspyglassinn.com, $130-160 d) has three guest rooms on two levels, private entrances and baths, Wi-Fi, fridges, and microwaves, along with king, queen, and handmade Murphy beds. Pat Melone cooks a fabulous breakfast, and co-owner Arden Jeffries' striking resemblance to Santa serves him well at Christmas.

Camping

Camping on the Spit is what most budget travelers, RVers, and backpackers do, although it's no picnic. It's within spitting distance of the noisy road, and it's barren and often windy. There are city-maintained camping areas on the Spit (camping-fee office across from the Fishing Hole, 907/235-1583, Apr.-Oct., tents $8, RVs $15 with no hookups), with bathrooms or portable toilets close by. Self-register at the campsites or pay at the camping-fee office. A few hardy folks try their luck in winter when the Spit is officially closed to camping. A quieter and more protected (but less scenic) seasonal campground is at **Karen Hornaday Park** (629 Fairview Ave., 907/235-3170, www.cityof-homer-ak.gov, tents $8, RVs $15) near the hospital on Fairview Avenue.

In addition to the city campsites, the Spit is home to three RV parks with full hookups. Close to the tip of the Spit, the privately run **Homer Spit Campground** (Homer Spit, 907/235-8206, mid-May-mid-Sept., tents $32, RVs $39-45) has rustic and crowded sites—some right on the beach—with electricity, showers, and Wi-Fi.

Sportsman's Supply (1114 Freight Dock Rd., 907/235-2617, RVs $40, Apr.-Sept.) has a few spots right across from the boat launch with full hookups and Wi-Fi.

THE KENAI PENINSULA

© DON PITCHER

camping on the Homer Spit

With a prime spot next to the Fishing Hole, plus all the latest amenities—including satellite TV, Wi-Fi, showers, a putting green, gift shop, and espresso—**Heritage RV Park** (3550 Homer Spit Rd., 907/226-4500 or 800/380-7787, www.alaskaheritagervpark.com, mid-May-early Sept., RVs $60) commands top dollar.

Driftwood Inn RV Park (907/235-8019 or 800/478-8019, www.thedriftwoodinn.com, $49) is in town close to Bishops Beach, with Wi-Fi, showers, and cable TV. It's open year-round.

Oceanview RV Park (455 Sterling Hwy., 907/235-3951, www.oceanview-rv.com, May-Sept., RVs $47, tents $25) is a crowded RV lot on the west edge of town with Wi-Fi and showers. It's right behind Jelly Beans Ice Cream Shop if you need to satisfy your sweet tooth.

At the crest of the hill before you roll into Homer, **Baycrest RV Park** (907/226-2886, www.baycrestrvpark.com, mid-May-mid-Sept., RVs $45) has full hookups and Wi-Fi, showers, and an adjacent gas station and convenience store. The location provides panoramic views of the bay, but is two miles from town.

If you're staying in the city campgrounds, showers are available at Sportsman's Supply or the Homer Spit Campground. Local coin laundries also have shower facilities; a good bet is **The Washboard** (1204 Ocean Dr., 907/235-6781), where you can even surf the Internet for free or get an espresso while watching the clothes spin or after showering. An even better deal is the high school pool, where they throw in a free swim for the cost of a shower.

FOOD

Homer's dining-out options are surprisingly varied, with several excellent choices. Many of the town's second- or third-tier eateries would be standouts almost anywhere else in Alaska, and the town's best restaurants are truly memorable.

Coffee

Homer is a coffee drinker's paradise, with two roasters and several excellent espresso joints. In business since 1995, **Captain's Coffee Roasting Co.** (528 E. Pioneer Ave., 907/235-4970, www.captainscoffee.com, Sun. 6:30am-5pm, Mon.-Sat. 6:30am-5:30pm, $3-6) has a downtown location and a bright airy space to relax. Ask friendly owner Ty Gates for tips on surfing in Homer. There's a second Captain's shop—open seasonally—near the base of the Spit.

A real surprise is **❰ K Bay Caffé** (397 E. Pioneer Ave., 907/235-1551, www.kbaycoffee.com, Mon.-Wed. 7am-9pm, Thurs.-Fri. 7am-10pm, Sat. 8am-10pm, Sun. 8am-9pm) in the center of town. Owner Michael McGuire really knows his (all-organic) coffee—he won top prize at a national barista contest a while back—-and is a connoisseur when it comes to creating the perfect roast.

Housed within an old homestead cabin, **Coal Town Coffee** (Coal Point Boardwalk, 907/235-4771, www.coaltowncoffee.com, daily 5am-8pm early May-mid-Sept.) serves the best espresso on the Spit, with K Bay coffee, baked goods from Vagabond Café, and a fine selection of teas.

Bakeries and Cafés

Just a block from Bishops Beach, **❰ Two Sisters Bakery** (233 E. Bunnell St., 907/235-2280, www.twosistersbakery.net, Sun. 9am-2pm, Mon.-Tues. 7am-6pm, Wed.-Sat. 7am-9pm, $16-18) is a great place to meet the locals any time of year. It's always warm and fragrant with the smell of fresh-baked pastries, daily breads, sticky buns, and ham and cheese savories from the wood-fired brick oven. For breakfast, try the quiche, biscuits and gravy, or housemade granola with a steaming espresso. Lunch includes sandwiches, focaccia, and deep-dish pizza by the slice. Dinners (served Wed.-Sat.) change seasonally, but always feature cioppino, scallop pasta, BBQ pork ribs, and nightly specials. A covered deck wraps around the back, and the backyard has a play area for families—or you can walk to nearby Bishops Beach.

Exceptionally popular with tourists but mostly unknown to locals, **Boardwalk Bakery** (4025 Homer Spit Rd., 907/235-2131, www. boardwalkbakery.biz, daily 5am-3pm May-early Sept., daily 5am-5pm mid-June-mid-Aug., $7-8, box lunch $12) has breakfast burritos, Belgian waffles, biscuits and gravy, sandwiches, and sweet treats, along with substantive box lunches for anyone headed out for a day of charter fishing. Sweets include lemon squares, pecan bars, cinnamon rolls, pies, cakes, and cookies. There's enough white sugar and frosting to keep your kids jumping for hours.

The Bagel Shop (East End Rd. at Kachemak Dr., 907/299-2099, Tues.-Sat. 6am-2pm year-round, under $10) makes best-in-Alaska bagels daily, including plain, poppy, sesame, onion-garlic, salt, and everything varieties. Bagels with spreads, breakfast and lunch sandwiches (on bagels of course), daily soups, and coffee round out the menu. The shop's bagels are also available at the Saturday Market.

Open seasonally since 1982 and a favorite with travelers, **Fresh Sourdough Express Bakery & Café** (1316 Ocean Dr., 907/235-7571, www.freshsourdoughexpress.com, daily 7am-9pm mid-May-mid-Sept., $25-28) is a homey Homer spot serving sourdough hotcakes, scrambles, granola, muffins, and monster pastries for breakfast. Lunch includes sandwiches, buffalo burgers, homemade soups, and salads, while dinners cover the salmon, chicken, and steak terrain. The mostly organic menu includes vegetarian meals, but also plenty of carnivorous protein.

La Baleine Café (near the end of Homer Spit, 907/299-6672, www.labaleinecafe.com, daily 6am-4pm late May-early Sept., $10-20)

provides rustic fare with a twist. Chef Mandy Dixon attended Le Cordon Bleu, and the café's name, French for "The Whale," plays on the mix of Alaska and France. La Baleine opens early for the fishing crowd, but the menu is anything but basic. No store-bought ketchup here; it's made on the premises. And the corned beef hash may be the best you've ever tasted. The café has a few tables inside, with picnic tables out front. Get the fish tacos or smoked salmon chowder for lunch.

American

Vegetarians will find slim pickings at **Boss Hoggz Restaurant** (4025 Homer Spit Rd., 907/235-5555, www.bosshoggz.com, $7-12), where the focus is on "awesome burgers and amazing barbeque." Meats come from local ranchers, the buns are freshly baked, fries are handcut, portions are hefty, and the staff is friendly. The menu covers pulled brisket, fried clam po'boys, the best burgers in town, and a ludicrous Big Boss Challenge for overeaters not-so-anonymous; consume it all and you get your $25 back and your photo on the wall of fame. Of course you might also die from the fat and calorie intake. Boz Hoggz is on the Spit, with a second restaurant along the Homer Bypass next to the Petro gas station.

A longtime favorite, **Duncan House Diner** (125 E. Pioneer Ave., 907/235-5344, www.duncanhousediner.com, daily 7am-2pm, $8-9) is a family place with substantial all-American meals for breakfast and lunch; it's often crowded on weekend mornings so get here early. Daily specials are often your best bet.

Sandwiches

One of Homer's few historic buildings houses both Bunnell Street Gallery and ◖ **Maura's Café Delicatessen** (106 W. Bunnell Ave., 907/235-1555, www.maurascafe.com, Mon.-Sat. 11am-7pm April-Aug., Mon.-Sat. 11am-5pm Sept.-Mar., $9-15). There's a fully stocked cheese case in this little Euro-style deli, with a menu of delicious sandwiches, soups, and salads. Try the open-faced Stella Vera sandwich, topped with roasted veggies and melted brie. Owner Maura Bernin is locally famous as a gourmet caterer.

Far from the hubbub on the Spit is **(Fritz Creek General Store** (55770 East End Rd., 907/235-6521, Sun. 10am-8pm, Mon.-Sat. 7am-9pm, $6-14), eight miles out on East End Road. The store has a small selection of groceries, a little post office, booze, and an eclectic video selection. The real attraction here is the deli, featuring daily breads, wonderful hot sandwiches, unusual burritos, tamales, pizza by the pie or slice, lemon bars, cakes, pies, and coffee. A 12-inch eggplant muffuletta sandwich is big enough to feed two, or just get a soup of the day with bread. Check the coolers for baby back ribs, pork adobo, potato knish, or hoisin noodles with smoked duck. Fritz Creek is a delightful place to hang out in an old-time country setting.

Meals on the Spit

Yes, Homer does have McDonald's and Subway, but you're much better off heading out on the Spit, where two summer-only places fish for your attention. The best-known is the perpetually crowded **Boardwalk Fish and Chips** (Homer Spit, 907/235-7749, www.boardwalkfishandchips.com, daily 11am-9pm early May-mid-Sept., hours vary, $11-20) across from the harbormaster and Salty Dawg, with crunchy halibut fish-on-a-stick and chips that will have you smackin' your chops. Save a few bucks with cod and chips or a handmade salmon burger. Eat inside or—if the wind isn't too strong— on the deck.

A few doors from Boardwalk is **(Finn's Pizza** (Homer Spit, 907/235-2878, daily noon-9pm early May-early Sept., large pizzas $24-32, slices $5), with hot-from-the-oven wood-fired pizzas, daily soups, and local beers on tap. Be sure to try the blue pear version, made with D'Anjou pears, Gorgonzola cheese, and roasted pine nuts. It's excellent, but, at $32 for an 18-inch pizza, it's the priciest pizza around. Climb the side stairs for rustic solarium dining with a beach vista.

Directly across the boardwalk is **Spit Sisters Café** (Homer Spit, 907/235-4921, www.spitsisterscafe.com, daily 5am-5pm mid-May-early Sept., $7-9, box lunch $9), serving pastries from Two Sisters, light breakfasts, wraps, and espresso. The café opens early to provide savory Danishes and box lunches for folks heading out on fishing charters.

International

Downtown's **Cosmic Kitchen** (510 E. Pioneer Ave., 907/235-6355, www.cosmickitchenalaska.com, Mon.-Sat. 9am-8pm late May-early Sept., 9am-6pm the rest of the year, $17-20) serves quick Mexican food such as cosmic burritos (with steak or chicken, rice, cheese, guacamole, and salsa), soft tacos, and steak enchiladas, plus avocado-bacon burgers, chicken tikka with chutney sandwiches, salads, and homemade soups. With more than 150 items on the menu—including plenty of vegetarian and kid-friendly options—you're bound to find something to your taste. It's all good and tasty, with a big choice of homemade salsas to spice things up. Cosmic is popular for lunch, when the front deck fills on a sunny day, but also serves dinner specials such as a fajita steak and shrimp platter and Greek gyros—*delicioso*. Beer, wine, smoothies, and even espresso are available.

Located five miles out East End Road, **(Wasabi's** (57219 East End Rd., 907/226-3663, www.wasabisrestaurant.com, daily 5pm-10pm late May-early Sept.; Wed.-Sat. 5pm-9pm winter, $24-40) provides a classy setting and Asian fusion fare; their motto is "Where East meets West, and ends up North." You'll discover a good choice of fresh sushi (try the Tutka Bay roll with shrimp, avocado, and masago for $12), along with fresh halibut, alderwood smoked ribeye steaks, baby back ribs, and tempura prawns. Get a window seat for bay vistas. Singles can sit at the wraparound bar for meals, and Wasabi's has a great selection of house-made infused rum and vodkas. The downstairs bar (Fusion) has live music or a DJ on weekends, and even the bathrooms are worth a look.

A bit hard to find, **Vida's Thai Food** (3585 East End Rd., 907/235-2585, Mon.-Fri. 11am-7pm, $9-11) is across from the Redden Marine store and next to a self-storage place. The Thai owners serve a limited menu with such standards as chicken satay, fresh rolls, *tom yum, pad see ew,* pad Thai, and Massaman beef curry. Eat at one of the few tables inside, or call for takeout.

Fine Dining

You can't miss **Café Cups** (162 W. Pioneer Ave., 907/235-8330, www.cafecupsofhomer. com, Tues.-Sat. 4:30pm-10:30pm, $26-32)—four Alaska-size teacups hang from the front of the converted house. Dinners encompass everything from vegetarian curry to filet mignon and "Dave's twisted fettuccine." You'll find eight or more daily specials, and these are the real attraction, particularly the fresh seafood. Typical offerings include a charbroiled combo of two local seafoods and a Mediterranean spice-rubbed breast of duck. Cups gets crowded and noisy, so call ahead for reservations; last reservation of the night can be made for 9:30pm. A small side patio is fun on warm afternoons.

One of Homer's special-occasion places, **C Mermaid Bistro** (3487 Main St., 907/235-7649, www.mermaidbistro.com, daily 11am-10pm summer; Mon.-Wed. 11am-4pm, Thurs.-Sun. 11am-8pm winter, light fare $10-15, $20-30) fills the back of Old Inlet Bookshop and is close to Bishops Beach. Light fare such as tapas, salads, and small pizzas are available all day, along with lunchtime sandwiches and a creative dinner menu that changes nightly. The emphasis is on fresh local fare whenever possible, including seafood and summer produce from the farmers market. This is a slow-food café, so come prepared to relax and enjoy a wonderful meal. Several tables on the deck are popular on mild summer afternoons. Reservations are not accepted.

Homer's fine-dining place, **C The Homestead Restaurant** (Mile 8.2 East End Rd., 907/235-8723, www.homesteadrestaurant.net, daily 5pm-10pm mid-May-mid-Sept., Wed.-Sat. 5pm-9pm mid-Mar.-mid-May and mid-Sept.-Dec., closed Jan.-mid-Mar., $25-37) is eight miles out on East End Road. The ever-changing menu specializes in fresh Alaskan seafood, including enormous plates of king crab legs ($75), but also features made-at-your-table Caesar salads and melt-in-your-mouth prime rib ($19 before 6pm). Homestead is open for dinner only, and it is where locals go for an elegant meal. Reservations are strongly advised, especially for the window seats. Visit in the off-season for a good choice of under-$20 dinners and Friday evening wine and appetizer pairings ($25).

Another place that gets high marks is **C Fat Olives Restaurant** (276 Olson Ln., 907/235-8488, daily 11am-9:30pm or later in summer, daily 11am-8:30pm winter, $16-26, pizza slice $4, extra large pizza $36). The setting evokes a trendy Italian bistro, and the menu stars wood-fired pizzas, calzones, fresh salmon, Kachemak Bay oysters, seafood pasta, pork loin, and delicious appetizers (including a three-cheese fondue). It's noisy and fun, perfect for kids and adults. Fat Olives is just off the Homer Bypass as you enter town. In a hurry? Get a giant thin-crust pizza slice to go or a gargantuan 28-inch cheese pizza—big enough to feed a hungry hockey team. The box is so big you'll have trouble getting it out the door!

At the very tip of the Spit is Land's End

Resort, where panoramic bay vistas and an expansive beachside deck are the main attractions. The **Chart Room Restaurant** (4786 Homer Spit Rd., 907/235-0400 or 800/478-0400, www.lands-end-resort.com, $18-30) here is open for three meals a day, serving seafood, steaks, prime rib, and daily dinner specials. There's a separate bar menu for lighter fare.

Groceries and Markets

On the Homer Bypass, **Safeway** (90 Sterling Hwy., 907/226-1000, www.safeway.com, daily 5am-midnight) is the main grocery store in town, with a pharmacy, floral shop, liquor, and deli.

Along the Homer Bypass near the visitor center, **Save-U-More** (3611 Greatland St., 907/235-8661, www.save-u-more.com) may be the most bizarre store in Alaska, selling everything from freshly baked bread to wheel barrows. Its concrete-floor industrial decor makes Costco look positively upscale, and half the products originated at Costco in Anchorage (with a Homer markup). The real surprise at Save-U-More is the diversity of items, with entire sections devoted to obscure items from Trader Joe's or imported Irish, Greek, or Indian specialty products. The so-so deli has pizza by the slice and very popular ice cream cones for just $0.99. You can check your email on the computers there for free.

SEAFOOD MARKETS

In addition to its reputation as a halibut fishing center, Homer is famous for oysters, and you'll find acclaimed **Kachemak Bay oysters** in local restaurants and from the Kachemak Shellfish Growers Co-op building (across from the Fishing Hole on the Homer Spit, 907/235-1935, www.alaskaoyster.com, daily 9am-5pm mid-May-early Sept.; Tues.-Sat. 11am-5pm winter, $14-19/dozen oysters). Also available here are K-Bay mussels, smoked oysters, and other Alaskan seafood, including Dungeness

and king crab, scallops, razor clams, and side-stripe shrimp.

On a summer afternoon **Coal Point Seafood** (Homer Spit, 907/235-3877 or 800/325-3877, www.welovefish.com, daily 8am-8pm April-Sept., Mon.-Sat. 10am-6pm winter) is one of the busiest places on the Homer Spit, with a queue of folks waiting to have their catch processed, packaged, and flash frozen. They'll box and ship your catch via FedEx. Sidle up to the seasonal bar for seafood chowder ($7), king crab ($17 for a half pound), salmon burgers ($10), and fresh K-Bay oysters on the half shell ($19/dozen). Fresh salmon, halibut, and scallops are sometimes available, and Coal Point always has frozen local seafood.

INFORMATION AND SERVICES

Stop by the Homer Chamber of Commerce **Visitors Information Center** (on the Homer Bypass at Main St., 907/235-7740, www.homeralaska.org, Mon.-Fri. 9am-6pm, Sat.-Sun. 10am-6pm late May-early Sept.; Mon.-Fri. 9am-5pm winter) for local details and a plethora of brochures.

Homer's gorgeous **library** (500 Hazel Ave., 907/235-3180, www.cityofhomer-ak.gov/library, Mon., Wed., and Fri.-Sat. 10am-6pm, Tues. and Thurs. 10am-8pm) has an atrium fireplace for relaxing, tall windows facing Kachemak Bay, a large kids' room, a fine choice of videos, and plenty of computers and free Wi-Fi for Internet users. Find the Homer Public Library a block up Heath Street from the post office.

A number of businesses—even a laundromat—provide free Wi-Fi hotspots, and one local company, **SPITwSPOTS** (www.spitwspots.com) has antennas on the Spit and around town providing Wi-Fi for a fee; pop open your laptop for details.

The **Homer post office** (Homer Bypass and Heath St., 907/235-6129) is a block beyond the Safeway store.

South Peninsula Hospital (4300 Bartlett St., 907/235-8101, www.sphosp.com) is a modern, fully staffed facility. If you really need to spend a night in a hospital, at least this one offers the views for which Homer is so famous!

One of the few Alaskan towns with its own newspapers, Homer actually has two award-winning weekly papers: the *Homer News* (www.homernews.com) and the *Homer Tribune* (www.homertribune.com).

GETTING THERE
Air
Homer Airport (www.cityofhomer-ak.gov/airport) is a half-mile out East Kachemak Road, which forks off from the Spit Road. Inside the terminal are racks filled with brochures from local businesses, plus free Wi-Fi and local newspapers. **Era Alaska** (907/235-5205 or 800/866-8394, www.flyera.com) flies between Homer and Anchorage several times a day, year-round.

Two local companies have daily flights from the airport to Seldovia ($120 round-trip) and the Native Alaskan villages of Nanwalek and Port Graham: **Homer Air** (907/235-8591 or 800/478-8591, www.homerair.com) and **Smokey Bay Air** (907/235-1511 or 888/482-1511, www.smokeybayair.com).

The Stage Line (907/235-2252, www.stagelineinhomer.com) runs vans between Homer (vans stop at 1213 Ocean Dr., across from the Washboard Laundromat) and Anchorage ($90), Soldotna ($50), and Seward ($80). Drivers can stop almost anywhere along the route to pick up or drop off passengers. Service is Monday-Friday to Anchorage or Seward in the summer, but decreases to once a week to Anchorage in winter. There are no winter runs to Seward.

Ferry
The **Alaska Marine Highway ferry terminal** (907/235-8449, www.dot.state.ak.us/amhs) is out near the end of the Homer Spit. From here, you can catch the *Tustumena* to Seldovia three times a week and to Kodiak four times weekly. Once a month in the summer it runs all the way out to Dutch Harbor in the Aleutians.

Operated by the Seldovia Village Tribe, the **Seldovia Ferry** (907/435-3299 or 877/703-3779, www.seldoviabayferry.com, late May-early Sept., $46 pp round-trip) provides twice-daily catamaran service to Seldovia. This is not a tour, just a quick and inexpensive connection to Seldovia. The ferry office is on the backside of the Homer harbor at Ramp 7; get there via Freight Dock Road. Reservations aren't needed since the ferry holds 150 passengers and usually has just a handful onboard.

GETTING AROUND
Car Rentals and Taxis
Rent cars at the airport from **Pioneer Car Rental/Hertz** (907/235-0734 or 800/654-3131, www.rentalcarhomeralaska.com) or **Active Car Rentals** (907/235-8640 or 888/460-2848, www.activecarrentals.com). Just a few blocks away, **Adventure Alaska Car Rental** (907/235-4022 or 800/882-2808, www.adventurealaskacars.com) has somewhat lower rates for used cars (starting at $70), and will pick you up anywhere in town. One-way rentals (i.e., leaving the car in Anchorage) are available.

Call **Kache Cab** (907/235-1950) or **Kosta's Taxi** (907/399-8008) for a taxi ride around town ($5) or from the Spit to downtown ($14).

Water Taxis
A small fleet of boats plies the waters of Kachemak Bay all summer ($75 pp round-trip to most places, $60 pp for Gull Island trips), offering wildlife-viewing trips to Gull Island, whale watching in the bay, transport for kayakers and hikers heading into the state park, and access to lodges across the bay. You'll find their offices on the Spit. A

two-person minimum is required, but if your time is flexible they can generally get singles onboard with another group heading in the same general direction.

The following are all excellent operators: **Bay Excursions** (907/235-7525, www.bay-excursions.com), **Bay Roamers Water Taxi** (907/399-6200, www.halibutcovealaska.com), **Mako's Water Taxi** (907/235-9055, www.makoswatertaxi.com), **Ashore Water Taxi** (907/399-2340, www.ashorewatertaxi.com), **Red Mountain Marine** (907/399-8230, www.redmountainmarine.com), and **Homer Ocean Charters** (907/235-6212 or 800/426-6212, www.homerocean.com). Most of these are seasonal, but both Mako's and Ashore operate year-round. Kayak rentals and a variety of specialized tours are offered by Mako and other operators. A round-trip water taxi to the park with a double kayak rental costs $190 for two people.

Across Kachemak Bay

◖ KACHEMAK BAY AND GULL ISLAND

If you have three days in Homer, spend at least one of them on beautiful Kachemak Bay. A great way to do this is through a **Natural History Tour** (907/235-6667, www.akcoastalstudies.org, late May-early Sept., $120, $80 children under 12) with professional naturalists from the nonprofit Center for Alaskan Coastal Studies. You'll spend time at bird rookeries, tide pools, rainforest trails, and prehistoric sites, and will gain a lifetime appreciation for the marine world. These eight-hour experiences are a bargain and include a visit to Gull Island during your boat ride across to Peterson Bay. Bring your own lunch, rubber boots, binoculars, and camera. Overnight stays (just $35 pp in a yurt) and kayak trips ($170 pp) are also available at the Peterson Bay field station. The Coastal Studies office is in a yurt behind Mako's Water Taxi on the Spit. At the non-profit's headquarters (708 Smokey Bay Way) there are additional displays on local flora and fauna and snowshoes for rent ($5) during the winter.

Local water taxis lead two-hour Gull Island and 60-Foot Rock tours ($60 pp); Karl Stolzfus of **Bay Excursions** (907/235-7525, www.bayexcursions.com) is especially good. He also guides three-hour K-Bay birding trips ($70). Watch the Gull Island action in real time through the "birdcam" (www.prattmuseum.org).

Biologist Glenn Seaman operates **Seaman's Ecotour Adventures** (907/235-2157, www.seamansadventures.com, May-Sept., full-day custom trip $550 for two people, $650 for four), providing a variety of boat-based environmental tours around Kachemak Bay, covering the gamut from birding to cultural history. All-day custom trips are geared to your interests. This means having your own private guide and boat for seven hours. As the former head of Kachemak Bay Research Reserve, Glenn has a deep knowledge of the region.

Both **Central Charters & Tours** (907/235-7847 or 800/478-7847, www.centralcharter.com) and **Rainbow Tours** (907/235-7272, www.rainbowtours.net) have daily sailings to Seldovia, stopping along the way at Gull Island and Eldridge Passage.

HALIBUT COVE

Even if you only have two days in Homer, spend half of one visiting this enchanted village across Kachemak Bay on Ismailof Island. At one time Halibut Cove (pop. 75, www.halibutcove.com) was the center for a thriving herring fishery, with 36 saltries operating. The fishery collapsed in 1928, and today the town is a small center for artists and fishers. Halibut

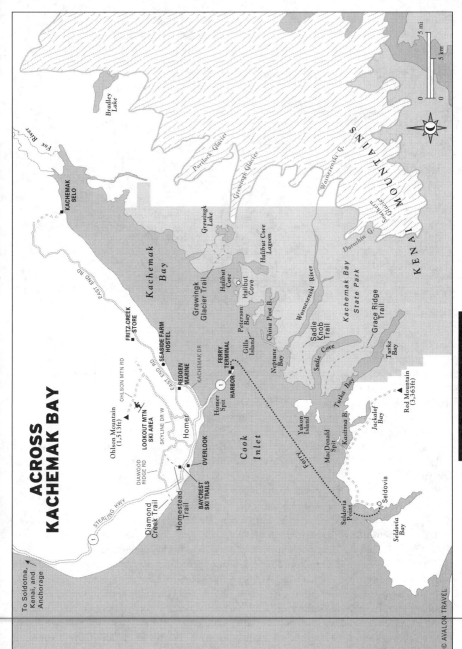

ACROSS KACHEMAK BAY

THE KENAI PENINSULA

© AVALON TRAVEL

© DON PITCHER

Halibut Cove

Cove has long been known for its picturesque harbor ringed by dense green forests; unfortunately, most of the trees were killed by a devastating spruce bark beetle infestation in the 1990s, so the land is in recovery mode now. The town consists of a long boardwalk that connects shorefront businesses and homes, so addresses have not been provided.

Sights

The boat to Halibut Cove docks in front of the Saltry Restaurant. Follow the boardwalk through an old boat barn, past the horses, and on to **Halibut Cove Experience Gallery** (907/296-2215, www.halibutcoveexperience. com, daily 1pm-4pm and 6pm-9pm late May-early Sept.), an excellent cooperative. A short distance down the boardwalk are side stairs climbing steeply to **Cove Gallery** (907/296-2207, closed winter) the studio of the late Diana Tillion, known for her subtle octopus-ink watercolors. The boardwalk passes Clem

Tillion's classic Alaskan home (a resident for over 80 years, Clem is jokingly called "the king of Halibut Cove") before ending at a sandy beach.

If you're looking for a little hike, walk along the boardwalk from the Saltry Restaurant till you see a gate on the left. Go through the gate and follow the trail up the hill for all-encompassing views of Halibut Cove, Kachemak Bay, eagles, and a rocky arch along the shore below.

Halibut Cove Adventures (907/299-0405 or 800/267-7581, www.halibutcoveadventures. com) provides guided hiking and kayaking trips and has kayak rentals. An informative and fun eight-hour natural history trip ($225 pp) from Homer includes water taxi, guide, kayak, boots, and lunch. These are private, customized trips, so each group gets its own guide and you set the pace. Kayak rentals ($75/day for a double) are available in Halibut Cove if you want to explore on your own.

kayakers at Gull Island

THE KENAI PENINSULA

Accommodations

At **Cove Country Cabins** (907/235-6374 or 888/353-2683, www.halibutcovealaska.com, $150-200 d, lighthouse guestrooms $300 d) stay in three attractive timber-frame cabins, each with a kitchenette, running water, and an outhouse, plus a central shower house. These range from a little unit to a two-story house with a fine view. The owners also have a newly built Victorian-style lighthouse with three guestrooms, where all meals are included. In addition, they operate Bay Roamers Water Taxi.

Quiet Place Lodge (907/235-1800, www.quietplace.com, $2,100 pp for three nights) features five romantic cabins facing the harbor. These are for groups only, and all-inclusive packages for a minimum of six people include access from Homer, lodging in luxurious cabins, meals, fishing trips, guided hikes, kayaking, rowboats, and a sauna.

Alaska's Ridgewood Lodge (907/296-2217, www.ridgewoodlodge.com, $1,130 pp for all-inclusive two-night stay) is a large and modern place in Halibut Cove.

Stillpoint in Halibut Cove (907/296-2283, www.stillpointlodge.com) hosts workshops, retreats, and weddings in an architecturally stunning setting.

A two-story house, **Sea Shanty** (on the boardwalk, 907/299-6120, www.halibutcoverental.com, mid-May-early Sept., $250 for up to four) contains two bedrooms, a bath, full kitchen, hardwood floors, wrap-around deck, and Wi-Fi. It's a short walk from the Saltry Restaurant and local trails. It shares the same owners as The Lighthouse, a quaint and remote two-story house perched atop a cliff. Call for details on The Lighthouse.

Food

Halibut Cove's acclaimed [**Saltry Restaurant** (907/296-2424 or 399-2683, www.thesaltry.com, daily 1pm-9pm late

May-early Sept., closed winter, $27-34) serves daily pasta specials, a wonderful seafood chowder ($10 with bread), Kachemak Bay oysters, Alaskan buffalo meatloaf, rack of lamb, and more. Everything is homemade, from the decorated plates to the fresh breads, pies, and a celebrated chocolate cheesecake. There's a waterfront deck for alfresco dining on a sunny afternoon, a full bar, a clamshell-shaped aquarium filled with tide-pool creatures (free talks are at 3:30pm), and a blazing fire in the outdoor pit. Dinner reservations are required.

Halibut Cove Coffee House (907/299-6120, www.halibutcoverental.com, daily 9am-4pm late May-early Sept.) is on the boardwalk a short distance from the Saltry. There is free Wi-Fi here.

Getting There

Most visitors arrive on board the *Danny J* (907/296-2424, www.thesaltry.com, twice daily late May-early Sept.), a classic wooden boat that has been transporting passengers from Homer Spit to Halibut Cove for decades. It carries a maximum of 34 people. The noon sailing ($58 pp) includes a tour of the Gull Island bird sanctuary, which Alfred Hitchcock should've known about; wear a hat and breathe through your mouth! After three hours onshore in Halibut Cove, the boat returns to Homer. Its second trip ($35 pp) leaves Homer at 5pm, and is only for visitors with dinner or lodging reservations. Reservations are made through the Saltry Restaurant.

As an alternative, **Bay Roamers Water Taxi** (907/399-6200, www.halibutcovealaska.com, $115 pp) has a "triangle" trip that combines a water taxi from Homer to Kachemak Bay State Park (typically Grewingk Glacier trails), an evening water taxi to the Saltry in Halibut Cove, and return on board the *Danny J.*

SELDOVIA

A sleepy fishing village (pop. 200), Seldovia (from the Russian for "herring") was once the bustling metropolis that Homer is now. The road, the

the *Danny J* ferry arriving in Homer Harbor

© DON PITCHER

THE KENAI PENINSULA

SELDOVIA

Kachemak Bay

WILDERNESS PARK

To Jakalof Bay

PICNIC AREA

Outside Beach

Tidal Slough

Lagoon

Irene Lake

Lagoon

Camel Rock

CEMETERY

SCALE NOT AVAILABLE

JAKOLOF BAY RD

SPRING ST

SPRUCE ST

INLET ST

Adventure Trail Loop

OTTERBAHN TRAILHEAD

WINIFRED AVE

YOUNG

AIRPORT

SHORELINE DR

SELDOVIA FISHING VENTURES

SUSAN B. ENGLISH GRADE SCHOOL

ENGLISH DR

ANDERSON WAY

PICNIC AREA

Lake Susan

FERRY DOCK

MAIN ST

RUSSIAN ORTHODOX CHURCH

ALDER ST

FULMORE AVE

CEDAR ST

Seldovia Bay

KAYAK 'ATAK

SELDOVIA HARBOR INN

ANDERSON WAY

Seldovia Slough

SEA PARROT INN

FULMORE AVE

AIRPORT AVE

Fish Creek

FENSKE'S

BOAT HARBOR

SELDOVIA MUSEUM AND VISITOR CENTER

KACHEMAK ST

breakwater

DANCING EAGLES CABIN RENTAL

BOARDWALK

ROCKY ST

FLOATPLANE DOCK

© AVALON TRAVEL

THE KENAI PENINSULA

earthquake, and fate exchanged their roles. On the same latitude as Oslo, Norway, Seldovia was first settled by Russians in the early 1800s and became an active fur-trading post. Through the years, Seldovia has had many ocean-oriented industries, from the short-lived herring boom to salmon, king crab, and tanner. The town has faced hard times in the last few years, and visitors will find boarded up storefronts and a growing crop of For Sale signs, along with several new mansions owned by outsiders.

Seldovia is a convenient place for really getting away from it all. Catch a ride over from Homer on the fast ferry, with its twice-daily service, or on a water taxi or tour boat. Not much to do in the town itself, but dirt roads and trails provide outstanding mountain biking and hiking.

Sights

Start out by strolling along Main Street. Interpretive signs describe Alaska's Russian history, commercial fishing, the earthquake, and more. The picturesque **Russian Orthodox Church** sits atop a small hill overlooking the town like a proud parent.

The Seldovia Village Tribe's (SVT) interesting **Seldovia Museum and Visitors Center** (across from the boat harbor, 907/234-7898, www.svt.org, daily 10am-5pm late May-early Sept., donations welcome) has exhibits on Native Alaskan culture and the town. SVT is the largest local employer, operating a gift shop, the fast ferry, and a medical center in Homer. Just up the road is **Seldovia Slough,** where you can walk the last remaining section of original boardwalk—the rest was wiped out in the 1964 earthquake.

Festivals and Events

In May, head to Seldovia for the **Human Powered Fishing Derby** (Memorial Day weekend) where contestants compete with rowboats, kayaks, and even peddle-powered boats for the biggest fish. A community fish fry ends the event. Simultaneously—and rather incongruously—another event takes place, the **Seldovia Craft Invitational Chainsaw Carving Competition.** You'll see dozens of the resulting sculptures scattered around town.

Held each June on the weekend closest to the solstice, the **Seldovia Summer Solstice festival** (www.seldoviamusicfestival.wordpress. com) features two nights of live music, workshops, and jam sessions.

Seldovia's biggest party arrives on the **Fourth of July,** when this sleepy town kicks into action with a parade, canoe jousting, log rolling, an egg toss, running race, and other events.

Recreation

One of the most fun things to do in Seldovia is to pedal out on the road to beautiful Outside Beach and Jakolof Bay, where you can savor the great views across Kachemak Bay. Well-marked **Otterbahn Trail** leads 1.5 miles from

the school grounds around the headland to Outside Beach.

For a real adventure, head out the road to the base of **Red Mountain.** A narrow 18-mile gravel road leads to a lovely mountain-rimmed alpine basin at Red Mountain. You'll find a pretty creek here, along with remnants of World War II-era chromium mines. Locals drive the road from town or ride up on 4-wheelers. It's a fun and challenging bike ride from town or from the Jakalof Bay dock (eight miles, much of it uphill). There are no bikes in Seldovia, so rent one in Homer and bring it over by water taxi.

For on-the-water fun, take a guided tour by Kirby Corwin of **Kayak'Atak** (907/234-7425, www.alaska.net/~kayaks, three-hour tours $80 pp). Kayak rentals are available for experienced kayakers.

Accommodations

Dancing Eagles Cabin Rental (907/268-5578, www.dancingeagles.com, late May-early Sept., $195 d, add $30 pp for extra guests) has perhaps the finest location in Seldovia, with a big deck perched on the water at the entrance to Seldovia Slough. A cabin sleeps six and includes a kitchen, bath, and Wi-Fi.

Seldovia Harbor Inn (273 Main St., 907/234-1414, www.seldoviaharborinn.com, May-Sept., $155-165 d) has three apartment units, each with a kitchen and private bath. Two of these open onto a deck, providing a fine harbor view.

Sea Parrot Inn (226 Main St., 907/234-7829, www.seaparrotinn.com, late May-early Sept., $125-145 d) contains four guest rooms with a communal living room, kitchen, deck, and continental breakfast.

Find three comfortable guest rooms, a big waterside deck, private baths, Wi-Fi, and delicious full breakfasts at **Seldovia Fishing Adventures** (907/234-7417, www.fishhalibut. com, $110 s, $164 d). Fishing charters are available onboard their 30-foot cabin cruiser.

Seldovia Slough

Harbor's Edge Vacation Suite (across from the harbor, 907/399-3195, www.seldovia.us, $150-170 d) is a clean, well-managed place with two guest rooms. Both include private baths, TV, and Wi-Fi, and one also has a full kitchen.

Camping

Pitch a tent or park RVs (no hookups) at **Wilderness RV Park** (Jakolof Bay Rd., 907/234-7643, tents $5, RVs $10) along Outside Beach. It's 1.5 miles out on Jakolof Bay Road, and there are a water pump and out-houses. Showers are available in town at Sea Parrot Inn, across from the boat harbor.

Food

Seldovia's dining choices are limited, and when winter comes the only place to find food is the grocery store. **Tide Pool Café** (907/234-7502, Sun.-Mon. 7am-3pm, Tues.-Sat. 7am-8pm mid-May-early Sept., $9-16) is a fine brunch spot, with breakfast burritos, pancakes and

crepes, waffles, and huevos rancheros, plus sandwiches, wraps, salads, burgers, and fish-and-chips for lunch. The dinner menu broadens out, with seafood plates, small pizzas, and mac and cheese. Tide Pool's deck faces the boat harbor, and the glass-top tables are inset with playful beach scenes.

Perry's Café (226 Main St., 907/234-7829, www.seaparrotinn.com, daily 9am-6pm late May-early Sept., $5-10) serves lunch sand-wiches, salads, quiche, and espresso, but the main attractions are ice cream cones and milk shakes. It's right across from the harbor.

Fenske's High Tide Originals (907/234-7850, late May-early Sept.) sells new and used books—along with coffee—from a tiny build-ing on pilings just up from the bridge. The covered deck is a nice spot to watch the tide come in.

Crabpot Grocery & Art Gallery (907/234-7435, Mon.-Sat. 10am-6pm) has a basic selec-tion of groceries. Find natural foods at **Auntie's**

Whole Foods (next to Tide Pool Café, 907/399-7315, Mon.-Sat. 10am-4pm).

Linwood Bar & Grill (907/234-7674, daily 6pm-10pm late May-early Sept., Thurs.-Sat. 5pm-9pm winter) is the local gin joint. There's a pool table inside and a deck out front, along with burgers, pizzas, and nightly specials in the summer.

Information

Find out more about Seldovia from the **Seldovia Chamber of Commerce** (907/234-7612, www.seldoviachamber.org) or the website for the **City of Seldovia** (www.cityof-seldovia.com). The free *Seldovia Visitor* publication (www.seldoviagazette.com) is available in visitor centers around Alaska, or visit www.seldovia.com for additional info.

Getting There

The **State Ferry** *Tustumena* (907/235-8449, www.dot.state.ak.us/amhs) sails over to Seldovia from Homer four times a week, taking 90 minutes and laying over for several hours before returning to Homer.

Operated by the Seldovia Village Tribe, the **Seldovia Ferry** (907/435-3299 or 877/703-3779, www.seldoviabayferry.com, twice-a-day service Thurs.-Mon. late May-early Sept., $46 pp round-trip, free for tots) is a high-speed catamaran ferry that makes the run from Homer to Seldovia in 45 minutes. This is not a tour, just a quick and inexpensive connection to Seldovia. The ferry office is on the backside of the Homer harbor at Ramp 7; get there via Freight Dock Road. The ferry overnights in Seldovia, departing at 9am the next morning, making for easy overnight trips to Seldovia. Reservations aren't necessary; just walk onboard.

The 75-foot *Discovery* (Central Charters & Tours: 907/235-7847 or 800/478-7847, www.centralcharter.com, late May-early Sept., adults $45, seniors $40, kids $30) departs Homer at 10am, stopping to watch the puffins and gulls at Gull Island and the sea otters near Sixty Foot Rock. They dock in Seldovia for three hours—perfect for lunch and a walk around town—before heading back across Kachemak Bay, arriving at 4:30pm. These are very informative tours.

Rainbow Tours (907/235-7272, www.rainbowtours.net, late May-early Sept., adults $45, seniors $40, kids $30) has a comfortable 65-foot boat with daily departures for Seldovia. It leaves Homer at 10:30am, stopping en route for a tour of Gull Island and then continuing through Eldridge Passage to Seldovia. After three hours in port, the boat heads directly back to Homer, arriving at 5pm.

Two Homer water taxis, **Mako's Water Taxi** (907/235-9055, www.makoswatertaxi.com) and **Ashore Water Taxi** (907/399-2340, www.ashorewatertaxi.com), will set up combo trips ($135 pp) that include a water taxi to Jakolof Bay, a taxi ride into Seldovia, and a return flight back to Homer. You can also do this as part of an overnight (or multiple-night) trip. There's a wonderful seven-mile mountain bike ride (or hike) up Red Mountain from Jakolof Bay if you're ambitious.

Both **Homer Air** (907/235-8591 or 800/478-8591, www.homerair.com) and **Smokey Bay Air** (907/235-1511 or 888/482-1511, www.smokeybayair.com) fly the 15 minutes from Homer ($100-120 round-trip) on a daily basis.

Getting Around

Seldovia Cab (907/234-7830) provides taxi service around town and even out the road to Jackalof Bay and Red Mountain (21 miles away). There are no bike rentals in Seldovia, so rent one in Homer and bring it over on the ferry.

Harbor's Edge (907/399-3195, www.seldovia.us, $50/hour) rents Polaris electric vehicles. They aren't fast (15 mph max), but are a good way to explore the area.

KACHEMAK BAY STATE PARK

One of the largest coastal parks in the nation, Kachemak Bay State Park spreads for 200 miles along the southwestern edge of the Kenai Peninsula. Within the park's 400,000 acres are glaciers, high mountains, lakes, islands, beaches, and a scenic rocky shoreline. Highlighted by constantly changing weather patterns, the park's outstanding scenery is a backdrop for high-quality recreation. Hiking and camping along the shoreline and in the surrounding forests and mountains are excellent. Above tree line, skiers and hikers will find glaciers and snowfields stretching for miles.

Almost three-quarters of the land is wilderness; it's officially called Kachemak Bay Wilderness State Park. Land mammals include moose, black bears, mountain goats, coyotes, and wolves. Kachemak Bay supports a rich diversity of marine life and is famous for its halibut and salmon fishing, plus the chance to view sea otters, seals, porpoises, and whales. Five very popular public-use cabins are available ($65), along with over 80 miles of hiking trails. Unfortunately, a major spruce bark beetle outbreak in the 1990s left massive stretches of dead trees within Kachemak Bay State Park (and in many other parts of Alaska). New trees are gradually moving into these areas.

The intermittently staffed **Kachemak Bay State Park office** (Sterling Hwy., 907/235-7024, www.alaskastateparks.org) is four miles northwest of Homer. Call the Soldotna office (907/262-5581) if Kachemak Bay State Park staff are out in the field.

Access

In addition to the daily summertime boat tours of Kachemak Bay, local **water taxis** ($75 round-trip) provide hiker or sea kayaker drop-offs within park waters. There is no extra charge for kayaks or bikes.

© DON PITCHER

Grewingk Glacier in Kachemak Bay State Park

© DON PITCHER

hiking on Grace Ridge in Kachemak Bay State Park

Backcountry Yurts

For something different, **Alaskan Yurt Rentals** (907/235-0132, www.alaskanyurtrentals.com, May-Sept., $77) maintains nine cozy yurts located at trailheads around the park, including China Poot Bay, Tutka Bay I and II, Halibut Lagoon, Kayak Beach, Quarry Beach, Humpy Creek, Right Beach, and Haystack Beach. Each includes a woodstove, sleeping space for six, foam mattresses, and a camp stove. These can also be booked through local water taxis. The yurts are made in Homer, and you can visit the facility where they are manufactured, **Nomad Shelter** (Sterling Hwy. and Olson Ln., www.nomadshelter.com).

Grewingk Glacier

For an outstanding day (or multiple-night) hike, have the water taxi ($75 pp round-trip) drop you at the Glacier Spit Trailhead, where an easy and very scenic two-mile hike leads to a lake in front of picture-perfect Grewingk Glacier. You can camp nearby, and return via the one-mile **Saddle Trail,** which takes you over a small ridge to Halibut Cove, where you can get a ride back to Homer. A multitude of side trips are available along this route, including ones that take you high into the alpine area over the glacier, and a delightful beach walk. Contact the park for many other hiking options.

Guided sea kayak tours to Grewingk are available through **Three Moose Meadow Guide Service** (907/299-1075 or 888/503-7160, www.threemoose.com, $169 pp). These include a guide, water taxi from Homer, a hike to the lake, and inflatable kayaks to paddle up to the glacier. Fly-in trips ($299 pp) are also available.

Grace Ridge

This challenging all-day hike begins at sea level, climbs steeply into the alpine, and then drops down the opposite side to another bay. You can hike up and back the same way or over the top and down for more variety. Access is by water taxi ($75 pp round-trip) from Homer to trailheads at Kayak Beach or South Grace, with campsites and yurts at both trailheads. Starting from Kayak Beach at the mouth of Sadie Cove, the trail rises through old growth Sitka spruce forests to an overlook at 2.3 miles, continuing into the alpine to the 3,100-foot summit of Grace Peak at approximately 4.5 miles. There are 360-degree views of Kachemak Bay, the Kenai Mountains, and a mix of coves, islands, glaciers, and forests. From the summit you can return the same way, or drop down to South Grace Trailhead along Tutka Bay, a total distance of nine miles. Grace Ridge Trail is equally fun from the other direction, too. If you have more time, book one of the yurts (907/235-0132, www.alaskanyurtrentals.com, $77) at Quarry Beach, Kayak Beach, or Tutka Bay.

Remote Cabins and Lodges

A number of delightful lodges fill coves surrounding Kachemak Bay State Park. Note, however, that spruce bark beetles have killed the forest in much of this area, so it may not look quite as nice as the photos online. One exception is Tutka Bay Wilderness Lodge, where the beetles have not wreaked havoc.

For a wonderful escape, **Porter's Alaskan Adventures** (Hesketh Island, 907/235-8060, www.portersak.com, May-Sept., weekdays $150 for four people, weekends $165 for four, add $80 pp round-trip water taxi from Homer) rents three modern cabins on the shore of Hesketh Island near the mouth of Tutka Bay, seven miles from Homer. All cabins contain full kitchens, decks, propane lights, BBQ grills, and waterfront views, but you'll need to bring sleeping bags, drinking water, and towels. There's a wood-fired sauna on the beach for bathing, and outhouses behind each cabin. Sea kayak rentals are available through **True North Kayak Adventures** (907/235-0708, www.truenorthkayak.com).

Sadie Cove Wilderness Lodge (907/235-2350 or 888/283-7234, www.sadiecove.com, $475 pp/day, add $150 round-trip water taxi from Homer) is an off-the-grid wilderness retreat in the heart of Kachemak Bay State Park. Guests stay in quaint cabins built by Keith and Randi Iverson, who have lived here since the 1970s. This is a place to escape to a quieter time, so you won't find in-room phones or TVs, though they do have Wi-Fi, a sauna and creek-side bathhouse, communal lounge, and professional chef. Lodging, three meals, and kayaks are included in the cost. A two-night minimum is required, but most guests book for five nights.

Tutka Bay Wilderness Lodge (907/235-3905 or 800/606-3909, www.withinthewild. com, mid-May-mid-Sept., $1,950 for two people for one day, up to $6,980 for four days) occupies the south shore of Kachemak Bay between Halibut Cove and Seldovia, nine water miles from the Spit. The lodge caters to nature lovers, photographers, bird-watchers, and anglers with an appreciation for the finer things in life and a willingness to pay dearly. The cost includes round-trip transportation from Homer, gourmet family-style meals, boat tours, sea kayaking, guided walks, beachcombing, clam digging, wildlife viewing, yoga classes, or just soaking in the hot tub. Also available for an extra fee are deep-sea fishing, flightseeing, and bear-viewing trips. Accommodations are luxurious; there is no roughing it here, and it's where you might run into the likes of Jim Carey and other celebrities.

Peterson Bay Lodge & Oyster Camp (907/235-7156 or 866/899-7156, www.petersonbaylodge.com, $145 pp per night, add $65 pp round-trip water taxi from Homer) occupies the head of this remote bay, where the owners raise famous Kachemak Bay oysters. Guests stay in four surprisingly comfortable canvas-walled cabins with screened porches, a sauna, and access to the lodge kitchen to cook meals.

Upon arrival, guests are given a tour of the oyster farm, along with the chance to sample fresh oysters and mussels. One night's lodging includes kayaks and a continental breakfast.

A classic Alaskan lodge, gorgeous **Kachemak Bay Wilderness Lodge** (907/235-8910, www.alaskawildernesslodge.com, $1,750 pp for two nights, $3,750 pp for five days) lies within China Poot Bay in the heart of the state park, with trails to nearby Peterson Bay. Guests stay in cozy artistic cabins, each with a cedar bath, a picture window, and homemade quilts, and are served gourmet organic meals. Rates are all-inclusive.

Located adjacent to a trailhead for Grewingk Glacier, **Hideaway Cove Wilderness Lodge** (907/299-1075 or 888/503-7160, www.hideawaycovelodge.com, mid-May-mid-Sept., from $299 pp all-inclusive) has four waterside cabins that share a separate bathhouse and two hillside cabins with private baths. A variety of packages are offered, starting with a one-night stay that includes water taxi from Homer, lodging, Internet access, and excellent meals in the central yurt, plus guided hiking and kayaking. Cabins have propane stoves and limited power; everything runs on solar cells.

BACKGROUND

The Land

Southcentral Alaska encompasses an extraordinary diversity of land, from deeply incised coastal fjords to 20,320-foot Mount McKinley, North America's highest mountain. Four major mountain ranges dominate the region: the Alaska Range, Talkeetna Mountains, Chugach Mountains, and Kenai Mountains.

Denali National Park lies near the center of the **Alaska Range,** comprising not just Mount McKinley (commonly called Denali by Alaskans), but many other high summits, including Mount Foraker (17,400 ft.), Mount Hunter (14,573 ft.), and Mount Huntington (12,240 ft.). Large glaciers flow from both sides of the mountains feeding the Toklat, Teklanika, McKinley, Kantishna, and Nenana Rivers that drain north into the Yukon River, and the Susitna, Yentna, Kahiltna, and Chulitna Rivers that drain south into Cook Inlet. Most visitors to Denali access it via the Park Road, a 92-mile gravel road along the north side of the Alaska Range. The southern side is only accessible by air or a very long hike.

The town of Talkeetna is south of Denali at the juncture of the Talkeetna, Chulitna, and Susitna Rivers. The **Talkeetna Mountains** rise

© DON PITCHER

BEST PLACES TO SEE DENALI

Seeing the massive 20,320-foot summit of Mount McKinley is a highlight for both newcomers to Alaska and locals. The mountain has notoriously fickle weather, and the summit is often obscured by clouds, but when it emerges, you have no doubt that it's the tallest mountain in North America. The peak is visible from many places in Southcentral Alaska; here are a few of the best.

- **Earthquake Park** in Anchorage. This city park is out West Northern Lights Boulevard near the airport.

- **Resolution Park** in downtown Anchorage.

- The rooftop bar at **Snow Goose Restaurant** in downtown Anchorage.

- Just outside **Talkeetna.** A turnout at Mile 13 of the Talkeetna Spur Road (one mile from Talkeetna) provides an excellent view of The Mountain. Across the way is the turnoff to Talkeetna Alaskan Lodge, with even more impressive Alaska Range vistas from the back deck.

- **Petersville Road.** This long gravel road turns west off the Parks Highway at Trapper Creek (Mile 115), with amazing views of Denali at several points along the way. If you continue out this road it leads to access points for Denali State Park, where a hike leads to dramatic south-side vistas.

- **Denali Viewpoint South** at Mile 135 Parks Highway. Within Denali State Park, this very popular highway stop has signs describing the Alaska Range and telescopes for a closer look.

- **Denali Viewpoint North** at Mile 163 Parks Highway. Another large turnout with views of Mount McKinley when it's out.

- **Eielson Visitor Center** in Denali National Park. You can't see Denali from the park entrance, though a pullout at Mile 9 of the Park Road has a limited view of the peak. It's an eight-hour round-trip bus ride into the park to reach the beautifully located visitor center at Eielson with panoramic views looking south to Mount McKinley. Just before the bus drops down to Eielson, it stops at Stony Hill for a higher perspective.

- **Wonder Lake and Reflection Pond.** Eighty-five miles out the Park Road (11 hours round-trip on the shuttle bus) is famous Wonder Lake, where the mountain is up close and personal. Nearby Reflection Pond is the perfect spot for photos of the mountain and its reflection.

east of here, with the Matanuska River just south of the Talkeetnas. Hatcher Pass (near Palmer) is a popular access point for the southern Talkeetna Mountains. The north side of the range is accessible from the Denali Highway that connects Cantwell with Paxson.

Cook Inlet reaches north into Southcentral Alaska, forming the region's western border. Two major rivers drain into Cook Inlet from the north, the Susitna River starting in the Alaska Range, and the Matanuska River with headwaters in the Chugach Mountains. The valley they jointly form is known as the Matanuska-Susitna Valley, or more commonly, the **Mat-Su Valley.** It's home to the fastest growing part of Alaska and the small cities of Wasilla and Palmer.

The city of **Anchorage** occupies a relatively flat area of coastal lowland jutting into upper Cook Inlet, with Knik Arm extending northward (it's fed by the Susitna and Matanuska Rivers) and Turnagain Arm separating the city from the Kenai Peninsula. The **Chugach Mountains** rise abruptly along the eastern side of Anchorage, with the lower areas dominated by upscale homes and the higher reaches within Chugach State Park.

The **Kenai Peninsula** has a rugged eastern half dominated by the **Kenai Mountains.** They extend across the peninsula from the southwestern tip to Turnagain Arm, encompassing Kachemak Bay State Park, Kenai Fjords National Park, Chugach National Forest, and

Kenai National Wildlife Refuge. Glaciers cover extensive parts of the peninsula, with massive Harding Icefield taking in 300 square miles and feeding 40 glaciers. The Kenai River is famous as a fishing destination, flowing across the western side of the peninsula. The town of Seward sits at the head of Resurrection Bay and is bordered by mountains on all sides. The western portion of Kenai Peninsula has extensive areas where Minnesotans would feel at home, with relatively flat forested country pockmarked with thousands of small lakes and several large ones: Tustumena Lake, Kenai Lake, and Skilak Lake. The almost-twin small cities of Soldotna and Kenai are near the mouth of the Kenai River, and Homer lies at the end of the road—literally—along beautiful Kachemak Bay.

GEOLOGY
Plate Tectonics
Briefly, the huge Pacific plate (the ocean floor) is drifting slowly northeast. It collides with the North American plate, on which the continent rests, along an arc that stretches from the western Aleutians in the Gulf of Alaska to the Inside Passage—defining one section of the famous Pacific "Ring of Fire." This meeting of plates jams the ocean floor under the continental landmass and gives rise to violent geological forces: upthrusting mountains, extensive and large earthquakes, volcanic rumblings and eruptions, and movement along fault lines.

Somewhere in the mists of early geological time, a particularly persistent and powerful collision between the two plates caused the Brooks Range to rise; erosion has whittled its highest peaks to 8,000 feet, half their original height. Later, a similar episode thrust the Alaska Range into shape. The Pacific plate even today continues to nose under the continental plate in the vicinity of Yakutat (near where Southeast meets Southcentral Alaska). The force pushes Mount Logan—Canada's

highest peak—slowly upward. Learn more about the geological forces shaping Alaska at www.gi.alaska.edu.

Earthquakes
One of the world's most seismically active regions, Alaska has withstood some of the most violent earthquakes and largest tidal waves ever recorded. In the last century, more than 80 Alaskan earthquakes registered higher than 7 on the Richter scale. The most destructive occurred at 5:35pm on March 27, 1964, when the most powerful earthquake ever recorded in North America rocked Southcentral Alaska. This 9.2 magnitude quake (80 times bigger than the famous 1906 San Francisco earthquake, which is estimated at around 7.8) had a devastating impact on the region, flattening 75 homes and businesses in Anchorage, creating tsunamis that wiped out nearly every coastal village in Southcentral Alaska, and wreaking havoc all the way to California. The quake and its tsunamis killed 131 people. It was the second strongest in the 20th century; only a 9.5 magnitude quake in Chile in 1960 was larger.

Anyone who spends more than a few months in Southwest or Southcentral Alaska will probably feel at least one earthquake, and residents of the Aleutian Islands barely take notice of anything with a magnitude less than 6. The **Alaska Earthquake Information Center's** website (www.aeic.alaska.edu) provides detailed information on Alaskan earthquakes, including today's activity. For additional background on earthquakes in Alaska, visit the **USGS Earthquake Hazards Program** website (www.earthquake.usgs.gov).

Tsunamis
An earthquake deep below the ocean floor in the Gulf of Alaska or the open Pacific is especially dangerous to the coasts of Alaska and Hawaii, along with the west coast of Canada and the United States. The activity creates

enormous tidal waves (tsunamis), which, although they are only 3-5 feet high in the open ocean, can travel at speeds exceeding 500 mph. Contrary to popular fears, a tsunami does not slam into the coast with 20 or 30 feet of water, washing away everything in its path like a flash flood. Instead, the water slowly inundates the land to a depth of 4-5 feet. Then, after a brief and chilling calm, the wave is sucked back out to sea in one vast undertow. Most of the destruction caused by the great Good Friday earthquake was of this nature, attested to by hair-raising pictures that you'll see in places like Valdez, Seward, and Kodiak. If you hear a tsunami warning, get to higher ground immediately. The **West Coast & Alaska Tsunami Warning Center** (http://wcatwc.arh.noaa.gov) is based in Palmer, and its website provides information on recent and historical tsunamis.

Volcanoes

Like its earthquakes, Alaska's major volcanoes are located along the Aleutian chain. In fact, 57 active volcanoes stretch along this arc, and

most have been active in the last 300 years. The largest recorded eruption occurred when Novarupta blew its top in 1912, the most cataclysmic natural disaster since Krakatoa had cracked 30 years earlier.

There's always an active volcano somewhere in the state, especially in the Aleutians and along the Alaska Peninsula. The University of Alaska Fairbanks **Alaska Volcano Observatory** (www.avo.alaska.edu) keeps track of volcanic activity, and its website has details on current and historic eruptions.

Several volcanoes get particular attention because of their recent activity and proximity to major population centers: **Mount Spurr** (78 miles west of Anchorage) erupted in 1992; **Mount Augustine** (171 miles southwest of Anchorage) in 2005; and **Mount Redoubt** (103 miles southwest of Anchorage) in 1989 and 2009. Each of these dumped ash in varying amounts on the region, closing schools and businesses, filling the air with ash (hazardous for people, electronics, and car engines), and creating havoc for air travel. The 1989 eruption

© DON PITCHER

Kenai Fjords National Park

of Mount Redoubt nearly brought down a KLM jet when it flew into the ash cloud, causing all four engines to shut down. The plane dove two miles before the pilots were able to restart the engines and land safely in Anchorage. That same year, Redoubt generated a massive debris flow down the Drift River, inundating an oil terminal and threatening to spill oil into Cook Inlet.

GLACIATION

A glacier forms in areas of high precipitation and elevation where the snow is allowed to pile up to great depths, compacting the bottom layers into solid ice. The great weight above the bottom ice (along with the force of gravity) pushes it slowly downward like a giant frozen river, scooping out huge valleys and shearing off entire mountainsides. When the rate of advance is balanced by melt-off, the face of the glacier remains more or less stationary. If the glacier flows more quickly than its face melts, it advances; if it melts faster than it flows, the glacier recedes. Air bubbles are squeezed out of the glacier by this tremendous pressure, which makes glacial ice extremely dense. It's so compact that the higher frequencies of light cannot escape or penetrate it, which explains the dark-blue tinge. And because of its density, it also melts at fantastically slow rates; a small chunk or two will keep beer in a cooler chilled for a day or two.

Signs of the Glaciers

As you travel up the coast or hike in the national parks of the Interior, you'll soon start to recognize and identify glacial landforms. While rivers typically erode V-shaped valleys, glaciers gouge out distinctly U-shaped **glacial troughs.** Valleys and ridges branching from the main valley are sliced off to create **hanging valleys** and **truncated spurs.** A side valley that once carried a tributary glacier may be left as a **hanging trough;** waterfalls often tumble from these hanging valleys and troughs. Alpine glaciers scoop out the headwalls of their accumulation basins to form **cirques.** Bare jagged ridges between cirques are known as **arêtes.**

As a glacier moves down a valley it bulldozes a load of rock, sand, and gravel—known as **glacial till**—ahead of it, or carries it on top. Glacial till that has been dumped is called a **moraine. Lateral moraines** are pushed to the sides of glaciers, while a **terminal moraine** is deposited at the farthest point of the face's advance. A **medial moraine** is formed when two glaciers unite. These ribbonlike strips of rubble can be followed back to the point where the lateral moraines converge between the glaciers.

When looking at a glaciated landscape, watch for gouges and scrape marks on the bedrock, which indicate the direction of glacial flow. Watch too for **erratics,** huge boulders carried long distances and deposited by the glacier that often differ from the surrounding rock. Glacial runoff is often suffused with finely powdered till or **glacial flour,** which gives it a distinctive milky-white color; the abundance of this silt in glacial streams creates a twisting, braided course. With a little practice, you'll soon learn to recognize glacial features at a glance.

The vast majority of Alaska's glaciers, like those in many other parts of the world, are retreating as the global climate warms. In some cases, glaciers have drawn back many miles in the last few decades, exposing newly formed bays and producing massive outflows of icebergs. The 1989 *Exxon Valdez* oil spill was caused when the ship diverted to avoid ice from nearby Columbia Glacier; it didn't help, of course, that the captain was drunk. Learn more about glaciers and ongoing Alaska research at the **U.S. Geological Survey's** glacier and snow website (http://ak.water.usgs.gov/glaciology).

Permafrost

To picture permafrost, imagine a veneer of

mud atop a slab of ice. In the colder places of the Lower 48, soil ecologists measure how much surface soil freezes in winter. In Alaska, they measure how much surface soil thaws in summer. True permafrost is ground that has stayed frozen for more than two years. To create and maintain permafrost, the annual average temperature must remain below freezing. The topsoil above the permafrost that thaws in the summer is known as the **active layer.** With the proper conditions, permafrost will penetrate downward until it meets heat from the earth's mantle. In the Arctic, permafrost begins a few feet below the surface and can extend 2,000-5,000 feet deep. This is known as **continuous permafrost,** which almost completely underlies the ground above the Arctic Circle. **Discontinuous permafrost,** with permafrost in scattered patches, covers extensive parts of Alaska, particularly boggy areas covered by black spruce forests.

CLIMATE

Granted, over the course of a year, in any given location, Alaska's weather can be extreme and unpredictable. Because of the harshness of the winters, comfortable travel to many popular destinations is difficult early October-late April. Contrary to popular perception, however, the weather can also be quite pleasant. Southcentral Alaska's spring, summer, and fall are not unlike these seasons in Minnesota. It's cool, it's warm; it's wet and dry; sometimes it's windy, sometimes it's foggy. For the latest outdoor forecast, visit the **National Weather Service's** Alaska website (www.arh.noaa.gov).

Though Alaska retains the reputation of the Great Frozen North, a distinct warming trend has had a noticeable effect on the state. Temperatures warmed abruptly in the summer of 1977 and have remained unusually warm ever since, throughout all the seasons. For the latest research, visit the website of the University of Alaska Fairbanks **International Arctic Research Center** (www.iarc.uaf.edu).

It's possible to generalize about Alaskan weather and distinguish three climatic zones: coastal maritime, interior, and Arctic. The main factor affecting the southern coasts is the warm Japanese Current, which causes temperatures to be much milder than the norm at those latitudes. This current also brings continuous rain as humid Pacific air is forced up over the coastal mountains. For example, it rains in Juneau two out of three days. However, these mountains shield the Interior plateaus from the maritime air streams, so yearly precipitation there is low—a mere 15 inches. The Interior experiences great temperature extremes, from biting cold in winter to summer heat waves. The mountains also protect the coastal areas from cold—and hot—Interior air masses. The Arctic zone is characterized by cool, cloudy, and windy summers (averaging 50°F) and cold, windy winters—though not as cold as in the Interior.

The **Alaska Climate Research Center** (http://climate.gi.alaska.edu) has detailed information on the state's climate, along with current weather conditions.

Northern Lights

One of the prime attractions for winter visitors to Alaska is the chance to view the aurora borealis—northern lights—in action. The finest viewing areas are in the northern part of the state, particularly around Fairbanks and Bettles, but when conditions are right, the sky lights up across Anchorage and the Kenai Peninsula. Denali National Park and Talkeetna are both far enough north to experience more aurora activity.

For detailed information on northern lights and predictions of upcoming aurora activity, visit the website of the University of Alaska's **Geophysical Institute** (www.gedds.alaska.edu/auroraforecast).

Flora

VEGETATION ZONES

Southcentral Alaskan forests are dominated by spruce, aspen, cottonwood, alder, birch, and willow. **Boreal forests** cover the western Kenai Peninsula. Much of the Interior lowlands north of Talkeetna consist primarily of scattered open stands of white spruce, paper birch, alpine fir, lodgepole pine, and balsam poplar (cottonwood). **Taiga,** the transition zone between boreal forest and tundra, is characterized by sparse and stunted black spruce, dwarf shrubbery (mostly the ubiquitous willow), and swampy areas known as "muskegs."

The lower-elevation **tundra,** also known as the "moist tundra," starts at the tree line, around 2,500 feet. There you find undergrowth similar to that of the taiga but without the trees. The higher-elevation alpine tundra consists of grasses, clinging mosses and lichens,

Alaska's state flower, the forget-me-not

© DON PITCHER

and an abundance of tiny, psychedelically bright wildflowers, including the unforgettable forget-me-not (state flower), with gaze-catching petals of light blue.

FLOWERS

While you're hiking, an excellent book to have along is *Field Guide to Alaskan Wildflowers* by Verna E. Pratt. The photographs are good, the descriptions are usable, and the flowers are conveniently arranged by color.

Fireweed is a wildflower you'll come to know intimately during your travels in the North. It enjoys sunlight and grows profusely in open areas along roads and rivers. Given proper conditions, tall fireweed can grow to seven feet high. Its long stalk of pink flowers blossoms from bottom to top; sourdoughs claim they can predict the arrival and severity of winter by the speed with which fireweed finishes blooming.

Three kinds of **primrose,** also a pinkish red, are another common sight on the tundra. Other red wildflowers of the tundra include **purple mountain saxifrage, moss campion,** and large bright-pink **poppies.**

White flowers include the **narcissus-flowered anemone,** similar to a **buttercup,** which also grows on the tundra. **Mountain avens** are easily recognizable—they look like white roses. A half-dozen kinds of white **saxifrage** are widespread throughout the state. Be careful of the local **water hemlock,** which is deadly poisonous. Similar is the **yarrow,** a medicinal herb with a disk of small white flowers and lacelike leaves. As soon as you identify **Labrador tea,** you'll notice it everywhere in the forest and taiga. **Cotton grass** looks exactly like its name. **Daisies** and **fleabane** complete this group of plants with white flowers.

Larkspur looks similar to fireweed, only it's

© DON PITCHER

fireweed

a dark purple. It grows on a long stalk and a dwarf bush. **Monkshood** is a beautiful dark-blue flower of the buttercup family; **harebells** and **bluebells** are easily identified around Denali. Three kinds of **violets** grow in the boreal forest. Light-purple **lupine** flowers grow in 20-inch clusters. **Asters,** resembling purple daisies, bloom all over the Interior.

BERRIES

Berries are the only fruits that grow naturally in Alaska, and luckily the many varieties are abundant, several are edible, a few even taste good, and only one is poisonous. If you're into berry collecting, get to know poisonous **baneberry** immediately. A member of the crowfoot family, it grows mostly in the

Southeast and the central Interior. The white berries look like black-eyed peas; they ripen to a scarlet red. **Juniper berries** grow throughout Alaska, but the **bog blueberries, Alaska blueberries,** and **huckleberries** are much tastier. Blueberries also grow on poorly drained, shady alpine slopes and are generally the first to ripen. **Salmonberries** turn a dark salmon-red in late summer, and are quite similar to raspberries.

Bunchberries are good tasting but have been known to upset a stomach or two. **Bog cranberries** are best after the first frost, especially when they're a deep purple—deliciously tart. **High-bush cranberries** are common but are best just before they're completely ripe. **Wild strawberries** are even better if you can get to them before the birds and rodents. The several kinds of **bearberries** (blue and red) are tasteless except to bears, and the **soapberry** will remind you of getting caught saying a dirty word as a kid. Pick up *Alaska Wild Berry Guide and Cookbook* for the complete lowdown on Alaska's berries.

FRANKENSTEIN CABBAGES

In 1941 the managers of the Alaska Railroad offered a $25 prize to the grower of the largest cabbage in the state, and since then cabbage growers have been competing. Usually the largest cabbages at the Tanana Valley State Fair (in Fairbanks in mid-August) weigh in at 65-70 pounds, but a world record was set in 2012 when a Palmer man grew a 138-pound cabbage. Ten-pound celery, 3-pound beets, 2-pound turnips, and 1-pound carrots have also been blue-ribbon earners. Find them and more at the Alaska State Fair in Palmer at the end of August.

Fauna

If any aspect of Alaska embodies the image of the "last frontier," it's the state's animal kingdom. For millennia, Native Alaskan hunters, with their small-scale weapons and limited needs, had little impact on wildlife populations. Eskimo and Aleut villages subsisted comfortably on fish, small mammals, and one or two whales per year; the interior Athabascan bands did well on a handful of moose and caribou. This all changed in the mid-1700s with the coming of the Russians and Americans. Sea otters, fur seals, and gray whales were quickly hunted to the verge of extinction. By the 1850s the Alaskan musk ox had been annihilated. Wolves, in part because they preyed on the same game as humans, were ruthlessly hunted.

Conservation measures have nurtured their numbers, and today Alaska boasts one of the largest concentrations of animal populations remaining on earth. For example, there are nearly twice as many caribou in Alaska as there are people. There's a moose and a Sitka black-tailed deer for every three people. If 80,000 sheep strikes you as an impressive number, consider 40,000 grizzly bears. Bald and golden eagles are commonplace, and while the magnificent trumpeter swan was believed near extinction in the Lower 48, it was thriving in Alaska. Marine mammals, from orcas to the recovering otters, are common (though they have recently experienced major declines in the Aleutians and western Alaska), and Alaskan waters also contain fish and other sea creatures in unimaginable quantities.

Wildlife Viewing

Alaska's wildlife is a major draw for both visitors and residents. The state's vast stretches of wilderness contain abundant mammals, birds, and fish, including some of the largest and most magnificent animals in the world. Land mammals such as brown (grizzly) and black bears, caribou, moose, Dall sheep, wolves, and musk ox are the main attractions, but the state also has incomparable populations of birds, including such favorites as bald eagles, puffins, loons, and sandhill cranes. Marine mammals include seals, Steller sea lions, and sea otters, along with beluga whales, orca (killer) whales, humpback whales, gray whales, and others.

The *Alaska Wildlife Viewing Guide,* by Michelle Sydeman and Annabel Lund, is a useful introduction to finding wild animals. Visit the Alaska Department of Fish and Game's website (www.wildlifeviewing.alaska.gov) for details on dozens of species of Alaskan animals in their "Wildlife Notebook" series, and for descriptions of places to see wildlife. The state also produces regional wildlife viewing guides, including **Anchorage Wildlife Viewing Hot Spots, Kenai Peninsula Wildlife Viewing Guide,** and **Kachemak Bay Watchable Wildlife Guide.** Pick up copies in visitors centers around the state or find them on the website above.

In Alaska, wildlife may be encountered up close almost anywhere outdoors. Many animals are well prepared to defend their territories against intruders (you), and even the smallest can bite. Never attempt to feed or touch wildlife. It is seldom good for it, you, or those who follow. Any animal that appears unafraid or "tame" can be quite unpredictable, so keep your distance. One thing you don't have to worry about is snakes; there are none in Alaska. Surprisingly, however, there *are* frogs, even above the Arctic Circle.

LAND MAMMALS
Brown Bears

The brown bear, also called grizzly, is the symbol of the wild country and a measure of its wildness. Grizzlies once roamed all over North

© DON PITCHER

brown bear

America. In 1800 there were over 100,000 of them; today, around 1,000 survive in the Lower 48. Ironically, the grizzly is the state animal of California, where it is now extinct. Things are very different in Alaska, where 40,000 of these magnificent creatures still inhabit the land.

Denali National Park offers some of the most accessible bear-viewing in the state. The estimated 200 Denali grizzlies are still wild, mostly in their natural state. This is especially important for the continued education of the cubs, who are taught how to dig roots, find berries, catch ground squirrels, and take moose calves. However, Denali grizzlies are not afraid of people, and they are extremely curious; some have tasted canned beans, veggie burgers, and Oreo cookies. While no one has been killed by a grizzly at Denali, maulings have occurred, usually because of the foolishness of novice hikers and photographers or as a result of improper food storage. Take care, but don't be afraid to go hiking.

The natural grizzly diet is 80 percent vegetarian. They eat berries, willows, and roots, as well as preying on anything they can take: from ground squirrels to caribou, from foxes to small black bears. And they're challenged by nothing, except humans with high-powered weapons. Grizzlies are racehorse-fast and have surprising endurance; they need about 50 square miles for home territory and travel several miles each night. During the day they like to eat, sleep in the sun—often on snow patches—and entertain tourists on the shuttle buses.

Grizzlies are solitary creatures. Full-grown boars and sows are seen together only during mating season, in early summer. The gestation period is a little over five months, and the sows give birth in December to 1-3 cubs. The cubs are hairless, weigh one pound each, and remain blind for a week. They stay with the mother for over 2.5 years—two full summers. They're then chased away sometime before

July of the third summer, when the sow is ready to mate again.

Contrary to popular belief, bears do not hibernate. They do sleep deeply in dens during the winter, sometimes for weeks. But they often get hungry, lonely, or restless, and step outside to forage for frozen roots, berries, and meat. Sometimes a bear will stay out all winter; that's the one that the Native Alaskans fear the most: the winter bear. Its fur tends to build up a thick layer of ice, rendering it nearly impenetrable, almost bulletproof. And of course, sows give birth in the deep winter, which they're certainly awake for.

Grizzlies and brown bears were once thought to be different species, but are now considered the same. The basic difference is in size, which is due to habitat. Grizzlies themselves are the world's largest land omnivores, growing to heights of 6-7 feet and weighing in at 500-600 pounds. However, they're the smaller of the two because they live in the Interior and feed mostly on vegetation. Brown bears are coastal, and with a rich source of fish protein, they have achieved near mythical sizes. Kodiak brown bears retain a reputation for being the largest, reaching heights of over 10 feet and weights of up to 1,400 pounds. On Admiralty Island in Southeast Alaska the brown bears are a bit smaller, but population densities are the highest anywhere: around one bear per square mile.

Hiking in bear country requires special precautions. A number of areas offer outstanding brown bear-viewing around Alaska; the most famous places are McNeil River, Katmai National Park, and Denali National Park.

Black Bears

Black bears are found in most forested parts of Alaska, though not on certain Southeast Alaskan islands. They are distinguished from grizzlies and brown bears by their size (much smaller), the shape of their face (much narrower), and the lack of a shoulder hump. Black bears are actually more dangerous to people than grizzlies: There have been more attacks and maulings in Alaska by black bears than by brown. **Polar bears** are not found in Southcentral Alaska. You'll need to visit the North Slope around Barrow or Kaktovik to see these amazing animals.

Moose

The moose is the largest member of the deer family, and Alaska has the largest moose. A bull moose in his prime gets to be about 7 feet tall and weighs around 1,200 pounds, all from eating willow stems—about 30 pounds per day. They also eat aspen and birch, but willow is the staple of choice. The antlers, which are bone, are shed and renewed every year. Full-size antlers can weigh up to 70 pounds—that's mostly in September during the rut, or mating time. Bulls of near-equal rank and size butt their heads together to vie for dominance. You want to be really careful of bulls then; they are touchy. The cows have one or two calves, rarely three, in May, and that's when you want to be really careful of the cows too. The calves stay with the cow exactly one year; then she chases away the yearlings. Sometimes at the start of the summer season you'll spot a huge pregnant cow with a frisky yearling on her heels, and you've never seen a more hassled-looking expression on an animal's face. But that's family life.

Moose don't cover too much territory—about 30 miles a year, mostly in the forest, which provides natural defense against predators. The word *moose* comes from the Massachusetts Algonquian dialect and means "muncher of little twigs." By the way, the little flap of hair under the moose's chin is known as the "moostache." (Just kidding, it's really called the "dewlap.")

Harsh winters are deadly to moose. Deep snow and bitter cold can cause one in three moose in central Alaska to perish. Annually,

© DON PITCHER

moose

hundreds of moose make their last stand along the snowless railroad tracks between Seward and Fairbanks and are killed by trains that don't stop for them. Hundreds of others starve to death. Those hit by cars along roadways are butchered and distributed to local people.

If Alaska moose are the world's largest, Kenai Peninsula moose are Alaska's largest. A Kenai moose holds the Alaskan record: at 10-11 years old, his antlers were just under 75 inches wide, he weighed 1,500-1,600 pounds.

Kenai National Wildlife Refuge was specifically established to protect moose, and these massive animals are a common sight along Kenai Peninsula roads at dusk. Other places to watch for moose are within the Anchorage bowl and in the Matanuska-Susitna Valley northeast of Anchorage. Drive with care, since moose can suddenly step onto the road without warning, and their massive bulk means that a collision could be fatal to both the moose and people in the vehicle.

Moose can be very aggressive, particularly in the winter months when food is scarce. A number of people have been killed by moose attacks, even in Anchorage. Always give moose a wide berth, especially if you're walking, on a bike or skis, or with a dog. If a moose appears ready to attack, quickly hide behind a tree, car, or other obstruction. Pepper spray may be effective if all else fails, or you can try to outrun a moose if you have no other options; they generally don't run far. If the moose knocks you down, curl up in a ball, protect your head with your hands, hold still, and say a few thousand Hail Marys.

Caribou

Caribou are travelin' fools. They're extremely flighty animals—restless, tireless, fast, and graceful. Run and eat, run and eat is pretty much all they do—oh, yeah, and reproduce. Reindeer, although of the same species, are smaller and often domesticated. Caribou are peaceful critters, and they'll outrun and outdistance their predators,

caribou

mostly wolves, rather than fight. They like to travel in groups, unlike moose, which are loners. And they cover 10 times as much territory. Their herding and migrating imperatives are similar to those of the plains bison; they gather in large numbers and think nothing of running 50 miles, almost on a lark.

Caribou are extremely well adapted to their winter environment. They have huge nasal passages and respiratory systems in order to breathe the bitterly cold winter air. Thick fur covers almost every inch of their bodies; the fur itself is protected by large, hollow, oily guard hairs. This tends to make caribou look much larger than they really are; a good-sized bull weighs 400-500 pounds, a cow about half that. Caribou have the richest milk in the animal kingdom: It's 20 percent fat. They've also got huge prancing hooves, immortalized in the Santa Claus myth, which are excellent for running, swimming, disco dancing, and pawing at the snow to uncover the moss and

lichens on which they subsist all through the harsh Arctic winter. The word *caribou* comes from the Maine Algonquian dialect and means "scraping hooves."

The caribou is the only member of the deer family whose females grow antlers. Babies are on their feet and nursing within an hour of birth, and at one week they can run 20 miles. If they can't, they'll most likely die, since the herd won't wait. But this helps to keep the herd healthy, controls population growth, and provides food for the carnivores.

Native Alaskans are among the caribou's natural predators. Historically, Native Alaskans ate the meat raw, roasted, and stewed. They ate all the organs, even the half-digested greens from the stomach. The little gobs of fat from behind the eyes were considered a delicacy. They used almost exclusively caribou hide for clothes, rugs, blankets, and tents. The leg skins were used to make mukluks; the long strands of stringy sinew provided sewing thread.

Nearly one million caribou roam across Alaska, with the largest herds in the Arctic, including within the Arctic National Wildlife Refuge. Caribou are commonly seen within Denali National Park and Preserve and along the Denali Highway.

Dall Sheep

Named for William H. Dall, one of the first people to survey the lower Yukon (1866), Dall sheep are sometimes called Alaska bighorn sheep, because the Rocky Mountain bighorn is a closely related species. Distinguished by their brilliant white color, the rams grow large curved horns, formed from a specialized skin structure made up of a compacted mass of hair and oil. The horns aren't shed; instead the sheep add another ring to them yearly, so the longer the horns, the older the ram, and the more dominant within the herd. The rams can weigh as much as 175 pounds; the ewes have small spiked horns and average 120 pounds.

Their habitat is the high alpine tundra, and they subsist on grasses, mosses, lichens, and flowers. Their bird's-eye view provides an excellent defense. They're also magnificent mountain climbers. Roughly 70,000 Dall sheep reside in the Chugach, Kenai, Alaska, and Wrangell mountain ranges. During summer, the rams migrate high into the ranges, leaving the prime lower grazing grounds for the ewes and lambs. It's natural that they migrate, the same way it's natural that they have predators. Their alpine tundra habitat is very fragile, and it can take decades to regenerate after overgrazing. Migration and predation thus keep the flock healthy, control population growth, and guarantee the survival of the habitat.

Dall sheep inhabit mountain hillsides throughout much of Alaska. They are frequently seen on rocky slopes in Denali National Park, near Cooper Landing on the Kenai Peninsula, and along Turnagain Arm 20 miles south of Anchorage.

Wolves

Wolves have traditionally been one of the most misunderstood, misrepresented, and maligned mammals in both fact and fable. We've come a long way from the days when it was believed that wolves were innately evil, with the visage of the devil himself, eating their hapless prey—or little girls in red hoods—alive. But it wasn't until the mid-1940s, when wildlife biologist Adolph Murie began a long-term and systematic study of the wolves in Mount McKinley National Park, that all the misconceptions of the accepted lore about wolves began to change.

For three years Murie tramped mainly on the plains below Polychrome Pass and became extremely intimate with several wolf families. (His book, *The Wolves of Mount McKinley,* published in 1944, is still considered a classic natural history text.) Though Murie concluded that a delicate balance is established between predator and prey to their mutual advantage, declining Dall sheep populations, political pressure, and, indeed, tradition forced the park service to kill wolves, which were considered, against Murie's conclusions, to be the cause of the sheep decline. Typically, though, the wolf population was in just as dire straits as the sheep, and for several years no wolves were killed in the feds' traps because of their scarcity.

Since then, many researchers and writers have come to incisive conclusions about the wolf. It has been determined that their social systems—within the pack and with their prey—are amazingly complex and sophisticated. The alpha male and female are the central players in the pack, surrounded by 4-7 pups, yearlings, and other adults. The dominant female receives a long involved courtship from the dominant male (though he might not necessarily be the biological father of the pups). Territories can be as small as 200 square miles and as large as 800 square miles, depending on a host of influences.

Perhaps the most complex and fascinating

aspect of wolf activity is the hunt. Barry Lopez, author of the brilliant *Of Wolves and Men,* argues persuasively that the individual prey is as responsible as the wolf for its own killing, in effect "giving itself to the wolf in ritual suicide." Lopez maintains that the eye contact between the wolf and its prey "is probably a complex exchange of information regarding the appropriateness of a chase and a kill." Lopez calls this the "conversation of death."

With the advent of radio collaring and tracking from airplanes, the movements of individual wolves and packs have continually surprised wildlife biologists. Wolves often travel 5-10 miles per hour for hours at a time. In a matter of days, an individual cut loose from a pack can wind up 500 miles away. Thus wolves are able to select and populate suitable habitats quickly.

Alaska's 7,500-10,000 wolves are thriving, even though roughly 15 percent of them are harvested yearly by trappers. They can be found all the way from the Southeastern panhandle to the Arctic slope, but are most common in Interior Alaska. Denali National Park offers travelers the best chance to see a wolf from the road system, but wolves may also be seen in other parts of the Alaska Range, in Brooks Range foothills, and in Wrangell-St. Elias National Park.

Captive wolves can be seen at the **Alaska Zoo** (www.alaskazoo.com) in Anchorage. A nonprofit organization, **Wolf Song of Alaska** (www.wolfsongalaska.org), has an education center in downtown Anchorage. A highly controversial state-sponsored hunting program has targeted wolves in some parts of the state to increase the survival of caribou and moose. The program includes the aerial killing of wolves and is widely opposed by environmental groups but applauded by some hunting organizations.

Musk Oxen

The musk ox is a stocky long-haired animal with a slight shoulder hump and a very short tail. Despite their name, musk oxen have no musk glands and are not oxen. The largest member of the sheep family, this shaggy prehistoric-looking creature was abundant in the North Country until it was hunted into extinction by the mid-1800s. In the 1930s, several dozen musk oxen were transplanted from Greenland to Nunivak Island in the Bering Sea. Like the elk on Afognak, the musk oxen on Nunivak thrived, and the resident Native Alaskans used the soft underwool to establish a small cottage industry knitting sweaters, scarves, and caps. And that's what it would have remained, a small cottage industry, if it hadn't been for Dr. John J. Teal, Jr., a student of Arctic explorer Vilhjalmur Stefansson. Stefansson recognized the potential of musk ox wool and inspired Teal to experiment with domesticating them. After spending 10 years with musk oxen on his farm in Vermont, Teal concluded that they were amiable, hardy, and easy to domesticate. So in 1964 he started the Musk Ox Project at the University of Alaska in Fairbanks.

In 1984 the project moved to a farm in the Matanuska Valley, where musk oxen are bred to produce *qiviut* (KEE-vee-oot), the soft underwool, which is renowned in Alaska for its insulation (eight times warmer by weight than sheep wool) and tactile (softer than the finest cashmere) properties. The *qiviut* is collected from the animals in the spring. The raw wool is sent to a mill in Rhode Island and then sold to Oomingmak (a Native Alaskan word for musk ox, meaning "bearded one"; www.qiviut.com), a co-op consisting of members in villages spread throughout western Alaska. Here the *qiviut* is knitted into garments, which are sold at retail outlets in Anchorage and at the farm near Palmer.

Today, wild musk oxen can be found on the Seward Peninsula near Nome, Nunivak and Nelson islands, the Yukon-Kuskokwim Delta, the North Slope near Prudhoe Bay, and the Arctic National Wildlife Refuge. The best places to see them up close are the **Musk Ox Farm** in Palmer (www.muskoxfarm.org) and the **Large Animal Research Station** (www.uaf.edu/lars) at the University of Alaska in Fairbanks.

Lynx

Alaska's only native cat, the lynx is the northern version of the bobcat. Weighing around 20-30 pounds, these extremely secretive animals prey primarily on snowshoe hare, a species that undergoes an 8-11 year cycle of abundance. Lynx numbers fluctuate with those of hare but lag one or two years behind. When a hare population crashes, lynx numbers soon decline, and they sometimes travel up to 400 miles in search of food. Although snowshoe hare are an important prey for lynx, when they are scarce lynx hunt grouse, ptarmigan, squirrels, and rodents, and may even take larger animals such as caribou or Dall sheep.

Lynx are sometimes seen during long periods of summer daylight, especially in years when they are abundant. Lynx have large broad feet that function as snowshoes for winter hunting and traveling.

Rodents

Ground squirrels and marmots are true hibernators: Unlike other mammals such as black, grizzly, and polar bears, they sleep for six months straight in a deep coma. This separation between life and death is one of the thinnest lines in the animal world. A ground squirrel's heart slows to about six beats a minute, and its body temperature lowers to just above freezing, around 38°F. (In fact, a zoologist at the University of Alaska Fairbanks has found that the core temperature of the Arctic ground squirrel, the northernmost hibernator, can drop to as low as 26°F—six degrees below freezing! Of course, the squirrels don't freeze; they "supercool.")

The hibernating squirrel takes a breath every couple of minutes. It uses up half its body weight, since it isn't eating. If you stuck a needle in a hibernating ground squirrel's paw, it would take the animal about 10 minutes to begin to feel it.

Ground squirrels provide a large part of the grizzly and wolf diet, and that of scavenger birds' as well, since they're a common type of roadkill.

Marmots, similar to woodchucks, are sometimes mistaken for wolverines. They live in large rock outcroppings for protection and have a piercing whistle, which warns of approaching predators or other possible danger. Look for marmots around Polychrome Pass at Denali Park; ask the driver where exactly to see them.

Alaska has a number of other members of the rodent family: shrews, mice, voles, lemmings, and porcupines. Long-tailed and least weasels occupy a wide habitat in the taiga and tundra. Martens are another member of the weasel family, similar to, though much more aggressive than, mink; the pine marten is one of Alaska's most valuable fur-bearers. Wolverines are in attendance, though you'd be very lucky to see one. Red foxes are common in the Interior and Southcentral Alaska, and you're likely to see one at Denali Park; the white Arctic fox is a gorgeous animal, though you'll only see one in pictures.

MARINE MAMMALS

Marine mammals are found all along the Alaskan coast, from Ketchikan in the Southeast to Barrow on the Arctic Ocean. Sea otters are frequently found in harbors, bays, and inlets, particularly around kelp beds. Good places to look for whales, seals, sea otters, sea lions, porpoises, and other marine mammals are the Inside Passage, Prince William Sound, Kodiak Island, Kachemak Bay, and Kenai Fjords. The Pribilof Islands serve as rearing and resting areas for thousands of northern fur seals,

sea otter

harbor seals, Steller sea lions, and walrus in the summer. Only Native Alaskans have the legal right to hunt marine mammals.

Sea Otters

A marine member of the weasel family, the sea otter had one characteristic that would seal its doom: a long, wide, beautiful pelt that's one of the warmest, most luxurious, and durable furs in existence. Otter fur catalyzed the Russian *promyshlenniki* to begin overrunning the Aleutians in the mid-late 18th century, sealing the doom of the Aleuts as well as the otters. In 1803, Alexander Baranov shipped 15,000 pelts back to eastern Russia. Up until the 1840s, otter hunting was the primary industry in the Pacific, and when the Americans bought Alaska in 1867, nearly one million otters had been killed in the northern Pacific.

During the extreme lawless period in the last quarter of the 19th century, the otters were annihilated. In 1906 schooners cruised the North Pacific for months without taking a single pelt. In 1910 a crack crew of 40 Aleut hunters managed to harvest 16 otters. In 1911 otters were added to the International Fur Seal Treaty, giving them complete protection from everybody. Small, isolated populations of otters had managed to survive in the western Aleutians, and their numbers have increased over the past century to roughly 100,000 today. Approximately 90 percent of the world's sea otter population can be found in coastal Alaska. For more on the current situation, visit the website of the Fish and Wildlife Service (http://alaska.fws.gov/fisheries/mmm).

Steller Sea Lions

George Wilhelm Steller was the naturalist aboard Vitus Bering's 1742 exploration of Alaska, and the first European to step on Alaskan soil. Two marine mammals ended up with his name: the Steller's sea cow, a coldwater relative of the manatee; and the Steller seal lion. The sea cow was driven to extinction just 26 years later, a casualty of not being afraid of humans and the tasty flavor of its flesh. Today, the sea lion in much of Alaska is equally endangered.

Steller sea lions are pinnipeds—marine mammals with flippers, not feet. Males can weigh up to 2,000 pounds; females peak at 600 pounds. Sea lions eat several kinds of fish, but mostly pollock. They range across the North Pacific from northern Japan and Siberia all the way to California. These playful but powerful animals were abundant in western Alaskan waters until quite recently. In the 1960s, for example, an estimated 177,000 sea lions lived in the Gulf of Alaska and along the Aleutians. Commercial hunting was halted in the mid-1970s, but the population continued to drop by more than 80 percent. By 2000, a mere 34,000 survived. The western Alaska population was officially listed as endangered in 1997, while sea lion populations in Southeast Alaska and farther south to California are considered threatened.

Researchers are unsure why Steller sea lions are disappearing at such an alarming rate, and there are a multitude of possible causes—including overfishing, toxic chemicals, and predation by sharks and killer whales. Most likely it is some combination of factors, but if something isn't done, the Southwest Alaska population could be headed for extinction. Learn more about these fascinating animals—including the latest research—at the National Marine Fisheries Service's website (www.fakr.noaa.gov/protectedresources).

Whales

The largest summer marine visitors to Alaska are the whales. Each spring **gray whales** are seen migrating north from along the coast off Seward; in the fall they return south. Also in the spring **humpback whales** move north from Hawaii. The humpback is easily distinguished

© DON PITCHER

humpback whales

by its humplike dorsal fin, large flippers, and huge tail, which shows as it dives. These 50-foot-long creatures often breach (jump) or beat the surface of the water with their tails, as if trying to send messages. Smaller (30-foot) **minke whales** are also common.

The **killer whale** (orca), which is not actually a whale but the largest of the dolphins (up to 24 feet long), travels in groups hunting fish and marine mammals. Its six-foot-high triangular dorsal fin and its black-and-white piebald pattern make it easily identifiable.

Look for **beluga whales** in Turnagain Arm along the Seward Highway south of Anchorage. These small white whales are approximately 15 feet long, with a blunt head. Although belugas are doing well in other parts of the North Pacific, the distinctive population within Cook Inlet is critically endangered, with fewer than 325 individuals; it had four times as many back in the 1970s and continues to decline due to overhunting and development.

Kenai Fjords National Park and Resurrection Bay—both accessible by boat tour from Seward—are popular places to spot killer whales and humpbacks, along with sea otters, seals, sea lions, and colonies of puffins. The spring migration of gray whales is a big Resurrection Bay attraction in April each year. There's also a fair chance of seeing humpback and killer whales on the Kachemak Bay wildlife boat trips that depart from Homer.

For more information on whales in Alaska, visit the National Marine Fisheries Service's website (www.fakr.noaa.gov/protectedresources).

BIRDS

Nearly 500 species of birds have been seen within Alaska, from tiny rufous hummingbirds to the nation's national emblem, the bald eagle. Because of Alaska's proximity to Siberia, many unusual species are sometimes seen, making

© DON PITCHER

bald eagle

islands in the Aleutians and within the Bering Sea of great interest to serious birders.

The **National Audubon Society** (www.audubon.org/chapter/ak) has an office in Anchorage (907/338-2473 birding hotline, www.anchorageaudubon.org). In Homer, visit www.birdinghomeralaska.org or call 907/235-7337 for unusual Kachemak Bay birds. All three websites provide details on local birding hot spots across the state.

Eagles

As many eagles are found in Alaska as in the rest of the United States combined. **Bald eagles** are common sights along the coasts, but with their unmistakable white heads, seven-foot wingspans, and dive-bombing, salmon-snatching performances, the thrill of watching them is not quickly lost.

Golden eagles, found throughout the Interior, come without the distinctive "baldness" but are no less magnificent for their size. Plentiful around Denali Park, golden eagles perched on the tundra, standing more than three feet tall, have been mistaken for everything from grizzly cubs to adolescent hikers.

Trumpeter Swans

The world's largest waterfowl, these swans boast wingspans as wide as eagles (7 ft.) and can weigh up to 40 pounds. They're pure white and so have figured prominently over the centuries in legends, drama, music, and metaphor. They fly as fast as 60 mph and as high as 10,000 feet on their migrations from Alaska to the Pacific Northwest for the winter (though a group of 500 overwinter in Alaska). They live to be 30 years old and have a hornlike call, which accounts for their common name.

Ptarmigan

The **willow ptarmigan** is the state bird, and one of the most popular targets of small-game hunters. Ptarmigan—willow, rock, and white-tailed—are similar to pheasant, quail, and partridge in the Lower 48. They reproduce in large quantities, molt from winter white to summer brown, and have a poor sense of self-preservation.

INSECTS
Mosquitoes

The mosquito—contrary to popular belief—is not Alaska's state bird. But skeeters are nearly as much a symbol of the Great North as glaciers, totem poles, and the aurora borealis. Mosquito eggs hatch in water, so the boggy, muskegy, marshy forests and tundra, plus all the ponds, lakes, creeks, sloughs, and braided rivers of Alaska, provide the ideal habitat for these bothersome creatures. Alaska hosts around three dozen varieties of mosquitoes.

Mosquitoes hibernate in the winter and emerge starting in March-April. Peak season is late June-early July. The males don't alight or bite, but they do buzz around people's eyes, noses, and ears, which can be as annoying, if not more so, than the bites. The males live 6-8 weeks, feeding on plant juices; their sole purpose in life is to fertilize the eggs the females produce. They also feed birds and larger insects.

The females live long lives producing batches of eggs, up to 500 at a time. To nourish the eggs they feed on the blood of mammals, using a piercing and sucking mouth tube. The tube also injects an anticoagulant, which causes the itch and swelling from a bite. No Alaskan mosquitoes carry the diseases that tropical mosquitoes are known to, such as malaria, yellow fever, encephalitis, and elephantiasis.

Mosquitoes are most active at dawn and dusk. Windy conditions and low temperatures depress mosquito feeding and breeding. Mosquitoes are attracted to dark colors, carbon dioxide, warmth, and moisture. Mosquito repellent containing DEET (diethyl-meta-toluamide) is the most effective. A head net

Mosquitos aren't really this big in Alaska.

popular and is now playing a more important role in Alaska's economy as tourism increases.

Salmon

Five kinds of salmon—king, red, pink, silver, and chum—all return to the same bend in the same little creek where they hatched to spawn and die, ending one of the most remarkable life cycles and feats of migration and single-minded endurance of any living creature. You'll be steeped in salmon lore if only by osmosis by the end of your trip, and you'll get more than your fill of this most delicious and pretty fish.

The **kings** (also known as chinooks) are the world's largest salmon, and the world's largest kings spawn in Alaskan waters. The average size for a king is 40-50 pounds. The world sport fish record is 97 pounds, and a few 100-pounders have been caught in commercial nets. Kings generally spend 5-6 years in saltwater before returning to freshwater to spawn: The more years spent in the ocean, the larger the fish. They run mostly mid-May-mid-July.

Reds (sockeye) are the best-tasting salmon and the mainstay of the commercial fishing industry. They average 6-10 pounds and run in June-July.

Pinks (humpback) are the most plentiful, with massive runs of more than 150 million fish late June-early September. They're smallish, 3-4 pounds, with soft flesh and a mild taste; they're mostly canned (or caught by tourists).

Silvers (coho) seem to be the most legendary of the salmon for their speed, agility, and sixth sense. Their spawning growth rate is no less than fantastic, more than doubling their weight in the last 90 days of their lives. Silvers grow 7-10 pounds and run late, from late July all the way to November.

Chum (dog) are the least valued of the five Pacific salmon, even though they average 10-20 pounds, are extremely feisty, and are the most far-ranging, running way above the Arctic

helps keep mosquitoes and other buggy critters away from your face and is a wise investment for anyone heading into remote parts of Interior Alaska or Kodiak Island. If you wear light-colored heavy clothing (the stinger can pierce light materials), camp in high and dry places that are apt to be breezy, and rub repellent on all exposed skin, you should be able to weather mosquito season without too much difficulty.

FISH

Get someone going on fishing in Alaska and you won't be able to shut him or her up or get a word in edgewise for the whole afternoon, guaranteed. The fisheries program in Alaska is extensive because commercial, sport, and recreational fishing are important to almost every state resident. Commercial fishing is Alaska's second-largest industry, and Alaska accounts for more than half of the nation's total seafood production. Sportfishing has always been

Circle. They're known as dog salmon because they've traditionally sustained working huskies, though chums remain popular with a hard-core group of sport anglers, who consider them terribly underrated. Surprisingly, they make some of the finest smoked fish.

Halibut

Halibut are Alaska's favorite monster fish and can grow so huge and strong that many anglers have an unsurpassed religious experience while catching one. "Chicken halibut" are the common 25-40 pounders, but 100- and 200-pounders are frequent sights in some ports; even 300-pounders are occasionally reeled in. The state-record halibut was a 464-pounder, more than 8 feet long, caught near Dutch Harbor in 1996. Even though halibut are huge and require 80-pound test line with 20-ounce lead sinkers, they're not the fiercest fighting fish, and just about anyone can catch one on a good day's charter from Homer, Seward, or Whittier. It has a very white flesh with a fine texture—many Alaskans regard it as the most flavorful (and least fishy-tasting) fish.

Smelt

The fattiest fish in northern waters is the Pacific Coast eulachon, also known as smelt, hooligans, and candlefish (legend claims that the dried fish are so fatty they can be wicked and lit like candles). These silver and white fish are roughly as long and slender as pencils, and they run in monumental numbers for three weeks in early summer from Northern California to the Pribilofs. A traditional source of oil, the females are dumped into pits or vats by the ton and left to rot for two weeks. Then freshwater is added, and the whole mess is boiled, during which the oil rises to the surface. After skimming, straining, filtering, and sterilizing, roughly 20 gallons of oil (reminiscent of cod-liver oil) can be processed from a ton of female smelt. The early males, in addition, are good tasting whether cooked, smoked, dried, or salted.

History

PREHISTORY

The Athabascan Indians of Canada have a legend that tells how, in the misty past, one of their ancestors helped a giant in Siberia slay a rival. The defeated giant fell into the sea, forming a bridge to North America. The forefathers of the Athabascans then crossed this bridge, bringing the caribou with them. Eventually the giant's body decomposed, but parts of his skeleton were left sticking above the ocean to form the Aleutian Islands.

In scientific terms, what probably happened was that low ocean levels—up to 450 feet below those at present—offered the nomadic peoples of northeastern Asia a 50-mile-long, 600-mile-wide land "bridge" over the Bering Sea. There is considerable controversy over exactly when humans crossed this isthmus, but it was certainly used at least 12,000 years ago, and perhaps considerably earlier.

One of the earliest records of humans in the Americas is a caribou bone with a serrated edge found at Old Crow in northern Yukon. Almost certainly used as a tool, the bone has been placed at 27,000 years old by carbon dating. The interior lowlands of Alaska and the Yukon Valley, which were never glaciated, provided an ice-free migration route. As the climate warmed and the great ice sheets receded toward the Rocky Mountains and the Canadian Shield, a corridor opened down the middle of the Great

Plains, allowing movement farther south. (Recent scientific evidence suggests that ancient peoples also sailed or paddled along the coast from Asia to North America.)

The Athabascans

The Athabascans and other Paleo-Indians were the first people to cross the Bering land bridge. Their language is spoken today from Interior Alaska to the American Southwest (among Navajos and Apaches). Way back when (anywhere from 12,000 to 40,000 years ago), these people of the Interior followed the mastodon, mammoth, and caribou herds that supplied them with most of their necessities. Agriculture was unknown to them, but they did fashion basic implements from the raw copper found in the region. Eventually, certain groups found their way to the coast. The Athabascan-related Tlingits, for example, migrated down the Nass River near Prince Rupert and then spread north through Southeast Alaska. The rich environment provided them with abundant fish and shellfish, as well as with the great cedar logs from which they fashioned community houses, totem poles, and long dugout canoes.

The Aleut

Marine mammals and fish provided the Eskimo-related Aleuts with food, clothing, and household materials. The Aleut were famous for their tightly woven baskets. Before the 1740s arrival of the Russians, 25,000 Aleuts inhabited almost all of the Aleutian Islands, but by 1800 only about 2,000 survived. The ruthless Russian fur traders murdered and kidnapped the men, enslaved or abandoned the women, and passed on their genes and diseases so successfully that today only 1,000 full-blooded Aleuts remain. The rest intermarried with the Russians, and scattered groups of their descendants are now found in the eastern Aleutians and the Pribilofs to the North.

EUROPEAN EXPLORATION
Vitus Bering

In the early 1700s, long before the New World colonists began manifesting their destiny by pushing the American frontier west to the Pacific coast, Russian *promyshlenniki* (explorers and traders) were already busy pushing their own frontier east to the Pacific. After these land conquerors had delineated Russia's inhospitable northeastern edges, they were followed by indomitable sea explorers who cast off from the coasts in search of answers to questions that had intrigued Europeans since Marco Polo's *Travels*—mainly, whether or not Asia was joined with America, the mysterious land to the east that was vaguely outlined on then-contemporary maps.

Danish-born Vitus Bering, a sailor in the Russian navy for nearly 20 years, set out in 1725 for Kamchatka Peninsula, Siberia, on orders from Peter the Great. It took him and his crew three years, dragging rigging, cable, and anchors 2,000 miles over trackless wilderness and suffering innumerable deprivations to reach the coast, where their real journey into the uncharted waters of the North Pacific would begin. Bering built his first boat, *Gabriel,* and sailed past St. Lawrence Island (south of present-day Nome) and the Diomedes, but fog prevented him from glimpsing North America. He returned and wintered in Kamchatka, sailed again in the spring, and charted most of the Kamchatka coast, but foul weather and a shortage of provisions again precluded exploring farther east.

Over the next 10 years, Bering shuttled between Moscow and his beloved coast, submitting patiently to royal politics and ridicule from the leading scientists and cartographers while planning and outfitting (though not commanding) a series of expeditions that charted the rest of the Siberian coast and Japan.

Finally, in 1741, at the age of 60, Bering undertook his remarkable voyage to America.

© DON PITCHER

Alaska's Russian heritage is revealed in the presence of many Russian Orthodox churches.

Bruno de Heceta were ordered north from Mexico in 1774 and 1775. Spanish explorer Juan Francisco Quadra sailed as far north as Sitka in 1775 and 1779, but in the end, Spain failed to back up its claim with any permanent settlement north of San Francisco. It was Englishmen James Cook (in 1776-1780) and George Vancouver (in 1791-1792) who first carefully explored and charted this northern coast. In 1778, Cook landed on Vancouver Island, then sailed north all the way to what is now called Cook Inlet in Southcentral Alaska, in search of the Northwest Passage from the Atlantic. He continued to the Aleutians and entered the Bering Sea and the Arctic Ocean. A decade and a half later, Vancouver, aboard his ship HMS *Discovery,* charted the coast from California to Southeast Alaska and claimed the region for Britain. His was the first extensive exploration of Puget Sound and circumnavigation of Vancouver Island; his maps and charts of this confounding coast were so accurate that they were used for another 100 years.

Exploration by Land

Meanwhile, explorers were reaching the Pacific overland from bases in eastern Canada and the United States. In 1789 a Northwest Company trader, Alexander Mackenzie, paddled down the Mackenzie River to the Arctic Ocean. Four years later, in 1793, he became the first person to cross the entire continent by land, reaching the Pacific at Bella Coola, British Columbia. Other employees of the same aggressive Montreal-based company explored farther south. In 1808, Simon Fraser followed the Fraser River, stopping near the present site of the city of Vancouver; in 1810-1811 David Thompson traveled from the headwaters of the North Saskatchewan River to the mouth of the Columbia River, near present-day Portland. In 1803, after the United States purchased 827,000 square miles of territory west of the Mississippi River from France, President

Commanding the *St. Peter,* he sailed southeast from Kamchatka, came up south of the Aleutians, passed Kodiak, and sighted Mount St. Elias on the mainland. By that time Bering, along with 31 members of his crew, was in the final throes of terminal scurvy. He died in December 1741 and was buried on what is now Bering Island, the westernmost of the Aleutians. Meanwhile, his lieutenant, Alexis Chirikov, commanding the *St. Paul,* had reached all the way to the site of Sitka. After much hardship, survivors from both ships made it back to Siberia—with a load of sea otter pelts. This bounty from the New World prompted a rush of Russian hunters and traders to Alaska.

Conflicting Claims

Reports of Russian advances alarmed the Spanish, who considered the entire west coast of North America theirs. Juan Pérez and

Thomas Jefferson ordered a military fact-finding mission into the area. Led by Lewis and Clark, a group of explorers paddled up the Missouri River to its headwaters and crossed to the Columbia, which they followed to the Pacific (1804-1806), helping to open vast expanses of western North America. American fur traders followed close behind. (The Alaskan Interior was not properly explored, however, until the gold rush at the end of the 19th century.)

The Fur Trade

The excesses of the *promyshlenniki,* who had massacred and enslaved the Aleut, prompted the czar in 1789 to create the Russian America Company, headed by Grigori Shelikov, a fur trader and merchant who in 1784 had established the first permanent settlement in Alaska at Three Saints Bay on Kodiak Island. Alexander Baranov, a salesman in Siberia, was the first director of the company; he moved the settlement to present-day Kodiak town, and for the next 20 years Baranov *was* the law. One of the most powerful men in Alaskan history, he enslaved the remaining Aleuts, warred with the Panhandle Indians, initiated trade with the British, Spanish, and Americans, and sent his trading vessels as far away as Hawaii, Japan, and Mexico. Exhausting the resources of Kodiak and its neighborhood, he moved the company to Sitka, where, according to Merle Colby in his classic 1939 Works Progress Administration *Guide to Alaska,*

> from his wooden "castle" on the hill surmounting the harbor he made Sitka the most brilliant capital in the new world. Yankee sailors, thrashing around the Horn, beating their way up the California coast, anchored at last in Sitka harbor and found the city an American Paris, its streets crowded with adventurers from half the world away, its nights gay with balls illuminated by brilliant uniforms and the evening dresses of Russian ladies.

Except for the Tlingit Indians, who fought bitterly against Russian imperialism, Baranov's rule, extending from Bristol Bay in western Alaska to Fort Ross, California, was complete. His one last dream, of returning to Russia, was never fulfilled: On the voyage back to his homeland, Baranov died at the age of 72.

THE 19TH CENTURY
Political Units Form

In 1824 and 1825, Russia signed agreements with the United States and Britain, fixing the southern limit of Russian America at 54 degrees 40 minutes north latitude, near present-day Ketchikan. But the vast territory south of this line was left up for grabs. The American claim to the Oregon Territory around the Columbia River was based on its discovery by Robert Gray in 1792, and on the first overland exploration by Lewis and Clark. Britain based its claim to the region on its effective occupation of the land by the Northwest Company, which in 1821 merged with the Hudson's Bay Company. As American settlers began to inhabit the area, feelings ran high—President Polk was elected in 1846 on the slogan "Fifty-four Forty or Fight," referring to the proposed northern boundary between American and British territory in the Pacific Northwest. War between Britain and the United States was averted when both agreed to draw the boundary line to the Pacific along the 49th parallel, which remains to this day the Canada-U.S. border. Vancouver Island went to Britain, and the new Canadian nation purchased all the territorial holdings of the Hudson's Bay Company (Rupert's Land) in 1870. In 1871, British Columbia joined the Canadian Confederation on a promise from the leaders of the infant country of a railroad to extend there from the east.

The Russians Bail Out

The year 1863 was a difficult one for the Russian America Company. Back in the motherland, Russia's feudal society was breaking down, threatening the aristocracy's privileged status. In Alaska, competition from English and American whalers and traders was intensifying. Food was scarce, and supply ships from California were unreliable and infrequent. The worst, perhaps, was the dwindled numbers of fur seals and sea otters, hunted nearly to extinction over the past century. In addition, bad relations with Britain in the aftermath of the Crimean War (1853-1856) prompted Czar Alexander I to fear losing his far-flung Alaskan possessions to the British by force. Finally, the czar did not renew the company's charter, and the Russian America Company officially closed up shop.

Meanwhile, American technology was performing miracles. Western Union had laid two cables under the Atlantic Ocean from the United States to Europe, but neither had yet worked. So they figured, let's go the other way around the world: They proposed laying a cable overland through British Columbia, along the Yukon River, across the Bering Strait into Siberia, then east and south into Europe. In 1865, the Western Union Telegraph Expedition to Alaska, led by William Dall, surveyed the interior of Alaska for the first time, revealing its vast land and resources. This stimulated considerable interest in frontier-minded Washington, D.C. In addition, Czar Alexander's Alaska salesman, Baron Eduard de Stoeckl, was spending $200,000 of his own money to make a positive impression on influential politicians and journalists.

Secretary of State William H. Seward purchased Alaska on March 30, 1867, for the all-time bargain-basement price of $7.2 million—*two cents* per acre. The American flag was hoisted over Sitka on October 18, 1867. According to Ernest Gruening, first U.S. senator from Alaska:

A year later when the House of Representatives was called upon to pay the bill, skeptical congressmen scornfully labeled Alaska "Icebergia," "Walrussia," "Seward's Icebox," and "[President] Johnson's Polar Bear Garden." If American forces had not already raised the Stars and Stripes in Sitka, the House might have refused to pick up the tab.

Stoeckl, meanwhile, reimbursed himself the $200,000 he'd invested and sent the other $7 million home to Alexander. Subsequently, Alaska faded into official oblivion for the next 15 years—universally regarded as a frozen wasteland and a colossal waste of money.

Organic Act of 1884

This act organized Alaska for the first time, providing a territorial governor and law enforcement (though not a local legislature or representation in Washington). President Chester Arthur appointed federal district court judges, U.S. attorneys, and marshals. From 1884 to 1900, only one U.S. judge, attorney, and marshal managed the whole territory, all residing in the capital, Sitka. The first three appointees to the court in Sitka were removed in disgrace amidst charges of "incompetence, wickedness, unfairness, and drunkenness." A succession of scandals dogged other federal appointees—and that was only in Sitka; the vast Interior had no law at all until 1900, when Congress divided the territory into three legal districts, with courts at Sitka, Nome, and Eagle.

William H. Dall wrote of Alaska at that time as a place where "no man could make a legal will, own a homestead or transfer it, or so much as cut wood for his fire without defying a Congressional prohibition; where polygamy and slavery and the lynching of witches prevailed, with no legal authority to stay or punish criminals." Kipling's line, "There's never law of God or man runs north of 53," also refers to the young territory of Alaska. In contrast, Colby in

homesteader's cabin near Homer

his WPA guide commented that the gold-rush stampeders,

> although technically without civil authority, created their own form of self-government. The miners organized "miners meetings" to enforce order, settle boundary disputes, and administer rough and ready justice. Too often this form of government failed to cope with [serious problems] yet the profound instinct of the American people for self-government and their tradition of democracy made local self-government effective until the creation of the Alaska Legislature in 1912.

Gold!

Alaska's gold rush changed everything. After the California stampede of 1849, the search moved north. In 1858 there was a rush up the Fraser River to the Cariboo gold fields. In 1872, gold was found in British Columbia's Cassiar region. Strikes in Alaska and the Yukon

followed one another in quick succession: at Juneau (1880), Fortymile (1886), Circle (1893), Dawson City (1896), Nome (1899), Fairbanks (1902), and Iditarod (1908).

A mobile group of men and women followed these discoveries on riverboats, dogsleds, and foot, creating instant outposts of civilization near the gold strikes. Gold also caused the Canadian and American governments to take a serious look at their northernmost possessions for the first time; the beginnings of Alaska's administrative infrastructure date from those times. Still, in 1896, when Siwash George Carmack and his two Athabascan brothers-in-law discovered gold where Bonanza Creek flowed into the Klondike River in Yukon Territory, this vast northern wilderness could barely be called "settled." Only a handful of tiny nonnative villages existed along the Yukon River from Ogilvie and Fortymile in western Yukon to Circle and Fort Yukon in eastern Alaska, and a single unoccupied cabin sat on a beach at the mouth of the Skagway River at the terminus of the Inside Passage.

But by the end of 1897, perhaps 20,000 stampeders had skirted the lone cabin on their way to the headwaters of the Yukon and the sure fortunes in gold that awaited them on the Klondike. The two trails from Skagway over the coastal mountains and on to the interior rivers proved to be the most "civilized" and successful routes to Dawson. But the fortune-frenzied hordes proceeded north, uninformed, aiming at Dawson from every direction on the compass. They suffered every conceivable hardship and misery, from which death (often by suicide) was sometimes the only relief. And those who finally burst through the barrier and landed at the Klondike and Dawson were already two years too late to partake of the "ready" gold.

But the North had been conquered by whites. And by the time the gold rush had spread to Nome, Fairbanks, Kantishna,

Commissary 1898

© DON PITCHER

old shovels at historic Crow Creek Mine in Girdwood

THE 20TH CENTURY

In the first decade of the 20th century, the sprawling wilderness was starting to be tamed. The military set up shop at Valdez and Eagle to maintain law and order, telegraph cables were laid across the Interior, the Northwest Passage had been found, railroads were begun at several locations, vast copper deposits were being mined, and thousands of independent pioneer types were surviving on their own wits and the country's resources. Footpaths widened into wagon trails. Mail deliveries were regularized. Limited self-government was initiated: The capital moved to Juneau from Sitka in 1905; Alaska's first congressional delegate arrived in Washington in 1906; and a territorial legislature convened in 1912. A year later, the first people stood atop the south peak of Mount McKinley, and the surrounding area was set aside as a national park in 1917. At that time, Alaska's white and Native Alaskan populations had reached equivalency, at around 35,000 each. Judge James Wickersham introduced the first statehood bill to the U.S. Congress in 1916, but Alaska drifted along in federal obscurity until the Japanese bombed Pearl Harbor.

Hatcher Pass, and Hope, Alaska could finally be called settled (if not civilized).

The consequences of this Anglo invasion were devastating for the people who had lived in this harsh land for thousands of years. Epidemics of measles, influenza, and pneumonia swept through the Native Alaskan communities, particularly in 1900 and 1918, sometimes killing every person in a village. Rescuers found entire families who had frozen to death because they did not have enough strength to keep the fire going. The impact of these deaths, combined with the sudden arrival of whites who introduced alcohol, depleted game and other food sources, and then brought Christianity as a replacement for indigenous beliefs, was profound. The consequences still ripple across Alaska, most notably in the form of rampant alcoholism, which is a factor in many Native Alaskan accidents and suicides.

War

It has been said that war is good for one thing: the rapid expansion of communications and mobility technology. Alaska proves that rule. In the early 1940s, military bases were established at Anchorage, Whittier, Fairbanks, Nome, Sitka, Delta, Kodiak, Dutch Harbor, and the tip of the Aleutians, which brought an immediate influx of military and support personnel and services. In addition, in 1942 alone, thousands of miles of road were punched through the trackless wilderness, finally connecting Alaska to the rest of the world: the 1,440-mile Alaska Highway from Dawson Creek, B.C., to Delta, Alaska; the 50 miles of the Klondike Highway from Whitehorse to Carcross; the

151-mile Haines Highway; and the 328-mile Glenn Highway from Tok to Anchorage, among others. At the war's peak, 150,000 troops were stationed in the territory; all told, the U.S. government spent almost $1 billion there during the war. After the war, as after the gold rush, Alaska's population increased dramatically, with service members remaining or returning. The number of residents nearly doubled between 1940 and 1950.

Statehood

The 1950s brought a boom in construction, logging, fishing, and bureaucracy to Alaska. The decade also saw the discovery of a large oil reserve off the western Kenai Peninsula in the Cook Inlet. The population continued to grow, yet Alaskans still felt like residents of a second-class colony of the United States and repeatedly asked for statehood status through the decade. Finally, on July 7, 1958, Congress voted to admit Alaska into the Union as the 49th state. On January 3, 1959, President Dwight D. Eisenhower signed the official proclamation—43 years after Judge James Wickersham had first introduced the idea.

In the 92 years between Alaska becoming a U.S. territory and becoming a state, much of the land was split up into Navy petroleum reserves, Bureau of Land Management parcels, national wildlife refuges, power projects, and the like to be administered by separate federal agencies, including national park, forest, and military services. By the time Alaska gained statehood in 1959, only 0.003 percent of the land was privately owned—mostly homesteads and mining operations—and just 0.01 percent had been set aside for Native Alaskan reservations, administered by the Bureau of Indian Affairs. The Statehood Act allowed Alaska to choose 104 million acres, but the issue of Native Alaskan land ownership was not considered,

and it would take oil discoveries in the late 1960s to force redress for that injustice.

A little over five years after statehood, the Good Friday earthquake struck Southcentral Alaska; at 9.2 on the Richter scale, it remains the largest earthquake ever recorded in North America. But Alaskans quickly recovered and rebuilt with the plucky determination and optimism that still characterize the young state.

Oil Changes Everything

Alaska entered the big time, experiencing its most recent boom, in 1968 when Atlantic Richfield discovered a 10 billion-barrel oil reserve at Prudhoe Bay. The following year, Alaska auctioned off leases to almost 500,000 acres of oil-rich country on the North Slope. A consortium of oil company leaseholders immediately began planning the Trans-Alaska Pipeline to carry the crude from Prudhoe Bay to Valdez. But conservationists, worried about its environmental impact, and Native Alaskan groups, concerned about land-use compensation, filed suit, delaying construction for four years.

This impasse was resolved in 1971, when Congress passed the Alaska Native Claims Settlement Act (ANCSA), the most extensive compensation to any indigenous people in the history of the United States. It gave Alaska's aboriginal groups title to 44 million acres of traditional-use lands, plus $1 billion to be divided among all American citizens with at least 25 percent Athabascan, Eskimo, or Aleut blood. The act also created a dozen regional Native Alaskan corporations, a "13th Corporation" for Native Alaskans in the Lower 48, plus more than 200 village and urban Native Alaskan corporations.

The pipeline was built in 1974-1977. Again, after years of uncertainty, Alaska boomed, both in revenues and population. Since then, the state's economic fortunes have risen and fallen with the volatile price of oil.

Preserving the Wild Places

The Alaska Native Claims Settlement Act (ANCSA) of 1971 had designated 80 million acres to be withdrawn from the public domain and set aside as national parks, wildlife refuges, and other preserves by 1978. In the mid-late 1970s, in the wake of the completion of the pipeline, this was the raging land issue, generally divided between fiercely independent Alaskans who protested the further "locking up" of their lands by Washington bureaucrats, and conservationists who lobbied to preserve Alaska's wildlife and wilderness. When Congress failed to act, President Jimmy Carter took a bold move that forever changed the way Alaskan lands are managed; he withdrew 114 million acres of Alaskan lands as national monuments on December 1, 1978. The withdrawal still rankles the state's right-wing politicians, who regard it as a criminal act that should be prosecuted.

Two years later, with Ronald Reagan waiting to take over the reins of power, Carter signed into law one of the most significant pieces of environmental legislation ever enacted, the Alaska National Interest Lands Conservation Act (ANILCA). The act set aside 106 million acres of federal property as "public-interest lands," to be managed by the National Park and National Forest Services, the Fish and Wildlife Service, and other agencies. These "d2 lands" (from section 17:d-2 of ANCSA) included the expansion of Mount McKinley National Park (renamed Denali); the expansion of Glacier Bay and Katmai National Monuments, which became national parks; and the creation of Gates of the Arctic, Kobuk Valley, Wrangell-St. Elias, Kenai Fjords, and Lake Clark National Parks, plus the designation of numerous national monuments and preserves, scenic and wild rivers, and new wildlife refuges.

INTO A NEW CENTURY

The late 1990s were hard on Alaska, as oil prices dropped, pulp mills closed down, logging declined, and commercial fishing suffered from low prices and a market flooded with cheap farmed salmon from Chile, Norway, and British Columbia. But the first several years of the 21st century brought a reversal, with sky-high oil and gold prices, a big push to develop a natural gas pipeline across the state, increased tourism, higher prices for Alaska's wild salmon, and major political upheavals as FBI investigations threatened the oil industry's stranglehold on state government.

In 2006 voters did the unthinkable by voting to tax and regulate the cruise ship industry while simultaneously throwing out an incumbent governor (and former U.S. Senator), Frank Murkowski, and replacing him with an almost unknown politician named Sarah Palin. This was followed by a series of scandals in 2007-2008 that sent legislators to prison on corruption charges and eventually brought down Senator Ted Stevens. His conviction was later overturned, but not before voters had thrown him out of office in the 2008 election. For the first time in decades Alaska now has one Democrat (Mark Begich) in the U.S. Senate. Across the aisle is Republican Lisa Murkowski, first appointed to her seat in 2004 by her dad, Frank Murkowski. The lone representative, Republican Don Young, has been in office for decades.

Going Rogue

Even bigger news in 2008 was the sudden ascendancy of **Sarah Palin,** Alaska's then-governor. When John McCain brought her onto his ticket as the Republican vice presidential candidate, Palin garnered intense international attention—not all of it positive. She resigned in 2009 after 2.5 years in office, but she remains a figure on the national stage.

Government and Economy

GOVERNMENT

Like Delaware, Wyoming, Vermont, and North Dakota, Alaska has only one representative to the U.S. Congress, along with two senators. There are 20 state senators elected to four-year terms and 40 state representatives elected to two-year terms. They meet in the capitol in Juneau January-March. Local government is a mishmash of 16 first- and second-class boroughs, first- and second-class unincorporated villages, and tribal governments.

Alaskan politics start on the conservative end of the spectrum and head west from there. The state has long been solidly Republican, but in 2008 corruption charges brought down some of the most powerful Republicans, all the way up to "Uncle Ted" Stevens, whose power and tenacity were legendary. He was replaced by moderate Democrat Mark Begich; the other U.S. Senator is Republican Lisa Murkowski. Representative Don Young remains in power. As of 2013, Republicans have the governorship (Sean Parnell), both houses of the legislature, and two of the three congressional seats.

LAND USE AND MANAGEMENT

The vast majority of Alaska's 375 million acres is publicly owned, with less than 1 percent in private hands. Some 60 percent of this land is under federal management, with most of the rest in state or Native Alaskan corporation hands. Get complete details on Alaska's public lands from **Alaska Public Lands Information Centers** (www.alaskacenters.gov) in Anchorage (907/271-2737), Ketchikan, Tok, and Fairbanks.

National Park Service

In the federal scheme of things, the National Park Service gets all the glory. The national parks are the country's scenic showcases, and visitors come by the millions, usually to look, occasionally to experience. Denali National Park and Preserve—home to North America's highest mountain—is Alaska's most famous and overloved park, attracting well over one million tourists each year. Other well-known Alaskan national parks—Glacier Bay National Park and Preserve, Katmai National Park and Preserve, Kenai Fjords National Park, Klondike Gold Rush National Historical Park, Sitka National Historical Park, and Wrangell-St. Elias National Park and Preserve—are high on the list for travelers, and offer both visitors centers and various park activities. The other eight national parks and preserves (Aniakchak, Bering Land Bridge, Cape Krusenstern, Gates of the Arctic, Kobuk Valley, Lake Clark, Noatak, and Yukon-Charley Rivers) are so inaccessible that those with any facilities at all are prohibitively expensive for the average traveler, and the others are really no more than a name and a set of boundaries on the map.

People accustomed to national parks in the Lower 48 are surprised to find that very few trails run through Alaska's 15 parks. Most of the 54 million acres of national parkland are unforested and in the moist alpine tundra, where trails are not only unnecessary but largely detrimental to the ecology: As soon as the insulating ground cover is removed, the melting permafrost turns the trail into a muddy, impassable quagmire. Even in Denali, the only trails are around the park entrance and hotel area. Some parks (such as Denali, Glacier Bay, and Katmai) require backpacking permits; in the rest you're on your own. Several of the more accessible parks (Denali, Kenai Fjords, Klondike Gold Rush, Katmai, and Glacier Bay) have designated camping areas, but in the others you can pitch your tent on any level patch.

For details on national parks in Alaska, request brochures from the **National Park Service** in Anchorage (907/271-2737, www.nps.gov/akso).

Forest Service

In Alaska, the U.S. Forest Service manages the nation's two largest national forests: Tongass National Forest in Southeast Alaska and Chugach National Forest in Southcentral Alaska. These forests cover 23 million acres of land, much of which is forested, but also comprising high mountains, glaciers, lakes, large rivers, and wild coastlines. Two national monuments within the Tongass—Admiralty Island and Misty Fiords—are popular with travelers, and 19 wilderness areas cover 5.7 million acres in the Tongass.

Chugach is a popular recreation destination, with hundreds of miles of hiking trails and a number of campgrounds and visitor centers. Also within these forests are more than 180 wilderness cabins, a few of which are reachable by road or trail, with the others accessible only by floatplane or boat. You must reserve them well in advance through Recreation.gov (518/885-3639 or 877/444-6777, www.recreaton.gov, $9 reservation fee). Brochures describing the cabins are available from Forest Service offices or from Alaska Public Lands Information Centers in Anchorage, Fairbanks, Tok, and Ketchikan.

For additional information, contact **Tongass National Forest** (907/586-7928, www.fs.fed.us/r10/tongass) and **Chugach National Forest** (907/271-3992, www.fs.fed.us/r10/chugach).

Fish and Wildlife Service

The Fish and Wildlife Service manages 16 different refuges covering more than 75 million acres in Alaska. Most of these are in remote regions that see little visitation (other than local subsistence hunters and anglers), but they provide vital habitat for birds and other animals. The best-known Alaskan refuges are Arctic National Wildlife Refuge on the North Slope, Kenai National Wildlife Refuge on the Kenai Peninsula, and Kodiak National Wildlife Refuge on Kodiak Island. Kenai sees the most tourists and has a visitors center, hiking trails, canoe routes, and campgrounds. Kodiak has a visitors center plus a number of public-use cabins available for rent. A large new visitors center in Homer provides a great introduction to the Alaska Maritime National Wildlife Refuge, which sprawls across 2,500 Alaskan islands. The nation's largest refuge (20 million acres) is Yukon Delta National Wildlife Refuge in Western Alaska. For details on all 16 refuges, contact the **Fish and Wildlife Service** (907/786-3909, http://alaska.fws.gov).

Bureau of Land Management

Alaska's largest land-management agency (over 90 million acres) is the Bureau of Land Management (BLM, 907/271-5960, www.blm.gov/ak). Most BLM land is undeveloped, but three popular recreation sites—White Mountains National Recreation Area, Chena River State Recreation Area, and Steese Natural Conservation Area—feature a handful of hiking trails, campgrounds, and public cabins in the vicinity of Fairbanks.

State Lands

The State of Alaska owns 89 million acres—almost a quarter of the state—and manages this land for a variety of purposes, from mineral and oil development to state forests. The state manages more than 110 state parks and recreation areas spread over three million acres. Located in western Alaska, Wood-Tikchik State Park is the largest state park in the country, encompassing 1.5 million acres. More accessible—it's the most popular state park in Alaska—is Chugach State Park, which covers nearly 500,000 acres bordering Anchorage. Most of these state parks and recreation sites have trails and campgrounds. Camping fees are typically $10 per night, with some parks charging a $5 day-use fee. A number of state parks have public-use cabins for $65 per night.

For additional state park information call 907/269-8400 to request brochures and a statewide park map, or visit www.alaskastateparks. org. You can also use this website to check cabin availability; reservations are made at Department of Natural Resources public information offices in Anchorage or Fairbanks or at state park offices.

The Alaska Department of Fish and Game manages more than 30 state refuges, critical habitat areas, and wildlife sanctuaries, including the world-famous bear-viewing area at McNeil River and the Walrus Islands near Dillingham. It also jointly manages (with the Forest Service) the Pack Creek brown bear-viewing area on Admiralty Island. Also popular is Creamer's Field Migratory Waterfowl Refuge in Fairbanks. The agency issues sport-fishing and hunting permits. For details on all its activities, contact the **Alaska Department of Fish and Game** (907/267-2253, www.adfg. alaska.gov).

Native Lands

Today, the 12 regional Native Alaskan corporations and more than 200 village and urban corporations created in 1971 by the ANCSA own some 37 million acres in Alaska. Much of this is closed to public access except with special permits; fees are commonly charged.

The ANCSA attempted to bring Native Alaskans into the mainstream of society, and it has succeeded in some ways while failing in others. Surprisingly, the corporations created by the act have become primary forces in logging, mining, and other developments around the state, in sharp contrast to the preserve-the-land policies that might have been anticipated. In parts of Southeast and Southcentral Alaska the Native Alaskan lands have been nearly all logged over; I know of one place where they logged almost within spitting distance of a

Native Alaskan cemetery and historic clan house. (Of course, these developments are driven by money, since corporations need profits to survive and to pay dividends to their Native Alaskan shareholders.)

COST OF LIVING

No doubt about it—this place is expensive. Alaska ranks near the top in cost of living among all the states. Numerous factors conspire to keep prices high. Most consumer goods must be imported from the Lower 48, and transportation costs are tacked on along the way. In addition, the transportation and shipping rates within Alaska are similarly high, further inflating the cost of goods and services. In more remote regions especially, lack of competition coupled with steady demand ensures top-dollar prices. And let's not forget how long and cold and dark Alaskan winters are: The cost of heat and utilities is a hardship, and Alaska ranks first in per capita energy consumption in the United States.

Prices in the North are much higher than Outside, and are generally the worst in the most remote bush communities. Food costs in places such as Galena or Fort Yukon are more than twice those in Anchorage. Even in Homer—which is on the road system—food is 20 percent more expensive than in Anchorage.

MONEY FOR NOTHIN'

In 1976, with oil wealth about to come gushing out of the south end of the pipeline, voters approved a state constitutional amendment calling for a percentage of all oil and mineral revenues to be placed in a **Permanent Fund** (www.apfc.org). Money from this account can only be used for investment, not for state operating expenses, which explains why, during recent Alaskan recessions, when hundreds of state workers were laid off and state funds were severely cut back, billions of surplus dollars sat untouched in the fund. It's the only one of its kind in the country, the only state fund that pays dividends to residents, and the largest pool of public money in the country. In 2011 it totaled more than $33 *billion*.

A portion of the interest and capital gains income from these assets is distributed to all Alaska residents—even children—in a yearly Permanent Fund Dividend check sent out each October. In 1982, the first year of the dividend, each Alaskan received $1,000, but it didn't reach that level again until the stock market boom of the late 1990s, when it topped out at nearly $2,000. The 2012 payout was around $900 per person. All this sudden cash doesn't go unnoticed by local businesses, especially car dealers, furniture stores, and airlines, who put out a plethora of special deals as soon as the money hits the banks.

MAKING A LIVING
Employment

Anyone thinking of moving to Alaska to get rich is in for a rude awakening. For a number of years after the oil boom, Alaskans earned the most per capita of any state, Alaska now ranks 8th for income—and near the top for cost of living. The state's unemployment figures are usually several percentage points above the national average, even during the peak summer season.

Despite this, you can still come to Alaska and make a decent living; after all, most Alaskans came from somewhere else (only a third of Alaskans were born in the state—the second-lowest such percentage in the country). But the opportunities, it should be stressed, are limited. For example, almost a third of the people collecting a paycheck in Alaska work for federal, state, or local government. And the industry that accounts for 87 percent of state revenues (oil and gas) accounts for just 3 percent of employment. The real growth of late has come at the bottom end, in service jobs and retail sales, where your income would probably leave

you officially listed with poverty status. So if a job as a Wal-Mart stocker is your dream, hop on the next flight to Anchorage.

For employment information, visit the Alaska Department of Labor's **Job Bank** (www.jobs.state.ak.us), with an up-to-date listing of openings around the state. Here you'll find details on jobs in all sectors, including seasonal cannery work, state positions, and relocation information.

Fishing

Alaska's fisheries account for over half of the country's commercial fish production. Three-quarters of the value is in groundfish (pollock and cod) and salmon, the rest in shellfish, halibut, herring, and others. Alaska produces almost all of the U.S. canned-salmon stock (200 million pounds), and eight Alaskan ports are among the country's top 50 producers, with Dutch Harbor/Unalaska almost always in the top three, and Kodiak not far behind.

Alaska's fisheries are probably the most carefully managed in the country, with healthy stocks of wild salmon and halibut. Fish farming is illegal in Alaska, but farmed salmon from other areas flooded the market in the 1990s. Since then, there has been a resurgence in demand for high-quality Alaskan wild salmon as consumers see problems caused by the farm-raised version—not to mention the difference in taste.

Learn more about Alaska's seafood industry (and get some good salmon and halibut recipes) from the **Alaska Seafood Marketing Institute** (www.alaskaseafood.org).

Agriculture

The percentage of Alaska's land used for farming is as minuscule as the percentage of Alaska's total economy that is accounted for by agriculture. Of the state's 375 million acres (17 million of it suitable for farming), only 910,000 acres are considered cultivable; of those, only 31,000 acres are occupied by crops. The Matanuska Valley (Palmer and Wasilla) and the Tanana Valley (Fairbanks and Delta) contain almost 90 percent of Alaska's usable farmland. Hay, potatoes, barley, and oats are the state's top agricultural products. Despite this, there has been a remarkable growth in small farms across Alaska, with summertime farmers markets from Sitka to Fairbanks.

In addition to legal crops, Alaska is famous for marijuana, and that crop is widely regarded as the state's biggest moneymaker. Cannabis-growing operations (most are indoor operations) are especially big in the Matanuska Valley. Medical marijuana was approved by the voters in 1998, but a measure to legalize pot failed in 2004.

Gold and Minerals

Thirty million ounces of gold were taken from Alaska between 1880 and 1980. Today, the Fort Knox Mine near Fairbanks is Alaska's biggest gold producer, extracting 1,000 ounces of gold per day.

Zinc is the state's most valuable mineral, mined at the enormous Red Dog Mine, 90 miles north of Kotzebue. The largest zinc mine in the world, it produces 575,000 tons of zinc and 100 million tons of lead per year. Coal is mined at Usibelli, near Denali National Park, and deposits of jade, molybdenum, chromite, nickel, platinum, and uranium are known, though the cost of mining in remote Alaska limits these ventures.

One highly controversial mine does not yet exist. Located in the upper reaches of the Bristol Bay watershed (home to the world's most productive red salmon fisheries) is an enormous gold, copper, and molybdenum deposit known as **Pebble Creek.** The mining company talks of valuations in the hundreds of *billions* of dollars, and a massive open pit mine has been proposed on the site. It is opposed, however, by an unlikely coalition that includes

fishers, Native Alaskan corporations, environmentalists, and wealthy lodge owners. Get their version at www.renewableresourcescoalition.org, and the mining company's story at www.pebblepartnership.com.

Oil and Gas

Everything that moves in Alaska is lubricated with oil, primarily North Slope crude. Without oil, the Alaskan economy would stiffen, shatter, and disappear into thin air. Oil and gas revenues account for 87 percent of the state's tax revenue. Alaska is so addicted to oil revenue that when the price of a barrel of oil drops by $1, the budget must be adjusted by $150 million. Though the industry accounts for just 3 percent of the total workforce, the average annual salary for these workers is $100,000. Few elected officials would dare speak out against the oil companies; they all know who pays the tab when election bills come in, and they don't want that cash going to their opponents.

At more than 350 million barrels of oil per year, Alaska accounts for around 17 percent of the nation's oil production, second only to Texas. Peak production was in 1988, when 738 million barrels of Prudhoe crude flowed through the pipeline. The Prudhoe Bay oilfield, the largest in North America and 18th in the world, had produced 14 billion barrels by 2003, but production continues to decline.

Enormous quantities of natural gas lie beneath the North Slope, and proposals have been made to build a gas pipeline paralleling the existing oil line, or to develop a gas-to-liquids technology so that the gas can be sent down the existing oil pipeline. Higher gas prices and increased demand may finally lead to its development within the next decade. In addition to the North Slope, both oil and gas are produced from offshore wells in Cook Inlet. The natural gas is used in Anchorage and Kenai, but production has declined in recent years.

Tourism

Tourism is Alaska's third-largest industry, behind petroleum production and commercial fishing. It's also the second-largest employer, accounting for thousands of seasonal jobs. More than one million visitors travel to Alaska each year, 90 percent of them arriving May-September from the continental United States and Canada. Approximately half of all visitors (including business travelers) travel independently; the rest come up on cruise ships and package tours.

Native Corporations

Native corporations are major players in Alaska's economy, and they also have large investments (we're talking billions of dollars) spread all over the nation. The corporations include **Arctic Slope Regional Corporation** (www.asrc.com), **Cook Inlet Regional Corporation (CIRI)** (www.ciri.com), **Chugach Alaska Corporation** (www.chugach-ak.com), **Doyon, Limited** (www.doyon.com), and **NANA Regional Corporation** (www.nana.com). Doyon, with more than 12 million acres, is the largest corporate landholder in the nation.

All of these companies are involved in tourism ventures around Alaska, but CIRI and NANA especially have major investments in tour companies, hotels, and other facilities. Another company that travelers to Southeast Alaska will certainly come into contact with is the Juneau-based village **Goldbelt Corporation** (www.goldbelt.com), which runs the Mount Roberts Tram, a hotel, and various other operations. If you travel in the North, you'll probably spend time in a Native Alaskan-owned facility or on one of their tour boats or buses.

The People

As of 2012, Alaska's population was 722,000. Of this, roughly 15 percent are of Native Alaskan descent. The nonnative population is predominantly white, with a small percentage of black, Hispanic, Asian, and Pacific Islanders. The Hispanic and Asian populations are growing rapidly in Alaska, and visitors to bush towns are often surprised to find that many of the restaurants are owned by Korean Americans, the cab drivers may be from the former Yugoslavia, and the cannery workers come from the Philippines or Mexico. Of course, the cruise ships that ply Inside Passage waters are staffed by workers from all over the globe. Anchorage has by far the most diverse population; more than one-third of its residents are Latino, Asian, black, or Native Alaskan.

ALASKAN NATIVES

Alaska Native people come from five cultural groupings: Athabascan; Aleutiq; Yup'ik and Cup'ik; Inupiaq and St. Lawrence Island Yupik; and Eyak, Tlingit, Haida, and Tsimshian. With intermarriage and migration the cultural groupings have blurred somewhat, but Native Alaskans are very proud of their heritage. Southcentral Alaska Natives were historically from two groups: Athabascan and Aleutiq. Athabascan peoples lived in interior parts of the region, while Aleutiq primarily occupied the coastline. On the Kenai Peninsula there are places where different groups were next to each other, with Kenaitze Dena'ina Athabascans in a village just a few miles from an Aleutiq settlement.

Athabascans

Nomadic hunters and migrants, the Athabascans are related to the Tlingit of Southeast Alaska and the Navajo and Apache of the American Southwest. They subsisted on salmon and the Interior's mammals, mostly caribou and moose. They passed the cruel winters in tiny villages of no more than six houses, with a *kashim,* or community center, as the focal point. They ice-fished and trapped in the dark, using dogsleds as transportation. Their arts were expressed primarily in beautifully embroidered clothing and beadwork. The men remained constantly occupied with survival tasks—finding food, building houses, and maintaining gear. When the first white explorers and traders arrived in the early 19th century, the Athabascans immediately began to trade with them, learning the new cultures and in turn educating the newcomers in local customs and skills, not the least of which was dogsledding.

Aleuts

As the Athabascans were almost entirely land-based people, the Aleuts (some prefer the terms Alutiiq or Sugpiaq) were almost entirely dependent on the sea. Clinging to the edge of tiny, treeless, windswept Aleutian Islands, they lived in small dwellings made of sealskin-covered frames, with fireplaces in the middle and steam baths attached on the sides. They made sea otter skins into clothing and processed walrus and seal intestines into parkas. Their kayaks (called *bidarka*) were made of marine mammal skins stretched over a wooden or whalebone frame. Basketry was their highest artistic achievement, and their dances were distinctly martial, with masks, rattles, and knives.

When the Russians invaded the Aleutians in the mid-1700s like furies from hell, around 25,000 Aleuts inhabited almost all the Aleutian Islands and the southern portion of the Alaska Peninsula. Within 50 years, over half had died through violence, starvation, or disease. Most of the rest became slaves and were dispersed around the New World to hunt the sea otter and fight for the Russians. In fact, Aleuts traveled as far south as Catalina Island off the Southern California coast, wiping out the Gabrieliño Indians there, along with the entire otter population, in 1810. Many of the women served as concubines to the Russian overlords, further diluting the Aleut lineage. Today, most Aleuts carry only half or a quarter Aleut blood; only 1,000 are considered full-blooded.

NATIVE ARTS AND CRAFTS

Not unlike most other aboriginal cultures, Native Alaskan arts and crafts were intricately intertwined with animism, religious ceremony, and utility. Each group worked with its abundant natural resources to produce all the necessities of a lifestyle in which subsistence, religion, and artistic expression were inseparable.

Alaskan tourism and Native Alaskan crafts have gone hand in hand since the first Russian stepped ashore. When John Muir arrived in Wrangell by steamer in 1890, he wrote,

> There was a grand rush on shore to buy curiosities and see totem poles. The shops were jammed and mobbed, high prices paid for shabby stuff manufactured expressly for tourist trade. Silver bracelets hammered out of dollars and half dollars by Indian smiths are the most popular articles, then baskets, yellow cedar toy canoes, paddles, etc. Most people who travel look only at what they are directed to look at. Great is the power of the guidebook-maker, however ignorant.

A similar observation holds today, especially in the shops selling made-in-China Alaskan trinkets or carved-in-Bali totem poles and masks. When buying Native Alaskan handicrafts from anyone other than the artist, always look for the **Silver Hand** logo that identifies the work as an authentic Native Alaskan piece. Get details from the **Alaska State Council on the Arts** (907/269-6610 or 888/278-7424, www.eed. state.ak.us/aksca/native.htm). Good places to buy Native Alaskan crafts are the various museum gift shops or directly from the artisans, if you visit remote villages.

Ivory

The Inupiat Eskimo of northern coastal Alaska are renowned for their use of ivory, harvested only by Native Alaskans from the tusks and teeth of walrus, as well as ivory from woolly mammoths and giant mastodons uncovered by miners or erosion. The ivory is carved, also known as "scrimshawed," and made into various implements. Today you'll see ivory jewelry, *ulu* handles, cribbage boards, and the like. The use of ivory for handicrafts is severely restricted by federal regulations established to protect the walrus. Native carvers can carve on ivory obtained from walrus killed for subsistence food, and nonnatives can legally carve on fossilized ivory (darker-colored ivory that was buried in the ground). But don't make the mistake of buying an ivory piece and then taking it through Canada, unless you have a written permit from the Convention on Trade in Endangered Species (www.cites.org). Avoid border confiscations and other legal problems by mailing your pieces home. You won't have any problems carrying them onboard an aircraft, unless your plane lands outside the United States.

Baskets

All Native Alaskan groups used available resources to fashion baskets for storage, carrying, and cooking. Birch-bark baskets, often lashed with spruce roots, were made by the forest Athabascans. The coastal Haida, Tlingit, and Tsimshian Indians used the bark of big cedar trees. They also made entire baskets of spruce roots, occasionally weaving in maidenhead ferns for decoration. The Yup'ik and Aleut indigenous people of Western Alaska are known for small, delicate baskets fashioned from coastal rye grass. They also process baleen, the long strips of cartilage-like teeth that hang from the upper jaw of whales, and weave the strips into baskets.

The finest examples of the different baskets are displayed in the largest Alaskan museums; commercial baskets sell for anywhere from $40 for simple birch-bark trays to several thousand dollars for large baleen baskets.

Masks

Each Native Alaskan culture had its traditional mask-making technology and its complex ceremonial uses for masks. Eskimo mask art and ritual were among the most highly developed in the world. Masks, like totems, represented the individual animals and birds that were worshipped, and each mask was believed to embody the spirit, or *inua,* of the animal. The masks of the Athabascans were worn by dancers, accompanied by a tribal choir, to dramatize the tribe's relationship to animal spirits as well as to entertain guests at feasts. Some believe Aleut masks symbolized the faces of ancient inhabitants of the western Alaska archipelago, though these people were only distantly related to the Aleut, if at all.

The use of masks has declined in Native Alaskan cultures, and the art of mask-making isn't as prevalent today as it's said to have been before contact with the Western world. But you will see commercial masks in Native Alaskan galleries and gift shops around the North; these bear a close resemblance to those of long ago.

Other Pieces

Fur parkas are the quintessential Eskimo garment and are available in remote villages and at shops in Anchorage and Fairbanks. The finest of these are custom-made and cost a small fortune; ask locally for the best seamstresses. Beautifully crafted **dolls** are a hallmark of Eskimo artists who typically use furs and other local materials. Other distinctively Alaskan items include **dance fans, beadwork,** and handcrafted silver or jade **jewelry.**

ESSENTIALS

Getting There and Around

BY AIR

Ted Stevens Anchorage International Airport (www.anchorageairport.com) is the hub for air travel into Alaska. The state's flagship carrier, **Alaska Airlines** (800/426-0333, www.alaskaair.com), has jet service to all the larger cities and towns in Alaska, as well as throughout the United States (including Hawaii) and all the way to Mexico, and the Alaska Air mileage plan is considered one of the best in the business.

Many of the big domestic carriers fly into and out of Anchorage from the Lower 48, including **Alaska Airlines** (800/426-0333, www. alaskaair.com), **American** (800/433-7300, www.aa.com), **Delta** (800/221-1212, www.delta.com), **Frontier** (800/432-1359, www.flyfrontier.com), **JetBlue** (800/538-2583, www.jetblue.com), **Sun Country Airlines** (800/359-6786, www.suncountry.com), and **United** (800/241-6522, www.united.com).

The following companies offer nonstop international service into Anchorage: **Air Canada** (888/247-2262, www.aircanada.com) from Vancouver, **Korean Air** (800/438-5000, www.koreanair.com) from Seoul, **Condor Airlines** (800/524-6975, www.condor.com) from

© DON PITCHER

© DON PITCHER

Alaska Airlines, the state's flagship carrier

Frankfurt, **Iceland Air** (800/223-5500, www.icelandair.us) from Reykjavik, and **Vladivostok Air** (www.vladivostokavia.ru/en) from Russia.

Regional Airlines

Alaska Airlines serves most larger towns around the state, including Fairbanks, Barrow, Nome, Bethel, Yakutat, Kodiak, and Dillingham. **Era Alaska** (907/266-8394 or 800/866-8394, www.flyera.com) has multiple flights daily connecting Anchorage with Homer and Kenai.

By Bush Plane

Flying in a real live Alaska bush plane is a spectacular way to see the state, and it's also the only practical way to access the vast majority of Alaska's roadless areas. You will never forget your first flight over Alaska, whether it's a floatplane heading to a lakeside lodge or a tiny Super Cub taking you to a remote wilderness camp. These airlines have regularly scheduled, though expensive, flights to towns and attractions that either have no public ground transportation or simply can't be reached overland—which accounts for more than three-quarters of the state. For many people who live in Alaska's bush, these planes provide a lifeline of mail, food, and supplies. The planes seat 2-12 passengers, and they fly for the regular fare no matter how many passengers are aboard (if the weather is cooperating).

But if you're heading to a really remote cabin, fjord, river, glacier, or park, that's when you'll encounter the famous Alaskan bush pilots, with their equally famous charter rates, which can make Alaska Airlines' fares look like the bargain of the century. Still, you'll have quite a ride—landing on tiny lakes with pontoons, on snow or ice with skis, on gravel bars with big fat tires, loaded to the gills with people, equipment, extra fuel, tools, mail, supplies, and anything else under the sun. Make sure you agree on all the details beforehand—charges, drop-off and pickup times and locations, emergency

Bush planes fly to the most remote corners of Alaska.

and alternative procedures, and tidal considerations. Never be in much of a hurry; time is told differently up here, and many variables come into play, especially the weather. If you're well prepared for complications and have a flexible schedule and a loose attitude, one of these bush hops will no doubt be among your most memorable experiences in Alaska, worth every penny and minute that you spend.

As far as what you can expect to pay, most flightseeing operations have preset itineraries and prices. Some companies flying out of the larger towns also have set rates to some of the more popular destinations. However, for most drop-off trips, you pay for the ride according to engine hours, both coming and going. So if your destination is a spot that's an hour from the airstrip, you pay for four hours of engine time (an hour out and an hour back, twice).

Safety in the Air

Before you head out into the wild blue yonder,

there are a few things you should know. Alaska has far more than its share of fatal airplane crashes every year, generally 3-4 times the national average for small planes. These have happened to even the best pilots flying for even the most conscientious companies, but certain operators cut corners in safety and allow their pilots to fly under risky weather conditions. You can't avoid all risks, of course, but you can improve your odds by taking a few precautions of your own.

First and foremost, you should choose your pilot and flight service with care. Just because someone has a pilot's license and is flying in Alaska doesn't mean that he or she is a seasoned bush pilot. You're well within your rights to ask about the pilot's qualifications, and about time spent flying *in Alaska*. The oft-repeated saying is, "There are old pilots and there are bold pilots, but there are no old bold pilots." Given a choice, you want an "old" one—not so much in chronological years, but one that has been flying in and out of the bush for a good long time. Ask locally about the air safety record of the various companies. Also ask which companies have the contracts with the Forest Service or other federal agencies, since they tend to be ones that aren't allowed to take chances. You can also search the Web for accident statistics for a specific company at the **National Transportation Safety Board's** website (www.ntsb.gov).

Even if you're just going on a 30-minute flightseeing tour, wear clothing appropriate for the ground conditions. Unplanned stops because of weather or mechanical problems aren't unusual. Warm comfortable hiking clothes, rain gear, and lightweight boots or sturdy shoes make reasonable bush plane apparel.

Weather is a major limiting factor in aviation. Small planes don't operate on airline-type schedules, with arrivals and departures down to the minute. Leave yourself plenty of leeway when scheduling trips, and don't pressure your pilot to get you back to the airstrip so you won't miss your bus, boat, train, dogsled ride, or salmon bake. More than one crash has been the result of subtle or not-so-subtle pressure by clients to fly when it was against the pilot's better judgment. Never pressure a pilot to fly, and always try to act as a second pair of eyes to look for any signs of danger, such as other aircraft in the vicinity.

Before taking off, your pilot should brief all passengers on the location of safety and survival equipment and airsickness bags, how to exit during an emergency landing (or crash), and the location and function of the Emergency Locator Transmitter (ELT) and survival kit. Ear protection may also be supplied, as most small planes are quite noisy. Just in case, buy a set of foam earplugs at a sporting-goods store before you go to the airport. They weigh nothing and are perfectly adequate for aircraft noise levels.

You'll probably be asked how much you weigh (don't be coy—lives are at stake) and told where you should sit. Weight and balance are critical in little planes, so don't whine about not getting to sit up front if you're told otherwise. Many companies place severe restrictions on how much gear they carry, charging excess baggage fees over a certain limit (sometimes less than 50 pounds).

Gear stowage can be a challenge in small planes, especially when transporting people who are heading out on long expeditions. Don't even think of showing up at the airfield with hard-sided luggage. Internal-frame backpacks, duffel bags, and other soft, easily compressed and stowed items are much easier to handle. Don't strap sleeping bags and other gear onto the outside of a pack. Lots of small items are much easier to arrange and find homes for than a few bulky things. Also, if you're carrying a canister of red pepper spray to deter bears, tell the pilot beforehand and follow directions for stowage. Pilots don't want the stuff inside the cabin (imagine what might happen if it went off in this enclosed space), but they'll store it in a float if the plane is so equipped, or you may be able to strap it to a strut with duct tape.

Whenever you fly, leave a flight route, destination, expected departure and arrival times, and a contact number for the flight service with a reliable friend. Then relax and enjoy the scenery. Flying in Alaska is a tremendous experience, one that relatively few people get to enjoy, and in spite of all the cautionary notes above, it is still a generally safe and reliable way to get to and see the wilderness.

FERRY SERVICE

The **Alaska Marine Highway** (907/465-3941 or 800/642-0066, www.dot.state.ak.us/amhs) operates two primary state networks: one from Bellingham, Washington and throughout Southeast Alaska; the other through Southcentral Alaska from Cordova all the way to Dutch Harbor in the Aleutians. In addition, a ferry sails between Whittier and

© DON PITCHER

Alaska Marine Highway ferries provide connections from Homer, Whittier, and Seldovia.

Juneau twice monthly in the summer, linking the two regions.

In Southcentral Alaska, Alaska Marine Highway ferries serve the communities of Whittier, Homer, and Seldovia. There is no ferry service to Anchorage or Seward. From Whittier, the ferries head east to Valdez and Cordova. From Homer, ferries head to Seldovia and on to Kodiak, with once-monthly summer sailings to the Aleutians.

The ferries have a relaxed and slow-paced atmosphere; it's impossible to be in a hurry here. Many travelers think of the ferry as a floating motel—a place to dry off, wash up, rest up, sleep, and meet other travelers while at the same time moving on to new sights and new adventures. Ferry food is reasonably priced and quite good, but many budget travelers stock up on groceries before they board. The hot water is free in the cafeteria if you're trying to save bucks by bringing along Cup-O-Noodles and instant oatmeal.

Staterooms or Solarium?

Alaska state ferries carry both passengers and vehicles, and offer food service, stateroom cabins, showers, storage lockers, gift shops, and cocktail lounges. Staterooms offer privacy, as well as a chance to get away from the hectic crowding of midsummer. These cabins have two or four bunk beds, and some also include private baths; other folks use the baths and showers down the hall.

If you don't mind hearing others snoring or talking nearby, you can save a bundle and make new friends with fellow voyagers. There's generally space to stretch out a sleeping bag in the recliner lounge (an inside area with airline-type seats), as well as in the solarium—a covered and heated area high atop the ship's rear deck. The solarium has several dozen deck chairs to sit and sleep on, and it can get so popular that at some embarkation points there's a mad dash to grab a place. To be assured of a deck chair, get in line five hours ahead of time if you're coming aboard in Bellingham in midsummer. When the weather is good you're also likely to see the rapid development of a tent city on the rear deck, often held down with duct tape (sold in gift shops on board).

Getting Tickets

The ferries operate year-round. Get schedules and make reservations by calling or going online (907/465-3941 or 800/642-0066, www. dot.state.ak.us/amhs). Reservations for the summer can be made as early as December, and travelers taking a vehicle should book as early as possible to be sure of a space. The ferry system charges an extra fee to carry bicycles, canoes, kayaks, and inflatable boats.

CRUISE SHIPS

For many people, particularly retirees, cruise ships offer a luxury way to see Alaska. A multitude of ships ply Alaska's Inside Passage and Gulf of Alaska waters, carrying nearly one million people each summer—two-thirds of all travelers to the state. Most ships depart from Vancouver, British Columbia, but some cruises also leave from Seattle or San Francisco. Many ships turn around in either Whittier or Seward, where buses or trains take passengers on to Anchorage to fly out or join a ground-based tour.

A good overall place to begin an exploration of cruise ship travel is the website of the **Cruise Lines International Association** (www. cruising.org). It has links to all the major players, plus general information. For specifics on Alaska cruising—including links to all the companies—visit www.alaskacruisingreport.com.

TRAIN

The **Alaska Railroad** (907/265-2494 or 800/544-0552, www.alaskarailroad.com) runs 470 miles between Seward and Fairbanks with a 7-mile spur between Portage and Whittier; it is the only state-owned railroad in the United States. The train—historic and a bit exotic—is also much roomier and slower than a tour bus but is about the same price (and is occasionally even on time). Dining service is available, and helpful tour guides are on board in the summer months. In addition, some of the trains will make flag stops to pick up hikers or people living in the Alaskan bush.

Two daily expresses (mid-May-mid-Sept.), one northbound and one southbound, run between Anchorage and Fairbanks ($167 one-way). The train connects Anchorage to Denali ($117) and Fairbanks to Denali ($51). The train also connects Seward with Anchorage ($79) and Anchorage with Whittier ($74) daily in the summer. The railroad has luxurious double-deck "GoldStar" cars ($202 for Anchorage to Denali) and a variety of package tours that combine train rides with boat trips and other activities. Princess Tours and Gray Line of Alaska hook double-decker superdome coaches to the end of the express trains in the summer.

A variety of rail-lodging and rail-lodging-boat tour options are listed in Alaska Railroad's brochure or online. Especially popular is the **Spencer Glacier float tour** ($211 round-trip from Anchorage), where the train stops in the Kenai Mountains for an easy rafting trip down the Placer River; return to Anchorage by motorcoach. Day-hikers and backpackers can also take advantage of special whistle-stop service at Spencer Glacier ($109 round-trip); the Forest Service provides free campsites near Spencer Lake a one-mile hike from here. **The Ascending Path** (907/783-0505, www.theascendingpath.com) leads a number of glacier hiking trips to the glacier, with access via the Alaska Railroad; see their website for details on these and other options.

BUSES

A number of companies provide bus or van service around Southcentral Alaska, including **Alaska/Yukon Trails** (907/479-2277 or 800/770-7275, www.alaskashuttle.com), **Alaska Bus Guy** (907/720-6541, www.alaskabusguy.com), **Anchorage Denali Express** (907/376-1992 or 877/376-1992, www.anchoragedenaliexpress.com), **Park Connection** (907/245-0200 or 800/266-8625, www.alaskacoach.com), **Seward Bus Lines** (907/563-0800 or 888/420-7788, www.sewardbuslines.net), **The Stage Line** (907/868-3914, www.stagelineinhomer.com), and **Interior Alaska Bus Line** (907/883-0207 or 800/770-6652, www.interioralaskabusline.com).

Green Tortoise (415/956-7500 or 800/867-8647, www.greentortoise.com) is more than just a bus ride—it's a vacation and a cultural experience in itself. The buses have bunks that convert to seats and tables in the day, and passengers enjoy communal meals. Green Tortoise has several trips each summer to Alaska: Some trips leave from San Francisco and wind up in Anchorage; others start and end in Anchorage.

CARS

Driving around Alaska by car is the most flexible means of mobility. You can start anywhere, and once there, you can go anywhere there's a road, anytime you feel like it, stopping along the way for however long you decide. The roads are especially fun, and you have some of them almost to yourself. On a few roads you'll rarely see another car. It's very open, unconfined, and uninhibiting—a large part of the spell of the North.

One essential for Alaskan drivers of all types is *The Milepost,* a fat annual book that's packed with mile-by-mile descriptions for virtually every road within or to Alaska (including, of course, the Alcan). The book is sold everywhere in Alaska—even at Costco—and is easy to find in Lower 48 bookstores or online at www.themilepost.com. Warning: Don't believe everything you read in *The Milepost;* much of the text is paid ads for specific businesses—watch for the small notice.

© DON PITCHER

Alaska travel can be confusing for the first-time visitor.

For current road conditions, construction delays, and more, contact the **Alaska Department of Transportation** (dial 511 toll-free anywhere in Alaska or 866/282-7577 outside Alaska, http://511.alaska.gov).

Winter Travel

During the winter months, travelers to Alaska need to take special precautions. Always call ahead for road and avalanche conditions before heading out. Studded snow tires and proper antifreeze levels are a necessity, but you should also have on hand a number of emergency supplies including tire chains, a shovel and a bag of sand in case you get stuck, a first-aid kit, booster cables, signal flares, a flashlight, a lighter and a candle, a transistor radio, nonperishable foods (granola bars, canned nuts, or dried fruit), a jug of water, an ice scraper, winter clothes, blankets, and a sleeping bag. The most valuable tool may well be a cell phone to call for help—assuming you're in an area with reception.

If you become stranded in a blizzard, stay in your car. You're more likely to be found, and the vehicle provides shelter from the weather. Run the engine and heater sparingly, occasionally opening a downwind window for ventilation. Avoid carbon monoxide poisoning by not running the engine if the tailpipe is blocked by snow.

Car Rentals

An increasingly popular way to see Alaska is by flying into the state and renting a car. This provides travelers with flexibility, and the costs have dropped in recent years. Rental cars are available in all the larger towns, but they are generally cheapest out of Anchorage, where most of the major car rental companies have airport booths. For long rentals, it's always best to get a car away from the airport, where the taxes are higher. In the peak summer season you should reserve up to two months in advance to get the best rates and to be assured of finding any car at all when you arrive.

If you plan to rent a car for an extended period, it's probably worth your while to check travel websites such as www.travelocity.com to see which company offers the best rates. When reserving a car, be sure to mention if you have a AAA card or are a member of Costco; you can often save substantially on the rates. Also be sure to ask about driving restrictions, since most car rental companies prohibit their use on gravel roads such as the Denali Highway.

RV and Camper Rentals

Recreational vehicles are among the most despised sights on Alaskan roads, but they seem to proliferate like rabbits as soon as the snow melts each spring. Motor homes are infamous for cruising slowly down the Seward Highway south of Anchorage, wagging a tail of impatient cars for a mile or more behind. Many snowbirds drive up to Alaska for the summer in their RVs, fleeing to Arizona for the winters. Other folks fly into Anchorage, Fairbanks, or Whitehorse and rent one of these land yachts.

Despite these criticisms, RVs can be a decent choice if the price of gas is not out of sight and if you can cram enough folks inside to cut your costs. But for just two people they are a profligate and environmentally disastrous investment.

Recreation

FISHING

Alaska is world-famous for its fish and fishing. More than half of the country's commercial seafood production comes from the state, and sportfishing is a favorite activity of both Alaska residents and visitors. Fishing options are equally vast in Alaska, where undeveloped areas stretch for hundreds of miles and the population is clustered onto a tiny portion of the land. The state is speckled with more than one million lakes—including some of the largest in the nation—along with 34,000 miles of pristine coastline and 42 Wild and Scenic Rivers.

The **Alaska Department of Fish and Game's** website (www.adfg.alaska.gov) has details on sportfishing, including descriptions of the various species, fishing regulations, news, and an abundance of other fish facts.

Alaska Fishing by Rene Limeres and Gunnar Pedersen is a comprehensive guide to fishing in Alaska, with detailed information on the when, where, and how to catch fish, along with natural history and other details. Locals, as always, are the best advice-givers about fishing techniques, spots, and regulations, and they might even share some secrets.

Popular Alaskan Fish

Salmon are the primary attraction for many sport anglers, and all five species of Pacific salmon are found in Alaska. Steelhead and rainbow trout, which are also salmonid, are famous for their beautiful coloration and fighting spirit. Rainbows are found in many streams and lakes around the state; the larger steelhead are the sea-run form.

Dolly Varden, also known as Arctic char, are a sea-run trout that flourish in many Alaska rivers. Arctic grayling occur in lakes and streams across the state, particularly in Interior Alaska and the Alaska Peninsula. The fish have a large

and distinctive sail-like dorsal fin, and they put up a big fight when hooked. Other important freshwater fish species include lake trout, brook trout (an introduced species), northern pike, sheefish, and whitefish.

Pacific halibut is a large flatfish that is commonly caught in saltwater, particularly in Southeast and Southcentral Alaska. Halibut sometimes reach the proverbial barn-door size, and it isn't uncommon to see ones that weigh in excess of 200 pounds. Many Alaskans consider halibut the best-tasting fish in the state. In addition to salmon caught in saltwater, other popular ocean-caught sport fish include rockfish and lingcod.

Catching 'Em

Fishing is not only great fun, it's the way to bag some super meals. All you need are a breakdown or retractable rod, a variety of hooks, flies, spinners, spoons, sinkers, line (4-8-pound for freshwater, 12-30-pound for saltwater, depending on what you're after), and a reel. All but the rod will fit in a small plastic case. For bait, get a small bottle of salmon eggs for freshwater, shrimp for saltwater. Have a filet knife to clean the fish. While fishing, watch for protected areas with deadfalls or rocks where fish like to hide. You'll have the best luck in the early morning or late evening, or on cloudy days when the sun leaks out to shimmer on the water. So as not to attract bears, keep your catch on a stringer well downstream.

Fishing Regulations

Fishing licenses are required. In Alaska, 1-day nonresident sportfishing licenses cost $20, 3-day $35, and 14-day $80. If you plan to catch king salmon, all these fees increase to $30, $55, and $130, respectively. The Alaskan license is valid in Denali and other national parks.

Homer and Seward are major ports for sport-caught halibut.

derby ticket first. Two of the biggest fishing derbies are in Seward and Homer.

Guided Fishing

Local knowledge is one of the best ways to be assured of a successful Alaska fishing trip. By using a charter or guide service, you're likely to have a more productive sportfishing excursion. Fishing guides can be found in most Alaskan communities, some offering float trips accessible by car and others going to more remote fly-in destinations. Charter fishing boats are available at coastal towns on the Kenai Peninsula, most notably Homer, Seward, and Ninilchik. Note that it's common to tip fishing guides, particularly if they're especially helpful or if you land a big one. There's no standard amount, but a 10 percent tip would certainly be appreciated.

INTO THE BACKCOUNTRY

Southcentral Alaska has an array of **hiking** options, whether you're looking for a waterside stroll along the Anchorage shoreline or a week-long backpacking trip into Denali National Park. Some of the best hiking trails are in Chugach State Park near Anchorage and on the Kenai Peninsula in Chugach National Forest. Check out *50 Hikes in Alaska's Kenai Peninsula* and *50 Hikes in Alaska's Chugach State Park* for details, or talk with folks at the **Alaska Public Lands Information Center** (www.alaskacenters.gov) in Anchorage. Few trails exist within Denali National Park, but the country is open enough for cross-country hiking.

Fishing licenses are sold in most outdoor stores and by charter fishing operators. Ask for brochures outlining local fishing regulations when you buy your license. Check open and closed seasons, bag limits, and the like to avoid trouble with the law. For the whole thing—spelled out in minute bureaucratic detail—request a copy of the regulations booklet from the **Alaska Department of Fish and Game** (907/267-2218, www.adfg.alaska.gov).

Fishing Derbies

Many Alaskan towns have salmon or halibut fishing derbies in the summer. If one is going on when you visit, it may be worth your while to buy a derby ticket before heading out on the water. The prize money gets into the thousands of dollars for some of these events, and more than a few anglers tell of the big one that would have made them rich if they'd only bought a

Public campgrounds are located throughout Chugach National Forest, Kenai National Wildlife Refuge, and Denali National Park, and in many smaller state and city parks. Most cost $10-15 and have potable water and vault toilets. Private RV parks can be found in nearly every town across Southcentral Alaska.

Several dozen **public-use cabins and yurts** are located within Chugach National Forest,

BIRDING

Alaska is an extraordinary place for birding enthusiasts. Nearly 500 species have been recorded in the state, and because of its immense size and diversity, Alaska has birds that are rarely seen anywhere else in North America.

INFORMATION

The Alaska Department of Fish and Game produces a helpful *Wings Over Alaska* (www.birding.alaska.gov) checklist of birds found in the state. The website also contains details on birding, bird identification, and hotspots to find unusual species.

Anchorage is home to a surprising diversity of bird species in the summer. The **Anchorage Audubon Society** (907/276-7034, www.anchorageaudubon.org) offers bird-watching field trips, sells a helpful Anchorage birding map, and maintains the **bird hotline** (907/338-2473) with the latest unusual sightings.

Alaska eBird (www.ebird.com/ak) is an online place to record bird observations, find birding hotspots, and share sightings. Maintained by the Cornell Laboratory of Ornithology and the Audubon Society, the site has a wealth of data on when and where to find birds, rare bird alerts, incredibly detailed range maps, and more.

LOCATIONS

One of the best local places to find birds is **Potter Marsh** on the south edge of Anchorage along Turnagain Arm. A quarter-mile wooden boardwalk provides a good vantage point through the marsh, and you may see Canada geese, Arctic terns, bale eagles, canvasback ducks, and even the occasional trumpeter swan.

TOURS

Based in Anchorage, **Wilderness Birding Adventures** (907/694-7442, www.wildernessbirding.com) has a cadre of Alaskan birders who lead trips to the Pribilofs, Adak, Gambel, Barrow, the Gulf of Alaska, and other remote places where you're likely to add new species to your life list.

Ken Marlow of **Alaska Birding Tours** (907/262-5218 or 800/725-3327, www.alaskabirdingtours.com, from $780 pp for a four-night package) is an expert on pelagic birds, and has a boat based in Seward. A four-night package includes lodging, birding trips, and lunches. Most trips are focused on the Kenai Peninsula, but he also guides birding adventures to Nome.

Another hardcore birding expert, Aaron Lang, has a website **Birding Alaska** (www.birdingak.com), which is a great source for unusual sightings, with links to regional rare bird alert websites.

EVENTS

In mid-May, the **Kenai Birding Festival** (www.kenaibirdfest.com) encompasses bird and nature photography walks, an art show, birding raft trips, and more. Most activities take place around Kenai.

On the first weekend of May, Homer's annual **Kachemak Bay Shorebird Festival** (www.homeralaska.org/shorebird.htm) brings bird walks, bay tours, an arts fair, speakers, and other activities, all in celebration of the great northward migration of shorebirds.

The **Kachemak Bay Birders** (www.kachemakbaybirders.org) keeps track of Homer area observations year-round, and has monthly meetings and birding events. Visit the website **A Birders Guide to Kachemak Bay** (www.birdinghomeralaska.org) for a species list, locations of birding hot spots, unusual sightings, and more. Both the Pratt Museum and Islands and Ocean Visitor Center in Homer have excellent natural history exhibits detailing the lives of seabirds and other species.

In spring, visitors to Homer are often thrilled by the presence of **sandhill cranes** in fields and yards throughout the area. Approximately 200 cranes return to the area each spring to nest (they winter 2,400 miles south in central California), and their arrival is a much-anticipated moment for locals. These loud and fascinating birds are always entertaining. Check with the Islands and Ocean Visitor Center for places to see them, and find more online at **Kachemak Bay Crane Watch** (www.cranewatch.org).

© DON PITCHER

Denali's wide-open spaces offer backcountry opportunities of all sorts.

Kenai National Wildlife Refuge, Kenai Fjords National Park, Kachemak Bay State Park, Chugach State Park, and Denali State Park. Most of these rent for around $45 a night, but advance reservations are needed. Cabins (and some campgrounds) in Chugach National Forest and Kenai National Wildlife Refuge can be rented through Recreation.gov (518/885-3639 or 877/444-6777, www.recreation.gov) for a $9 reservation fee.

A number of prominent organizations guide **mountaineering expeditions** in Alaska, particularly climbs up Mount McKinley within Denali National Park. Good wilderness guiding companies include **Alaska Mountaineering School** (907/733-1016, www.climbalaska.org), **Alaska Mountain Guides & Climbing School** (907/766-3366 or 800/766-3396, www.alaskamountainguides.com), and **NOLS** (907/745-4047, www.nols.edu).

BICYCLING

Bicycles are available for rent in Anchorage, Denali Park, Talkeetna, Homer, and Seward, providing an excellent way to see the local sights, especially in fair weather. Winter has not traditionally been a time for cycling, but the advent of fat tire bikes has created a boom in snow and ice riding. Bike shops in Anchorage, Seward, and Homer all rent fat bikes (with bizarre balloon tires) if you want to check out this fun winter sport.

The most popular mountain biking trails are in the Anchorage area and include many miles of paths (both paved and unpaved) along the shore and within a couple of city parks. Paved biking paths can also be found paralleling portions of the Seward Highway south of Anchorage, and in Homer, Talkeetna, and other cities. Many Forest Service trails are open to mountain biking, but some of these are muddy and challenging to ride. Especially popular is the Resurrection Pass Trail on the Kenai Peninsula.

The Anchorage-based **Arctic Bicycle Club** (www.arcticbike.org) organizes road races, mountain bike races, and tours, and its website is an excellent source for anyone interested in cycling in Alaska. Useful books are *Alaska*

PANNING FOR GOLD

Panning for gold is not only great fun, it's also a good way to get involved in the history of Alaska. Besides, there's the chance you'll find a nugget that will become a lifelong souvenir. You might even strike it rich! The amount of equipment required is minimal: an 18-inch plastic gravity-trap gold pan (buy one at any local surplus or sporting-goods store for a few dollars), tweezers and an eyedropper to pick out the gold flakes, and a small vial to hold them. Ordinary rubber gloves will protect your hands from icy creek water. An automobile oil dipstick bent at one end is handy for poking into crevices, and a small garden trowel helps dig out the dirt under rocks. Look for a gravel bar where the creek takes a turn, for larger rocks forming eddies during high water, for crevices in the bedrock, or for exposed tree roots growing near the waterline; these are places where gold will lodge. Try your luck on any of the old gold-rush creeks; tourist offices can often suggest likely areas. Stay away from commercial mining operations, and always ask permission if you're on someone's claim.

The principle behind panning is that gold, twice as heavy as lead, will settle to the bottom of your pan. Fill the pan half full of pay dirt you've scooped up from a likely spot and cover it with water. Hit the rim of the pan seven or eight times, or shake it back and forth. Break up lumps of dirt or clay with your hands and discard any rocks after rinsing them in the pan. Shake the pan again, moving it in a circular motion. Dip the front edge of the pan into the stream and carefully wash off excess sand and gravel until only a small amount of black sand remains. If you see gold specks too small to remove with tweezers, take the black sand out and let it dry. Later dump it on a clean sheet of paper and gently blow away the sand. The gold will remain. That's the basic procedure, though there are many ways to do it. It does take practice; ask a friendly sourdough for advice. Also, a number of spiked gold-panning facilities are found along the roads in Alaska—they are commercial, but good places to refine your technique.

Bicycle Touring Guide by Pete Praetorius and Alys Culhane and *Mountain Bike Alaska: 49 Trails in the 49th State* by Richard Larson.

For bicycle tours, check out **Alaskabike** (907/538-2392 or 888/320-2453, www.alaskabike.com), **Alaska Backcountry Bike Tours** (907/746-5018, www.mountainbikealaska.com), or **Backroads** (510/527-1555 or 800/462-2848, www.backroads.com).

ON THE WATER
River Rafting

White-water rafting trips are offered by numerous adventure-travel outfitters around the state. Several of the more reasonable, short, and accessible trips include floats down the Sixmile Creek south of Anchorage, Nenana River at Denali, Kenai River at Sterling, and Susitna River near Talkeetna.

Sea Kayaking

Sea kayaks are quiet and fairly stable, providing an outstanding way to explore hidden Alaskan coves or to watch wildlife. Because of this, kayaking has increased in popularity in recent years, both for independent travelers who rent a kayak and for those who choose a package trip with a professional guiding company. Companies offering sea kayak rentals and tours are in Homer, Seldovia, Seward, Whittier, and Eklutna Lake north of Anchorage.

Canoeing

Canoeing is a common activity on lakes and rivers in Alaska. Two canoe routes (Swanson River Route and Swan Lake Route) connect lakes within the Kenai National Wildlife Refuge; canoe rentals are available in the nearby town of Sterling. Canoe rentals are also available in Talkeetna, Nancy Lake north of Wasilla, and Matanuska Lakes near Palmer.

Sailing

Alaska has a small but active community of sailing enthusiasts. Resurrection Bay near Seward generally offers the state's top wind conditions, with day trips, sailing lessons, and bareboat charters. Kachemak Bay near Homer is another popular sailing area, with weekend races throughout the summer.

Surfing and SUPs

Surprisingly, surfing is growing in popularity in Alaska. It will never be a particularly common sight, but Homer has a few hardcore souls who head out when conditions are right. Homer is also an increasingly popular destination for kite-surfers, with good winds most afternoons. Stand up paddleboards (SUP) and surfboards (with wetsuits) can be rented in Homer.

WINTER SPORTS
Skiing and Snowboarding

Downhill ski and snowboard areas are near Anchorage (Alyeska Resort, Hilltop Ski Area, and Alpenglow). Alaska's largest ski area, **Alyeska Resort** (www.alyeskaresort.com), is south of Anchorage in the town of Girdwood, with 500 skiable acres, 60 trails, a 60-passenger aerial tram, eight chair lifts, and two pony lifts. Hilltop Ski Area and Arctic Valley are smaller areas near Anchorage, and Homer has a little community rope tow.

Cross-country skiing (both classic and skate) is very popular in Alaska, particularly in Anchorage, where many miles of lighted and groomed trails are available throughout the winter. Anchorage may well have the finest cross-country skiing of any American city, and a number of the nation's best Olympic skiers come from here. The city's main cross-country ski areas are in Kincaid Park, Hillside Ski Area, and the Tony Knowles Coastal Trail.

cross-country skiing near Homer

© DON PITCHER

dog-mushing

Additional groomed ski trails are around Homer, Talkeetna, Kenai, Palmer, Eagle River, Seward, and Soldotna. The **Nordic Skiing Association of Anchorage** (907/276-7609, www.anchoragenordicski.com) is Alaska's largest cross-country association, and its website has links to the state's other Nordic skiing groups.

Dog Mushing

Dogsledding has a rich history in Alaska, and sled dog races are a major winter staple across much of the state. The most famous is the **Iditarod Trail Sled Dog Race** (www.iditarod. com) from Anchorage to Nome in March. A number of companies offer wintertime dogsled tours.

During the summer months, visitors can ride on wheeled sleds behind teams of dogs, providing a chance to get the feel of the real thing. These very popular rides—some led by Iditarod mushers—are offered in Seward, Wasilla, and

Denali. In addition, summertime dogsled tours take place on glaciers near Girdwood and Anchorage. Tourists are flown up to the glacier by helicopter and given a chance to ride along as the dogs head across the ice and snow. It's a unique—but very expensive—experience.

Snowmobiling

Snowmobiling—or snowmachining, as it's called in Alaska—is both a bush necessity in the winter and a favorite of the motor-head crowd in urban centers. The **Alaska State Snowmobile Association** (www.aksnow.org) has additional info on their website. Rentals and tours are available in Anchorage and Fairbanks.

SPECTATOR SPORTS

The **Alaska Baseball League** (www.alaskabaseballleague.org) consists of six semi-professional teams, five of which are in Southcentral: Mat-Su Miners, Peninsula

Oilers, Anchorage Bucs, Anchorage Glacier Pilots, and Chugiak Chinooks. The teams include talented college players from throughout the country who come to Alaska to play in June and July. Alaska Baseball League teams play each other, along with Outside teams from the West Coast and Hawaii, with the top teams ending up at the National Baseball Congress World Series in Wichita, Kansas. Alaskan teams have won these World Series many times, and quite a few famous players have spent a summer on Alaska turf, including Mark McGwire, Tom Seaver, Graig Nettles, and Dave Winfield.

Hockey is very big in Alaska, especially in Anchorage, where overachiever parents push their kids onto the ice by age four. The **Alaska Aces** (www.alaskaaces.com) play professional hockey in the minor-league West Coast Hockey League, and the University of Alaska Anchorage (UAA) has a nationally competitive hockey team.

In bush Alaska, no sport is bigger than basketball, and any visitor who can play well stands a good chance of immediately being accepted by the locals. There's intense competition among high school teams at the state level, and UAA has its own basketball squad. The state's biggest basketball event is the **Great Alaska Shootout** (www.goseawolves.com) held in Anchorage each November and featuring eight college teams.

Tips for Travelers

ACCESSIBLE ALASKA

Because of the undeveloped character of Alaska, much of the state is not readily accessible to those with disabilities. This is particularly true in parts of bush Alaska, where even having a flush toilet may be a luxury, and entering small aircraft is a major challenge. Despite this, many towns and cities—particularly those that see an influx of seniors as cruise ship passengers each summer—have made great strides in recent years. Even in remote areas, some Forest Service and State of Alaska cabins have wheelchair ramps, outsized outhouses, and fishing platforms. In addition, quite a few trails around Alaska have been built for wheelchairs, including popular ones in Ketchikan, Juneau, and Anchorage. Hotels, buses, trains, cruise ships, tour boats, and ferries throughout the state all have some sort of accommodation for travelers in wheelchairs or with limited mobility.

A good place for travelers with disabilities is **Access Alaska** (121 W. Fireweed Ln., 907/248-4777 or 800/770-4488, www.accessalaska.org), a nonprofit independent-living center in Anchorage that can assist travelers with specific needs, including wheelchair-accessible hotels and restaurants, along with accessible horseback rides and river trips. Satellite offices are in Soldotna and Wasilla.

In Anchorage, **Hertz** (800/654-3131, www.hertz.com) has rental cars with hand controls, and **Alaska Yellow Cab** (907/222-2222, www.akyellowcab.com) offers lift-equipped van service.

TRAVELING WITH CHILDREN

Long a destination for seniors and couples, Alaska is increasingly popular with families, and even the cruise lines have gotten into the act with all sorts of kid-friendly activities and childcare onboard the larger vessels. Disney Cruise Line offers trips to Alaska, providing another option. The small adventure cruise ships are primarily the domain of couples, and children can get in the way or become bored. They're welcome on all state ferries, but parents need to keep a close watch due to the onboard hazards. Fortunately, the leisurely pace,

FESTIVALS AND EVENTS

The biggest events in Alaska revolve around the sun and snow. A number of Alaskans, especially those who live in the Interior and the north, believe that the purpose of summer solstice is to compress all the partying encouraged by the light and heat of summer into a single 24-hour period. There are fishing derbies in the waters off the coastal towns, and athletic competitions, such as triathlons and mountain races, everywhere.

The most famous winter festivals are Anchorage's Fur Rendezvous and the Iditarod. Every town has some sort of winter carnival that frequently includes dog mushing, a snow sports competition, and accompanying arts and crafts fairs.

Typically, the major public holidays are also a cause for celebration, including Memorial Day (last Mon. in May), July 4th (Independence Day), Labor Day (first Mon. in Sept.), Thanksgiving Day (last Thurs. in Nov.), Christmas, and New Year's Eve. The happiest days of the year, though, are in mid-October when the big Permanent Fund dividend checks show up in the mailboxes of state residents.

JANUARY
Anchorage–Anchorage Folk Festival; Seward–Polar Bear Jump Off

FEBRUARY
Anchorage–Fur Rendezvous

MARCH
Anchorage and Wasilla–Iditarod Trail Sled Dog Race

APRIL
Girdwood–Alyeska Spring Carnival

MAY
Homer–Kachemak Bay Shorebird Festival and K-Bay SeaFest

JUNE
Anchorage–Mayor's Midnight Sun Marathon, Joint Base Elmendorf-Richardson Open House and Air Show, Taste of Anchorage; Palmer–Colony Days

JULY
Eagle River–Bear Paw Festival; Girdwood–Girdwood Forest Fair; Homer–KBBI Concert on the Lawn; Seward–Mount Marathon Race

AUGUST
Ninilchik–Salmonstock and Kenai Peninsula State Fair; Palmer–Alaska State Fair; Seward–Silver Salmon Derby; Talkeetna–Bluegrass Festival

SEPTEMBER
Kenai and Whittier–Silver Salmon Derby

OCTOBER
Anchorage–Alaska Federation of Natives Convention

NOVEMBER
Anchorage–Great Alaska Shootout

DECEMBER
Talkeetna–Winterfest

engaging scenery, good food, naturalist talks, and free movies make the traveling easier.

Anyone traveling with kids today should consider bringing a portable DVD player, a laptop computer, or a smartphone with a stock of movies and games for those times when you need the kids to quiet down. Don't forget the headphones.

Most attractions and activities have lower rates for children, and some also offer one-size-fits-all family rates. Be sure to get your children into the great outdoors since that's really what Alaska is all about. The long bus ride into Denali National Park can be challenging for little ones, but the chance to see bears, moose, and wolves makes the trip worthwhile for everyone. Of special interest is the Park Service's **Junior Ranger Program,** in which children attend a nature program, hike a trail, or complete other activities. They're rewarded with an official Junior Ranger patch and are sworn in. It's always a big hit, but your kids may later try to arrest you if you get too close to a ground squirrel.

Be sure to set aside time for a special kid-friendly place such as the Anchorage Zoo, the

Alaska SeaLife Center in Seward, Islands and Ocean Visitor Center in Homer, or the one place all children love—H2Oasis Indoor Water Park in Anchorage.

Many tours are open to children, but the more hazardous ones (including helicopter flights, sea kayaking, white-water rafting, and zip-lines) impose age restrictions. Children are accepted in most Alaskan lodging places, but they will not do well in certain wilderness lodges or bed-and-breakfasts.

TRAVELING WITH PETS

In general, travelers visiting Alaska should leave their pets at home. Dogs may be good hiking companions, but if not kept under control they could bring a bear charging in your direction. Most hotels do not allow pets, and those that do typically tack on an extra charge for the privilege. Folks driving up the Alaska Highway—particularly RVers—frequently bring along a small dog or cat, but a current rabies certificate is required when crossing into Canada.

GAY AND LESBIAN TRAVELERS

Openly gay individuals may feel uncomfortable in politically conservative Alaska, so discretion may be wise, especially in rural areas such as Glennallen, where Rush Limbaugh is regarded as a socialist. Anchorage, not surprisingly, is the primary center for gays and lesbians in Alaska. The nonprofit group Identity Inc. runs a **Gay and Lesbian Community Center** (336 E. 5th Ave., 907/929-4528, www.identityinc.org), promotes the PrideFest event (www.anchoragepride.com) each June, and operates a help line. Two Anchorage bars—**Mad Myrna's** (530 E. 5th Ave., 907/276-9762, www.madmyrnas.com) and **The Raven** (708 E. 4th Ave., 907/276-9672)—are favorite meeting places. **Out North Contemporary Art House** (3800 DeBarr Rd., 907/279-8099, www.outnorth.

org) sometimes presents plays with a gay and lesbian slant, and several Anchorage B&Bs promote themselves for gay travelers and couples.

SENIORS

Alaska is a very popular summer destination for seniors traveling by cruise ship or RV, and for a surprising number of retirees who move to the state. Alaska Marine Highway ferries offer half-price senior discounts on certain smaller vessels in the summer and on most wintertime sailings. Most museums and some restaurants have discounted rates for those over age 65, and visitors to national parks can get an **Interagency Senior Pass** (www.fs.fed.us/passespermits/senior.shtml) that allows entry to all parks for a one-time charge of $10.

Travelers over age 55 should consider joining a **Road Scholar** (formerly Elderhostel, www.roadscholar.org) educational adventure, with dozens to choose from in Alaska. **AARP** (www.aarp.org) also has discounted Alaskan trips and other benefits.

WILDERNESS SAFETY TIPS

The most important part of enjoying—and surviving—the backcountry is to be prepared. Know where you're going; get maps, camping information, weather, and trail conditions from a ranger before setting out. Don't hike alone. Two are better than one, and three are better than two; if one gets hurt, one person can stay with the injured person and one can go for help. Bring more than enough food so hunger won't cause you to continue when weather conditions say stop. Tell someone where you're going and when you'll be back.

Always carry the **essentials:** a map, a compass, a water bottle, a first-aid kit, a flashlight, matches or a lighter, and fire starter (Vaseline and cotton balls work great), a knife, extra clothing (a full set, in case you fall in a stream), rain gear, extra food, and sunglasses—especially if you're hiking on snow. Many travelers

PACK THE ESSENTIALS

The following items assume that your trip to Alaska takes place in the summer months. If you plan to travel before May or after September, additional winter supplies will certainly be needed. In general, plan on cool and wet weather for your trip.

Even if you arrive in Alaska without the correct gear, almost anything you need is available in the larger towns, and in Anchorage the prices are really not much higher than in Lower 48 cities. In addition, the larger cities typically have at least one place that rents outdoor gear such as tents and stoves.

A **cell phone** can be especially useful if you want to stay in contact with friends and family while traveling, but coverage varies, so check with your service provider for specifics. And of course, don't forget your camera!

CLOTHING ESSENTIALS

- base layers
- hiking boots
- hiking socks
- light water-resistant coat (Gore-Tex works well)
- lightweight gloves
- liner socks
- rain pants
- sweater or wind-block jacket
- swimsuit
- sunglasses
- walking shoes
- warm cap

CAMPING ESSENTIALS

- 50 feet of line
- camp stove and fuel bottle
- compass
- cooking pot
- day pack
- first-aid kit
- fishing tackle (or get this in Alaska)
- insect repellent
- internal-frame backpack
- jackknife or Leatherman tool (a better option)
- plastic bags
- plates, cups, spoons, and forks
- sewing kit
- sleeping bag
- small towel
- sunscreen
- tent and ground cloth
- Thermarest pad
- water bottle
- water filter
- waterproof matches and lighter

now also carry along a GPS unit to stay oriented. Cell phones are popular but often don't work in remote areas. Satellite phones are the ultimate safety toy, but they are a pricey addition to your trip.

Check your ego at the trailhead; stop for the night when the weather gets bad, even if it's 2pm, or head back, and don't press on when you're exhausted—tired hikers are sloppy hikers, and even a small injury can be disastrous in the woods.

Hypothermia

Anyone who spends much time in the outdoors will discover the dangers of exposure to cold, wet, and windy conditions. Even at temperatures well above freezing, hypothermia—the reduction of the body's inner core temperature—can prove fatal.

In the early stages, hypothermia causes uncontrollable shivering, followed by a loss of coordination, slurred speech, and then a rapid descent into unconsciousness and death.

SAFETY IN AVALANCHE COUNTRY

Skiing and snowmobiling are becoming increasingly popular in Alaska's limitless backcountry. Unfortunately, many winter outdoor enthusiasts fail to take necessary precautions before heading out. Given the heavy snowfalls that occur, the steep slopes the snow piles up on, and the high winds that accompany many storms, it should come as no surprise that avalanches are a real danger in Alaska. Nearly all avalanches are triggered by the victims. This is particularly true for snowmobilers, who often attempt such dangerous practices as "high-marking"—riding as high as they can up steep slopes—and are killed in avalanches that result.

To avoid avalanches, ski only on groomed trails or "bombproof" slopes that, because of aspect, shape, and slope angle, never seem to slide. This isn't always possible, so backcountry skiers and snowmobilers need to understand the conditions that lead to avalanches. The best way to learn is from a class such as the avalanche safety programs taught by the **Alaska Avalanche School** (907/345-0878, www.alaskaavalanche.com) in Anchorage.

An avalanche safety course is extremely valuable, but you can also help protect yourself by following these precautions when you head into the backcountry:

Before leaving, get up-to-date avalanche information. The **Chugach National Forest Avalanche Information Center** (907/754-2346, www.cnfaic.org) has current snow conditions for the Kenai Peninsula; it's updated several times a week in the winter.

Be sure to carry extra warm clothes, as well as water, high-energy snacks, an avalanche transceiver, a lightweight snow shovel (for digging snow pits or excavating avalanche victims), an emergency snow shelter, a cell phone, first-aid supplies, a Swiss Army or Leatherman knife, a topographic map, an extra plastic ski tip, a flashlight, matches, and a compass or GPS unit. Many skiers also carry that cure-all, duct tape, wrapped around a ski pole. Let a responsible person know exactly where you are going and when you expect to return. It's also a good idea to carry special ski poles that extend into probes in case of an avalanche.

Avalanche airbags are the latest safety devices. They are designed to provide instantaneous floatation and head protection if you're caught in an avalanche. They're made by a number of companies, but are expensive, starting around $500.

Check the angle of an area before you ski through it. Slopes of 30-45 degrees are the most dangerous, while lesser slopes do not slide as frequently.

Watch the weather. Winds over 15 mph can pile snow much more deeply on lee slopes, causing dangerous loading on the snowpack. Especially avoid skiing on or below cornices.

Avoid skiing on the leeward side (the side facing into the wind) of ridges, where snow loading can be greatest.

Be aware of gullies and bowls. They're more likely to slip than flat open slopes or ridgetops. Stay out of gullies at the bottom of wide bowls; these are natural avalanche chutes.

Look out for cracks in the snow. Additionally, listen for hollow snow underfoot. These are strong signs of dangerous conditions.

Look at the trees. Smaller trees may indicate that avalanches rip through an area frequently, knocking over the larger trees. Avalanches can also run through forested areas, however.

Know how much new snow has fallen recently. Heavy new snow over older, weak snow layers is a sure sign of extreme danger on potential avalanche slopes. Most avalanches slip during or immediately after a storm.

Learn how to dig a snow pit. Learn how to read the various snow layers. Particularly important are the very weak layers of depth hoar or surface hoar that have been buried under heavy new snow.

Always travel prepared for sudden changes in the weather. Wear clothing that insulates well and that holds its heat when wet. Wool and polypro are far better than cotton, and clothes should be worn in layers to provide better heat trapping and a chance to adjust to conditions more easily. Always carry a wool hat, since your head loses more heat than any other part of your body. Bring a waterproof shell to cut the wind. Put on rain gear *before* it starts raining; head back or set up camp when the weather looks threatening; eat candy bars, keep active, or snuggle with a friend in a down bag to generate warmth.

If someone in your party begins to show signs of hypothermia, don't take any chances, even if the person denies needing help. Get the victim out of the wind, strip off his clothes, and put him in a dry sleeping bag on an insulating pad. Skin-to-skin contact is the best way to warm a hypothermic person, and that means you'll also need to strip and climb in the sleeping bag. If you weren't friends before, this should heat up the relationship! Do not give the victim alcohol or hot drinks, and do not try to warm the person too quickly since it could lead to heart failure. Once the victim has recovered, get medical help as soon as possible. Actually, you're far better off keeping close tabs on everyone in the group and seeking shelter *before* exhaustion and hypothermia set in.

Frostbite

Frostbite is a less serious but quite painful problem for the cold-weather hiker; it is caused by direct exposure or by heat loss because of wet socks and boots. Frostbitten areas will look white or gray and feel hard on the surface, softer underneath. The best way to warm the area is with other skin: Put your hand under your arm, your feet on your friend's belly. Don't rub it with snow or warm it near a fire. In cases of severe frostbite, in which the skin is white, quite hard, and numb, immerse the frozen area in water warmed to 99-104°F until it's thawed. Avoid refreezing the frostbitten area. If you're a long way from medical assistance and the frostbite is extensive, it's better to keep the area frozen and get out of the woods for help; thawing is very painful, and it would be nearly impossible to walk on a thawed foot.

Beaver Fever

Although lakes and streams in Alaska may appear clean, you could be risking a debilitating sickness by drinking the water without treating it first. The protozoan *Giardia lamblia* is found throughout the state, spread by both humans and animals (including beavers). The disease is curable with drugs, but it's always best to carry safe drinking water on any trip, or to boil any water taken from creeks or lakes. Bringing water to a full boil for one minute is sufficient to kill *Giardia* and other harmful organisms. Another option—most folks choose this one— is to use a water filter (available in camping stores). Note, however, that these may not filter out other organisms such as *Campylobacter jejuni,* bacteria that are just 0.2 microns in size. Chlorine and iodine are not always reliable, taste foul, and can be unhealthy.

CRIME

Alaska has a surprisingly high violent-crime rate; the most recent figures put the state at 10th in the nation in terms of violent crimes, with 588 such crimes per 100,000 residents. Part of this is due to simple demographics, since Alaska has the second-highest percentage of young people in the nation, but it is also a reflection of the impact of alcohol abuse. Alaska has a sexual-assault rate more than twice the national average, and the child sexual-assault rate is a shocking six times the national average.

The good news is that crime has dropped in recent years, especially in Anchorage, where many of the worst incidents have taken place. In general you're quite safe traveling in Alaska, though you should take the standard precautions, such as not leaving belongings in an unlocked vehicle and not walking around certain Anchorage neighborhoods after dark. Also, it's wise to avoid situations where people have been drinking heavily, even in bush Alaska. To be honest, after 25 years in the North, my only experience with crime took place when gear was stolen from me in Prince Rupert, British Columbia, and (equally shocking) in my hometown of Homer. I'm not saying crime doesn't exist, but many Alaskan towns are so safe that folks leave their doors unlocked and their keys in the cars.

MONEY

Most consumer goods must be imported from the Lower 48, and transportation costs are tacked on along the way. In addition, the transportation and shipping rates within Alaska are similarly high, further inflating the cost of goods and services. In more remote regions especially, lack of competition coupled with steady demand ensures top-dollar prices.

Visitors to Anchorage will be pleased to find that prices are not totally out of line with the Lower 48, and large discount-chain stores help keep prices more reasonable. The big chains have also spread to Wasilla, Palmer, Soldotna, and Kenai, driving down prices in those areas (and squeezing local businesses).

Beyond these exceptions, the prices in the North are much higher than Outside, and are generally the worst in the most remote bush communities. Food costs in places such as bush villages are more than twice those in Anchorage. Even in Homer, food is almost 20 percent more expensive than in Anchorage.

I travel almost exclusively using credit cards and an ATM card, but a few people still prefer traveler's checks. The major **credit cards**—especially Visa and MasterCard—are accepted almost everywhere in the larger towns. This is probably the easiest way to travel, especially if you can get airline mileage credit at the same time. Note, however, that credit cards may not be accepted by businesses in bush Alaska, so call ahead if you aren't traveling with cash or traveler's checks.

You'll find **ATMs** in all the larger towns and increasingly even in the more remote settlements. For locations, head to www.mastercard.com and www.visa.com/atms.

Traveler's checks from American Express, Bank of America, or Visa are accepted by most businesses; but don't arrive with traveler's checks in non-U.S. currency since they're only accepted at a few banks. In some remote villages, even traveler's checks may not be accepted.

Most Wells Fargo offices in Anchorage and some other cities will exchange Canadian dollars, Japanese yen, and euros for U.S. dollars.

Tipping (usually 15 percent of the bill) is expected at most sit-down eating places fancier than snack bars or takeaway counters. Tourism employees, fishing guides, and others providing personal service often depend on tips for their real income.

Information and Services

TOURIST INFORMATION

If you want to leave the trip-planning to others, you may want to contact one of the many itinerary planners who specialize in Alaska. These could be as close as your local travel agent, or one of the online information sources such as www.alaska.com or www.alaskaone.com.

A great starting point when planning a trip to Alaska is the official *Alaska State Vacation Planner,* produced annually through a joint partnership between the state and private businesses. It's distributed by the **Alaska Travel Industry Association** (907/929-2200, www.travelalaska.com). Find chambers of commerce around the state at www.alaskachamber.com.

LAND MANAGEMENT AGENCIES

The following phone numbers and websites provide contact information for major public land-management agencies in Southcentral Alaska:

- **Alaska Maritime National Wildlife Refuge,** 95 Sterling Hwy. in Homer, 907/235-6961, www.islandsandocean.org
- **Alaska Public Lands Information Center,** 605 W. 4th Ave. in Anchorage, 907/644-3661 or 866/869-6887, www.alaskacenters.gov
- **Bureau of Land Management,** 4700 BLM Rd. in Anchorage, 907/267-1246 or 800/478-1263, www.blm.gov/ak
- **Chugach State Park,** 18620 Seward Hwy. in Anchorage, 907/345-5014, www.alaskastateparks.org
- **Chugach National Forest,** 161 E. 1st Ave. in Anchorage, 907/743-9500, www.fs.usda.gov/chugach
- **Denali National Park & Preserve,** 907/683-9532, www.nps.gov/dena

- **Denali State Park,** 7278 E. Bogard Rd. in Wasilla, 907/745-3975, www.alaskastateparks.org
- **Department of Natural Resources,** 550 W. 7th Ave. in Anchorage, 907/269-8400, www.alaskastateparks.org
- **Kachemak Bay State Park,** Homer, 907/235-7024, www.alaskastateparks.org
- **Kenai Fjords National Park,** Seward, 907/422-0500, www.nps.gov/kefj
- **Kenai National Wildlife Refuge,** Ski Hill Rd. in Soldotna, 907/262-7021 or 877/285-5628, http://kenai.fws.gov
- **Alaska Department of Fish and Game,** 333 Raspberry Rd. in Anchorage, 907/267-2253, www.adfg.alaska.gov

COMMUNICATIONS AND MEDIA
Newspapers

Newspapers are becoming thinner with each passing year as the Internet cuts into their business. Alaska's unofficial state newspaper is the *Anchorage Daily News* (www.adn.com), and its website contains current stories, news blogs, classified ads, upcoming events, weather, and video. The company also produces a free *Alaska Visitors Guide* that can be found in the larger visitors centers or online at www.alaska.com.

The *Anchorage Press* (www.anchoragepress.com) is a free weekly newspaper available from racks all around Anchorage. Weekly newspapers come out in Homer, Soldotna, Seward, and Wasilla.

Radio

Commercial radio stations are in all the larger towns, and the state is blessed to have the **Alaska Public Radio Network** (www.aprn.org), one of the finest public radio networks in the country. Anchorage's **KSKA** (91.1 FM, www.kska.org) is the flagship station, but many Alaskan towns have their own versions. Anchorage's noncommercial **KNBA** (90.3 FM, www.knba.org) is one of the only Native Alaskan-owned radio stations in the nation, and it broadcasts some of the best music programming in Alaska. Two other notable stations are **KBBI** (890 AM, www.kbbi.org) in Homer and **KTNA** (88.5 FM, www.ktna.org) in Talkeetna.

Post Offices

Post offices are generally open 9am-5pm Monday-Friday, though a few open their doors on Saturday. Anchorage's airport post office is open 24 hours a day year-round. When post offices are closed, their outer doors usually remain open, so you can go in to buy stamps from the machines. Many grocery store checkout counters also sell books of stamps at no markup.

Phones and Internet

Telephone service is excellent to all the major towns and cities in Alaska, though you may experience a delay in some remote areas, and the wilderness lodges often depend on radio or satellite phones. Cellular phone coverage is variable, but generally quite good on the main highways. It's nonexistent in many backcountry areas, so don't expect to be able to pull out your iPhone and surf the Internet at a remote campsite! Not all companies provide coverage even when services exist, so contact your carrier for a coverage map ahead of your trip.

If you're traveling into remote areas and are worried about keeping in touch, satellite phone rental kits are available from **Surveyors Exchange** (907/561-6501, www.satellitephone-sak.com).

Alaska is surprisingly well wired, and even the most remote towns now have some sort of online connection. Nearly every library in the state has at least one computer where you can check your email or surf the Internet for free, though you may need to wait in line or sign up ahead of time. In addition, nearly all towns now have commercial businesses where you can rent computers by the hour for the same purpose. Wireless Internet (Wi-Fi) is becoming the norm for Alaskan hotels and bed-and-breakfasts, along with many local businesses. It's even available on some state ferries. Visit www.free-hotspot.com for updated listings around the state.

RESOURCES

Suggested Reading

ART AND LITERATURE

Bodett, Tom. *As Far as You Can Go Without a Passport*. New York, NY: Perseus Publishing, 1986. A collection of wry, bring-a-smile-to-your-face Alaska tales. Bodett's other books include *The End of the Road* and *Small Comforts*. This book is out of print.

Krakauer, Jon. *Into the Wild*. New York, NY: Random House, 1997. Now a Hollywood movie, this is the tale of Chris McCandless, a young man whose 1992 death in the bush north of Denali does not merit the attention it received. The story is loved by many Outsiders, but viewed with disdain by many Alaskans.

McGinniss, Joe. *Going to Extremes*. New York, NY: Plume, 1989. One man's journey to Alaska leads him to a series of characters as diverse as the state itself. This reissue of a 1980 book, though quite dated, is still popular with travelers.

McPhee, John. *Coming into the Country*. New York, NY: Noonday Press, 2003. Even though it was actually written in the 1970s, this remains perhaps the best portrayal of Alaskan bush lifestyles ever written. It's the book you'll still see folks reading on the long ferry ride north.

Schooler, Lynn. *Blue Bear: A True Story of Friendship, Tragedy and Survival in the Alaskan Wilderness*. New York, NY: Harper-Collins Publishers, 2002. This beautifully crafted memoir chronicles Schooler's life and how it was changed by Michio Hoshino, the renowned wildlife photographer killed by a grizzly in 1996.

DESCRIPTION AND TRAVEL

Alaska Almanac. Anchorage, AK: Alaska Northwest Books, published annually. A rich source of useful information about the state, all in one compact volume.

Alaska Atlas & Gazetteer. Freeport, ME: De-Lorme Mapping, 2004. This large book of up-to-date topographic maps is a wise investment if you plan to explore the more remote parts of Alaska. It's very easy to use.

Greiner, James. *Wager with the Wind: The Don Sheldon Story*. New York: St. Martin's Press, 1982. The true story of one of the state's most famous bush pilots.

Larson, Richard. *Mountain Bike Alaska—49 Trails in the 49th State*. Anchorage, AK: Glacier House Publications, 1991. An outdated but reasonably complete look at mountain biking in Alaska.

The Milepost. Augusta, GA: Morris Communications, published annually. For motorists, this publication—in existence for more than 60 years—is the best guidebook to Alaska. The highway maps and description make it a must if you're driving north. Although the information is accurate and comprehensive, specific listings of hotels, bars, and restaurants are limited to advertisers, and the ads don't tell the whole story.

Moore, Terris. *Mt. McKinley: The Pioneer Climbs.* Seattle, WA: The Mountaineers, 1981. An exciting history of the challenge to climb North America's highest mountain.

Nienhueser, Helen, and John Wolfe Jr. *55 Ways to the Wilderness in Southcentral Alaska.* Seattle, WA: The Mountaineers, 2002. A compact trail guide, complete with maps, photos, and descriptions of the best the region has to offer.

Quick, Daniel L. *Kenai Canoe Trails.* Anchorage, AK: Todd Publications, 1997. A very helpful guide to canoe routes within Kenai National Wildlife Refuge.

Romano-Lax, Andromeda. *How to Rent a Public Cabin in Southcentral Alaska.* Berkeley, CA: Wilderness Press, 2003. An enjoyable and detailed guide to dozens of Forest Service and state park cabins.

Shepherd, Shane, and Owen Wozniak. *50 Hikes in Alaska's Chugach State Park.* Woodstock, VT: Countryman Press, 2008. An informative guide to hiking in the second-largest state park in the country.

Tally, Taz. *50 Hikes in Alaska's Kenai Peninsula.* Seattle, WA: The Mountaineers, 2000. This is the authoritative guide to Kenai Peninsula trails.

NATURAL HISTORY

Hulten, Eric. *Flora of Alaska and Neighboring Territories.* Stanford, CA: Stanford University Press, 1968. A huge manual of vascular plants—highly technical, but easy to consult.

Murie, Adolph. *A Naturalist in Alaska.* Tucson, AZ: University of Arizona Press, 1990. This reprint of a 1961 classic still offers excellent insight into the fauna of Alaska.

Murie, Adolph. *The Wolves of Mount McKinley.* Seattle, WA: University of Washington Press, 1985. Another Murie classic, originally published in 1944.

Sydeman, Michelle, and Annabel Lund. *Alaska Wildlife Viewing Guide.* Old Saybrook, CT: Globe Pequot Press, 1996. A small helpful guide to the state's animals.

Internet Resources

Alaska Climate Research Center
http://climate.gi.alaska.edu
This site includes climatic data, current weather conditions, and Alaskan forecasts.

Alaska.com
www.alaska.com
This website is a great resource, with tons of links. It's operated by the *Anchorage Daily News,* whose website, www.adn.com, has current Alaska news, fishing info, and much more.

Alaska Department of Fish and Game
www.adfg.alaska.gov
The Fish and Game website is a good starting place for details on sportfishing and wildlife viewing around Alaska.

Alaska Marine Highway System
www.dot.state.ak.us/amhs
Visit this website for current Alaska Marine Highway ferry schedules and fares.

Alaska State Parks
www.alaskastateparks.org
Find details on Alaska's state parks and recreation areas on this useful site.

Alaska Travel Industry Association
www.travelalaska.com
This organization distributes the official *Alaska State Vacation Planner.*

Alaska Wilderness Recreation and Tourism Association
www.awrta.org
Find a complete listing of Alaskan environmental groups, with links to their websites.

Don Pitcher
www.donpitcher.com

www.facebook.com/donpitcherphotography
Author Don Pitcher's website provides details on all his books and photographic projects. Visit his Facebook page and become a fan!

511.Alaska.gov
http://511.alaska.gov
Especially useful for winter travel in Alaska, this site has details on road conditions, winter travel tips, highway construction updates, and more.

National Park Service
www.nps.gov/akso
The National Park Service's Alaska website has details on 15 national parks in Alaska, including Denali and Kenai Fjords.

Public Lands Information Centers
www.alaskacenters.gov
The Alaska Public Lands Information Center in Anchorage is an excellent resource, and their website offers an overview of federal lands in Alaska.

Recreation.gov
www.recreation.gov
Head here to reserve Chugach National Forest and Kenai National Wildlife Refuge cabins and campgrounds.

State of Alaska
www.state.ak.us
The State of Alaska website has links to state agencies and tourism sites.

U.S. Fish and Wildlife Service
http://alaska.fws.gov
Head here for details on the Fish and Wildlife Service, which manages 16 refuges across the state.

Index

List of Maps

Acknowledgments

For Rio Jalen

Whose sense of humor and effusive ways
  make each day a pleasure

Thanks for your adventurous spirit and
  joyfulness of discovery

Don't ever lose your inquisitive mind and
  desire to learn

This book grew out of a much larger guidebook covering the entire state of Alaska. As a resident of Alaska for three decades, I have been involved with *Moon Alaska* for much of that time. This book is more focused, covering some of the most popular and accessible parts of this massive state. If you've never visited before, south-central Alaska provides an outstanding and diverse sampling of some of the finest the state has to offer. This first edition of *Moon Anchorage, Denali & the Kenai Peninsula* was the product of not just my own labors, but the people of Avalon Travel, most notably my helpful editor, Leah Gordon. Thanks to her and the rest of the staff at Avalon for getting this book into your hands.

A big thank you goes to the following people who opened doors to their hometowns and provided details on local sights and attractions: Chris Smith at the Alaska Public Lands Information Center in Anchorage, Alex McLain at Chugach National Forest in Anchorage, Sarah Henning at Anchorage Museum, Cindy Clock at Seward Chamber of Commerce, Tami Murray at Greater Soldotna Chamber of Commerce, Trisha Costello at Talkeetna Roadhouse, Bill Madsen at Denali Mountain Morning Hostel, Katy Odneal and Brian McCullough at Out of the Wild in Talkeetna, and the staff and pilots of Talkeetna Air Taxi.

I offer special gratitude to my wife, Karen Shemet, and our two kids—Aziza and Ri—for keeping my priorities straight and helping me carve out the time for this book.

www.moon.com

DESTINATIONS | ACTIVITIES | BLOGS | MAPS | BOOKS

MOON.COM is ready to help plan your next trip! Filled with fresh trip ideas and strategies, author interviews, informative travel blogs, a detailed map library, and descriptions of all the Moon guidebooks, Moon.com is all you need to get out and explore the world—or even places in your own backyard. While at Moon.com, sign up for our monthly e-newsletter for updates on new releases, travel tips, and expert advice from our on-the-go Moon authors. As always, when you travel with Moon, expect an experience that is uncommon and truly unique.

KEEP UP WITH MOON ON FACEBOOK AND TWITTER
JOIN THE MOON PHOTO GROUP ON FLICKR